The Twilight Lords

The Twilight Lords

AN IRISH CHRONICLE

RICHARD BERLETH

Alfred A. Knopf   New York   1978

THIS IS A BORZOI BOOK
PUBLISHED BY ALFRED A. KNOPF, INC.

Grateful acknowledgment is made to the following for permission
to reprint previously published material:

The Devin-Adair Company, Old Greenwich, Conn.: Excerpt from
"The Downfall of the Gaol" as it appears in *1,000 Years of Irish
Poetry*, edited by Kathleen M. Hoagland. Copyright © 1947 by The
Devin-Adair Company.

A. D. Peters & Company Ltd.: Excerpt from "A Grey Eye Weeping" by Egan O'Rahilly, translated by Frank O'Connor; from *The
Penguin Book of Irish Verse.*

Library of Congress Cataloging in Publication Data
Berleth, Richard.
The twilight lords.
Bibliography: p.
Includes index.
1. Ireland—History—1558–1603. 2. Great
Britain—Politics and government—1558–1603.
3. Munster, Ire.—History.   I. Title.
DA937.B47   1978   941.505   77–15125
ISBN 0–394–49667–1

Manufactured in the United States of America

First Edition

For Emily,

who remembers Kilcredan

Contents

Maps and Genealogies

Acknowledgments

This book has benefited from much help and advice. I would like to thank Professor John O'Connor, who listened to my ideas and taught me much, and Professor Bruce Berlind, who first introduced me to the Elizabethans. To Angus Cameron, who believed in this book and encouraged the writing, and to Carol Janeway, who talked it over and always understood, I owe the most. My thanks also to Mr. and Mrs. Richard Ridgway for helping me to explore Spenser's Kilcolman and the heart of the old Munster Plantation, and to Commander Jephson and his family for access to Mallow Castle and the history of the Norris family. Like any New Yorker with a book to write, my debt to the New York Public Library has been incalculable, and I especially wish to thank the staffs of the Rare Book Room and Cartographical Division for their generous help. Likewise the staffs of the New York University Library; the Rutgers University Library; the Brooklyn Public Library; and the Library of Congress. Finally, to my wife, for her help and support, my gratitude as always.

Preface

During the reign of Elizabeth I, England succeeded in conquering and colonizing large tracts of Irish land. In a series of squalid, destructive wars the face of Ireland was altered permanently, and the estrangement of the two countries, which had had no exact beginning, hardened finally into a lasting emnity.

Elizabeth's actions in Ireland are disastrous in retrospect, but at the time they seemed like good ideas. And they were carried out by a succession of the best of men. This book tells part of that story. It is concerned with the gradual invasion of Southern Ireland, Munster especially, during twenty years of Elizabeth's reign. Yet it is not about Ireland so much as about the Elizabethan statesmen, soldiers, idealists, and adventurers who, in their fervor to act against real and imagined menaces there, were drawn into a political, military, and moral quagmire. Few emerged from the ordeal with credit or lasting gain.

The Twilight Lords is not based on a single central historical figure but takes as its center a historical generation. The account ranges back and forth in time, and back and forth between the English perspective and the Irish. The twilight lords themselves were the great feudal barons of Ireland: Gerald Fitzgerald, Earl of Desmond; James Fitzmaurice, Captain of Desmond; and the greatest rebel of them all, Hugh O'Neill, Earl of Tyrone. Caught between them and the invading English, the common people, the pawns at risk, were sacrificed by both sides without compunction.

The tragedy of Elizabeth's Ireland took place a long time ago, and it is fair to ask what conceivable interest it can have for modern readers. The glories of Elizabethan England are well fixed in the popular mind. The drama of Mary Stuart, the epic of the Spanish Armada, the swashbuckling romance of Drake and the Voyagers—all are at the heart of that age which

was also the flowering time of English-speaking culture and national senti-
ment. Now to insert the Irish debacle seems rude, except for the fact that
popular accounts have passed silently over that subject, relegating it to the
backwater of specialized history or dismissing its brutal nature as evidence
of an unfortunate residual barbarity in people already much improved by
the Renaissance. Ireland, however, was not a minor theater. Unlike Mary
Stuart's fall, Ireland's was not a foregone conclusion. Unlike the Spanish
Armada's defeat, Ireland's was not accomplished in a season. The conquest
progressed in stages. In modern parlance, the pacification of Ireland began
with a policing action, which escalated to full-scale operations, which
resulted in a near total depopulation of the countryside, which was
amended by wholesale colonization and usurpation. On the other hand,
Ireland gobbled up the Queen's men, resources, and energy for more than
thirty years. The Irish wars destroyed reputations, bankrupted great families, and culminated in the first authentic colonial venture in English
history.

The Twilight Lords opens this matter not to revel in old horrors or to
deflate the triumphs of a legendary reign. The book only means to suggest
the underside of Elizabethan virtues, the negative force of certain Renaissance values, for those values have surely descended to us. That the thinking of Elizabeth's advisors was often flawed, that their understanding of
reality was not always applicable, is an inevitable conclusion. Nothing
about this assertion is original. I owe a general debt to Winthrop D.
Jordan's *White Over Black* for his comments on Elizabethan racial attitudes
and another to H. R. Trevor-Roper for fresh elucidations of the sixteenth
century.

The book found its inception, however, in an observation by the very
great Anglo-Irish historian W. E. H. Lecky: "The pictures of the condition
of Ireland at this time are as terrible as anything in human history. . . . It
needs, indeed, the widest stretch of historic charity—it needs the fullest
realization of the manner in which, in the sixteenth century, civilized men
were accustomed to look upon races they regarded as inferior—to judge
this history with equity or moderation." Intolerance, perhaps even more
than greed and ambition, explains the failure of Elizabeth's best men,
though at the time they could not recognize their failure. Peter Carew
found in County Carlow the property and wealth which had eluded him
most of his life. Warham St. Leger exchanged a tenement in Southwark
for a manor house in County Waterford. Edmund Spenser acquired an
estate in County Cork. Walter Raleigh made his service in Kerry a step-
ping-stone to royal favor. Francis Walsingham voided the threat of Spain
in Ireland; Henry Sidney, John Perrot, William Pelham, Nicholas Maltby,
and Arthur Grey all achieved victories over the Queen's Irish. But despite

Preface

these successes, they managed in the end only to awaken a corresponding intolerance in the Irish, and the history of James Fitzmaurice, Gerald Fitzgerald, and Hugh O'Neill related here illustrates the contagiousness of a narrow nationalism. Beyond these remarks, *The Twilight Lords* ventures no conclusions; my hope is that the story will suffice.

A few words are necessary on the method. Wherever possible I prefer to let the Elizabethans speak for themselves, without comment or interruption. In the interest of readability, the extracts have been edited and modernized to remove as many obstacles as possible while preserving the meaning and flavor. Those interested in the modern sources informing and underlying the narrative should consult the select chapter bibliographies. In synthesizing this history from English and Irish annals I have depended almost exclusively on printed sources. No claim is made to new authority or fresh discoveries. I have relied heavily on the one or two Irish histories which are indispensable for the period and on a wide range of contemporary literary sources.

Anyone venturing for the first time into the chaos of sixteenth-century Irish politics must be overwhelmed by the profusion of clans and chieftains, feudal and tribal relationships, regional and hereditary conflicts, which impart their great energy to Irish history at this time. I have spared the reader as much needless complexity as possible, searching out unbroken lines in both the English and the Irish accounts. Some material is necessarily skipped, some is simplified, and some issues, judged unessential to my purposes, are neglected. All of which is to say that this book does not aspire to be a definitive history. The interpretation of motives, the portrayals of English and Irish participants, may be controversial and are largely my own. For them, and for any mistakes, distortions, or omissions, I take full responsibility.

Brooklyn, New York
1977

WHITEHALL, 1579
The English

As the second decade of her reign drew to a close, Elizabeth's Ireland was a possession still largely outside the Tudor order, a land always to be reformed tomorrow, never today. To the Queen, the island was a wilderness. She preferred to ignore it. England faced expensive choices elsewhere, and neglect, though lacking majesty, was a serviceable alternative, not without benefit to both countries. But in the autumn of 1579 the Irish rebelled and thrust themselves into the forefront of a grave international crisis, cancelling the blessings of neglect.

At home the Queen's opponents seized on the Irish uprising to discredit her foreign policy. Influential men warned that Catholic Spain and agents of the Holy See had entered this back door of England to overthrow the Crown, that the situation warranted all-out action. These men believed that the Irish emergency was part of a vast conspiracy. Elizabeth did not. She was convinced that the rebellion was just another Irish rebellion, to be met with available force, customary negotiations, and, at the requisite moment, a discreet bribe. In the meantime, she declined action and turned once more to her great concern.

In the view of her trusted advisors, the English state faced questions far more grave. Elizabeth celebrated her forty-sixth birthday in September; she was unmarried, without acceptable heirs, and now arrived at the limit of childbearing age. Either she would marry soon, and conceive, or the nation would drift toward the chaos of a contested succession. Her closest advisors were committed to a marriage solution and, this late in the day, not particular where she found her husband. The preceding spring they were gratified to learn that the Queen had settled on a match. He was French and nominally Catholic, but well disposed toward the Protestant powers. Through this marriage England hoped to rejoin the Continent, forming with France a counterpoise to Spanish hegemony. By one stroke the issue of the royal succession could be resolved, and threats to England's internal security, such as in Ireland, averted. The answer had everything to recommend it but one—the majority of Englishmen were opposed.

In 1579 it also happened that the Crown stood petitioned to join in common cause with other Protestant powers against Roman Catholicism and the Counter-Reformation. The cockpit of the religious wars was then the Netherlands, and that spring there arrived at Court Dutch patriots requesting English support in their struggle against Spain and the Inquisition. Elizabeth considered them a nuisance, the advocates of the marriage an embarrassment, and they were bustled into Whitehall Palace and out with abbreviated ceremony. The Queen did not desire entangling foreign commitments, though to be sure she voiced her warmest regards for coreligionists battling against Spanish tyranny and Popish oppression. Such was t. ʔ official position, measured and moderate, seeking to hide beneath it the risː g indignation and frustration of her subjects. Elizabeth was daughter of aı ʔxcommunicated King, herself illegitimate by papal decree, and therefo ʾ by birth and precedence the foremost Protestant ruler in Europe. . ʾl that her Protestant countrymen asked was that she act Protestant; lumpː g all the issues together, they demanded that she subjugate Ireland, strik at Spain through the Low Countries, and deny herself a French marriag Those most importuning were the so-called puritans, and by 1579 they were numerous in her government. In September of that year she was driven to dismiss several, banishing them from her sight and her Court. They advanced a notably virulent love of nation, a government by principle which could not avoid encroaching on the personalizing prerogatives of majesty. The ardent Protestants, the puritan party, preferred war, while all the Queen wished was a husband, a last chance to marry and be happy. Behind her determination lay the time-honored conviction that a monarch's welfare *was* his country's. The marriage controversy was the great test and crisis of Elizabeth's middle years, and on its outcome depended, beyond all expectation, the future of Ireland.

In that season nothing offended responsible and sober Englishmen more than the antics at Whitehall. Love was all the talk at Court, music and dancing were the diversion, and flattery ruled. Elizabeth doted on the portrait of her intended, Francis of Valois, Duke of Alençon, and, waiting his return, sported with his confidant and envoy, Jehan de Simier. Since January she had been continually in Simier's company, and for all the bickering over marriage terms, he sustained her light, flirtatious mood until Alençon arrived in August. She was utterly charmed with her suitors, and Simier became affectionately "her monkey," Alençon "her frog." Outside the palace, where courtesy was nothing, they were "the ape and the fox," a pair of posturing "mounsieurs," plain opportunists. Alençon was twenty years younger than Elizabeth, short and slight, his face ravaged by smallpox. The Crown's ambassador to France found him pliant, "a good fellow and a lusty prince, not so tall perhaps, nor so fair as his brother the King, but, on the other hand, not so obstinate or papistical, and if rumors be true, apt for the getting of children." Elizabeth gave out that he was actually handsome, and all agreed who wished to avoid her wrath. But marriage or no marriage, Alençon was also in the way. By September battles were imminent in Ireland; the Union of Utrecht had consolidated the Dutch position in the Low Countries; yet any concerned with this urgent business found the Queen indisposed. She walked with Simier, wrote passionate letters to the Duke, and passed the nights in dancing. All that now stood between her and her heart's desire was the Privy Council, and there the puritans were in retreat. During the first week in September they made a last bid to bring the government to their view.

The Council had been meeting on the marriage question since April, and in her rages the Queen had decimated her opponents. The Earl of Leicester, barred from her presence, continued in disfavor; the Earl of Sussex had given in; and of the strong men, her Foreign Secretary, Sir Francis Walsingham, alone remained. He could count on Sir Christopher Hatton, Vice Chamberlain, and Sir Francis Knollys, Lord Steward, to resist the marriage, but of all Principal Secretaries, he was the least suited to argue against love. Walsingham was fifty and every bit his age; he was stern, hardworking, and loyal, with strong Calvinist leanings, and, as he once described himself, "a man of the night." He was Elizabeth's spymaster, who ran perhaps the most ingenious network of informers Europe ever knew, and was to his adversaries "the spider." The very talents which distinguished his career worked against him during the marriage crisis, above all his commendable logic. Oblique, cautious, accustomed to traffic in facts, he failed to understand how one moment Elizabeth was content to play Alençon against Spanish interests and the next, was in love with him. Now he was pitted against Elizabeth's Lord Treasurer, William Cecil, Lord Burghley, who favored the marriage and opposed him on every point, and rather than cross the Lord Treasurer, Walsingham sought a private audience with Her Majesty. The Spanish ambassador at Court, Bernardino de Mendoza, relished the outcome. "Yesterday Walsingham, Hatton, and Knollys went to see the Queen. Their decision was that, on no account, ought the Queen to marry Alençon or any other personage of the House of France; this being the opinion of all, with the exception of Sussex and Burghley." In fact, they threatened to refer the issue to Parliament, and Elizabeth, after politely stating that she would not summon Parliament, "wept and remained extremely sad after the conversation and was so cross and melancholy that it was noticed by everyone who approached her." But after Knollys and Hatton had left, she exploded at Walsingham, shouting "the only thing you're good for is to protect heretics." She had no further use for him and warned him to get out of her sight. Sir Francis joined his closest associates in exile and was to remain in banishment for the rest of the year.

At home and shaken, he could scarcely credit the transformation he had witnessed, and wrote, "Would to God her Majesty would forbear. . . . No one thing hath procured her so much hatred abroad as these wooing matters." Even once the blow had struck, Walsingham did not know where he had failed. The marriage made no sense; it was against God and an abrogation of everything English. Francis of Valois' mother was Catherine de Medici; his younger brother, King Charles IX of France; and between the two they had permitted the massacre of untold numbers of Protestant men, women, and children in Paris on St. Bartholomew's Day, 1572. Walsingham had been in Paris then, had narrowly escaped, and had seen the blood of innocent people splashed against the door of his house. He could never after accept a Valois as the consort of England. The Queen pleaded for a child, the continuance of her line, but she was only a few years younger than himself and might easily be carried off in childbirth. And here, it appears, was his mistake. In arguing against the marriage, Walsingham offended the woman, calling attention to her sagging body. His want of tact nullified the effect of his arguments. Walsingham had recognized how the Queen need not marry at all. No match could call back the Jesuits then beginning to infiltrate England or cast the Spanish influence out of Ireland. War had grown preferable to a shoddy peace by ineffectual marriage alliance. Bitter in his temporary retirement, he weighed the risks of action and judged the nation ready.

London, and the realm at large, needed time to consider. Elizabeth's subjects were inured to marriage maneuvers; various matches had been arranged since the start of the reign and had always miscarried. Few doubted that future stability depended on marriage, but whether a French match was wise or seemly had become the source of heated debate. The puritan pulpits of the City of London thundered against the marriage, while more orthodox churchmen remained silent. At times the envy and ancient malice felt toward France boiled to the surface in the streets, and there were disturbances. In Southwark the odds makers gave three to one the marriage would not take place, and common gossips blamed everything on Alençon from the weather to the price of wine. The simpleminded suspected witchcraft in his triumph, blaming the whole arcanum of love possets and enchantments for his easy success. And merchants, well traveled and knowledgeable, speculated on the price of grain in the wake of a union of Anjou and Aylesbury. William Cecil, Lord Burghley, saw no harm in this confusion, and he listened as intently as Walsingham for the rumors of a coalescing disaffection. In September only the Spaniard Mendoza, his hopes running forward, predicted civil war. But serious disorders were not out of the question, and Cecil weighed them with other risks in recommending the marriage. Elizabeth had appealed to her people: "Might not she, no less than common women, desire to have children?" Many of her countrymen grumbled but understood, and Cecil had not yet lost the struggle for public opinion.

In Council he had more to fear. Separating the issues, proclaiming Ireland irrelevant, throwing influence and prestige against the mounting paranoia which could lead to a disastrous war with Spain, he held by far the least attractive position. What he possessed, however, from his years and long service, was a generosity toward women and a profound understanding of the Queen. He recognized that the safest course was to give direction to those instincts of rule which seldom betrayed Elizabeth. In defense of the marriage he praised her physique and readiness to bear children, and if there is much flattery in his speeches, there is also a surer statecraft: "Elizabeth is a person of most pure complexion, of the largest and goodliest stature of well-shaped women, with all limbs set and proportioned in the best sort, and one whom, in the sight of all men, nature cannot amend in any part to make her more likely to conceive and bear children without peril." The Queen's body was a treacherous subject, and part of the bitter comedy of these months is that Burghley left his adversaries no choice but to disagree over the Queen's comeliness and shape. While they did so to their misfortune, he elicited assurances that Alençon's affections, unlike his brother Henry's, ran to women and not young boys.

After Walsingham's defeat, the Queen demanded silence on the subject of her marriage. She withdrew the matter from consideration, chastising her Council, as Burghley records: "She said she condemned herself for simplicity in committing this matter to be argued by them, for that she thought to have rather had a universal request made to her to proceed in the marriage than to have doubt made of it." Her mind was made up; for the moment she would not even entertain doubts. But Elizabeth was not unaware that she had still to convince her people. During the weeks that followed, her letters to Alençon were filled with advice about the way he was to act in England. One caution in particular is offered: if he would appear Protestant in public, he might worship as he pleased in private. His replies are grateful, compliant; he is Her Majesty's complete servant, willing to abide by whatever she says. By mid-September the Court was certain that the marriage would take place, but outside the Court the crisis had not passed. The Queen was estranged from her most loyal servants; the machinery of government had slowed, and her officers and deputies stuck in such places as Kerry and Connaught waited in vain for her instructions. History concurs that Elizabeth picked an awkward moment to love. "She was by time surprised," Raleigh would say later, and for those few critical months while she tried to make up years, her realm drifted close to dissolution.

Those she had discarded were no less intent on saving her, and they now made Leicester House the center of their activities. During 1579 no one of consequence, and opposed to the marriage, failed to visit this tall brick mansion along the Thames, and following his fall, Walsingham; Sir Henry Sidney, previously Lord Deputy of Ireland; Henry Herbert, the Earl of Pembroke, and a company of young, highborn gentlemen met there regularly. Foreign reports were received at Leicester House daily, and by September this large establishment had become the headquarters of the puritan faction. From there, late in 1578, the Sidneys had issued their *Discourse on Irish Affairs,* intended to spur a review of the government's policies. There, in February, 1579, Count Casimir, commander of the largest Protestant army on the Continent, had been lodged while visiting incognito, his journey to London an attempt to interest the Queen in the Low Countries war. And from there, in mid-August, went out a 4500-word discourse, written by Sir Philip Sidney, denouncing the marriage and acquainting the Queen with reasons. Walsingham's thinking was apparent throughout, and no answer is known to have been made. In the spring Leicester House railed against Simier, in the summer, against Sussex, in the fall, against Burghley, whose machinations were suddenly seen everywhere. Agitation bordered on the seditious, but Elizabeth was content to bar her puritans from government, refraining from sterner reprimands for the time. Neither she nor Burghley could afford a definitive break. What she would not countenance, however, was the return of Robert Dudley, Earl of Leicester, to Court and let it be known that Dudley belonged more in the Tower than in the Privy Council.

In better days he had received his titles, his houses, and the better share of his now-dwindling fortune from the Queen. He had been her "Robin," her enduring favorite, her chief courtier and constant companion. But with time and familiarity he had abused her affection, his errors in judgment and numerous *affaires de coeur* stretching her indulgence. At Court the Earl of Leicester was no longer a paragon of service, although in 1579 he was still a man invested with immense influence. At the height of his brilliance, Elizabeth had presented him sixteen choice estates, the Chancellorship of Oxford, the post of Master of the Horse, and an annual revenue far surpassing any other earldom. Ceremonially, Leicester approximated a marshal of the realm, with lines of patronage and authority extending into the Queen's army and navy. Six feet two, he towered above his contemporaries as much in physical presence as in style and ambition. He affected the gorgeous dress, the magnificence, the magnanimity more appropriate to Henry VIII than to the grandson of Henry's tax collector. And he had seized his early opportunities to create a formidable dynasty. His sister was Sir Henry Sidney's wife; his wife was Sir Francis Knollys' daughter; his nephew, Philip Sidney, was to be Sir Francis Walsingham's son-in-law. By virtue of wealth and rank, Leicester was the true head of the puritan faction, and he served as a magnet to the ambitious young of other noble houses. Men might question the sincerity of his religious fervor, his devotion to puritan principles, but Leicester was a soldier, and none doubted that at forty-six his great hope was to command a Protestant army in the Netherlands. He craved action, however, only on the central stage. Ireland would never do; victories there were more obscure than defeats. Other men could campaign in Ireland. Dudley would lead Englishmen onto the Continent. In his enormous pride he may have mistaken his competence, but he never mistook his obligations to the Queen. His absolute allegiance to the Tudor regime was such that he was first and always Elizabeth's creature. Nothing ever struck him harder, therefore, than his precipitous fall from grace in June, 1579, and the cause of his hurt was Jehan de Simier.

The previous April he still sat on the Privy Council, deliberating against the marriage, struggling arduously to sway Burghley against the Queen's proposal. Each morning at seven he passed through the columned water gate of Leicester House, pushing his way through beggars and supplicants, to be rowed upriver to Whitehall and the Council Chamber. Each evening at eight he returned more despondent than before. On one occasion he gathered his household in the darkened hall to pray for the Queen and, beginning with "God only now must defend her and us all," seemed to vent his frustration in sanctimony. Dudley, it should be recognized, was not beyond projecting his private interests as the interests of the realm. What must have frightened him most was the prospect of losing

9

everything he had gained over the years, and he would certainly lose if the Queen married. His politics, therefore, were determined; he would do anything to block a marriage alliance and gladly accept war as the alternative. Precisely how much he did do, however, was the great question. Elizabeth suspected that he ordered Simier murdered.

Sinister rumors had always dogged Leicester. It was claimed by some that he murdered his first wife, Amy Robsart, when a marriage with Elizabeth seemed possible; by others that he had had Lettice Knollys' previous husband, the Earl of Essex, poisoned in Ireland; and now that he had paid for Simier's assassination. The tales of Leicester's alleged indiscretions, his bloody misdeeds, his debaucheries, his innumerable bastards would fill a book; indeed, somewhat later in the reign they did, with the Jesuit publication of *Leicester's Commonwealth*. But the essential fact, and only fact, is that Simier feared Leicester and surmised that the Earl wanted him dead. Doubtless Leicester did, but so did many others, and there is no evidence that Dudley went so far as to hire assassins. Normally Elizabeth disregarded stories of Leicester, but she had experienced an attempt on Simier's life first hand, and the incident left her shaken. On a hot, humid day in early June, while she and Simier were taking the air on the Thames in the royal barge, shots rang out from the shore and bullets splattered the water around them. The helmsman was hit in the arm, and as the Queen coolly dressed his wound with a strip of her gown, Simier reportedly cowered in terror. He later informed Her Majesty that he held certain enemies accountable for the episode. Nor in his view was this the first attempt on his life. A few weeks earlier, at Whitehall, a trigger-happy guard mistakenly fired on the Frenchman in the dark. The case was dismissed as accidental by the Lord Steward, but Simier harbored doubts.

Now out of an instinct for self-preservation, or the pleasure of doing an enemy mischief, he exposed the Queen to an interesting item of intelligence. Robert Dudley had secretly married Lettice Knollys, cousin and Lady-in-Waiting to the Queen, without Elizabeth's consent or knowledge. The response to this news was immediate and predictable. Arrested at once and dragged before her, Leicester was denounced as an ingrate traitor, his bride as a calculating wanton. As a wedding gift, the Queen confined Leicester alone and indefinitely to a tower in Greenwich Park, and only Burghley's intervention prevented him from being flung into the great Tower of London. Her pride stung, her jealousy aroused, Elizabeth remained inconsolable for days, and some were always to believe that Leicester's defection drove her to the extravagances with Alençon. In any event, Simier dealt a telling blow to his opponents; in one stroke he temporarily removed Leicester, discredited his party, and advanced the French courtship.

Leicester's followers preferred to think that he fell because of his convictions, a martyr to the cause of a new and independent nation-state. They were mistaken in their earnestness. Dudley stumbled because of the jealousy of two women: one whom he had served all his life and one whom he had seduced most recently. He could pretend to the new politics, but he belonged to an earlier time, to Elizabeth's youth. Walsingham and the Sidneys brought integrity and experience to puritan policies, and their sense, far more than Leicester's example, carried the cause forward. The puritan faction was more than a Court coterie or a religious persuasion; rather it was a national constituency, diverse and transcending sectarian disputes and the interests of Robert Dudley. As the crisis deepened, the Earls of Warwick, Bedford, and Pembroke reaffirmed their strong puritan sympathies, opposing themselves to the influential Catholic families of the aristocracy. Among the Queen's soldiers, Lord Grey and Sir Nicholas Maltby were staunch puritans, with Sir John Norris and Lord Willoughby sharing their foreign outlook, though not their theology. In Cornwall and Devon, Drake, Grenville, the Raleighs, Gilberts, Carews, and Godolphins favored puritan aims and welcomed war. The profane, hard-bitten mariners of this region were already raiding French and Spanish shipping and stood to gain by an official declaration of hostilities. Moreover, these men commanded the ready vessels Elizabeth would need in an emergency.

If the Western ports supplied the brawn, Cambridge molded the puritan intellect. Down from the university, Christopher Marlowe enlisted as a secret agent in Walsingham's service; Edmund Spenser was employed as a secretary in Leicester's household; Fulke Greville, Lord Brooke, became a protégé of the Sidneys; and Sir Edward Dyer carried dispatches between Dublin and Leicester House. Thomas Cartwright, the Cambridge scholar and exiled divine, had inspired a generation of undergraduates, and his students found their way naturally into service of the puritan cause. Even at its lowest ebb, the party had secured the future; standing for national expansion, it was inevitably the party of young and ambitious men. Nor is it surprising that many of these names appear over the next twenty years in the bitter chronicles of Ireland and the popular accounts of fighting in the Low Countries. Some of these men would meet the Great Armada, forgetting by then how they had provoked it, and would in time be woven into the heroic legends of Elizabethan England. But their aspirations were not Elizabeth's or Burghley's. They envisioned another world, impelled by other terrors, and by 1579 had finally reduced their general sentiments to a program of demands.

———◆———

Walsingham came back from the Continent in 1578. He had reached two conclusions and was groping toward a third. At Amsterdam he was given the latest reports on the colleges at Rheims and Douai, then preparing English Jesuits to enter England and minister to the recusants, or English Catholics, remaining in the country in the face of persecution. The Catholic menace was growing within the realm, and Walsingham concluded that the Queen's life was in danger. To some extent he was correct. In 1570 Pius V committed the folly of excommunicating Elizabeth, thereby forcing English Catholics to choose between their ruler and their faith. The Pope's act succeeded in destroying any hope of religious toleration and, by intensifying the government's suppression of recusants, loosed a wave of terror and counterterror which continued throughout the reign. Walsingham had determined to ferret out English Catholics, loyal and otherwise, and his agents had soon infiltrated both Rheims and Douai. At home, informers had been planted in heavily Catholic shires and even within the homes of principal Catholic families. But now if the Queen married Alençon, her husband would become the chief recusant of England. He would be beyond the law and free to act as a magnet for Catholic intrigues. For her own security the match had to be prevented.

But Walsingham was also apprised of extensive Spanish preparations in the Low Countries. At Antwerp concentrations of coastal shipping were being gathered, and the stock of munitions was growing monthly. These developments seemed out of proportion to the needs of the Spanish army then in Flanders, and Walsingham concluded that within a few short years Spain would attempt a Channel crossing against England. Again, he was near the mark. From this conclusion it followed that the Crown would do well to delay Spanish designs by fielding an expeditionary force in support of the Dutch. Since the threat was not immediate, there was time to wheedle the forces out of Elizabeth.

The danger that was imminent and required urgent measures was Ireland. Abroad Walsingham had received fragmentary reports of a convoy readying at Corunna for a voyage against Ireland. The details were obscure. On sound evidence he knew that the expedition contained a papal legate, an English Jesuit by the name of Nicholas Sanders. He was led to believe that ten or twelve bottoms were being readied for the invasion and that they would transport Italian mercenaries and Spanish volunteers. The contingent was placed at several thousand troops, most in the pay of Spain and the Holy See, and they would land under a papal banner, commanded by the redoubtable rebel James Fitzmaurice, Captain of Desmond. The only good news was that a co-conspirator in the adventure, Thomas Stukeley, had become embroiled in a Moroccan war while en route to Corunna and had been killed with most of his men. Thus, as Sir Francis returned to London at the end of 1578, he surmised that a fresh rebellion was being hatched in Ireland; that it would be stiffened by foreign troops; and that it would likely overpower the Queen's scattered garrisons in that island within a few months. This was the critical issue, the one palpable threat, and Walsingham was about to conclude that large reinforcements were needed in Ireland when he was drawn headlong into the marriage controversy.

The pending invasion was hardly discussed during the first part of the new year, but in the last week of April word reached London that the expedition had finally sailed. Rebellion was now a certainty in Ireland unless the convoy was intercepted before reaching the coast. The likely landfall was Valencia Island on Dingle Bay and the probable point of landing somewhere on the desolate shore of Kerry. From there the invading force could make its way into the heart of Munster, Desmond Ireland, where the English were certain a warm welcome was prepared. So apparent was the peril that Elizabeth finally consented to consider the matter and for the moment put aside her obsession. The Privy Council voted unanimously to dispatch an intercepting squadron, and orders were rushed early in June to Dartmouth. The command of the naval detachment was given to Humphrey Gilbert and his half brother Walter Raleigh. The royal fleet had been badly battered by winter weather and was unready to sail immediately. It was late June before Gilbert was at sea, and he quickly lost himself in fog and heavy rains off Land's End. Never the best navigator, Gilbert had difficulties just keeping his ships together. He and Raleigh sailed to windward of the Spanish convoy, missing it by several leagues, and on July 17 Fitzmaurice, Sanders, and their party landed dry-shod in Dingle Bay. Considering the fateful consequences of this event it would be fitting to report a grand, triumphant entry. But in truth, the invasion was more delusion than reality, a pathetic remnant cast ashore at little cost and less risk. Fitzmaurice's "army" actually numbered 700 men; 80 were Spanish soldiers; 300 were Italians impressed from the jails of Rome; and the balance, exiled Irish clerics and adventurers. The force transported four cannon and had more shovels for entrenching than muskets for battle. James Fitzmaurice thought they would be enough; in any event, they were all he had to show for five years of scraping and begging at Rome and Madrid. He was home, and that was what counted.

Gilbert buried the account of his failure in dispatches concerning supplies and the state of the fleet, and Elizabeth was not informed of Fitzmaurice's arrival until the last week in July. By then she was in a rage with Leicester and ill disposed to other business. She clearly resented the exaggerated reports of the rebel's strength, and now that he was ashore she counted complacently on the chaotic conditions of Ireland to impede his progress. In this estimation Elizabeth and Burghley were close to the truth. They believed that they had time, that the marriage would do more to settle the state of Ireland than all the expeditions the Crown could send. Without help from Spain, no Irishman could mount a successful rebellion. Therefore, the landing at Dingle Bay was dismissed and forgotten.

At Leicester House, Fitzmaurice was not held so lightly. Sir John Perrot, acting for Sir Henry Sidney, had taken his surrender seven years before, amid the ashes and collapsing walls of a church at Kilmallock. The surrender marked the end of the First Desmond War, a four year struggle which wasted wide tracts of the South. And the intrepid leader of the Irish resistance had been James Fitzmaurice, a regular soldier, a formidable field commander, a religious visionary. To disregard such a man seemed the height of irresponsibility, but that is just what the Crown proposed to do. Leicester was powerless to reverse the decision; he was then in the throes of his disgrace and wrote Walsingham, "Our remedy must be prayer, for other help I see none." His chaplain, Dr. Thomas Wilson, the Cambridge humanist and Council Secretary, delivered himself of a similar sermon at Leicester House. "You must be contented and make of necessity a virtue," he lectured, "and say with yourselves that this world is not governed by wisdom and policy but by a secret purpose or rather fatal destiny." Pride, however, opposed this counsel; fatalism was not an attitude congenial to Dudley or his generation, and they tormented themselves over Fitzmaurice's easy victory. He had been beaten once, and if the Crown acted, he would be beaten again. To do less not only was cowardly but was to lose Ireland. No one knew better than Sir Henry Sidney. He was the onetime Lord Deputy of Ireland, had spent more years and more of his family wealth administering that country than any living Englishman, and he was what later times would call "an expert consultant."

In the summer of 1579 Sir Henry was also unemployed. After long, arduous service, he had fallen from favor in a dispute over taxes, the cess, or land tax, opposed by influential Irish nobles and therefore opposed by Burghley and the Queen. Sir Henry had returned to England to nurse his resources and lobby persistently for changes in Irish government. He was a frequent guest at Leicester House and, with Walsingham, one of the chief architects of puritan foreign policy. Whitehall made a point of ignoring him. No one questioned his distinguished record or doubted his capacities; his family alliances were the real hindrance and prompted Elizabeth to suspect that he and his son were too ambitious. She looked for a pretext to remove him and in 1578 charged him as governor of Ireland with squandering her money and seeking to extort unjust taxes from her loyal Irish subjects. In fact, the office of Lord Deputy was then filled with a candidate of Burghley's choice, and Sidney's decline reflected Leicester's. There was nothing for it but to agitate and wait. Sir Henry's health had suffered from campaigns in Ireland, and between his disabilities and growing disillusionment, he relied increasingly on his son Philip. Together they drafted seven treatises, or position papers, on the Irish question, and these were circulated throughout the government during 1579.

Fitzmaurice's return certainly pained Sidney. He had ruined his health and his fortune pursuing the rebel for four long years. There was hardly a bog or a mountain in Munster he had not crossed chasing Fitzmaurice's ragged army, and he had seen the devastation and waste of an Irish uprising at first hand. When Fitzmaurice was in Ireland, every theft of cattle, every murdered townsman, every stir and bordrag in the night found an excuse. Violence was endemic, but Fitzmaurice gave it direction. The man was a fanatical Papist and made of religion a unifying principle, a justification for resistance to the Crown. In Sidney's estimation, the use of religion to raise resistance among the disheveled chieftaincies was a perilous precedent. In the end the English had made Fitzmaurice kneel in the muddy ashes of a church burned by the war, the blade of the Lord Deputy's sword of office held to his bare breast, and Fitzmaurice had spoken his words of contrition and obedience in clear English, not Gaelic. The temptation to use the sword had been great. But the Queen's policy had swung once more to treaty, to offering a second chance to the Desmond lords. And as usual, her clemency masked the same, familiar parsimony: the war had cost too much; the peace might cost more. It was cheaper to let the few surviving rebels go, stripped of arms and broken, than to fill the vacuum their summary execution would create. Burghley's hand was visible here. To make good inadequacies in the army, to repair Dublin Castle, to build defenses, Sidney had spent his own money. Now his condition was so impecunious that his son Philip was thrown on the generosity of Leicester, his uncle, to maintain himself decently at Court and to travel abroad. Moreover, it had all gone for nothing. Fitzmaurice escaped to France in 1573. By the next year he was in Rome, demanding an army with which to return. By 1576 he was in Spain, training and outfitting a fighting force. His projects and whereabouts were continually reported to Whitehall, but they did nothing. Worse still, Fitzmaurice's cousin in Ireland, the Earl of Desmond, commanded virtually the whole of the South, and his loyalty to the Crown was always questionable. If Fitzmaurice returned, Sidney was certain that the weak, impressionable Earl of Desmond would soon join him. These were the reasons for the alarm at Leicester House.

James Fitzmaurice landed in Ireland with a declared mission. He sought to overthrow the English Crown, the heretical religion of the excommunicant Queen, and to establish Pope Gregory XIII's nephew on an Irish throne. From this monarchy would then follow the ratification of all lordships and chieftaincies in accord with right religion and love of country. What Sir Henry offered in place of this plan is worth considering. A talented administrator, before the word "administrator" was commonly applied, he understood that the wellspring of all civil order was uniformity of justice and law. Therefore, he stood for the development of strong central government and against the prerogatives of the hereditary lords and Gaelic chieftains. The reformed religion advanced these principles, in his opinion, and helped eradicate the evils of superstition and ignorance. He was not insensitive to the plight of the common Irish countrymen, those sheltered by neither the clans nor the lordships, and called for agrarian reform in their interest, including taxation according to means. The five ancient provinces or kingdoms of Ireland—Ulster, Connaught, Meath, Leinster, and Munster—organized as they were into counties, were to become shirelands. Sidney hoped to encourage yeomen farms, a form of shire administration, and the extension of arable land. His goal might in fact have been more revolutionary than Fitzmaurice's, but it amounted to Anglicizing Ireland. His plan has been called "modern," "progressive," and indeed, it possessed the merits of generosity and humaneness. But it was also out-and-out colonialism, the seed from which sprang later versions of colonial rule and administration. As they were in 1579, the Irish would never accept the plan; they might not accept Fitzmaurice's either, but he was of them and entitled to try. Sidney was perhaps the best governor Ireland had during Elizabeth's reign; at least many Irishmen honored his name and reputation. In all likelihood he was as fair and merciful a man as the age could offer, but to bring to fruition his hopes for Ireland would require immense effort, a struggle spanning twenty years, and a cost of thousands of lives. The price was apparent mostly in hindsight, but one official foresaw many of the obstacles; he was the Lord Treasurer, William Cecil, Lord Burghley, and as much as he supported the Queen's marriage, he resisted large-scale military intervention in Ireland.

Burghley was fifty-nine in September, old for the responsibilities he bore, but age had concentrated his mind wonderfully. He was never more determined to avoid impulsive acts and foreign adventures than now. He was never more secure in his dislike of military answers or the pomp and gallantry of war. Elizabeth tended to concur, for there was little in either her politics or his that pretended to boldness or grandeur. Together, they were a cautious pair, socially conservative and distrustful of visionary solutions. Burghley once remarked, "I have gained more by my temperance and forebearance than ever I did by wit or daring." He never meant that he was without cunning; only that he preferred method and study to spontaneous reaction. A masterful negotiator, he was most at home in the known world of diplomacy, where knowledge and nuance won advantage. Diffident, discreet, he had learned to distinguish between personal interests and public duties and, in a disciplined, understated style, set the example for generations of future civil servants. Privately he inclined to puritan religion; publicly he was a firm upholder of the Anglican Church compromise. In solitude he admitted his sympathies for the Protestant minority on the Continent, but publicly he was prepared to compromise his allies, to conserve England's force, to wait. The very complexity of his mind left him open to the charges of hypocrisy and duplicity, and to his opponents he was always to be "the old fox." To Elizabeth, he was simply the most perceptive and knowledgeable man in her service, which was to say that he often anticipated her views. The strategy on which they most frequently agreed was that of limited objectives and a maximum economy of force. Either principle applied to the issues of 1579 dictated a French marriage.

Few of his contemporaries were as content as Cecil to remain peacefully at home among familiar things. He never relished long journeys or sea passages, and with advancing age even his visits to London became infrequent. The Queen's messengers grew accustomed to finding him riding a small white mule in his gardens as he supervised the completion of his great houses or saw to the planting of trees and hedges. Cecil had a desire to be remembered for his building, and so far as leisure permitted, he devoted himself to constructions and plantings. Theobalds and Burghley House were not just tourist attractions in their day; they embodied all that Cecil could not express elsewhere: his delight in sensual beauty, his sensitivity, his fondness for order amid multiplicity. No architect designed for him; the work was his own. And in the solid materiality of these houses may lie an explanation for his disregard of flamboyance and heroics. Like all true dynasts, Cecil cared too deeply for substance to waste it on gestures or speculation.

During the height of the marriage crisis he busied himself repaving a street by his house in London. Probably nothing galled his opponents more than to see Cecil supervising the laying of stones in Ivy Lane only a few hundred yards along the Strand from Leicester House. Small matters like Ivy Lane were the tinder of Dudley's anger. Burghley's cool, methodical labors spoke of a situation under control, but his behavior also suggested how little he valued Leicester's pretensions. The Cecil family had origins in the small gentry, and though Burghley was to found a dynasty of grandees on the merit of his service, he would not adopt the manner of hereditary lords. The fact remained that he was not comfortable with the aristocratic ethos of courage and honor. Renaissance humanism held out the twofold excellence of heroic action and contemplation, and Cecil's devotion was clearly to the latter. "Learning will serve you in all ages and in all places and fortunes," he wrote to his son Thomas, and believing strongly in the moral and utilitarian worth of education, he was the generous patron of teachers like Roger Ascham and William Camden. His habit of study had no small effect on his policies. He gathered historians and geographers to him as Leicester gathered poets. For all his retiring ways, his simple domesticity, Cecil remained the best-informed official. His perception, regard for facts, his careful logic repeatedly served as a foil in Council for Walsingham's zeal and Leicester's pomposities. "Did they know a better way?" was the frequent question, and with their "ifs" and "shoulds" discounted, the answer was usually that they did not.

What most worried Burghley as the decade drew to an end was the continued presence in England of Mary Stuart, Queen of Scots. Should she outlive Elizabeth, she was heir apparent to the English throne, and her ascension meant certain civil war. A Catholic Queen, she was the great hope of Catholics in England and abroad and was already at the center of numerous intrigues. Her greatest power lay not in Scotland, but in France. Therefore, short of the terrible and unprecedented act of executing her, Alençon offered the surest answer. French power would follow him, not Mary, and though he was not the perfect match, he was far preferable to her. Moreover, the presence of Spain in the Low Countries threatened French sovereignty as much as English. Alençon was committed to leading a French army in support of the Dutch; he would call on England for financial backing, but the military risk would be his. The marriage promised everything Burghley could ask, including the possibility of a legitimate heir to the throne. So much for economy of force; the match was also attainable, even ardently desired, and offered certainty, whereas an English expedition to the Low Countries was anything but a certain success. Cecil held the English army in low estimation, fearing that it could never meet the Spanish on equal terms and, in the event, his analysis proved correct. The war fever at Leicester House, should it gain headway, might plunge the realm into a disastrous confrontation with Spain, a conflict for which England, and more specifically the English navy, were not ready. The principle of limited objectives was violated by most recommendations Walsingham and Leicester made, and nowhere more than in regard to Ireland.

The problem with Ireland was that no reasonable objective could be seen clearly. The country was partly unknown; the local conditions were confused and ill reported; and above all, the place had little bearing on the crucial conflict. Spain could create inexpensive diversions in Ireland; England, on the contrary, could pour men and arms into the countryside and never see a shilling's worth of difference. This is precisely what had happened ten years before during Fitzmaurice's rebellion, the First Desmond War. Cecil granted that Ireland was a dangerous corner, but he shrank from dissipating the Crown's energies in an attempt to govern it. What could be learned about the country he assiduously digested, but the difficulty lay in how little was definitely known.

Centuries of English presence had resulted in a few hundred square miles of tamed earth surrounding coastal towns; these were the pales, where English law, manners, and speech prevailed to the exclusion of Gaelic. The largest was around Dublin, the smaller environing Cork, Waterford, Galway, and Limerick. Beyond the pales, however, Gaelic Ireland was largely obscure to Englishmen. Elizabethans had only begun to explore their own past and the topography of their island, to say nothing of Ireland's. The chief chroniclers, topographers, and cartographers of the age dedicated their work to Burghley and drew from him sustaining patronage. But Ireland was beyond their reach, a land of different language and culture, difficult to travel through, as exotic to them as the lands across the Atlantic. Brittany, Cornwall, Wales possessed remnants of an ancient Celtic civilization and tongue, but these were relatively peaceful provinces which could hardly prepare the sixteenth-century traveler for the shock of Ireland. Years would pass before reliable maps appeared of Ulster and the mountain fastnesses of Kerry. In the meantime, English armies paid dearly for the lack. The land itself was treacherous; 40 percent of it was covered with bogs and forested mountains; and through war and famine, the people clung to their customs. Gaelic Ireland remained a herding culture, indifferent to tillage and settled agriculture. In the most insular form, Irish society was tribal, still emulating the values and traditions of the heroic age. But where modern European civilization had penetrated, the old ways were in disarray, adding a new confusion to the land. Not until early in the seventeenth century did thoughtful men begin to perceive the unique culture which had sustained Gaelic life and which had subsequently disintegrated.

Burghley had evidence of the chaos, but not a clue to the emerging patterns. His papers at Hatfield House expose the informers, Irish as well as English, on whom he relied for intelligence. The reports are contradictory, vague, merely hearsay. They are filled with rumors of tribal clashes, murders, vacant chieftaincies, and cattle raids. How to make sense of this world beyond the pale troubled Cecil no less than Walsingham, and in 1570 he commissioned a young scholar named Edmund Campion to undertake an exploratory journey through Hibernia. The project seems to have been conceived as a compilation and chronicle of Irish antiquities and current customs, a geopolitical history not unlike Camden's encyclopedic *Britannia*. It was intended to uncover facts helpful to the government; what it turned out to be, however, was a minor classic in English travel literature, a book of charming digressions, totally useless. Outside of a survey on English education in Ireland, a condition well-nigh nonexistent, Campion reports such oddities as how Irish salmon catch their tails in their teeth and, letting go suddenly, flip themselves over weirs. Barnacles attract his attention because they were numerous and posed a dietary dilemma for Irish Catholics. Since everyone agreed that barnacles hatched into sea gulls, it stood to reason they were both fish and meat. No guidance is offered those who hanker after sea gull, but the author recommends abstaining from barnacles on Fridays and holy days. Campion scoffs at some notions: even he declines to believe that Ireland was peopled by Noah's niece who landed with three men and fifty women. This curious work was, of course, rejected out of hand, as much for its English as for its waywardness. Cecil demanded the precision of Latin and had no patience with literary pretensions. In 1572 Campion's history appeared under the patronage of Sir Henry Sidney and dedicated to the Earl of Leicester. They were right to appreciate its merits, for as an impressionist account the work was not to be surpassed. But Campion himself was not satisfied to remain, as he was, a Catholic in conscience. He found his way to Prague and a Jesuit seminary. Ten years later, having taken orders, he was smuggled back into England as a secret agent. A harmless enthusiast, he managed to be captured quickly, was tried by his former patrons, and executed a few months later as an example to his brethren.

Ireland seemed possessed of a curious property for assimilating and subverting reasonable men. The interior was almost lawless by English standards; Gaelic society was not without restraints, but conventional Elizabethan morality seldom applied beyond the pale. Ireland could invigorate ambitious men with a breath of freedom, and instances of officials and officers of the Queen's forces "going native" were not uncommon. Burghley would eventually be drawn into the strange case of Captain Thomas Lee. Here was one of the most energetic commanders Elizabeth sent over, a relentless flail of rebels, a fighter of no mean ability. From 1575 on he was in continual communication with London first as Sir Henry Sidney's man and then as Essex's. But as the years passed, his letters began to show a deterioration of mind and an odd cast of expression. No one thought seriously of his peculiarities until the head of the outlaw Fiach MacHugh arrived before the Queen's august Council at Whitehall, salted, boxed, and addressed to Elizabeth from her loyal "bog soldier," Captain Thomas Lee. The practice of head money was upheld throughout the era,

THE IRISH LAND
ABOUT 1600

MILES
0   50
0   KM   50

N

NORTH CHANNEL

LOUGH SWILLY

RATHLIN ISLAND

DERRYVEAGH MTS.

DONEGAL

FOYLE
LOUGH FOYLE

FINN
STRULE

SPERRIN MTS.

ANTRIM HILLS

BANN

ULSTER

BLUE STACK MTS.

LOWER LOUGH ERNE

DUNGANNON

LOUGH NEAGH

BELFAST LOUGH

DONEGAL BAY

BLACKWATER N.

DARTRY MTS.

Sligo

UPPER LOUGH ERNE

PASS OF THE NORTH

Armagh

STRANGFORD LOUGH

MOURNE MTS.

Newry

OX MTS.

MOY

LOUGH ALLEN

CAVAN

Dundalk

LOUTH

DUNDALK BAY

CLARE ISLAND

CLEW BAY

LOUGH CONN

CONNAUGHT

LOUGH MASK

SUCK

LOUGH REE

INNY

MEATH

BOYNE

Drogheda

PARTRY MTS.

TWELVE PINS

LOUGH CORRIB

Galway

SLIEVE AUGHTY MTS.

Athlone

SHANNON

BOG OF ALLEN

LIFFEY

Dublin

IRISH SEA

GALWAY BAY

ATLANTIC OCEAN

LOUGH DERG

WICKLOW MTS.

Idrone MTS.

LEINSTER

OWR

SHANNON

Limerick

Askeaton

FOREST

LOUGH GUR

GOLDEN VALE

AHERLOW VALLEY

Cashel

Kilkenny

NORE

Smerwick

MULLAGHAREIRK MTS.

Tralee

SLIEVE MISH MTS.

DINGLE BAY

DEEL

MAIGUE

FUNCHEON

BALLYHOURA HILLS

GALTEE MTS.

Clonmel

SUIR

COMERAGH MTS.

Wexford

NORE

BARROW

LOUGH LEANE

BLACKWATER

KNOCKMEALDOWN MTS.

Lismore

Waterford

MACGILLYCUDDY'S REEKS

BOGGERAGH MTS.

MUNSTER

LEE

Cork

Dungarvan

Youghal

ST. GEORGE'S CHANNEL

BANTRY BAY

Kinsale

ELEVATIONS

▲ 2,000' to 3,000'
△ 3,000' and over

palacios

and there was nothing extraordinary in Fiach's dismemberment. Yet remains were never posted to Her Majesty as if she were some petty chieftain to be placated by trophies. After upsetting the Council's sensibilities, the head had the mischance to become lost in London, passing from one fastidious official to the next until it came to rest in someone's garden. The loss of Fiach's head was enough to bring supporters of Lee's initiative down on the necks of Burghley and the Council, with the result that the Lord Treasurer felt constrained to write: "Her Majesty is surely not well contented that the head of such a base Robin Hood is brought so solemnly to England. It is no such trophy of a notable victory, and yet of it Lee's friends make great advantage." But it was not Fiach for whom condolences were in order so much as Lee. Stung by what he took to be official disregard, he turned outlaw in his own right and soon fell to despoiling his own people. Ireland had become his home, Irish chieftains his companions, and several years later he was captured, dragged to London, and hanged at Tyburn like any other Irish renegade. The records make a point of stating that he died a Christian.

A racial as well as cultural bias is met in official accounts of the Irish. What made defections such as Lee's so alarming and inexplicable was the belief that the Gaels, as Celts, were less developed, capable, and moral than the English themselves. During the sixteenth century the Irish were commonly referred to in government documents as savage, lazy, unwashed, ignorant, superstitious, and promiscuous—hardly a propitious start toward governance. Burghley's generation lacked the intellectual vantage point from which to view the evolution of Irish conditions or the impact on the country's habits and institutions of several centuries of English domination. From bald chronicles and patchy annals it was known that the Danes had invaded the island during the Viking Age, built coastal towns, and vanished without a trace into the interior. The Normans then overran Ireland in the wake of their conquest of England. Norman nobility, flowing into the country, brought practical arts and feudal administration, but the Normans too blended with the native population. The principal aristocratic families of Elizabeth's day—the Ormond Butlers, the Desmond and Kildare Fitzgeralds, the Clanricarde Burkes—were descended directly from Norman conquerors, but as lines they had long ago become Irish, speaking Gaelic, marrying Gaels, becoming chieftains in their own right. The problem with Ireland, from Burghley's viewpoint, was that assimilation too often went the wrong way. He knew that the Crown had never sent a force to Ireland which was not eventually reduced 50 percent or more by desertion, defection, and an erosion of patriotism. So poorly fed and maintained were the Queen's soldiers in Ireland that they frequently sold their arms to the Irish for food and vanished into the local populace for protection.

Neither Cecil nor Elizabeth ever visited Ireland to learn why plans invariably miscarried. But early in the reign Ireland visited them in the person of Shane O'Neill, the great Ulster chieftain, and the furor O'Neill caused left a lasting impression. In fact, had the Irish lords banded together, they could not have mounted a more eloquent argument against English interference than Shane's performance.

O'Neill was that unparalleled example of the Celtic chieftain, the tribal king, as different from Irish Earls as they were from English. He was not even nominally faithful to the Crown and came to London not out of a sense of feudal obeisance but because the Queen's bog soldiers were hot on his heels. Whatever else Shane was, or legend has made him, he was emphatically not an Irish patriot. Few of his countrymen ever led the English a merrier chase or cost them more treasury, but in outlook he was pure warlord. His policies, if they could be called that, were as devoid of national instinct as they were of gentlemanly scruple. He had one great passion in life: killing O'Donnells, and he dispatched many until they caught him in their turn. His own family hardly fared better: Bacach, his father, was stripped of his rule and ended his life in Shane's dungeon; Matthew, his bastard brother, he had murdered; and several cousins experienced fatal and abrupt accidents. This mayhem and slaughter did not especially disturb the English; what they held against Shane was that he persisted in calling himself "the O'Neill" in defiance of the "Earl of Tir-Oen."

It is generally recognized that nothing ever contributed more to the social chaos and decay of Ireland than the long-standing English policy of forcing chieftains to conform to English titles and laws of inheritance. Shane, however unlovable, was a victim of this practice. When Henry VIII came to the throne, the King of England was still styled Prince of Ireland; when he left, the King of England was also King of Ireland. Henry began the destruction of the clans and did so by compelling elected chieftains to accept from his hands English lordships and privileges. The laws of feudal monarchy were imposed on the Irish. Throughout Irish lands the observance of primogeniture, or inheritance by the eldest legitimate son, was enforced, with the result that the old clan system of designating and publicly confirming heirs was broken, and with it the ancient ties binding together Gaelic society. The Irish chieftain was intended to become an instrument of the Crown in perpetuity, and through him his people would be governed, despite the fact that the Irish chieftain traditionally owed more to his clansmen than they did to him. Bacach, for example, was persuaded to renounce his chieftaincy of the O'Neills in exchange for the title Earl of Tyrone, and he designated his son Matthew his eldest, legitimate heir. Shane, who knew Matthew to be illegitimate and who commanded the loyalty of the O'Neills, had Matthew murdered and himself elected to the chieftaincy in spite of the English and their law. He put his old father away, summoned the clan to his island fort on Lough Neagh, and there, in the time-honored way, tossed a silver slipper over his head and declared himself the O'Neill, duly designated and ratified by the might of the clan. His election was "barbarous," to quote the English historian Camden, and Elizabeth had no choice but to pursue him. Several months of desultory fighting followed, in which Shane took more hurt than he gave, and he finally resolved to come to London, beg the Queen's pardon, and embrace the very system for which he had denounced Bacach. The occasion was more momentous than anyone realized, for Shane's submission marked the end of the Gaelic world. Perhaps he appreciated its significance and therefore made it all the more Irish.

Only Shane ever dared to inflict tribal Ireland on the splendors of the Elizabethan Court. The Council, the peers, foreign ambassadors, highborn and low suddenly found themselves struck dumb as this Celtic apparition entered the audience chamber. Shane's saffron mantle swept around him in great folds. His black hair curled down his back. He walked forward slowly in measured steps, swaying slightly, eyes fixed ahead on the Queen. Behind him came two columns of warriors—their heads shaved, wolfskins flung over their shoulders. The menacing attitude of the henchmen was not lost on the spectators, a few of whom recalled later how each was clad from neck to knees in old-fashioned leaf mail and gripped a three-foot battle-ax in front of him. As the procession neared the throne, Shane let out with a deafening howl and, throwing himself flat before the Queen, began to beg her pardon in Gaelic and defend his rights at the same time. The gist of his apology has survived in rough translation. "It was his right," he claimed, "being the certain and lawful son of Bacach, born of a legitimate woman, to take the succession, and that Matthew was the issue of a locksmith of Dundalk married with a woman named Alison, and not withstanding had been deceitfully supposed by his mother Con to be her son, to the end falsely to take away the dignity of the O'Neill." Any who understood Shane's gibberish knew at once that Matthew was in his grave and that the issue of succession really did not matter anymore. But very few present understood Gaelic, including Elizabeth, and for them the outlandish effect of the entrance was overwhelming. Now Shane spoke English as well as any subject. But Elizabeth demanded an Irish submission, and an Irish submission she would get. The decorum of the royal audience was so rudely upset that few of the attending ministers could recall protocol, and as O'Neill rose, those closest to the Queen groped for a style of addressing him. Someone struck on the idea of calling him "the Great O'Neill," since he could not be called just *the* O'Neill" and had not been recognized as Earl of Tyrone by the Crown. And thereafter during his stay he was announced as "O'Neill the Great, cousin to St. Patrick, friend to the Queen of England, enemy to all the world besides." Camden commented: "The English admired him no less than they should do at this day to see those savages of China or America." Shane disarmed the English Court with his bizarre behavior, and doubtless he strove for this result. Behind closed doors, however, those who knew better named him "the Grand Disturber" and never mistook his power, and the power of those like him, to mar the peace of Ireland.

Shane came to London in 1562, and in the years immediately following, the Crown studied to avoid direct intervention in Ireland. Instead, it pitted James Fitzmaurice against his cousin, the Earl of Desmond, and balanced Desmond's influence with the Earl of Ormond's. It thrust Turlough O'Neill against Shane, and once Shane had been murdered by the O'Donnells, endowed Turlough with Shane's power. The solution was to contain and countermine Irish forces, never permitting any clan or chieftain to consolidate his position. The process was tedious and, in the end, not very profitable. During this period of internecine squabbles the Crown's income from excise and land taxes plunged. The Irish morass swallowed much but gave nothing up. Thus, in 1568 Cecil and Elizabeth allowed themselves to be persuaded that direct rule was preferable. Certain West Country gentlemen believed that the answer to the Crown's Irish difficulties lay in establishing English settlements in the South. The native Gaels were to be evicted, and a purely English colony planted in Desmond Munster, the most fertile province. Among the entrepreneurs and adventurers who profited most from this plan were such famous warriors as Sir Richard Grenville, Humphrey Gilbert, Walter Raleigh, and Sir Peter Carew. Haughty and cruel beyond all reason, they managed to steal huge tracts of land, but their hated presence united the Desmond Irish under James Fitzmaurice, and there began a bitter guerrilla war. When Sir Henry Sidney finally succeeded in capturing Fitzmaurice and ending the rebellion four years later, the Munster colony, the settlers, and a large part of Elizabeth's army and resources had vanished. Burghley could look back on the experiment in 1579 and see that nothing remained. Ireland had again proved the medieval dictum *Hibernia Hibernescit,* Ireland makes all things Irish.

Let the Irish govern themselves, he concluded, let them fight among themselves, thrash about and murder their own leaders, so long as they remained nominally loyal to the Crown. The country was a hopeless quagmire, on the edge of the known world, a place that could prove as inimical to Spanish order as it had to English. As the marriage crisis grew and Ireland came to obsess his opponents, Cecil was determined to stem any precipitous rush toward war.

In August, 1579, an event seemed to confirm his judgment and to remove Ireland as an issue from the marriage dispute. James Fitzmaurice, now at the head of a swelling army, fell to arguing with a peasant over a horse. One argument led to another, and in the end Fitzmaurice was shot and killed. The hostile invasion was all at once without a leader. Rejoicing, however, was short-lived, for shortly the Earl of Desmond, Fitzmaurice's kinsman and supporter, proclaimed himself head of the rebellion, and with his immense power and prestige was already moving toward an attack on the Queen's coastal cities. In October word reached Whitehall that the Queen's forces had suffered a sharp defeat. The information was suppressed. By early October the Crown also knew that William Drury, its Lord Deputy in Ireland, was dead and by the end of the month that another battle had resulted in a costly and indecisive victory. The situation was deteriorating rapidly, and as the puritan faction learned of these developments, it pressed harder for new initiatives and an end to the marriage negotiations.

The final stage in this long conflict began in an unlikely place. In a garret room at Lincoln's Inn, London, a puritan zealot named John Stubbs completed a book which would undo a decade of diplomacy. The manuscript was so manifestly seditious that it passed through many hands before finding its way surreptitiously to a printer. On August 6 and 7 the book was handed in parts to Hugh Singleton by Francis Chamberlain, and on August 18, the day of Alençon's arrival, William Page of London "maliciously, contemptuously, and seditiously imprinted and caused to be imprinted a thousand of the aforesaid false and feigned books." Writers have noted fondly how Stubbs's pen was more potent than Leicester's sword in averting the French alliance, but in truth it is unlikely that many Londoners had time to read *The Discovery of a Gaping Gulf Whereinto England Is Like to Be Swallowed by Another French Marriage* . . . before it was called in, or confiscated. Rather what set loose the resentment dammed up against Alençon and Burghley and brought the London populace to the brink of riot was the cruel punishment meted out to Stubbs and his accomplices by the Queen.

The *Gaping Gulf* is trenchant political slander, an attack so wrongheaded and irritating that even today it stirs anger. Such stuff was common to puritan pamphlets, yet had hardly ever been directed against the Queen without a masking of allegory and biblical allusion. Understandably she was distraught; marriage was her prerogative, but now every scribbler and pulpit pounder had taken it into his head to infringe on her rights. Her anger grew violent, and she could not be brought to discuss the subject rationally. Nothing delighted her enemies more than to see her at cross-purposes with her subjects, and Mendoza lost no time in communicating her overreaction to Philip of Spain: "the Queen prohibited possession of the book under pain of death, and great efforts were used to collect all the copies, and to discover the author, in order to prevent the circulation of the facts before Parliament meets." Spain had no cause to welcome the marriage, and Mendoza hoped that Parliament might balk at Elizabeth's plan. Elizabeth's behavior left open the possibility that Parliament would oppose her. Besides calling in all copies of the *Gaping Gulf* and arresting possessors, she had ordered her clergy to deliver sermons against the book, with the consequence that Stubbs was shortly famous whereas he had previously been obscure. Then, as though one miscalculation were not enough, Her Majesty pronounced that he and Page should be hanged, drawn, and quartered. Cecil argued with her to commute the sentence, but she was adamant. Her justices tried to convince her that death and mutilation were not fitting punishment for sedition. A few provoked her anger and ended in the Tower. It was not until the end of September that the Queen relented, as it was certain she would, and commuted Stubbs's sentence. But still furious, she resorted to an obscure statute proclaimed by her sister, Mary, and smacking to everyone of persecution, Popery, and the Inquisition: Stubbs and Page were condemned to lose their right hands by knife and block. Instantly the sentence was denounced as un-English. The Privy Council was at wit's end; Parliament was in turmoil; and Cecil, sensing the mood in the streets, was alarmed by the specter of disorder and riot. Even Elizabeth found the outcry sobering, and if she refused to reduce the sentence further, she at least sent her own physicians to attend Stubbs and Page on the scaffold.

What the marriage party had clearly underestimated in opposing Leicester House was the mood of the people. Nothing is more difficult to discern in this age than the attitudes of ordinary subjects, but on the issue of Francis, Duke of Alençon, the evidence is apparent. The people, Englishmen of all classes and persuasions, puritan or established church, were united in a distaste for the Frenchman and in a desire to reverse the Crown's policy. The bare truth is that the people were more nationalistic than Elizabeth or Cecil. The Queen, of course, was lost in a reverie of love, but Burghley clearly saw the disaffection of her subjects and sensed too late their growing militancy. The nation was confident, cocky, ready to fight. During that summer dozens of ballads circulated among the citizens of London and larger towns, and one which has come down conveys the public mood:

> *The King of France shall not advance his ships in English sand,*
> *Nor shall his brother Francis have ruling of the land:*
> *We subjects true unto our Queen, the foreign yoke defy,*
> *Whereto we plight our faithful hearts, our limbs, our lives, and all,*

> *Thereby to have our honor rise, or take our fatal fall.*
> *Therefore, good Francis, rule at home, resist not our desire;*
> *For here is nothing else for thee, but only sword and fire.*

Doggerel of this sort was set to dance music, called "Monsieur's Al-lemagne" or "The Frog's Galliard," and, though it was often good-humored, spoke a world of contempt for the Queen's chosen consort. A cheerful bravado marked popular outbursts against Alençon, but the Queen was invariably held in affectionate esteem. The puritan rant, unlike tavern verse, was aimed at the educated classes. The *Gaping Gulf* was hardly the work of an itinerant preacher or ballad monger; Stubbs's intel-lectual credentials were excellent. At the time of the writing he was a barrister at Lincoln's Inn and a member of a circle which included Robert Southwell, the Catholic poet; Thomas Cartwright, the puritan divine; and Sir Edward Coke, the future Chief Justice of England. As a gentleman of some means Stubbs spoke for the middle estate of Elizabeth's common-wealth, and he put forth what was properly a manifesto announcing Eng-land's mission and place in the world. His assumptions are by now famil-iar, for they were to be invoked generation after generation in shaping and justifying the expansion and outflow of English power and influence. The *Gaping Gulf* foretells an active and godly nation, a sovereign state guided not by unprincipled diplomacy or the amoral machinations of royalty, but by conformance to the inner voice, compliance to the will of God. The nation should take pride, Stubbs insisted, in being without friends, for to be alone in an unrighteous world is never to be lost. Divine election is never easy. Inevitably the analogy is Old Testament, to Abraham and Isaac, who "cared not to have their sons match with the Canaaneans dwelling at their next door but sent further off for the daughters of God. What a contradiction of religion it were for us dwelling among Christians to admit from overseas the sons of men in marriage." Stubbs is convinced that the English are a chosen people. He is equally convinced that they are, therefore, in danger of losing their souls through idolatry, and the root of this evil is ingratitude for the insular blessings God has bestowed—in other words, their traffic with foreign infidels. But this argument is not in itself what made the *Gaping Gulf* offensive to Elizabeth. Stubbs possessed a positive knack for unconscious double entendre. Fantastically, he equates Catholicism with syphilis and the French pox and equates the proposed marriage with the Fall of Man: "This sickness of mind have the French drawn from those eastern parts of the world, as they did that other horrible disease of the body, and, having already too far westward communicated the one contagion, do now seek notably to infect our minds with the other. And because this infection spreads itself after another manner from the first, they have sent us hither not Satan in the body of a serpent, but the old serpent in shape of a man, whose sting is in his mouth, and who doth his endeavor to seduce our Eve, that she and we may lose this English Paradise."

Stubbs generally succeeds in making flesh loathsome—and this on behalf of a Queen ever conscious of her age and loss of physical beauty. Certainly the English Diana, Gloriana, Phoebe, and Eliza did not appreciate comparison with Eve; she must have enjoyed even less Stubbs's treatment of her intended. Noting the high hopes for a royal heir, he ridiculed Alençon, whose right buttock was rumored to be missing: "Assuredly there is a measure of his wickedness measured out, and a time for his judgment whensoever the saints of God have filled his bottle with tears. The common plague of his house he hath. That is he wants one of his loins to sit upon his seat. So that we see by proof in three brothers that the Lord will not leave one of Ahab's house." Reports of Alençon's deficiencies pinned the blame on venereal disease, while in fact, his condition was probably attributable to smallpox and in no way affected his potency.

Given the bald insolence of Stubbs's attack, it is no wonder that Elizabeth wanted him hanged. She fell headlong, however, into the censor's fallacy by destroying most of the evidence that might have told against him with the public. What survived in the popular mind was not Stubbs's mania but a general impression of his xenophobia, and xenophobia was a fashion of the day. The *Gaping Gulf,* for example, strikes hardest at the bordering peoples, at the Scots and the Irish. By the time the book was published Fitzmaurice was dead, yet he lived on in Stubbs's imagination, linked to Alençon and a widespread Catholic conspiracy: "Yea, unless we ourselves close our own eyes, we may see that it is a very French Popish wooing to send hither smooth-tongued Simiers to gloss and glaver and hold talk of marriage, and yet, in the meanwhile Fitzmaurice, who hath been in France . . . even now came immediately thence into Ireland to invade our Queen's dominion. . . . Is it possible for the breath of marriage well meant to England and war performed in Ireland to come out of one mouth?" With a complete disregard for life and wealth, Stubbs concludes that England does not need help in liberating the Netherlands or protecting its own borders: "English money and Englishmen must do this enterprise. It may be much better achieved now while we have the law in our own hands and may command than when we shall have put our sword into another hand; we have not so much need of him for a captain as he hath of our strength to serve him." For many the issue could not have been more succinctly stated. The Queen might set Lord Henry Howard to drafting a reply to the *Gaping Gulf,* alert her bishops, and denounce the work as treason and demagoguery, but Stubbs was destined to have the last say.

He was carried with the publisher Page to the scaffold at Westminster on November 3. Those present recall how they were astonished at the mood of the crowd, for public punishment was a favorite diversion, and execution days were normally boisterous. This day was not. The atmosphere was charged with resentment. As Stubbs and Page mounted the platform, the Londoners grew sullen, and the Lord Mayor wondered whether his guards could restrain the crowd. Stubbs was the first to suffer the penalty, but before the executioner placed the knife to his wrist and raised the mallet, the prisoner was permitted to address the people. His speech survives in the words of Camden; it affirmed his loyalty to Elizabeth, the innocence of his intentions, and his disappointment at the severity of his sentence. At his mention of the Queen, however, the crowd broke into jeers and hisses. Then, following Stubbs's benediction, "If I am to suffer, grant me this grace, that the loss of my hand do not withdraw any part of my duty and affection toward Her Majesty," Camden tells how "his hand was smitten off with three blows, and Stubbs put off his hat with his left and said with a loud voice, 'God save the Queen.' " Thereafter he swooned and was taken into the charge of the attendant physicians. The response of the people was ominous; the report goes on, "the multitude standing about was altogether silent, either out of horror of this new and unwonted punishment . . . or else out of hatred of the marriage, which most men presaged would be the overthrow of religion." If they were appalled, Page was naturally more so. As his turn came, he recalled his days as a simple plowman, saying, "This hand did I put to the plow and got my living by it many years. If it would have pleased Her Highness to have pardoned it and have taken my left hand, or my life, she had dealt more favorably with me, for now I have no means to live." Page may have regretted ever leaving his Devonshire farm, but his simple courage moved observers to tears when, after his hand was struck off with two blows of the mallet, he lifted the stump into the air and cried, "I have left here a true Englishman's hand."

Even as the crowd dispersed and the victims were carried away, Elizabeth began to yield. Her passion for Francis did not wane; she continued to assert her right to marry, but her uncanny instinct for judging how far she could lead her people began to undermine her determination. The patriotic fervor which was arousing London was contagious and she began to respond to it. Elizabeth's complexities would often take Burghley by surprise. He had struggled to hold to a reasonable course, and now he felt her veering away from the French strategy. A few months later, when the *Golden Hind* sailed in from its circumnavigation, loaded to the boards with Spanish plunder, Cecil warned her to ignore Drake's triumphant homecoming. England was not yet at war with Philip, and any royal gesture supportive of privateers could be construed as a hostile act. Elizabeth disregarded Cecil's advice. She possessed an unerring sense for singular and dramatic moments, and no sooner had the *Golden Hind* docked than she was aboard congratulating the seamen, knighting Drake, and commending his officers for "singeing the beard of Spain."

As Elizabeth proceeded to change her mind, the brunt of criticism was increasingly borne by Cecil and Alençon himself. In Paris the Duke began to appreciate the the the extent of public resistance and wrote to Elizabeth, as Mendoza records: "he was very sorry they had cut off the hands of the men concerned . . . and he would indeed be glad if he could remedy it, even at the cost of two fingers of his own hand; but as that was impossible, he entreated her to pardon the men and award them some recompense." He had begun to sense that the marriage game was up; he had come close to the great prize, but now all he could hope for was English support of his expedition to the Low Countries. Support would be forthcoming; indeed, the possibility of a marriage continued to be discussed, but after 1579 the likelihood of a match grew increasingly remote. Five years later, after fulfilling his pledge to campaign in the Netherlands, Alençon fell ill with a fever and succumbed. Elizabeth was heart-stricken at the news; the recollection of their courtship flooded back, but by then she was married to her people.

For Cecil, the period during and immediately following the marriage crisis was to be the most trying in his long political life. He was now virtually assured a spinster Queen, war with Spain, and intervention in Ireland. He would do his part to meet each of these challenges, but none would cause him more grief or lasting distress than the Irish decision. His analysis of that situation proved true. England was opening a wound which would not be closed or healed in his lifetime or the Queen's. During the next ten years Ireland's native population would be reduced 30 percent, the land wasted, and the towns laid ruin. The indigenous culture was uprooted and destroyed. But the price was also high. The energy and resources of Elizabethan England were deflected, and of those men who pressed hardest for war in 1579, not one escaped personal loss. A profound decision had been reached, a political turning point, and Cecil forgave his opponents. Though he continued to exert a restraining influence, he henceforth worked closely with Walsingham and Leicester. Some years later, when the government's practice of imprisoning and executing Jesuit agents was challenged, Burghley replied in an elaborate defense, *The Execution of Justice in England,* a work drafted for him by Francis Walsingham's man, the attorney John Stubbs.

Cecil was ridiculed for what many thought his opportunism and lack of scruple, yet beneath these charges can be sensed a resentment of established order and authority. Burghley was old and honored, but an earlier age had shaped his ideas, and by now a brilliant younger generation had begun to crowd him. Sir Philip Sidney and Edmund Spenser, England's illustrious poets, both played a prominent role in the marriage crisis and paid for their presumptuous attacks on Cecil. Sir Philip, in a second letter denouncing the French marriage, made a point of baiting the Queen's advisor for his timidity and base abdication to Simier and Alençon. Fortunately for Sidney, the letter did not come to Elizabeth's attention until January; it angered her, of course, but did not provoke the destructive wrath it might have in September. She reflected on a suitable rebuke. Meanwhile, Cecil said nothing. Sidney continued to appear at Whitehall and a short time after was drawn into a violent dispute on the tennis court with Cecil's son-in-law, the Earl of Oxford. Insults were exchanged, blows tendered, and each called the other out. Both were strong swordsmen, and it is possible that Sidney's ridicule of Cecil might have ended in bloodshed had the Queen not learned of the duel and banished Sidney from London.

Sir Philip's impatience with Burghley was rooted in his desire to supplant cynicism and to imbue the state with a new spirit. His noble impetuousness was to end tragically. At twenty-five he was a promising young statesman, raised and educated to foreign service, and, apart from his literary genius, had already shown a remarkable aptitude for administration and affairs. Perhaps inevitably he was caught up in the war to free the Netherlands. Nor was he content to remain in an administrative post, but insisted on leading troops in battle. In 1586, outside the town of Zutphen, a few miles from Arnhem, he fell fatally wounded in a skirmish with Spanish infantry. Sidney's body was shipped home in the *Ark Royal*, Elizabeth's flagship, the vessel draped from stem to stern in black crepe, and he was brought ashore to the cries and lamentations of his countrymen. He was their perfect knight, their model; he was also their first war hero, more honored in death than life. His funeral at St. Paul's was the highest tribute paid a soldier during Elizabeth's reign, but the Queen contributed not a farthing to it. Since Sir Henry had left nothing to his son but creditors, Sir Philip's father-in-law, Francis Walsingham, paid the charges, and it was said that the old man's fortune never recovered from this honor done the Sidneys.

If anything, Edmund Spenser slandered Cecil worse, and without the security and assured position Sidney enjoyed. He was the son of a poor tailor, penniless, and newly wed. In 1579 he was Leicester's personal secretary, commuting daily from Mistress Kerke's house in Westminster to the City. He was employed in celebrating Dudley's origins by drafting from his genealogy an epic poem, to be called the *Stemmata Dudleiana*. Of more consequence, Spenser was also the poet of *The Shepheardes Calendar*, already circulating in manuscript by mid-1579 and the first harbinger of greatness in Elizabethan verse. If anyone could benefit from the cosmopolitan atmosphere and influence of London, Spenser could, but his participation in the marriage crisis assured his virtual banishment. The cause of his troubles was a satiric allegory, based on *Reynard the Fox*, and called *Mother Hubberds Tale*. The plot turns on the antics of an ape and a fox, all too unmistakably similar to Simier and Burghley, and their scurvy adventures in the animal kingdom. They are seen to subvert the natural order of things; they cheat and defraud, undermine religion and morality, and eventually succeed in overthrowing the regal lion. Once they have filched the lion's crown and once the ape has mounted his throne, an army of foreign beasts is invited into the kingdom to complete the despoliation. *Mother Hubberds Tale* is accomplished satire, perhaps one of the finest animal fables in the language, but, insofar as it treats Cecil as a species of chicken thief, more than a little mad. Spenser, in his enthusiasm for Leicester and his opposition to a foreign marriage, overstepped reasonable bounds. It is more or less certain that his poem was called in; that it occasioned some embarrassment to Dudley, who was struggling to regain the Queen's confidence; and that it resulted in Spenser's dispatch to Ireland. Within a few months he and his bride were en route to Cork with an English army. He never saw the heroic war in the Netherlands, just the footslogging misery of the interminable Irish campaign, and he was to be both witness and participant in the conquest of that country. For the next twenty years Ireland conditioned his life as an official and as a poet and, for all its barbarity and desolation, became the setting of his mature verse. Dudley, however, on the advice of Henry Sidney, had disposed of him, and Spenser found this ingratitude hard to forget. Henceforth his great work moves to define the essence of power, loyalty, and justice, and though, understandably, Burghley was never his friend, his powerful idealizations of monarchy and the moral order won him the patronage of the Queen.

Leicester, for his part, achieved his heart's desire. In 1586 he led an English expeditionary force to the Netherlands, some of his troops survivors of the earlier Irish ordeal. Once there, he attempted to seize command of all Protestant forces in the struggle and, by doing so, alienated Elizabeth. Dudley overestimated his capacities. Within a short time his army was laughed at by allies and enemies alike, its logistics hopelessly tangled, its troops poorly led and deserting. Dudley found himself baffled at every opportunity. He despaired over the senseless death of his nephew Philip and began to lose his nerve. During the worst he turned to Burghley, begging him not to desert him in his hour of need: "Good my lord, have me thus far only in your care that in these things which Her Majesty and you have all agreed and confirmed for me to do, that I be not made a metamorphosis, that I shall not know what to do." Leicester was not abandoned, but he was fortunate to be extricated from Dutch mud and brought home to confront Elizabeth's disgust and disappointment. The expedition which he led suffered appalling attrition and in the final analysis accomplished only an extravagant expenditure of treasury. Broken by defeat and recrimination, saddened by his family's losses, Dudley returned to England a tired man. Within two years he was dead.

But in 1579 the expansion had only begun. Ireland now lay open to English arms, and what caused that poor island to become an objective was the very confusion and instability of the Gaelic world.

MUNSTER, 1565
The Irish

Long before the marriage crisis, Elizabeth had begun to lose patience with her Desmond lords. Among the many provocations she endured, one in particular could not be borne. On a May morning in 1565 the feudal levies of Gerald Fitzgerald, Earl of Desmond, and Thomas Butler, Earl of Ormond, collided a short distance below Lismore Castle, on the Blackwater River. The field was called Affane, and there in one hour the frail peace of Ireland was shattered. Affane was the last private, pitched battle fought in the British Isles between neighbors, the last meeting of autonomous armies. That morning Fitzgerald brought his MacCarthys, O'Sullivans, McSheehys, and O'Connors to the field; Butler his O'Kennedys, Gillapatricks, and Burkes, and before the day ended Fitzgerald's men had been driven headlong into the Blackwater and hacked to pieces along the banks. More than 300 Geraldines, as the Earl of Desmond's supporters were known, died at this place, and Fitzgerald himself was left abandoned on the field, his right hip broken by a pistol ball. As the victorious Butlers lifted him onto their shoulders to be borne away, they jeered, "Where now is the mighty Earl of Desmond?" To which Fitzgerald replied, "Where he belongs—on the backs of the Butlers." The feud which resulted in Affane was by now several generations old, and neither Gerald Fitzgerald nor Thomas Butler imagined this battle to be their last. The ostensible reason for the fighting was a dispute over rents; the real reason, control of Munster, the vast sprawling province of the South. Elizabeth was of an opinion that Desmond Munster belonged to her realm, with the rest of Ireland, but she had no warning of Affane.

Neither lord thought much about the Crown or the Queen's displeasure. She was young, immersed in English affairs, and not inclined to meddle with her Irish peers. Thomas Butler, tenth Earl of Ormond, was Elizabeth's "Black Tom," her childhood playmate, a cousin on the Boleyn side. He had been reared at Court and, almost alone among the Irish magnates, was a staunch Protestant. Gerald Fitzgerald, fourteenth Earl of Desmond, was the second husband of Butler's mother, and for all that the Countess of Desmond had been unable to keep her husband and son from one another's throats, her intercession with Elizabeth had sheltered Gerald. There should have been no reason to look for English interference. But both Butler and Fitzgerald miscalculated. The Queen was furious with her Irish lords; Affane was the last indignity. "No sword shall be drawn in this realm but the Queen's, which shall touch only the guilty," she had warned them on several occasions, and they had disregarded her. They had fought a battle without reference to her, her government, or the welfare of her realm. She therefore summoned them both to London to stand trial. Ormond could be counted on to obey; Desmond could not, but since Fitzgerald was in Butler's hands and unable to walk, "Black Tom" was ordered to carry him to London on a stretcher if need be. So it happened that Gerald Fitzgerald left Ireland. He would not return for seven years, and in that time momentous changes would overtake the land.

Gerald was brought before the Privy Council on a litter, his dress unchanged and filthy since the day of the battle, his strong constitution broken by weeks in Ormond's dungeon. He had received no medication for his wound, and now, almost six weeks after Affane, the bone was mending poorly. Feverish and in pain, he frequently lost consciousness during the arraignment and had no idea to what he confessed. The Crown had not yet decided what to do with him, but since he had admitted to violating the Queen's peace, he was placed in the custody of the Lieutenant of the Tower to await further trial. His antagonist, Butler, was likewise reprimanded but allowed his liberty on parole.

The Desmonds were no strangers to the Tower. During his youth, Gerald had been detained there. His father had escaped imprisonment there by dying in Ireland, but his grandfather had died in the Tower, and his great-uncle Silken Thomas had been penned there for eighteen months before he was carted to Tyburn with five kinsmen, hanged, drawn, and quartered. The Tower symbolized everything the Fitzgeralds were born to hate: English rule and English law—tyranny and injustice. It fell to Gerald, once he had recovered, to conduct himself there with noblesse and bravado. The Fitzgeralds were Catholic and, when they chose, pronouncedly Gaelic. Unlike Butler, Gerald despised the capital and visited London only under constraint. Even then, he traveled with an entourage of harpists, bards, family retainers, and squires or kern. In the wake of Affane more than a hundred dependents flocked to London to eat at his table in the Tower and share his hardships. They soon turned his prison into a hostel and, until the money ran out, kept up the brave show. But the money did run out. The Council denied Gerald credit, and since his rents were temporarily impounded pending his trial, he was thrown onto a bare allowance from the Queen.

Gerald's second wife and son came to live with him at the Tower, but even after two months in confinement he still believed that he would be freed. His transgressions did not warrant severe measures; he was prepared to pledge his obedience to the Crown as he had in the past, stand his trial *pro forma*, pay his fine, and listen to the usual admonitions from Cecil or Sussex. Then he would be in Ireland again. But Gerald was not brought to trial in 1565 or 1566; he languished in the Tower a favored prisoner, but a prisoner nonetheless. The reason for the long delay had nothing to do with Affane, Butler, or Gerald's many infractions of the Queen's laws. During these months a heated debate persisted over the future of Ireland, and Gerald bore on the question for the same reasons the Desmonds always had—they were without exception the largest titled landholders in the country.

By ancient grant and right of chieftaincy Desmond claimed more than 800,000 acres of Southern Ireland, 1550 square miles in Munster, Leinster, and Connaught. His domains far exceeded those of any English lord and, though less productive than shireland, were also largely outside the surveillance of the Crown. The revenues of his fiefdoms might pay for the entire per annum administration of Ireland or, much the same, support an army of 4000 men to enforce Her Majesty's rule. The painful fact, as matters stood, was that the Crown received virtually nothing from Gerald, neither rent on grants and leases nor cess. Money that might have gone to defray the cost of government went instead to pay Gerald's private armies, and these forces broke more laws than they ever helped enforce. In the absence of strong English government in Ireland, Desmond squandered his great wealth through maladministration and petty warfare. He was an indefatigable schemer and annually increased the aggregate of his holdings. Yet should he prove a more capable ruler with age and maturity, he would present a formidable challenge to the Crown itself. The temptation was there from the start to remove him entirely.

Until Affane, it was all that Whitehall could do to balance the other principal earldoms of Ireland against Desmond. The Earls of Ormond, Kildare, Thomond, and Clanricarde hemmed him in, and beyond them, the Earl of Tyrone, isolated in the Celtic fastnesses of the North. The North, however, lay in another sphere, cut off by lakes and mountains from the South, and the English were no more loved in Ulster than they were in Munster. Ormond, Kildare, Clanricarde, and Thomond were left to contain Gerald, and they were barely sufficient to do so. Kildare was a Fitzgerald, uncle to Desmond, and inclined to strict neutrality. The Earl of Thomond, an O'Brien, and the Earl of Clanricarde, a Burke, were too weak to challenge Gerald alone and were as often in conflict with Ormond as with Desmond. Balance was not working, and no solution was in sight when Affane suddenly changed all. Gerald had fallen into the government's hands, and understandably, it was reluctant to turn him free. What to do with Desmond absorbed the attentions of the Council during the next year. Cecil argued that Ireland was better off without him, and Henry Sidney, concerned with the vacuum left in the South, held that he should be returned. Unavoidably the dispute coincided with a clash of politics at Court, and the lines were drawn between those who favored Desmond and those who supported Ormond. Walsingham suspected Desmond's links to Spain and Rome and expressed disgust at his degeneracy into chieftaincy and Gaelic forms. Attempts to establish the Church of England in Munster had been continually frustrated, while Common Law made no headway whatever against Gaelic Brehon Law. The Queen distrusted Gerald and favored her kinsman Ormond, but she refused to judge, and while the matter remained unsettled, Desmond was made to vanish from the public eye. By 1567 his Irish supporters believed that he had died in the Tower.

Actually the Council chose to remove him across the Thames to Southwark, to bury him in the house of Warham St. Leger, a city knight with connections to Ireland. Gerald was permitted the company of his second wife, Eleanor, and a son by his first marriage, Garet, but he was restricted to house arrest. He also found himself in unaccustomed squalor. The small stipend allowed him by the Council was inadequate to maintain his family. His retinue had disappeared; his money was gone; and to assure his helplessness and forestall the rise of another Fitzgerald, the Crown had arrested and brought to London his two brothers, Sir John of Desmond and James. Gerald's links to Munster were severed completely.

He had never recovered entirely from his wound, and throughout 1567 he was in poor health. That he was also hungry and ragged is certain from his correspondence and the niggardly provisions the Queen provided. Sir Warham probably aided him from his own slender means, or so their later relations would suggest, but St. Leger House was dark and cramped; it was

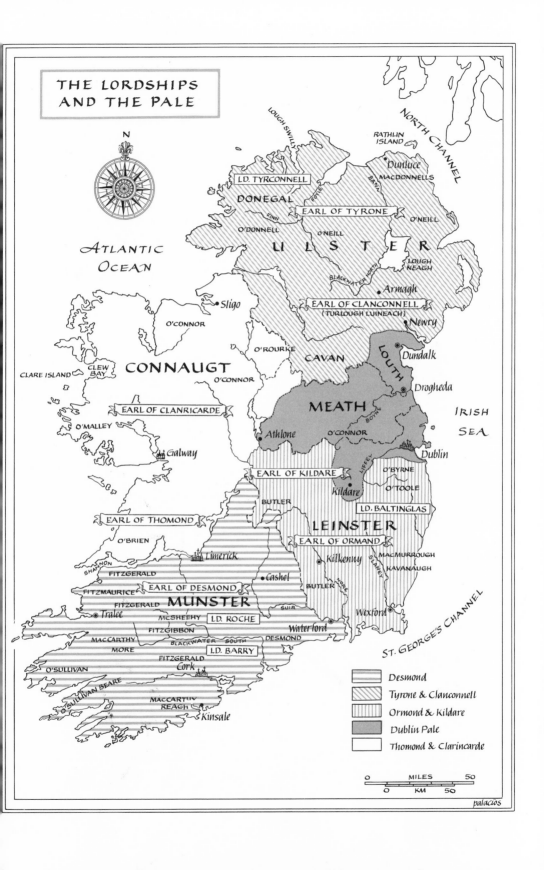

THE LORDSHIPS
AND THE PALE

N

NORTH CHANNEL

ATLANTIC
OCEAN

LOUGH SWILLY

RATHLIN
ISLAND

LD. TYRCONNELL

• Dunluce
MACDONNELLS

DONEGAL

EARL OF TYRONE

O'NEILL

O'DONNELL

O'NEILL

U L S T E R

LOUGH
NEAGH

BLACKWATER NORTH

• Armagh

EARL OF CLANCONNELL
(TURLOUGH LUINEACH)

• Sligo

O'CONNOR

• Newry

O'ROURKE

CAVAN

• Dundalk

LOUTH

CLEW
BAY

CONNAUGT

O'CONNOR

• Drogheda

CLARE ISLAND

IRISH
SEA

O'MALLEY

EARL OF CLANRICARDE

MEATH

BOYNE

• Athlone

O'CONNOR

• Galway

• Dublin

EARL OF KILDARE

O'BYRNE

O'TOOLE

BUTLER

LIFFEY

• Kildare

EARL OF THOMOND

LD. BALTINGLAS

O'BRIEN

LEINSTER

EARL OF ORMAND

SHANNON

• Limerick

MACMURROUGH

FITZGERALD

• Kilkenny

KAVANAUGH

EARL OF DESMOND

• Cashel

NORE

SLANEY

FITZMAURICE

MUNSTER

BUTLER

FITZGERALD

SUIR

• Wexford

• Tralee

MCSHEEHY

LD. ROCHE

• Waterford

ST. GEORGE'S CHANNEL

FITZGIBBON

DESMOND

MACCARTHY

BLACKWATER SOUTH

MORE

LD. BARRY

FITZGERALD

O'SULLIVAN

Cork

O'SULLIVAN BEARE

MACCARTHY
REAGH

• Kinsale

	Desmond
	Tyrone & Clanconnell
	Ormond & Kildare
	Dublin Pale
	Thomond & Clarincarde

0   MILES   50

0   KM   50

palacios

located just east of London Bridge beside a depot for municipal building materials. The house had once been a friary in the country, but grown up around it was Bankside, a rowdy neighborhood of breweries, brothels, the Clink Prison, and Paris Garden bear-pits. In this environment Lady Eleanor, Countess of Desmond, was with child in 1568 and delivered of a son, James, early the next year.

By the spring of 1568 the Earl of Desmond was largely forgotten outside Munster, yet there were also signs that Whitehall was finally coming to a decision. Gerald was suddenly granted the liberty of Southwark, Bankside, and the marshes west of Lambeth Palace, which was to say that he could move freely outside the City of London. His allowance was increased, and he was encouraged for his health and pleasure to enlarge his knowledge of the neighborhood. Since he was known for looseness and carousing ways, no one was surprised to learn that he was soon frequenting low taverns near the Clink, visiting the stews, and plotting with disreputable waterfront types. In any event no effort was made to interfere with his pastimes. And in June, after Lady Eleanor had begun her lying-in, Gerald fell in with Martin Frobisher, the famous sea dog and privateer, somewhere along Bankside. What he needed was a discreet captain with a knowledge of the Irish coastline and a penchant for dangerous money. Frobisher assured him that he was the man, and between them they hatched a plot to smuggle Desmond down the Thames and to sea before his disappearance could be discovered. After three years in captivity Gerald was desperate, his judgment—never the strongest—seriously affected, or he would not have plotted escape and treason with Frobisher. Desmond had never obeyed the Crown, but he had never dared hope for its overthrow or imagine that he possessed the power to expel the English from Ireland. Now he spoke wildly, and though the details of his conversations with Frobisher are not known, they were all that Whitehall could have wished. By accepting Frobisher's proposal, Gerald played directly into the hands of Frobisher's employers. Desmond never reached a ship; he was retaken on a London wharf, armed and incognito, and hauled before Francis Walsingham to be charged with violating his parole and plotting treason. Before Frobisher had consented to play Judas, the Crown had already decided its course in Ireland, and the Earl of Desmond was the necessary sacrifice to the success of a new policy.

The outcome of the long-awaited trial was never in doubt; Gerald was judged guilty of treason, and his doom sealed by the testimony of Frobisher. One hope was held out for his salvation: he was required to admit his guilt, to renounce his earldom and his claim to land and privileges, and to receive back from Elizabeth whatever she pleased to give him. His ill-considered act had left him no choice but total surrender, and to save his life, he forfeited the inheritance of his house and the independence of Irish Munster. Though Gerald had been set up, incited, he acted predictably and the trick was a way to remove him, short of assassination or the block. Elizabeth could no longer permit him to return to Ireland, but she could also no longer permit a vacuum in Munster, into which his cousin Fitzmaurice or some other lordling might move. Gerald's holdings were to be broken up and his lands occupied by English settlers, and to this end the great domains of Desmond Ireland were to be attainted and confiscated. It would prove one thing, however, to seize Munster, another to hold it. Gerald's capitulation would haunt him for the rest of his long life, and the words of his surrender, spoken under duress, were to echo down the years of Elizabeth's reign: "I, the Earl of Desmond, on the 12th day of July, 1568, hereby acknowledge my offenses, my life being in peril, my goods liable to forfeiture, and myself in danger to her Highness for the forfeiture of 20,000 pounds; I here by my security relinquish into her Majesty's hands all my lands, tenements, houses, castles, signories, all I stand possessed of, to receive back what her Majesty please allow me, and engaging to make a full and complete assurance to her Majesty of all which she might be pleased to keep." What Elizabeth pleased to allow Gerald was four more years in Southwark. She increased his support and pension, but he was still residing at St. Leger House long after Sir Warham had left for Ireland in the first land rush.

If the way lay open to Munster, the means of resettlement continued in question, for only by a thorough colonization could the Crown realize its hopes of increasing political stability, revenue, and allegiance. Colonization, however, meant dispossession of the native Irish, and dispossession required a substantial commitment of force. Few planters, or settlers, were willing to undertake the hazards of working Irish land so long as the great clans remained loyal to the Fitzgeralds. What was needed was colonization with strong military muscle, and in order to lure soldiers to Ireland, large tracts of Desmond land would have to be awarded. Therefore, it became both convenient and necessary to discover discrepancies in the Fitzgeralds' patents of ownership. Even before his betrayal at the hands of Frobisher, questions were raised about the legality of Desmond's titles and the authenticity of his ancient grants, many dating back to the Norman conquest of Ireland. Whether the scheme to disown the Fitzgeralds and their dependent clans was conceived before or after the Earl's conviction is not known. Nor is there certainty whether the plan originated with Walsingham or, as the government would always contend, with Sir Peter Carew.

But by late 1568 a movement was under way to award substantial estates to any wellborn gentleman, with military experience, who could prove a prior claim to Desmond lands.

Sir Peter Carew was only the first to discover an ancient and lapsed patrimony in Ireland. The occasion of this revelation was described by his solicitor and biographer, John Hooker: "At leisure in Devon, Sir Peter thought to himself of such lands as he persuaded himself he should have in Ireland, and having some evidence of the same, and being old and unlearned, he was referred to Hooker as a man greatly given to seek and search old records and ancient writings . . . and that he was best able of any in the city of Exeter to do him pleasure in this behalf." Hooker is remembered now principally as the historian of the first Munster colony, yet in 1568 he was a poor solicitor eking out a living from illiterate Devonshire gentlemen. It was to be his good fortune to discover in Sir Peter a lifelong patron and friend, the more so because this aging client was soon to be rich beyond his dreams.

The documents which transformed Carew from a ne'er-do-well country knight to an Irish grandee were illegible. Whether their obscurities resulted from negligence, for Sir Peter was not a careful man, or from forgery remains open to question. But Hooker, by his own admittance, was singularly prepared to decipher them to Sir Peter's satisfaction. He recalled his first view of these controversial documents: "He did forthwith show and part unto him [Hooker] two or three old writings of evidence concerning the said lands, and of which one was very old and had been trodden under the foot, and by that means the letters were almost worn out: nevertheless he [Hooker] did read them and declare the effect unto him: which he did like so well, that then he committed unto him the view and search of all his evidence." An agreement consummated, Hooker was dispatched at once to Dublin Castle, the center of English government in Ireland, to search out further proof of Sir Peter's rights and compile a book supporting his claims. All was accomplished within the month, and armed with pedigrees and patents attesting to his distant kinship with the Fitzgeralds, Sir Peter left Devon for London and Whitehall. As for the validity of his suit, Hooker only commented in his *Life of Peter Carew,* "No thing could be found to prejudice or impeach his title"; neither could anything be found really to substantiate it, and history has weighed Carew's case and found it slight.

But more must be said of Carew than that he proceeded from dubious legalities to outright theft. For he was neither the best nor the worst of Elizabethan entrepreneurs. His age resorted gladly to litigation, and he was no less conversant with writs and depositions than many others. With Desmond's fall he discerned an opportunity, and few blame him overly for having seized it. He could never have foreseen the consequences of his adventure. Hooker wrote that Sir Peter was "of mean stature, somewhat broad, big boned and strong sinewed," and the portrait which emerges is of a man large in action but small in thought. To be sure, his abilities were limited, but he was inordinately ambitious and had been taught perseverance in a harsh school. Hooker told a revealing anecdote about his youth. Peter, who was sent by his father to school in Exeter when he was about twelve, came under the tutelage of a teacher named Freers, the master of the grammar school. And whether because Freers was "counted to be a very hard and cruel master, or whether it were for that Peter had no affection to his learning, true it is, he would never keep his school, but was daily a truant." The scholars would look for him and find him invariably on the city walls, unwilling to climb down. Finally, because he was so generally troublesome, his father was sent for, "who, at his next coming to Exeter, calling his son before him, tied him in a line and delivered him to one of his servants, to be carried about the town as one of his hounds, led him home to Mohonesotrey like a dog: and after that he being come to his home, he coupled him to one of his hounds and so continued him for a time. Finally, he took him to London, to the schoolmaster of Paul's, but do the schoolmaster what he could, he in no wise could frame this young Peter to smell to a book, or to like of any schooling."

Carew spent many years escaping from the shadow of his father, soldiering on the Continent, going to sea, squabbling with his Devonshire neighbors. Yet in 1568 he was still mired in the provinces, and the fact galled him. Despite his age, he was prepared to begin all over again, and it is essential to recognize that his quest was less for riches than reputation. Like so many other men of his time, he was a conscious dynast, more concerned with posterity, that monument which could withstand the ravages of time, than with wealth for its own sake. That he should have chosen to build in Ireland, where nothing ever lasted, is a great irony. But he also commissioned his companion Hooker to record his exploits, and this work, full of extravagant flattery and compliment, is Carew's lasting epitaph— and the Munster colony's.

Sir Peter's suit met with an enthusiasm from the Queen which could only have confused and overwhelmed him. Not only was his evidence taken at face value, but his plan to found a nation of Englishmen in the midst of Ireland was welcomed. Where one solicitor could go, however, others could also, and as Sir Peter returned home to ready himself and his servants for their journey, scores of lackland English knights rushed to follow his example. Among them was the redoubtable soldier Sir Richard Grenville; Gerald's jailer, Sir Warham St. Leger; and Carew's kinsman Humphrey Gilbert. The Crown was eager to recognize their claims, too.

For on these men would eventually fall the defense of the Munster Plantations.

To the Irish the invasion of Munster would always seem a coming of the locusts. Across the English westward ports—Bristol, Chester, Mount's Bay, Plymouth—yeoman and laborers, artisans and militia gathered from every shire, paying exorbitantly for their passage, ignorant of what they would find in Desmond's Ireland, and unprepared. Had Elizabeth realized then what forces she was loosing on her Irish subjects, she might well have reconsidered. Cecil, for his part, despaired at the extent of the proposed evictions, and until the last moment he counseled against the scheme. But Elizabeth had grown weary with Ireland. Year after year the issues confronting her multiplied; by 1568 she was threatened with revolt in Scotland and the North Country, with the complicity of Mary Stuart and Mary's French allies abroad. It is little wonder perhaps that the beset Queen grasped at Carew's promises and the hope of a stable Ireland. The plan was not new to her. What Carew proposed to carry out, Sir Henry Sidney had advised several years before. In a private letter to Her Majesty, he wrote: "The Earl of Desmond enjoyeth under his rule, or rather tyranny, the third part of this great country, which, I assure your Majesty, to be greater than all Yorkshire. In all which his limits, neither is your name reverenced, nor your laws obeyed. Neither dare any sheriff execute any part of his office therein. . . . If you will have this country free from annoyance, your Majesty must plant (as I have often written) justice to be resident in those quarters. But surely it will never be thoroughly so, till the same land be made shire-ground and your Highness' writ and tongue as current there as in your other counties." The theme which Sidney struck here was constant with him: it is the insufficiency of English officers under Irish chieftains and Irish laws which leads to disorder. Translate the shire administration of England to Ireland, Sidney argued, and there will be peace, so long as there are Englishmen to govern. How much Elizabeth came to believe in this idea is apparent in a letter to Sidney at the time of Desmond's warfare with Ormond. She advised Sir Henry to burn the message and treat its contents as a routine communication: "Harry, suffer not that Desmond's designing deeds, far wide of his promises, but trust to the other [Ormond]. A strength to harm is perilous in the hand of an ambitious head. . . . If we always deliberate, we shall never do; thus are we ever knitting a knot, never tied. Yea, and if our web be framed with rotten hurdles, when our loom is wellnigh done, our work is new to begin. God send the weaver true prentices again." The Queen's phrases are intentionally elliptical. Yet there is no doubt that she rejected Gerald for Ormond, and as she chose Thomas Butler to be the foundation of a new peace in Ireland, she chose Carew's Englishmen to be the sound hurdles of her web.

The more alarming, then, was to be the outcome. Final permission was granted to the undertakers, as they were called, of the First Munster Plantation, and without delay Sir Peter Carew's hordes sailed for Cork, Waterford, and Youghal. They sailed also, as events were to prove, for the First Desmond War—the long nightmare Cecil was to recall in 1579.

Sir Peter's adventure began propitiously with his appearance before the members of the Dublin Parliament, the instrument of English rule in Ireland. If any governing body might have blocked his advance, it was this assembly of Anglo-Irish magnates. Before them he presented his claims, *inveniens rotulam evidentiarum*, to the barony of Idrone in County Carlow and to one-half the *kingdom* of Cork, a kingdom which never existed. To everyone's amazement, his arguments were not only heard but credited. Doubtless encouraged, Carew immediately produced additional evidence supporting his demands to territory in Imokilly, Tyrbarry, Muskerry, Tyrcourcy, Carberry, Collymore, Collybeg, Castle Donovan, Bantry, Clandonough, Kerricurrihy, Dunhallow, and Coshbride—virtually the heart of Desmond Munster and MacCarthy Muskerry. That the Irish lords sat still for these demands is a testimony to Elizabeth's power, Sidney's eloquence, and the sad state of Munster under Desmond's thumb. Common interests were not easily grasped in midcentury Ireland, and Gerald's fall had gladdened more hearts than it dismayed. The situation was explained succinctly by Sir Henry Sidney when he wrote: "The lesser lords and others, with open mouths and held-up hands to heaven, cry out for justice and that it might please your Majesty to cause your name to be known amongst them, with reverence and your laws obeyed."

As always there was dissension among the chiefs; one's right was the other's wrong, and the loser first to the throne. Never once in the midst of their squabbling did they suspect the full possibilities of Carew's mission, and their pettiness, no less than Whitehall's duplicity, lay at the root of his whirlwind success. Carew not only was granted the flaithlands, or clan jurisdictions, of the Fitzgeralds, but was yielded the flaithlands of the More-MacCarthys, the MacMurrough-Kavanaughs, the Connaught Burkes, all as staunchly opposed to the Earl of Desmond as any clans in Ireland. With the flaithlands went those portions known in Gaelic as *cumhal senorba*, lands set aside for the maintenance of widows, orphans, and old childless people. There went also the *gabhailcine*, or gavelkind lands, possessed in common by a clan and tenanted by younger sons. It is apparent that Carew and his fellow undertakers intruded unwittingly on a unique system of land tenure, one prescribed by ancient Irish or Brehon Law and already in precarious condition through the lawlessness of the Irish themselves. No stability could result from such an invasion, only mounting disorder and social collapse.

No wonder that the allowance of Carew's claims by the Dublin Council eventually alarmed the countryside and those few Irish who appreciated the comparative state of Ireland and England. One in particular, the shrewd, accomplished MacTeige MacCarthy, Sheriff of Cork, recognized the danger and, familiar with usual English motives, offered to buy off Sir Peter. Together with other flaiths, or chieftains, MacTeige promised a handsome tribute if Carew would return whence he came and remain an absentee landlord, resigned to collecting rents. Hooker left his master's side and journeyed to Cork; there he received on Carew's behalf a large house in the city and a prosperous manor at Kinsale. But the bribe once taken, Carew reneged, proceeding first to strip the Kavanaughs of their lands. MacCarthy had misjudged him. Within a few weeks Sir Peter had seized the barony of Idrone, and by early autumn was evicting Irish families across the length of his domains. Simultaneously, Sir Richard Grenville had established an estate west of Cork at Tracton, Sir Warham St. Leger had settled nearby, and Humphrey Gilbert had pushed west with others beyond the Blackwater River into the very center of Munster.

The clan Kavanaugh was first to bear the yoke of this new order, and they, by an accident of history, were least able to resist it. The Irish clan, or *fine*, had been recognized by English law since the beginning of the thirteenth century. At this time the clans were denominated the *naciones et cognomina*, the nations and families, of the land. They became bound to the administration of English justice by the Brehon principle of *cin comhfhocuis*, through which clan and chief were made responsible for the misdeeds of their kin. This gradual synthesis of Irish law and English Common Law encouraged social evolution. By Elizabeth's day some of the clans were more feudal than tribal and had in large measure abandoned the practice of communal land tenure and an elected chieftaincy. Now the flaiths were made barons; their families, vassals. And perhaps more than others the Kavanaughs epitomized this transition. For while the MacMurrough-Kavanaughs traced descent from one of the five lines of Irish kings, they had long ago surrendered their native prerogatives. They were reared and educated in England; they were welcome at the English Court; and it is little wonder that, being civil men, they attempted to fight Carew with his own weapons. Resorting to law, they took their case first to the Dublin Council, then to the Queen. Both suits were lost before begun. Their claim to Idrone and Carlow had been recognized by the Crown since the mid-twelfth century, but pressed to prove their ownership, they could produce no deeds, no patents, no pedigrees or rolls. For the lack of a parchment, the Kavanaughs lost their lands and way of life. They awoke to find themselves trapped between their English friends and their Irish countrymen. No longer warriors, most of the Kavanaughs had neither the means nor the inclination to resist Carew, and they relinquished their lands grudgingly, becoming subjects where they had once ruled. Their subjugation was not uniform. But the code of *cin comhfhocuis* now worked against them. Solidarity was the law of the *fine*, and disobedience by some meant that all would suffer. Consequently where some Kavanaughs rose against the English intruders, fighting for their homesteads, they were suppressed and driven off by their own kinsmen fearing reprisals. The dilemma was not theirs alone; during Elizabeth's Irish wars other clans found themselves torn between their English overlords and the desperate needs of their fellow Irish. The final decision was often based on the local strength of either side and, once made, would change with circumstances.

Sir Peter acquired tne barony of Idrone without force, and he would hold the estate through war and troubled peace until his natural death in 1575. The barony then passed to his son, Peter, who in turn held the land until the Desmonds swept into Carlow in 1580, murdering him, the English, and the Kavanaughs alike. But in the winter of 1568–1569 the Kavanaughs either submitted at home or froze in the mountains, and the Fitzgeralds, MacCarthys, and Butlers nearby were fortunate to escape.

Of Sir Peter's life at Idrone little is known beyond Hooker's account, and Hooker was no doubt concerned with presenting his client in the best light. He wrote of Carew that he was a perfect, temperate, noble knight, kind, just, modest, "and of one fault: too generous to his guests when feeding them." As for his ambition after the seizure of Idrone, Hooker said only that "he contented himself with that which was his own, as that he neither inordinately sought any other men's goods." With some truth to this report allowed, it seems no less probable that Sir Peter responded to Ireland as other Englishmen had before him—that he was struck by the backwardness of the land. He would not have found the Irish a model of good yeomanry; the inhabitants of his estates were certainly not plowmen or herdsmen by shire standards. They were instead either freemen or serfs, in Gaelic *saer-ceile* or *daer-ceile,* and their compliance was not to be assured overnight like the Anglicized Kavanaughs'. Carew seems to have characterized them as slothful, dishonest, and lascivious, and overlooking how a few months earlier he had been an estate-hunting soldier of fortune, he came to look upon his task in Ireland as a civilizing mission. In any event a restless strain in his nature was to become the source of much trouble, for Sir Peter had won Idrone easily and thereafter underestimated the diffculties of Ireland. Possibly the land had begun to affect his judgment. Wide, far-stretching meadows suddenly seemed hostile; the forests of Carlow appeared forbidding, and a note of paranoia was struck by Hooker when he recalled, "Sundry conspiracies had been and daily were contrived against Sir Peter, and for no other cause but because he did not only abolish in his own country, but also inveighed against everywhere the wicked and detestable Irish customs, the same being but the spoiling of the honest subjects and true laborers, and the maintenance of thieves, murderers and the maintenance of all loose and disordered people."

Unfortunately, Sir Peter's attention was drawn during this period to Sir Edmund and Sir Edward Butler. These brothers of the Earl of Ormond were occupied in his absence with raiding their neighbors, and having lost several plowlands to Carew, they carried their marauding across the border of Kilkenny into Carlow. Rustling, or reiving as it was known, had long been a fact of life in Ireland, where wealth was still measured in cattle and herding provided more subsistence than farming. The Butlers were likely taking the measure of Carew, and in the process some cattle changed hands, a church was burned, and a small loss of life occurred among the churls. MacTeige MacCarthy had feared and expected just such a provocation. More experienced authorities than Sir Peter might have ignored the Butlers, but he mistook their careless exuberance for malice. As a result, he resolved to punish them, disregarding that their brother, Thomas, had been the first cause of Desmond's removal and Carew's own good fortune. To this day it is difficult to understand Sir Peter's decision. Hooker offers no clarification, only the slightly ominous observation that while Sir Peter read little, he preferred books on military history and the martial arts. Conceivably, Carew was lured into the field against the Butlers by the prospect of a swift and glorious campaign. From all that is known of him, this explanation cannot be discounted. But just as likely Ireland, stubborn and irredeemable, had tried his patience to the last and overpowered his good sense. For nothing that Carew might have done could have been more ill advised than his invasion of Ormond's territory.

To the purpose he gathered English militia, Kavanaughs, and the dreaded mercenaries of Ireland, the bonaghts. He would live to regret his pick of troops. For the bonaght was drawn from the disintegrating center of Celtic life; he was the masterless man, the drifter, the outcast of the clans. On account of him, wars in Ireland were easier to start than stop. He was a ravenous plunderer of both sides, despised by English and Irish alike, and, even under the firmest command, near uncontrollable. So much the worse, then, for a novice like Sir Peter. As his motley force crossed into County Kilkenny, it struck the deathblow of the first Munster settlement.

Before the onslaught of his troops the Butlers recoiled and fell back, at first into their fortified houses and castles. Sir Edmund and Sir Edward were not inexperienced, but they were taken completely by surprise. Along the River Nore and the road to Dublin the invaders cut a swath of burned homesteads and devastated pastures up to the walls of Kilkenny.

And there they should have stopped. Kilkenny town was no cluster of wattle huts. A medieval settlement, a merchant center, this thriving seat of Thomas, Earl of Ormond, was one of the few prosperous county towns in Ireland. Rising above the town to the west stood St. Canice's Cathedral, the burial place of the Butler family and one of the country's fine Gothic structures. Eastward from St. Canice's, and visible across the gabled roof-tops of the town, rose Kilkenny Castle on a sloping hill beside the rapid Nore. Even then the residence of the Earl of Ormond was a splendid home, a Norman stronghold opened to light and air by Tudor windows, a mansion of long galleries and tapestried halls. Kilkenny and its famous castle would withstand far worse than Carew's rabble before the century was out, but on this occasion the attack came so suddenly that townsmen and warders were caught completely unaware. Within a few hours the town fell. The ferocity of the raid startled Ireland, and in many counties lords and chieftains refused to credit the first reports. For now either the English beast had begun to devour itself, or else Carew's mad stroke was only the first in a planned eradication of the Irish nobility.

Whatever the implications, Kilkenny town had burned. Carew's troops had rampaged through the merchant houses, despoiled the treasury of St. Canice's, and broken through the battlements of the castle. Inside, Sir Edward had taken command of the Earl's household and with a few retainers fought to bar the great south portal. But hundreds of bonaghts forced their way into the chambers, plundered the household goods, and took Sir Edward prisoner with his family. It was reported that Edward's wife was violated publicly by the troops, that many of the Earl's personal servants were put to the sword in the orgy of pillage and flame. Whether such accounts were exaggerated or not, there was no denying that within a few days Sir Peter had despoiled one of the finest towns in Ireland, sacked one of the richest earldoms, and turned the Queen's cousin into the laughingstock of the Fitzgeralds. For while his property was being razed, Thomas Butler was at Court in London suing for his share of the Desmond estates. It is hardly conceivable that Carew planned and executed the sack of Kilkenny; in all likelihood his army broke loose of its own accord against the defenseless citizenry. But now, with the whole of the South in turmoil and the Butlers in arms, Sir Peter had little recourse except to brazen out his invasion. He pursued Sir Edmund, the remaining brother, from stronghold to stronghold, and Hooker left an account of how one castle was captured during this campaign: "Sir Peter was able within a few days to lay siege to Clogrennan Castle. . . . Being hard pressed the commandant did ask if Sir Henry Sidney was present, and being told that he was, went out on safe conduct. Finding himself deceived, he returned then into the house, but a soldier named Baker followed, shot or stabbed him in the back and threw a log of wood between the doors, so that they could not be shut. The men then entered in, and killed not only the garrison but the women and children, including an honest gentleman's son, not three years old." Throughout that frightful summer Butlers everywhere hoped that Elizabeth would learn of their plight and send Sir Henry Sidney to compose their differences with Carew. Indeed the Queen eventually would send both Sidney and Ormond; by then, though, more than intermediaries were needed. The country was aflame with war.

As he pressed on into Kilkenny, Carew captured Sir Edmund as well. He now had both brothers in his custody and was assured by both that they would honor their parole if released. He had good reason to relax his severity. Ambushes awaited his men down every road, villages were burned to the ground by inhabitants or fought for fiercely, and by July attrition and desertion had begun to decimate his force. The terrible heat of that summer was long remembered. Forage grew scant, and dead cattle were flung into streams and wells by the Butlers to poison the waters. Before long Carew was seen fleeing toward the borders of Carlow as fast as his plunder-laden troops could travel, which was not very fast, and at each encampment skirmishes broke out and continued through the night. The clans of Ireland fought less frequently to the sound of war pipes than to their own shrill howling, and survivors of Carew's campaign long remembered the savage battle cries. From morning to night they heard them in every field and wood, at every river crossing, along the march home.

But their worst discovery in defeat was that the Butlers were receiving aid from their traditional enemies, the Fitzgeralds, and also from the MacCarthys, Burkes, O'Connors, Kavanaughs, Barrys, Roches, McSheehys, McSweenys, and O'Neills. What had begun as a punitive expedition against cattle thieves had succeeded in uniting the major Midland clans and Munster, and Carew's withdrawal quickly assumed aspects of a rout. Fearing a piecemeal suppression of their kind, the lords and chieftains banded together to destroy the Munster colony before it could be reinforced. Despite their weaknesses, the clans were practiced in guerrilla tactics. And over the next twenty years guerrilla warfare would remain their most successful strategy against the more heavily armed English. Ambush came naturally in this land of numerous fords, forests, bogs, and hedgerows and was suited to Irish weaponry such as the crossbow and dart, the matchlock, broad-bladed sword, and battle-ax. The relay ambush in particular devastated Sir Peter's ill-disciplined and fleeing columns. Hiding along the forest trails, the Irish moved parallel with the column, sniping with crossbows and muskets, until they passed their scarce arms to others farther down the line of march. The dead lay thick along Sir

Peter's line of retreat, and silver and gold plundered from Kilkenny was left littering the roadways.

Under the circumstances it is not surprising that Carew freed Sir Edmund and Sir Edward Butler. Perhaps he hoped by this show of clemency to propitiate the angry clansmen or to compensate for the damages of the invasion. He did not need to be told what effect his action had had on Whitehall or on the Earl of Ormond, and no doubt he feared the Earl's return. Thus, with admonishments, the brothers were turned loose; they took their leave submissively, returned to their people, and the following day were pressing home attacks into Carlow and Idrone. Parole was a concept little honored in Ireland. His army melting away, his flanks exposed, Sir Peter raced forward now, only to find that the Irish had crossed into Carlow ahead of him and were despoiling his settlers. From Kilkenny, where he had left Sir Warham St. Leger in charge, reports came that the Butlers were allied firmly with the Fitzgeralds and were raiding along with them into Counties Cork and Waterford. Most upsetting to the government was a dashing, flamboyant affair which turned the Fair of Inniscort upside down and left the citizens of Wexford bereft of their cattle and horses, silver and goods. The Irish Chronicle tells who commanded Butlers and Fitzgeralds alike on this occasion: "James, the son of Maurice, son of the Earl, was a warlike man of many troops this year; and the English and Irish of Munster; from the Barrow to Carn-Ui-Neid, entered into a unanimous and firm confederacy with him against the Queen's Parliament. The Earl of Ormond, Thomas, the son of James, son of Pierce, son of James, son of Edmund, being at this time in England, his two brothers, Edmund of Caladh and Edward, had confederated with James Fitzmaurice. These two sons of the Earl went to the fair of Inis-corr on Great Lady-Day; and it would be difficult to enumerate or describe all the steeds, horses, gold, silver, and foreign wares they seized upon at that fair. The Earl returned to Ireland the same year, and his brothers were reconciled to the State." It should be remembered that "son" is used broadly in Irish to signify relationship of blood and fosterage as well as direct descent. The James of this quotation is James Fitzmaurice, the same whose return would cause such consternation ten years later, and with his appearance on the scene in Munster, Carew's border raid had passed from an incident to the convulsion which historians have called the First Desmond War.

It should be assumed that embarrassment at Whitehall gave way finally to anger, not over Carew's aggression, but over his target—the ever-loyal Butlers and Earl of Ormond. Elizabeth had her hands full with revolt in Scotland, and an Irish debacle at this juncture was exceedingly awkward. In the crisis atmosphere of those days the apportionment of blame became secondary. Carew, after all, had attempted nothing he had not promised; he had planted English settlers on Irish soil, restored respect for English law, and punished wrongdoers. There could be no question now of removing him and, in the face of widespread revolt, no question of capitulating to the Irish. She ordered him only to release Butler hostages, this to mollify Ormond, and to stay at home and leave the settling of issues to other men. Sir Peter was apparently happy to comply; he remained only so long in Ireland as his properties required and was home in Devonshire by 1571. Possibly he had grown weary with Irish life, for he did not return until 1573 in an expedition to Ulster led by the Earl of Essex. Regarding this last adventure, the faithful Hooker wrote: "Sir Peter passed over with Essex, where, when he had remained awhile and considered the continual troubles, the daily encountering with the enemies, the excessive expenses and the doubtful events, and for a soil of land, though fertile of itself, yet a savage, wild and desolate country, environed with deadly enemies, did think then of his own country." For Carew, worn out by the harsh land, Ireland was no longer worth the struggle. He abandoned Essex in the North and, stopping at Idrone on his way back to England, died on November 27, 1575. Sir Peter Carew had sought fame no less than wealth in Ireland; his recompense was to be one line in William Camden's history of Elizabeth's reign: "The Earl of Ormond's brethren were proclaimed traitors, and Sir Peter Carew the elder skirmished with them sundry times with variable success."

From the English point of view, Carew left a perilous legacy. Intimidated by his rash acts, the chieftains and lords of the South and Midlands sought for common ground and found it in the cause of James Fitzmaurice. James was likely the most redoubtable soldier then in Ireland, and by the confiscation of Geraldine lands and Carew's acts, the Crown had presented him with an unhoped-for opportunity. In the absence of Gerald and his brothers, Fitzmaurice usurped the title "Captain of Desmond," and while Carew., Grenville, Gilbert, and others were consolidating their domains, he had won support of Desmond's henchmen at swordpoint. Now he proclaimed his intentions across Ireland, and his intentions rose above petty revenge and self-aggrandizement. For all that he despised his cousin the Earl, he made the restoration of Gerald's rights synonymous with native rule, with the hereditary privileges of every lord and chieftain. But his grand stroke, following from conviction no less than policy, was the denunciation of the Act of Religious Uniformity and Oath of Supremacy by which the Established Church of England was established in Ireland. Fitzmaurice recognized, as no Irish leader had yet, the remarkable unifying power of a spiritual cause, and his campaign to extirpate the Munster Plantation also became a crusade to restore the Church of Rome to Ireland. That year, before the walls of Cork, he would denounce Elizabeth, not because she was Queen of the English, but because she was a heretic, illegitimate, and an antichrist. Such views were hardly unknown in certain corners of Europe, and after Fitzmaurice's flamboyant bid to capture Cork, Philip of Spain dispatched Juan Mendoza to treat with him. But religion as such was not the whole issue. If reports about the sorry state of the churches are credited, piety of any persuasion was rare in sixteenth-century Ireland. What Fitzmaurice may have inspired, therefore, was less a religious fanaticism than a dawning awareness of cultural difference, and under Elizabeth's suppression the Church of Rome came increasingly to stand for and champion these native differences. Whatever the explanation, Fitzmaurice succeeded in winning support of the major clans and great Earls. By the close of 1569 the Earls of Clanricarde, Thomond, and Clanconnel had joined the rebellion; the Earl of Kildare was aiding him surreptitiously; and the kinsmen of the Earl of Ormond, who could not accept Fitzmaurice's religious convictions, were nevertheless fighting beside him.

Carew's troops had not even crossed back into Carlow when reports began to reach Whitehall of imminent danger to the coastal towns. The Mayors of Cork and Youghal wrote to Sir Henry Sidney on June 20, 1569: "The rebels brag that they will take Kinsale and Cork, that help cometh from Spain, and that the Butlers are of the confederacy. All the country betwixt Cork and Kinsale is destroyed." The Mayor and Corporation of Youghal added a postscript: "We beg her Majesty for 60 soldiers and a barrel of good powder for their protection. Unless his Lordship come with a main army, the whole country is like to be overthrown." "Good" powder held a special meaning for the Mayor and citizens of Youghal; much of the gunpowder sent to Ireland before the outbreak of the rebellion was found to be worthless. At Waterford, much closer to the zone of fierce fighting between the Butlers and Carew, the situation was worse. The Mayor and Corporation wrote to Sir William Cecil on July 8, 1569: "The good subjects in the country are forced by the rebels to become partners of their confederacy, or else to end their wretched lives by famine. The traitors are not contented, only to spoil the kine and garrons [small horses], but also send naked to this city the men, not sparing (a shameful thing to be reported) to use the honest housewives of the country in like manner, and torment them with more cruel pains than either Phalaris or any of the old tyrants could invent. The chieftains of this rebellion are James Fitzmaurice, called Captain of the Geraldines, and MacCarthy More, who refuses the new titles of Earl, and is offended with any one that calleth him Earl of Clancar.

These and other rebels have forced Kinsale to compound. Great need of munition and victual." The spectacle of English settlers being driven toward the gates of Waterford naked and scourged did nothing to reassure Whitehall that the situation could be contained. Far worse, it was evident from this report that the Irish chiefs had taken to casting off their English titles and were returning to Celtic customs. Finally, on July 12, Whitehall received news that Fitzmaurice was outside the gates of Cork. The gist of his long, rhetorical message to the Mayor of that city is entered in the *Calendar of State Papers* as: "He requires them to abolish out of that city the old heresy newly raised and invented, and namely Barnaby Daly, bishop, and all them that be Huguenots [Protestants], both men and women."

From these and other reports dated July through September, it appears that William Cecil's gloomiest predictions were coming true. The plan to dispossess the Irish and colonize Ireland with English settlers was beyond the power and scope of the Crown. In fact, the very settlers who had flocked to the Irish ports in 1568 were now dying in isolated pockets all across Munster. The fate of many would never be known. The following winter English patrols came upon many blackened peel towers, small stone keeps that can still be seen in the Irish countryside. From the peat ashes banked against the walls, the scene could be imagined: alarm in the night; fire; choking smoke; and finally the possessors driven out into the waiting arms of the dispossessed. Henceforth the Queen's deputies knew that an evicted Irish farmer living meant an English colonist dead.

But in several respects the fate of the settlers was least important. Fitzmaurice had seized practically the whole countryside, and prepared or not, Elizabeth was in danger of losing Ireland forever. To begin with, she ordered Sidney to depart for Cork; an army under Sir John Perrot's command was to join him there shortly, and together Sidney and Perrot were to cut a swath across Munster from Cork to the relief of Limerick in the West. Meanwhile, Thomas Butler was ordered home to pacify his family. It was absolutely essential that the Butlers be realigned with the Crown, and to this end Elizabeth was prepared to pardon his brothers. Sir Edmund had written to Sidney: "I do not make war against the Queen, but against those that banish Ireland, and mean conquest. . . . Aye, my lord brother come to apprehend me, I will not in this quarrel be ruled by him nor come into his hands." Sir Edmund and Sir Edward, however, thought twice about the offer. In Camden's words: "the Earl's continual intercession for them to the Queen obtained that they were not brought to trial, as their offenses deserved, and one means also to procure this favor was the nearness of blood between them and the Queen." Even in the case of the Butlers, mercy was hard bought, and it would be one year before Thomas was able to undo Carew's damages and lead a loyal body of troops into the field on the Queen's behalf. By then the Queen's orders had largely been carried out, and as her instructions to Sidney make clear, those orders were uncompromising: "It shall be lawful to prosecute and oppress any rebel or rebels with sword and with fire, and for the doing of the same, to levy in warlike manner and array, and with the same to march such and so many of the Queen's Highness's subjects, as to his discretion shall seem convenient." Conscription among the Anglo-Irish was thus authorized, along with the most desperate measures required to suppress the rebellion.

Between the resolution and the deed, however, stretched more than 375 miles—the distance from London to Cork—and the 55 miles of St. George's Channel. The usual port of embarkation for English armies bound for Ireland was Chester, but Cork could be reached more quickly by way of Bristol and Mount's Bay. All these points were at best four days' hard riding from London. Sidney reached Cork by late summer, 1569, but months would elapse before Perrot could assemble his forces and press on into the interior. Before an English army could take to the field, ordinance, powder, victuals, and horses had to be procured and the bottoms required to transport them leased from private merchants. During the sixteenth century the Crown did not possess sufficient transport to land or support a large field force. Perrot's cavalry, therefore, arrived in Cork without its horses, his infantry arrived without its powder, and all his men arrived without adequate provisions—most that they had brought with them proving spoiled or sour. The cost was, of course, staggering and was only compounded by the ambushes, the desertions, the camp fevers which afflicted the army before it marched.

While Sidney was en route to Ireland, the situation darkened further. Warham St. Leger wrote to him: "The citizens of Cork are robbed whenever they venture out, and all the lords of the country are overawed or in sympathy with Fitzmaurice, who vows to give no peace to Cork until the English, including Lady St. Leger and Lady Grenville, are given up, as well as some Irish prisoners. The City is in want both of provisions and powder, and the town of Youghal hourly expects attack. English farmers in the neighborhood have been already put to the sword." St. Leger's report was probably second hand, written at Kilkenny, and prompted by anxieties over his wife. If anything, conditions in the city were more desperate than he realized. In 1569 Cork was little more than a walled town. It was situated then between the constricting arms of the River Lee, and this space, walled and fortified with a gate tower, was overcrowded even in peacetime. In war, as soldiers and refugees swelled the population, the city spilled over its walls into a vast, palisaded encampment that was often stricken with disease and hunger. And the citizens of Cork, by all accounts, were seldom helpful. English settlers fleeing to the city from the countryside discovered that at best they were tolerated, for as one Elizabethan official recognized, "the citizens so distrust the country adjoining, that they match in wedlock only among themselves, so that the whole city is well nigh linked one to the other in affinity." The people of Cork never forgot that they were an island in a hostile sea, or that fall what may, they would remain long after the refugees were gone. If they could not bar their gates against the Queen's subjects, they knew better than to make them welcome. How damaging generosity became in times of war and famine is evident from the plight of Waterford a few months later. The Mayor wrote to Cecil: "On Good Friday the city opened its gates to 1100 starving men, who, when they had eaten, fell to plundering and housebreaking and it took three weeks to get rid of them by beating out the stronger ones and coaxing the weaker."

Similar disorders occurred at Cork shortly before Sidney's arrival. The refugees who had fled from Fitzmaurice lived in hovels improvised beneath the city walls. Stripped of all possessions, starving, and hardly knowing what would become of them, they ran through the streets like wild men as news of Fitzmaurice's approach reached them. Fitzmaurice was fully informed of the city's plight, and it is one measure of his shrewdness that he refrained from assaulting the fortifications or calling for an unconditional surrender. The Captain of Desmond had neither the troops nor the artillery required to breach the walls; instead, he attempted to turn the defenders against one another. By offering to abandon his siege if the city gave up its Protestants, along with Ladies St. Leger and Grenville, Fitzmaurice played on the antipathy between townsman and refugee, Catholic and Protestant. Lady Grenville had escaped from the sack of Tracton alone and had reached the gates of Cork on horseback only a few yards in front of her pursuing tenants. For all her courage, neither she nor Lady St. Leger was worth a city, but since their husbands were among the most influential Englishmen in Ireland, the women would have made useful hostages. Only a grudging admiration for their pluck in ever reaching the city alive and the admonitions of MacTeige MacCarthy swayed the Mayor and Corporation of the city from surrendering them. The acrimony between townsmen and refugees did not abate overnight, yet once the city had determined to hold out, Fitzmaurice had no alternative than to break off the siege.

Though the Irish hordes that overran the South were experienced skirmishers, they were incapable of sustained siege or field operations. In 1569 the loose army assembled and manhandled across Munster by Fitzmaurice resembled few others in Europe. Where it possessed a semblance of order, the Irish force seemed a throwback to the armies of earlier invaders, the Vikings and Normans. Unquestionably it was ill disciplined and ill equipped for modern warfare. In its vanguard rode clan horsemen, armed with leather and steel headpieces, shirts of mail, broad-bladed swords, daggers, and spears. They rode on stuffed saddles fitted with pillions in place of stirrups, and since without stirrups they could not hold their seat in a charge, they held their lances above their heads, gripped in the middle, ready for thrusting. Europe had seldom seen their like since the close of the eleventh century. Steel breastplates and morions had long ago replaced mail and plated leather, and the stirrupless rider had vanished from England with the Battle of Hastings. Fitzmaurice's cavalry would therefore never be a match for even a small squadron of regular horse.

His infantry was similarly disadvantaged. The mainstay of the Irish battle line had long been the *galloglaigh*, or young foreign warrior—a name corrupted to gallowglass in English and soon to become synonymous with blind savagery and valor. To an English soldier who fought them, gallowglass were "picked and selected men of great and mighty bodies, cruel without compassion. The greatest force of the battle consisteth in them, choosing rather to die than to yield, so that when it cometh to bandy blows, they are quickly slain or win the field. They are armed with a shirt of mail, a skullcap of steel, and a skein [dagger]: the weapon they most use is a battle-axe, six foot long, the blade whereof is somewhat like a shoemaker's knife; the stroke whereof is deadly where it lighteth." While in fact gallowglass could be Irish or Scottish, they had their origin in the Scottish Isles and, along with the redshanks, or Scottish highlanders, constituted the professional mercenaries on which every Irish chieftain was dependent. The employment was seasonal, and the gallowglass often returned to Scotland during the winter months. In Ireland, they were maintained at the expense of a lord's peasantry, their feeding called coynage and their stabling livery. The gallowglass might be helpless against musketeers and pikemen, but in ambush or the first rush of battle they could justify their keep, working terrible harm at close quarters. Fitzmaurice led the famous Desmond gallowglass—the MacSheehys and MacSweenys—and these families lost heavily in many of his engagements.

Finally, the Irish force employed a light infantryman, who, armed only with a sword and a few darts, usually skirmished in front and to the flanks of the advancing gallowglass. The kern, not to be confused with the "woodkern" or outlaw, "cast with wonderful facility and nearness, a weapon more noisome to the enemy, especially horsemen, than it is deadly —the short dart or spear." In Fitzmaurice's day the kern was not yet armed with musket or pistol; he was no match for regular soldiery and was easily dispersed in numbers by a square of English troops. Along with these fixed elements, it was not unusual to find *diolmhaineach*, delonies, hobboys, or mounted irregulars. Of these, the bonaghts of Carew's expedition, their opponents wrote "they are the very scum, and outcast of the country, and not less serviceable in the camp for meating and dressing horses than hurtful to the enemy with their darts." Scavengers by necessity, the *diolmbaineach* were feared by everyone left wounded on a battlefield.

Though James Fitzmaurice had learned formal war in France, he was sufficiently flexible to compensate for the shortcomings of his men. When Sidney advanced to the relief of Cork, hoping to engage him, Fitzmaurice and his Irish army vanished abruptly. For the next three years he conducted a war that is still best described by the English who endured it: "The lurking rebels will plash down whole trees over passes, and so intricately wind them, or lay them, that they shall be a strong barricade, and then lurk in ambush amongst the standing wood, playing upon all comers as if they intend to go headlong forward. On the bog they likewise presume with naked celerity to come as near our foot and horse as is possible, and then fly off again, tripping after their pipes as in a morris dance, knowing we cannot or indeed dare not follow them. And thus they serve us in the narrow entrances into their glens and quagmires of their mountains, where a few muskets well placed, will stagger a pretty army."

Sir Henry Sidney faced a formidable task; he was required to pacify the countryside while opening the overland route between Cork and Limerick, Limerick and Dublin. To accomplish this mission, he was understrength. Without sufficient troops to post garrisons behind him, Sidney was compelled to destroy everything in front of him, and following his capture of Castlemartyr and Glanmire along the approaches to Cork, he put to death all Irish found in arms. His main objective was to divide the confederacy which had formed around Fitzmaurice, and to this end he ravaged the castles and lands of the rebels one by one, forcing them to break off from Fitzmaurice to defend their own holdings. The Lord Justice's progress across Munster was marked by burning fields, slaughtered cattle, and hanging trees. The earth scorched once by Fitzmaurice was scorched a second time by Sidney and for years would lie fallow—a cause of widespread famine.

Sir Henry knew that Fitzmaurice could not retreat indefinitely. He must stand and fight somewhere between Cork and Limerick, and the site would be dictated by the forests and mountains of Munster. On a direct line from Cork to Limerick, Kilmallock was the key to the West. This fortress town, astride the east-west axis of Munster, was the one place Fitzmaurice had to hold, and the place Sidney had to capture. Today Kilmallock is a dingy little town on the main railroad line between Cork and Dublin. A bit of the old town wall remains, and the portico of a great house. Hardly a tree is visible. Yet when Kilmallock stood at a crossroads in Great Kilmore Wood, it was called the "sally port of the Geraldines" and commanded a wooded defile through the Ballyhoura Hills. It was a strong town, built and walled in gray stone, a flourishing center of trade until the Desmond Wars. In September, 1569, Fitzmaurice occupied Kilmallock in strength, and there Sidney found and attacked him without delay. The struggle continued for several days in high winds and heavy rain, and in the end English firepower and the disciplined ranks of English pikemen decided the issue. Through Kilmallock Sidney broke into the West, and behind him he left Humphrey Gilbert to garrison the town and neutralize the neighborhood.

During October and November the Lord Justice pursued his advantage, marching first to Limerick, then to Galway and Athlone, and finally to Dublin by early December. Along the way he received the submission of the Earl of Thomond, the Earl of Clanricarde, and dozens of petty chieftains. The loss of Kilmallock and the presence of an English army in the West effectively ended the Geraldine confederacy, and Fitzmaurice fell back alone into the mountain fastnesses of Kerry, powerless to inflict further harm that year. Sidney had bought time for Elizabeth; in the words of the Irish Chronicle "he returned to Dublin in victory and triumph, and no deputy of the Kings of Ireland had ever before made a more successful expedition, with a like number of warriors, than that journey performed by him."

But the campaign was not decisive. The guerrilla war continued. Humphrey Gilbert came under attack early in the new year at Kilmallock, and Fitzmaurice threw all that he could muster against him. As the English record reveals, it was not much: "Fitzmaurice and Clancar brought 1500 foot and 60 horse before Kilmallock, intending to starve out the garrison, but Gilbert sallied forth with about 100 men and put them to flight." If this astonishing feat proved the poor quality of Fitzmaurice's troops, it also showed Gilbert's reckless courage and audacity. During an inspection Sidney was so moved by the wreckage of the Irish camp and the heaps of slain gallowglass that he knighted Gilbert on the spot. But there was another side to Sir Humphrey's nature. Left to his own methods, he pursued a course of pacification which grew monstrous even in the eyes of many of his countrymen. Visitors to his headquarters at Kilmallock were greeted by impaled heads lining the path to his door. His half brother, Sir Walter Raleigh, said of him, "I never heard nor read of any man more feared than he is among the Irish nation." Raleigh's remark was an understatement. While he held Kilmallock, Gilbert could boast with justice that "Kerry is so quiet that I have but to send my horse-boy for any man and he will come." In a letter to Sir Henry, revealing of Elizabethan policy, he set forth his views on managing the Irish: "My manner of dealing was to show them all that they had more need of her Majesty than she of their service; neither yet that we were afraid of any number of them, our quarrel being so good. I slew all those from time to time that did belong to, feed, accompany, or maintain any outlaws or traitors; and after my first summoning of any castle or fort, if they would not presently yield it, I would not afterwards take it of their gift, but perforce, how many lives so ever it cost, putting man, women, and child of them to the sword. Neither did I spare any malefactors unexecuted that came to my hands in any respect, being for my part constantly of this opinion that no conquered nation will ever yield willingly of their obedience for love, but rather for fear."

Gilbert was not back in England more than a month before the efficacy of his method was put to the test. Kilmallock fell to Fitzmaurice, and this time the large English garrison was overcome by "120 naked villains afoot." Aided from within the town, the rebels achieved a stunning success, as the Irish Chronicle relates: "Before sunrise in the morning those who had gone to sleep happily and comfortably were aroused from their slumber by a furious attack made by the warlike troops of the Clan-Sweeny and Clan-Sheehy, who were along with James Fitzmaurice; and they proceeded to divide among themselves its gold, silver, various riches, and valuable jewels, which the father would not have acknowledged to his heir, or the mother to her daughter, on the day before. They were engaged for the space of three days and nights in carrying away the several kinds of riches and precious goods, as cups and ornamental goblets, upon their horses and steeds, to the woods and forests of Aherlow, and sending others of them privately to their friends and companions. They then set fire to the town, and raised a dense heavy . . . shroud of smoke about it, after they had torn down and demolished its houses of stone and wood; so that Kilmallock became the receptacle and abode of wolves in addition to all the other misfortunes up to that time."

With the destruction of Kilmallock the Crown concluded reluctantly that the rebellion which it had believed suppressed was in fact as strong as ever. Sidney now passed from the scene as commander of English forces, and Sir John Perrot began a two-year campaign to track down and capture the elusive Fitzmaurice. At the outbreak of the rebellion Perrot was called from retirement at his Pembrokeshire estate; he would pass his next fifteen years in and out of Ireland. But he would grow more in the Irish service than other soldiers, until during his final years he opposed the Queen herself on behalf of her Irish subjects. An immensely fat man, his beard and mane still red, Perrot was too old for active campaigning, too active for administration. And one sees in his outlook and actions the spirit of the previous era. He had grown to manhood amid the reckless splendor of Henry's Court, and the rumor persisted throughout his life that he was Henry VIII's bastard son. If tales of his appetites are true, there were indeed similarities. His coarse good humor endeared him to ordinary soldiers, yet the suspicion lingers that Whitehall's grave and somber statesmen looked down on Sir John. Large, generous to a fault, he would never be accused of malfeasance or cruelty—just foolishness. For Perrot began badly in Munster; he required time to learn; yet unlike many of his contemporaries, he stayed in Ireland to the end, never relinquishing his post for a higher preferment.

As the new Lord President of Munster, Perrot attempted to restore order in the province with customary forthrightness. Naturally he began by assuming the prejudices of English settlers, and since in their eyes the Irish were little else than savages, Munster became subject to brutal proscriptions and a suspension of ordinary justice. In country under the Crown's control, Perrot forbade native dress and native customs, travel, Brehon Law, the civil usages of Gaelic. Not unlike Carew, he may have thought that to suppress Celtic practices was to suppress the crime and violence endemic to Irish life. He forbade the growing of glibs, the long forelocks worn by men of all stations, because the thick mass of hair could be combed down over the face to hide identity. He prohibited the gray woolen mantles, the common dress of country people, because stolen goods could be concealed in the folds. Perrot never intended to leave the Irish naked; he merely ordered them on pain of fine and imprisonment to dress like Englishmen: "wearing clerk's gowns, jackets, jerkins, and some civil garments." The immodesty of Irishwomen had always particularly exercised the authorities, and the new Lord President made an end to their display by commanding that no woman wear "any great roll or kercher or linen cloth upon her head, neither any open smock with great sleeves, nor bracelets or crucifixes about her neck, but put on hats, and cloth herself in decent closing attire."

If Perrot's code of dress was harsh, his effort to remake Irish society in the image of English was still harsher. He outlawed bards and rhymers categorically, even the carrying of messages, on grounds that loose words and idle songs moved simple people to defiance and stirred kern and gallowglass to deeds of blood. Penalty for rhyming or harping began at twelve months in prison. But by banishing the news gatherers and communal historians of Munster, Perrot did not wean the Irish from their love of war and glorious exploits. Harps and poetry were not the only cause of disorder. To halt the decay of agricultural life in Ireland, he ordered the sons of poor farmers and plowmen to "follow the same occupation as their fathers. If the son of a husbandman will become a kern, gallowglass, or horseboy, or will take any other idle trade of life, he shall be imprisoned for a twelve month and fined." Even more to the point, Perrot inveighed against the payment of *éraic*—the blood money owed for the death of a clansmen to his friends and kinfolk. This vestige of tribal law survived nowhere in Europe with comparable authority, and because it made murder an affordable luxury, Perrot punished payment with death. On this count and others, Perrot claimed to have hanged no fewer than 500 people during his first year in Munster. Ten times that number would not have been enough to change the life of the province, and furthermore, Sir John's threats proved worse than his deeds. At Whitehall evidence was found to contradict his tally of hangings; not only did the Irish war continue to go badly, but the number of brigands and rebels in Munster gave every sign of increasing.

History questions Perrot's severities, for having once passed his draconian measures, he seems to have realized that all of them were unenforceable. In his own words, he was whistling into the wind. The Desmond uprising raged on. Munster was ruined and desolate. Available forces were needed in the West in pursuit of Fitzmaurice. Against this background Perrot's proclamations take on the appearance of formal gestures, and before long he obviously tired of governorship, of trials and arraignments, suppliants and sycophants. By the close of 1571 he was found leading his own troops, slogging through the bogs around Castlemaine, doing what he knew best—soldiering. No one has ever denied that the Irish of the sixteenth century gloried in war for its own sake; the problem would be that the man sent out from England to break them of their habit gloried in it no less.

"This work of trotting the mountains and marching the bogs is not suited to English soldiers," Perrot wrote to Burghley, but through the bleak winter months of 1571–1572 he kept up the pressure on Fitzmaurice. Now that the war had passed into the West the advantages enjoyed by the English army were lost. The mountainous terrain south of Tralee and along the shore of Dingle Bay discouraged large formations, and the war had settled down to bloody patrols and slow attrition. The Lord President besieged Castlemaine, failed to carry the fortress by assault, and fell back to try again unsuccessfully in the new year. London grew impatient with his progress, for the longer Fitzmaurice held out, the more French and Spanish interests inclined to support him. But Perrot grew impatient also, impatient for replacements and decent provisions as he watched his men die of Irish ague contracted on the wet bogs and mountainsides. Elizabeth was never solicitous of soldiers, and the provisions she sent westward were reduced for economy's sake. As for replacements, Perrot was made to make do with gallows bait, the outcast souls of the English shires. Despite his difficulties and the miseries of his army, he developed a talent for improvisation, a technique for leading demoralized men in battle. He learned to fight as the Irish fought; he armed his men to meet the prevailing conditions and, throwing away his infantry manual, met Fitzmaurice on his own terms. Perrot does not exaggerate when he claims to have become half Irish. Evidently he found pleasure in a well-executed ambush, for in early 1572 he wrote to Burghley: "The Irish ran from our trap and fled into the bogs, where my soldiers followed them barefooted, carrying light cavalry lances which there serve better than pikes. They returned with a trophy of 50 heads, with which I decorated the market cross at Kilmallock." Perrot's few victories were hard bought; his officers recollect trudging ceaselessly over hills, wading for days through bogs, and they testify to their commander's determination and endurance. For most there was nothing more extraordinary than to watch Perrot, Lord President of Munster, overweight and panting, struggle along with common troopers. A Captain White writes to Walsingham recalling how "On one occasion Sir John's foot hurt him as he was struggling through a bog in pursuit of the rebels. 'My lord,' said an officer, 'you have lost your shoe.' 'It matters not,' he says, 'as long as the legs last we shall find the shoes.' "

Perrot did not take Castlemaine that year. He was fortunate to hold Tralee and to keep open his lines of communication with Limerick. His troops mutinied at Kilmallock, and he was forced to march East to relieve the garrison. Perhaps by then it was becoming clear to him that the Desmond War could not be won. No decisive victory could be expected, for while Fitzmaurice was near exhaustion, the Queen's forces were also. The fury of the Irish war was moving northward into Ulster, Ormond was occupied just holding Kilkenny and the passes north to Dublin, and Sidney was committed to protection of the Dublin Pale. Alone in the South, Perrot evinced every sign of losing his grip. By 1572 Munster was too ravaged to support an army in the field, yet garrisoned, the English companies sank into ennui, diminishing their numbers daily through desertion and sickness. Such was the price of stalemate. Whitehall might press for a decisive victory, but to the bog soldier who did the fighting it seemed that no eleventh-hour triumph could ever restore the devastated plantations. The war had lost its slender reason. Possibly in this mood Perrot resolved on his next course of action, a course for which full explanation has never been offered. Weary of killing perhaps, dismayed at official blindness, or determined to go Fitzmaurice one better, the Lord President of Munster challenged the Captain of Desmond to single combat—winner take all.

Accounts of Perrot's *affaire d'honneur* are fabulous; doubtless they have passed down heightened in the retelling. But reliable witnesses verify the main details and communiqués testify to the outcome. Generally all agree that Perrot offered to meet Fitzmaurice on horseback not far from Kilmallock, in a clearing of Kilmore Wood. As befitted great captains, their duel was to take place between their armies and was to be fought to the death with lance, sword, and shield. To the victor would belong the field and, by extension, the portion of Munster he then controlled, though the Lord President had no authority to surrender Crown territory. Defeat, however, seems not to have entered Perrot's mind. He had been a formidable jouster, a champion of the English Court—twenty years before—and chivalric battle held no terrors for him. That he expected Fitzmaurice to abide by the code is only evidence of how desperate he had become. In any event the challenge was duly brought to the Irish camp by a paroled prisoner, and if it is allowed that Fitzmaurice was stunned, his surprise was like nothing compared with the English. No settler holding tenuously to a few acres of Munster was happy to trust his future to the prowess of a middle-aged knight, but then he was given no choice. For Fitzmaurice graciously accepted the gauntlet—with a condition. As the challenged he reserved the right to name the terms of combat. And since he did not like fighting on English horses with English weapons, or trust Perrot anyway, he required that the battle be fought on Irish hobs.

Perrot was counting on the long lance to unhorse his adversary, for at 280 pounds' weight and mounted on a heavy charger, he possessed a natural advantage. Nevertheless, a gallant enemy, he consented to the terms and settled on an Irish pony with Irish bridle and saddle. As the duel approached, however, Fitzmaurice raised another objection. He did not care for English battle gear; he suggested that both wear native Irish dress, discard their lances, and fight at close quarters with darts and broad-bladed Irish swords. In the English camp the outrage which greeted these conditions was tempered somewhat by Perrot's unshaken confidence; if Fitzmaurice would fight Hibernian style, Sir John was determined to kill him Hibernian style. He wanted Fitzmaurice out in the open, and no question of breeches was going to spoil his plan. Thus, on the appointed day at the appointed hour, Perrot rode to the hilltop where the combat was to take place; he wore scarlet breeches under a flowing cape of saffron, and at his side he carried a broad-bladed sword. The day began fair, as the story goes, and during the first hours of morning Sir John waited for Fitzmaurice. Toward noon a light drizzle began to fall, but still Perrot waited, the army growing restless behind him. Finally, as the rain began in earnest, he cast his sword aside and wheeled his mount to depart, but just then an Irish messenger appeared out of the woods below and galloped up the slope to meet him. In disgust Perrot tore the parchment message open impatiently and read, the eyes of the army fixed on him. And if a modicum of fiction

appears in the setting and circumstances of the scene, certainly there is
none in the note Perrot read. "If I do kill the great Sir John Perrot," it
began, "the Queen of England will but send another President into this
province; but if he do kill me, there is none in Ireland to succeed me, or
to command as I do now." Fitzmaurice did not come; most likely he had
never intended to come, and Perrot rode back alone in the rain.

His humiliation was complete. By the time news of the event reached
London, Whitehall was beside itself. The scene in the clearing had been
one to make a Secretary of State's blood run cold: an English governor
behaving more like the legendary Irish Achilles, Cuchulain, than St.
George. Admittedly, Perrot had risked only his own life, but his ill-considered adventure had also risked the Queen's imperial dignity and the authority of the Munster presidency. Nothing but Burghley's adroit intervention staved off his immediate recall.

In the following months England reinforced its position. Stung by
Whitehall's rebuke, Perrot drove westward with an avenging fury, capturing Castlemaine and dispersing his enemy's main force. He sallied north
from Limerick, surrounded 100 Scots gallowglass in a wood, and destroyed
them. He probed the rebel nest of Aherlow in a joint expedition with
Ormond and cut off access to Cashel and Tipperary. But his efforts were
unnecessary. The real Desmond War was over. It had ended in Kilmore
Wood with the Lord President of Munster on a sagging Irish pony, waiting
in the rain for an Irish rebel, who never came. The Queen could scourge
Ireland from end to end; she would never erase the significance of that
moment. For Perrot had begun by attempting to Anglicize Munster, and
in the end Munster had changed Perrot, reducing him to the stature of an
Irish warlord. The Irish had reason to laugh, but they did so in grudging
admiration; and while Sir John remained in Ireland, he enjoyed the affection of many of the Queen's Irish subjects.

The government had learned that there were many ways to win a war.
It now blockaded its enemy in the ravaged hills of Kerry and waited for
starvation to tell against the small band. So exhausted and reduced were
the Irish forces that the stratagem worked. In the spring of 1573 Fitzmaurice surrendered; he came to Kilmallock and before the town's ruined
church, knelt in submission to Perrot, a sword pointed at his breast. He
was worn out, his men were scattered, and because he came freely, he was
allowed to depart freely. A few days later he had escaped to France. Sidney
wrote in his letters of having beaten the Desmonds, but the fact was
inescapable that the Munster Plantations were gone. Carew was gone, and
the men whom he had brought with him. The confiscated property of the
Earl of Desmond had not paid the Crown's revenues; it had nearly bankrupted the Dublin exchequer. And where a rich, fertile grassland had once

been, there was devastation and famine. Sidney wrote of victory but knew full well that the Desmond War had settled nothing. A phase had ended; the violence had abated, nothing more.

Now the Queen's Irish policy veered again. Direct rule was abandoned, and Burghley came forward to suggest the only logical alternative, a return of the Earl of Desmond. Elizabeth was not sure; she hesitated between the counsel of her advisors, one moment willing to release Gerald, another, not. Perhaps it was Gerald's proved distaste for his cousin Fitzmaurice which finally persuaded, or the questionable assumption that so long as the Earl of Desmond held Munster under her, the Captain of Desmond would not return. In any case she made trial of the solution. At St. Leger House, Gerald was approached with the conditions for his restoration, and after seven years in exile he was amenable. He was not far behind Irish events. A few months earlier he had dispatched his wife, Eleanor, to report on his domains, and the letters which passed between them left no doubt that she blamed Fitzmaurice for the destruction of Munster. This correspondence is the testament of a marriage as well as a report, a reminder of the lives torn apart by the Irish wars. Eleanor wrote in the summer of 1573 that the countryside of Munster was so wasted by Fitzmaurice that she could not get as much money from loyal servants as would pay her traveling charge, the Earl being, of course, in straitened circumstances. "I pray God," she concluded, "send us joyful meeting or me short departure out of this world. If you make any provisions for me, I beseech you let the same be in readiness in Bristol against my return, and upon information thereof I will in all haste repair towards you. Your loving, miserable wife." Eleanor could not wait to be clear of Ireland, of its poverty and wretchedness. Her husband did not share her feelings.

Gerald was escorted to Dublin by the Queen's officers and entrusted to the Lieutenant of Dublin Castle to await Elizabeth's pleasure. Her Majesty was halfway to a decision. But Gerald did not intend to lie patiently in a new prison. Dublin was always a poor cage to hold a Fitzgerald, and he slipped out of the castle, out of Dublin, and out of Kildare before he was missed. On the road south he was met by Maurice McSheehy, his *marasgal*, or marshal, and as word raced ahead of his coming, peasants crawled out of the woods and dells to cheer him. According to tradition, Gerald threw off his English clothes as he rode and donned the dress of a clan chieftain; of this there is no certainty, but reliable reports indicate that by the time he had reached Askeaton more than several hundred warriors had joined his progress. McSheehys, McSweenys, Dalys, O'Flahertys flocked to him, acknowledging him the Desmond returned from exile. In some towns and fortified villages English officials were hanged or driven out, and before Gerald was at Askeaton a week, his followers had reclaimed Castlemaine, Kilmallock, Castlemartyr, the battlegrounds of a few months ago. In the words of the Irish Chronicle, he overturned the very order Perrot and his predecessors had been at pains to establish: "By the end of the month he had not left a proprietor of a single townland, from the meeting of the Three Waters to Bealach-Chonglais, and from Bealach-Chonglais to Limerick, whom he did not subdue and bring under the control of his bonaghtmen and stewards. He ordained that the Church and the men of knowledge should be restored to the possession of their privileges; and he reestablished the religious orders in their own respective places, according to the law of the Pope, as was right."

In Dublin the Irish Council meanwhile met to deliberate the emergency. A vote was taken whether a reward should be offered for Gerald's head, but the measure was defeated by a margin of one. Oddly, Elizabeth sustained the decision of the Council. She had lost her stomach for the business, and now, rather than renew the Irish war, she would compromise. Sidney was quickly empowered to negotiate a settlement, and though he may not have relished the assignment, he moved to entice Gerald into a new amnesty. Speed was of the essence, for by New Year's, 1574, Gerald had already strong-armed the Geraldine chiefs into signing a combination supporting him against the Crown. Flushed with success, his strength growing daily, he was in a position to drive a hard bargain. But Sidney offered more than a pardon; he offered the substance of the earldom as well as the title, the revenues, and privileges of the province at peace under the Crown. Suddenly Gerald was where he had started, seven years ago, before Ormond had captured him wounded at the Battle of Affane. And on September 2, 1574, he submitted to Sidney at Cork, receiving in exchange the full right to his hereditary estates. He had once agreed "to receive back what her Majesty would please to allow me," and now Elizabeth had pleased to give back everything. The test of her wisdom, however, would come in the fateful spring of 1579, with Gerald at Askeaton and James Fitzmaurice on the high seas bound for Ireland.

ASKEATON, 1573

Lord of the South

Few pardons have provoked a more voluminous correspondence than the one which passed between the English Crown and Gerald Fitzgerald in the aftermath of the First Desmond War. At the height of their communications, between 1574 and 1576, the Earl of Desmond wrote profusely to Elizabeth and her Council, apprising them of Irish affairs, professing his undying devotion. Yet the more Gerald sought to disarm the Council, the more the Council inclined to distrust Gerald—and for good reason. His letters are transparent. They were read before long for what they were: lies, alibis, and pretenses. During the communicative years, Gerald's duplicities stunned Whitehall; his caprice earned him the epithet "mad-brained Earl," and only after 1576, when all regards ceased, was he at last called "the deaf Earl."

What Gerald called the Council is conjecture. His bard, Angus O'Daly, perhaps caught the gist when he wrote: "that pushing and aggressive English crowd." For despite protestations of loyalty and respect, Gerald never once advanced English interests in Munster. His letters were red herrings, his compliance was illusory, and the wonder remains that he dared to play Elizabeth as he did. Possibly his temerity can be traced to a salient misunderstanding; for Gerald, the very fact of his restoration to a prized earldom argued the weakness and indecisiveness of the Crown. He mistook Elizabeth's intentions, her love of sound economy, and thereby mistook his own position. The fabric of the Cork agreement began to unravel, and between the squabblings of Gerald, Cecil, and Walsingham it would not survive the decade.

Burghley, for instance, believed rightly that coyne and livery lay at the root of the island's disorders, that this quartering of mercenaries on the population was a source of internecine war. Therefore, on several occasions, he wrote to Gerald requiring that the Earl desist from coynage. Gerald, however, replied that without coyne and livery he could not support adequate forces to maintain the Queen's laws or guarantee the safety of her subjects. He boasted of hunting down woodkern and outlaws. Burghley reminded him that he had apprehended precious few outlaws and that by report, he was escorted on progresses by more than 500 gallowglass. Desmond answered that he could not be blamed for having many enemies in Ireland. Burghley replied that enemies or not, he had too many gallowglass. Desmond next denied that he had *any* gallowglass and interjected that the Irish were no good against the Queen's soldiers anyway, as his cousin Fitzmaurice discovered. His excuses were of little avail; the Privy Council ordered him to disband his feudal army. Gerald complied, retaining only a handful of musketeers, but his heavy infantrymen were now reported in the service of his brother, Sir John of Desmond, and his uncle, the Seneschal of Imokilly. Once more Burghley reiterated his demand that the gallowglass be sent home. But by this time winter had come to Ireland, and Desmond's henchmen had served out their season; in the spring they would return and the dispute begin again.

During 1575 Gerald wrote to Walsingham requesting that the strongholds of Kilmallock, Castlemaine, and Castlemartyr be ceded to him in perpetuity. Since the Queen's garrisons were being withdrawn, Desmond contended that only he remain to keep the defenses in repair. Understandably he was reluctant to spend money on English walls and English breastworks without some guarantee of control. The curious fact, however, was that he already possessed all but Kilmallock. Castlemartyr was then held by Sir John of Desmond, and Castlemaine, that thorn in Perrot's side, had been retaken by Sir James of Desmond, Gerald's youngest brother, while the garrison played cards. Walsingham probed for Gerald's object; he must have found the obvious explanation incredible. Desmond was angling for Kilmallock, the gate to the West, and, failing that, for royal subsidy of his own castles. Of course, Walsingham turned him down. As matters stood, Gerald was already erecting towers along the lines of supply to the Crown's major fortresses, and the Secretary of State particularly warned him against continuing work on Castle Cullen astride the Limerick road. Dutifully the Geraldines suspended building at Cullen—at least during the daytime—and the Crown was astonished to learn several years later that the stronghold had been completed, secretly at night.

Disputes over feudal rights and assignments are the common stuff of the *State Papers,* and in Ireland negotiations commenced promptly with peace and concluded abruptly with the outbreak of war. The balance of power normally altered little. In his dealings with Gerald it may be said that Cecil surrendered more than he gained, but until 1576 he also remained reasonably confident that Desmond's ambitions were local and dynastic rather than patriotic. There was comfort perhaps in the Earl's endless conniving, for so long as Desmond avoided direct antagonism, the odds were that he had not yet subscribed to the religious fanaticism and national pride which made Fitzmaurice a formidable adversary. The Crown could not afford such distractions again. By 1575 Cecil had begun marriage negotiations with Alençon; he had forestalled Elizabeth's precipitous involvement in the French religious wars; he had nullified Walsingham's dangerous affinity for the Dutch Calvinists. A permanent Irish solution was now beyond his reach, and short of armed insurrection, Cecil was disposed to ignore Gerald's lesser provocations. Forbearance did not preclude a show of loyalty, however, and Cecil asked that Desmond maintain English law in Munster and the Religious Settlement of 1559.

Like his English counterparts, the Earl of Desmond was permitted freedom of conscience in private; in public he was expected to support the Church of England in Ireland. No sooner was he at large, though, than priests and friars of the old religion returned out of hiding. At Askeaton, his ancestral home, Gerald refurbished the ancient friary; at St. Mary's Cathedral, Limerick, he installed a papal bishop; at St. Mary's, Youghal, he advanced Roman prebendaries and a canon. Those closest to Walsingham already believed that Gerald had gone too far when they learned that everywhere in Munster clerics of the new religion were being driven from their benefices and replaced by Catholic priests. Sidney brushed Cecil aside and wrote directly to the Queen: "Most dear Mistress, and most honored sovereign, I solely address to you, as to the only sovereign salve-giver to this your sore and sick Realm, the lamentable state of the most noble and principal limb thereof, the Church I mean, as foul, deformed, and as cruelly crushed, as any other part thereof. . . . I would not have believed, had I not for a great part viewed the same throughout the whole Realm . . . the particular state of each church. All are leased out for years, and great gain reaped out of them above the rent which your Majesty receiveth. . . . No parson or vicar is resident upon any of them, and among the curates, only 18 were found able to speak English; the rest Irish priests, or rather Irish rogues, having little Latin, less learning, or civility. All these live upon the gain of masses, dirges, shrivings and such like trumpery, goodly abolished by your Majesty; no one house standing for any of them to dwell in. In many places, the very walls of the churches are down, very few chancels covered, windows and doors ruined or spoiled." Yet despite such evidence of Gerald's negligence, Cecil gave no indication of alarm. He appreciated the futility of religious reform in Munster. Old habits faded slowly among England's aristocracy, to say nothing of Ireland's, and in a recalcitrant and backward country, change was predictably slow. Besides, practical considerations made enforcement of the religious laws difficult. Few English clerics wished to risk their lives and fortunes in Munster; there was a perennial shortage of Protestant clergy; and as a consequence, the ebb and flow of Reformation in Ireland would be tied closely to military conquest and occupation. The cure of souls had usually to await the winnowing advances of war and famine.

Cecil had little desire to free Ireland from its medieval bonds so long as those bonds served the Crown. From the outset of the Geraldine compromise he appears to have placed more store in legal reform than religious. And in Ireland legal reform usually signified suppression of Brehon Law in favor of Common Law. By the terms of his restoration Gerald was pledged to uphold the Queen's justice; he was committed to protect and aid the Sheriffs of Cork, Dublin, and Waterford and to preside at assizes and session days. Forgotten perhaps was the fact that Gerald's experience of Common Law had been anything but fortunate. The Earl of Desmond had been carried before the Privy Council on a litter, wounded and unconscious; he certainly had no reason to honor English justice, and how little he did so was soon apparent. Cecil gambled that orderly government in Ireland depended more on acceptance of English law than on adoption of English customs, and now he learned with dismay how Gerald had permitted English sheriffs to be abused and the assizes of 1576 broken up by bonaght horsemen.

In 1576 the law of Munster was once more Brehon Law, and the judges, or Brehons, of the Geraldines moved through the countryside with impunity. *Éraic,* or blood money, was paid again; tanistry, or the election of chiefs by the assembled heads of the septs, was practiced again; and outside the coastal pale, the cloaked and bearded Brehons lived among the people, negotiating disputes in the time-honored Gaelic fashion. How this hereditary legal caste appeared to outsiders is seen in Edmund Campion's account: "Lawyers they have, liable to certain families, which after the custom of the country determine and judge causes. These consider of wrongs offered and received among their neighbors, be it murder or felony or trespass, all is redeemed by composition (except the grudge of parties seek revenge) and the time they have to spare from spoiling and 'proyning' (robbing) they lightly bestow in 'parling' (talking) about such matters. The

Brehon sitteth him down on a bank, the lords and gentlemen at variance round about him, and then they proceed." It is hardly to be wondered that negotiated justice shocked English moral sense. *Éraic*, after all, condoned homicide; tanists, after all, could be violent men, elected by bloody feud. Since they were invested with chieftaincy only for their lifetimes, they felt no responsibility to posterity or their Queen. To the English observer, the Brehon, along with other hereditary castes such as the bard and chronicler, was a root cause of civil strife. Few on either side of St. George's Channel denied this, but the problem was never agreement; the problem was what could be done about it. To expect Gerald Fitzgerald to root out a system which had always favored the Gaelic lords was too much to ask, and in any event Cecil probably did not possess the power to do so. From the thirteenth century onward the Gaelic Irish had been excluded from the Common Law, being treated as aliens, except for those who purchased charters of denizenship or those who belonged to the five great ruling dynasties of pre-Norman Ireland. Naturally, as Gaelic Ireland expanded over the years, the area of Brehon Law expanded, too, pressing in on areas of Common Law, until by the sixteenth century Cecil's hopes of encompassing the Irish under one legal system were sure to fail. In the spring of 1576 the fragile peace, of which he was the architect, seemed to be crumbling before his eyes.

Elizabeth had by then been apprised of Gerald's behavior and all at once was demanding swift retribution. Unfortunately her anger outstripped her means. Years of parsimony had reduced Elizabeth's garrisons in Munster. Perrot's urgent requests for men and arms could now be recalled, but Perrot himself was on indefinite leave to Wales. At neither Cork, Limerick, Waterford, nor Youghal did sufficient force stand ready to find Gerald, let alone apprehend him. For once everyone, including Cecil, favored a demonstration of strength, but there was no strength. Elizabeth had no choice except to bluff. She therefore commanded that Gerald come to her and answer the charges brought against him. But Desmond had heeded a similar request in his youth; as a result, he had spent three years in the Tower, and he was by no means prepared to commit the same mistake twice. He wrote, instead, requesting that he be allowed to meet with the Earl of Essex at Waterford, his uncle the Earl of Kildare to act as intermediary, and there answer all questions the Queen wished addressed to him. Since Essex acceded to the suggestion, it was quickly determined that Gerald join Essex at Waterford, proceed with him to Dublin, and there offer his submission to Lord Deputy Fitzwilliams,

Sidney's successor. The difficulty in the way of this plan, however, was that Elizabeth in the meanwhile had changed her mind; she sent new instructions to Essex, requiring that Gerald repair immediately to London. Desmond did not search long for an answer; he remembered his years cooped up in St. Leger's Southwark villa and told Essex, "I'd rather wear an old mantle in Munster than a torn silk gown in England." Of course, Essex could do nothing; he had pledged his honor for Gerald's safety. Now he escorted him to the frontier of the Waterford Pale and permitted him to go.

A few weeks later military operations were begun against Desmond. He was declared a traitor and a price of 500 pounds was set on his head. Yet when in the opening stages of the new war a fortress on the Suir River fell and its entire garrison was killed, resistance ceased inexplicably. Gerald had apparently weighed the gains of rebellion, and, since he already held Munster, found them slight. Consequently, he did nothing. What may be the shortest rebellion in the history of Ireland sputtered out over the following weeks of inaction, and by midyear Whitehall was tendering new terms. Some have blamed Desmond's capitulation on his lack of character, miscalculations, or indecisiveness, but Gerald had been negotiating with the English Crown for most of his life. One may assume, if nothing more, that he recognized his own best interests. As matters turned out, he was not summoned to London. He was forced to surrender Castlemartyr and Castlemaine, he was commanded to stem the decline of law and religion within his province, but otherwise, his authority remained intact. In the first flush of an easy triumph the Crown inclined to mercy, and Gerald perhaps had counted on just such generosity. Once more he had escaped Elizabeth's wrath with no diminution of his estates.

But behind the events of the year were possibly more sinister developments. Catholicism and Brehon Law were hardly new discoveries in Ireland; they alone were little reason to risk war and further destruction of the Queen's domains. Proof of Gerald's collusion with foreign powers, however, would have justified the risk. And the question occurs whether Walsingham presented such proof to Elizabeth. The links to Fitzmaurice and Spain are found in a most unlikely place, for indeed if Gerald was collaborating with his "despised" cousin, he covered his tracks meticulously.

Lady Eleanor passed much of her time during 1575 at Dublin and Whitehall. She was accompanied by her son, James, Gerald's heir, born at St. Leger House in Southwark, and in England and Ireland the homes of the influential were always open to her. A Butler by birth, a woman of great charm and perception, the Countess of Desmond was universally pitied for her husband's excesses. Yet her devotion never wavered; during his lifetime she supported him as emissary, partisan, and wife. Ostensibly, Eleanor's *bête noire* was James Fitzmaurice, and in society she never ceased to condemn the Captain of Desmond for the destruction of Munster. Perhaps her credibility was enhanced by her efforts to confiscate his rents and property while he was abroad or by her violent denunciations. For in 1575 it was widely believed, on her authority, that Fitzmaurice intended to supplant Gerald, that he had styled himself "Earl of Desmond" and was preparing to invade Munster from France. So far as is known, Eleanor succeeded in diverting the official gaze from her husband. She had good reason. It is apparent that the cousins were anything but enemies. Yet the more she reminded Whitehall of Fitzmaurice, the more her husband must have seemed the model of duty and obedience.

If Eleanor's behavior was feigned, she did not deceive anyone for long. No reference to James Fitzmaurice as Earl of Desmond has ever been found in the records of the Spanish Court or French, and the indications are that Walsingham knew as much. Fitzmaurice was called "James of Desmond," "Captain of Desmond," even "King of Ireland" by the Parisians, but never "Earl of Desmond." Nor was there the slightest sign of estrangement between him and the Earl. Walsingham's agents shadowed Fitzmaurice on the Continent; in 1575 they reported that a servant in the Earl of Desmond's livery had been spied at the Spanish Court. The servant, one William of Danubi, was observed conferring with James and the Spanish ambassador to Paris, Count Olivares. By 1575 Walsingham was aware that Fitzmaurice was in league with Thomas Stukeley, an English adventurer in the service of the Holy See, that he was supported in his bid for French ships by the French privateer De la Roche, and that he was receiving the help of the Countess of Northumberland and other English Catholics in Rome. Now he must have suspected that the Earl of Desmond was abetting James in his plan to invade Ireland from Spain. Indeed, a letter from William of Danubi to James has survived; it is of uncertain date, though not later than 1577, and urges Fitzmaurice to descend on the Irish coast immediately. Neither France nor Spain honored Fitzmaurice's request for men and arms, but by 1576 he had made his way to Rome, where he was welcomed warmly by Pope Gregory XIII. Surveillance became difficult. Father Allen, a Jesuit priest known to be close to Gerald, was seen in Rome; he was in communication with James and Stukeley. Undoubtedly, Walsingham surmised that a plot was under way, yet he could not determine its strength and timing. And for such reasons he, more than anyone, wanted Gerald's overthrow in 1576, before Fitzmaurice could act with the aid of the Holy See. It may be said that cost was no object with Walsingham; he recognized the need to secure Ireland for once and for all, and not for a moment did he trust Gerald, Eleanor, or anyone in the service of Desmond. But the preemptive measures he recommended were too expensive; moreover, they were soon forgotten in the mounting controversy over Elizabeth's French courtship.

After the abortive rebellion of 1576 Gerald was watched closely. For his part, he visited Cork and Dublin less frequently and communicated reluctantly with his masters. Where he had once been a nuisance, he grew silent. Elizabeth and Cecil were lulled into believing that their compromises had succeeded, and only their Irish veterans, Sidney, Perrot, Fitzwilliams, could see the clouds gathering over Munster. Gerald had removed to his birthplace, Askeaton Castle, and in all his domains he could not have found a more secluded refuge. Askeaton lay far from the base of English power, the coastal towns, and its approaches were well guarded. The castle was built on an island in the River Deel, a few miles above where the Deel flows placidly into the Shannon estuary. And at this time the surrounding countryside was largely forest and bog, a labyrinth of deep streams, traversed infrequently by roads. Fifteen miles of dense woodland stood between the castle and the nearest English garrison at Limerick, and more than fifty miles of wild Desmond Munster between Askeaton and the walls of Cork. At Askeaton Gerald could feel safe, and by 1577 he had retired there, purportedly to regain his health and look after his estates.

Askeaton is itself worth examining. After Gerald's return, the castle became by slow degrees an Irish counterpart to Whitehall, an anti-Court, Catholic and indisputably Gaelic. Gerald thought it impregnable, but he was never a good tactician and hopelessly underestimated the value of siege artillery. Along with Maynooth, Kilkenny, and Dublin Castle, it was a great Norman stronghold. But Askeaton flourished untouched by the Renaissance. The castle had been renovated in the early fifteenth century by James, the "builder Earl," sixth in the line of Desmond, and with Newcastle O'Connell remained one of the two great homes of the Desmond Fitzgeralds. The sixth Earl happened to be inordinately proud of his family's Florentine lineage, its pre-Norman ties to the Gherardinis. He appears to have traveled widely and appreciatively in Italy, yet nothing Italianate survives in his works. Grace had little place in an Irish home, and even a century and a half later the square keep still prevailed as the dominant architectural structure. In Gerald's day, Limerick had 300 stone keeps, County Cork 400, and nearly all were in the possession of the Geraldines. Outside and within, the life of Askeaton was unmistakably medieval, Irish medieval to be sure, but ages apart from the grandeur of Burghley House, Knole, or Hatfield.

A description of the castle's interior has passed down and provides some insight into the life of the Desmonds. In the survey of the Earl of Desmond's properties made by the Crown in 1583, Askeaton is called: "The one great castle built of square plan, a chief house of the Earl of Desmond, having at each angle of the same a round tower, with various places and chambers in each tower. And there is at the south corner on the western side at the south part, a high square tower or peel, built for defence within the walls; and also there were within the walls of the said castle many buildings—namely a large hall, a large room, and an excellent chamber, one garden and in the same two fishponds. And outside the walls, and near them, are divers orchards and gardens." From contemporary visitors it is known that the rooms had little furniture, that they were carpeted with rushes in the medieval manner and not with the woven mats commonly found in Elizabethan houses, and that in the main hall "the Irish recline at their meals, couches being supplied." The English found little to their liking in the rusticity of Irish home life. They remarked, however, the lavish hospitality of the Irish and their fondness for strong drink. Excerpts from one account suggest the typical menu: "The castles are built very strong, and with narrow stairs, for security. . . . The hall is the uppermost room . . . go up, and you come not down until the morrow. . . . The lady of the house meets you, and salutations passed, you shall be presented with all the drinks in the house: first, the ordinary beer, then aqua vitae (us-quebagh), then sack, then old ale. The lady tastes it; you must not refuse to drink. The fire is prepared in the middle of the hall; the table is spread plentifully furnished with meats but ill-cooked and without sauce. . . . When you come to your chamber, do not expect canopy and curtains. . . ."

Life at Askeaton was evidently crowded and noisy, especially after Gerald's return, when the remnants of Gaelic society, uprooted by the late war, flocked to his doors. Traditions of feudal dependence were not yet broken. It is notable that the sixth Earl's bard had also been an O'Daly; his Seneschal a McSheehy; his Brehon, like Gerald's, an O'Donnell. And there were friars in the village of Askeaton. On the south bank of the Deel, across from the castle, stood a Franciscan abbey erected by James and enlarged by succeeding Earls. The abbot and brothers reemerged with Gerald's restoration, and into their keeping he commended the graves of his parents and his first wife. Though little is known of the Earl's private passions, his attachment to this venerable abbey, the sepulcher of the Desmonds, is evident in letters to Thomas Butler and the Crown.

The countryside was little more than a stone's throw from the walls of Askeaton; beyond a village of thatched houses and a timbered keep belonging to Lombard merchants, the plowlands spread out into meadows and woods, the flaithlands of the Desmond clans. The predominance of sky and green rolling hills lends to the vicinity a strong feeling of seclusion, and after London, Gerald apparently reveled in the freedom of his home.

Along the road to Cork, almost up to Rathkirk Castle, extended an arm of Kilmore Wood, and here Gerald hunted red deer as his fathers had. During 1577 and 1578 he was often seen riding to the hunt with his brothers John and James or hosting the marches of his lands with bands of riders. Gerald planted his banner, the pine tree ensign, where people had answered his cousin's call to rebellion; where they had not, his henchmen extorted a high price in cattle and grain. The English presence was receding, and now the poor churls who had fled to the Crown for protection against the marauding sides, were left at the mercy of the rebels. It was never otherwise in Munster. Gerald stirred pride in many, but also fear and hatred, and the brutal and summary justice he meted out to his countrymen was the response of a hunted man, no stranger to betrayal. The figure Desmond cut on his progresses through the countryside is reflected still in local lore. To some he was the "silken Lord" because of his finery and the bold livery of his servants. To others he was the "black Earl," black for the color of his beard and hair, his eyes and pale complexion. But to the majority who viewed him during his resurgent years, Gerald was the "pale Earl," the cripple who grimaced and twisted painfully in his saddle, who feted his bonaghts on the fat of the land.

If ever a time was sweet for him, the years 1576 to 1579 were, and yet Munster was not at peace. Desmond squabbled with the Burkes. He skirmished with Rory Oge, who burned the large town of Naas to the ground amid frightful slaughter; he mustered Irish against Irish as if Peter Carew had never been. An account of his maladministration was offered by an English traveler named Collins: "Not long before my arrival there . . . a principal servant of the Earl of Desmond, after that he had burnt sundry villages and destroyed a great piece of country, there were certain poor women come to him who sought to have been spared; but too late. Yet so soon after the horrible fact committed, their children were felt and seen to stir in the bodies of the dead mothers. And yet did the same Earl lodge and banquet in the house of the same murderer his servant, after the fact committed." Gerald did not murder women who pleaded their bellies; what shocked Collins rather was his unspoiled appetite, his callous indifference to suffering and the excesses of his captains. Collins discovered the truth about home rule first hand whereas the old men in London arrived at the same conclusion by deduction. There comes to mind Cecil's contempt for Irish law, his conviction that the Brehon system indulged the strong by stripping the weak of their rights—not because the Brehon was himself corrupt, but because his society was. Yet how much English intervention in Ireland contributed to corruption and disorder is conveniently forgotten. Collins' description of peacetime Munster appalls: "And there I heard such lamentable cries and doleful complaints made by that small

remain of poor people which yet are left. Who, hardly escaping the fury
of the sword and fire of their outrageous neighbors, and famine with the
same, which their extortionist lords hath driven them unto, have their
goods taken from them by the extort of coign and livery, all making
demonstration of the miserable state of that country. Besides this, such
horrible and lamentable spectacles there are to behold as the burning of
villages, the view of the bones and skulls of the dead subjects, who, partly
by murder, partly by famine, have died in the fields; as, in truth, any
Christian with dry eyes could not behold."

Gerald might have asked, had the occasion arisen, what Christianity
had to do with holding Munster. At forty-three he had already fought a
full-scale feudal war, spent a total of ten years imprisoned in a foreign
country, had his worldly possessions and honors stripped from him, and
watched powerlessly while his domains were methodically ravaged. By
loyalty, not by virtue, a lord judged men, and before Gerald was a Christian or an Irishman, he was a lord. Munster would never owe him gratitude, but it would never disown him. Cruel he undoubtedly was, but he
belonged to Munster; Sir Henry Sidney, Sir John Perrot, and Peter Carew
did not.

Gerald's behavior until 1579, and during the eventful years which
followed, has given rise to no little controversy. Irish apologists have
tended to minimize the brutality of his government by referring to England's far worse transgressions. Here atrocity is used to obscure atrocity.
Opponents, not without justification, point to Gerald's plain lack of character, his self-indulgence and indecisiveness, as final proof of his inability
to rule at all. To be sure, the Earl of Desmond was unsteady. One moment
he is England's grateful client, the next, its implacable foe, and had circumstances permitted, he would have likely continued equivocation indefinitely. Yet how far his actions derived from indecision and how far from
a keen sense of self-preservation is virtually impossible to tell. The pressures and temptations through which Desmond lived were perhaps as
harrowing as any endured by an Irish leader during the century. He
perpetually walked the fine line between subservience, with a resultant
loss of Irish support, and rebellion, with a resultant loss of his life and
lands. Always the slightest miscalculation was apt to plunge Desmond, the
Fitzgeralds, and Munster into catastrophe. Who is to say, therefore, how
much longer Gerald might have kept his balance? That he kept it as long
as he did is something of an achievement. But critics who accuse him of
lacking principles are nonetheless right. Principles, or moral standards, no

more concerned him than they had England's great feudal barons during the War of the Roses 100 years before. Gerald was no revolutionary. He never desired change or progress; he harbored no national vision, cherished no dream of Irish independence. He wished only to remain the Earl of Desmond, and beyond defense of his prerogatives, he probably recognized neither purpose nor politics. One admits that seen against a background of religious and national wars, he is an anachronism, but his very obsolescence argues against accusing him of duplicity, treachery, or treason—crimes given point by allegiance to a modern state. What appears cruel and capricious in his case was perhaps only careless, for Gerald cannot be compared with the Sidneys, Perrots, or Fitzmaurices of Irish history. He was far above them in station, reared to enjoy princely wealth and power, and, an aristocrat first and last, Gerald disdained administration.

His father, the thirteenth Earl, had also disdained statecraft. An enemy of prudence and restraint, James, the thirteenth Earl, had the remarkable distinction of crossing Elizabeth's father twice and dying peacefully in his bed. In 1541 Henry proposed to rear young Gerald at the English Court, a companion to Prince Edward, later Edward VI of England. A more enviable offer was never made an Irish Earl, but James rejected the honor, arguing that his eight-year-old son would learn all he need know about courts and affairs of state at home in Ireland. His refusal did not have dire consequences, as it might have a few years later in Henry's reign, but his covert negotiations with Pope Paul III for sovereignty of Munster was another matter. James was cited in correspondence as the "traitor Earl," and the King's justice was in motion against him when he died unexpectedly at Askeaton, Gerald his designated heir.

When James died, it was said in Ireland that "the loss of this man is woeful to his country, for there was no need to watch cattle or close doors from Duncaoin in Kerry to the green-bordered meeting of the three waters on the confines of the province of Leinster." Gerald would change all that. He had been nurtured in the hard school of reiving and raiding; the O'Daly chronicle boasts that at thirteen he led incursions against the lords of Muskerry, the Lords Barry, and his old antagonists the Butlers. These raids were most likely mere adventures, bordrags, but they foreshadowed what was to come. Gerald, however, did not plunge headlong into hostilities without reflecting on the power of the Crown. No sooner had he leveled the Butler village of Kilfekille than he repaired to the English Court in full pomp and panoply. The history of the Geraldines, written years later by Dominicus De Rosario O'Daly, states that "shortly after assuming the earldom, young Gerald and one hundred noble youths, the flower of all Ireland, journeyed to London to do homage to the Queen and she received them graciously." One suspects that this visit began as an embassy and ended as a lark, for Gerald's prodigality was universally noted, and if his largess did not impress Cecil, Sussex, and their like, it charmed many. Manners aside, Gerald was being tested for submissiveness, and in 1559 he was eager for warm relations with the English. At home he had other ambitions. Two years later, when Gerald renewed his submission to the Crown under forced detainment in London, he was pardoned of murder, piracy, and kidnapping by no one less than Elizabeth herself. It appears that in addition to destroying his neighbors' lands during the interim, Gerald had seized the wine ships of Youghal on the high seas.

Elizabeth's conservativism, her reluctance to dismember ancient patrimonies, was surely one reason why Gerald escaped his crimes with impunity. Joan Butler Fitzgerald was another. No account of Gerald can disregard the fact that he exercised a peculiar attraction on influential and admired women. Joan, Countess of Ormond, was one such, and why she chose Gerald among all the lords in Ireland, is the occasion of some speculation. That he may have been a perfect lover is conceivable, though it is more a matter of record that he looked a perfect lover. Some years later it would be all the rage among Elizabeth's courtiers to affect the melancholic pose of dejected lovers and heartbroken swains. Painters like Nicholas Hilliard and Isaac Oliver were to capture the conventions of the melancholic pose in their portraits of reclining nobles and sad, pensive youths shaded by overarching trees and sunk in despair at the follies of mankind. Gerald anticipated the vogue, for without pretense he was born to the "humour," endowed by nature with a dark melancholic aspect, handsome and ascetic. Contemporaries saw him as frail, wan, "fantastical" in gestures and conversation, and the image which emerges of sickliness and hypersensitivity suggests the modern equivalent "consumptive." Yet Gerald was anything but an invalid. To the strong women who desired him, he appeared consumed and tormented, but to the men who fought him in the light of common day he was a violent, wasteful adversary, coarse and, above all, vain. These contradictions cannot be resolved. Behind him Desmond left no cool-eyed observers; he moved through his age enveloped in rumors and turmoil, and if his actions repelled some, the riddle of his personality irresistibly drew others.

That Joan Fitzgerald Butler pursued him shamelessly while her second husband lived, and married him despite being twenty years his elder is significant for more than its human interest. Joan, the Countess of Ormond, was the mother of Black Tom Butler, and through her dalliance with young Gerald she turned the politics of baronial Ireland upside down. Joan did not come by the name "Fitzgerald" through her union with Desmond; she was the daughter and heiress of the eleventh Earl, and by her marriage to the ninth Earl of Ormond she bore Thomas and his brothers, Edmund and Edward. Black Tom was only two years Gerald's senior; it is said that he was twenty when his mother's liaison with Desmond began. By then the ninth Earl was dead and Joan had remarried one Sir Francis Bryan. Now while Bryan lay on his deathbed, his wife went hunting with Gerald along the bounds of Leinster, visited Askeaton, accompanied her lover to fairs and festivals. The Countess of Ormond's success with young Desmond is a tribute to her lasting charm and beauty. Evidently Joan preferred marriage to widowhood, young men to old, yet nothing could be further from the truth than to think her a light-headed gentlewoman with a hankering for boys at middle life. By birth she was among the noblest women of the realm, by inheritance one of the richest, and on both sides of St. George's Channel she was justly admired for her maturity and intellect. To be sure, she played Gerald, but she played him partly from love and partly from a genuine desire to erase the hereditary animosities between her father's house and her first husband's. And much good came of the match. For a while the new Countess of Desmond had a wholesome effect on her husband's habits and rowdy household. But even her healing graces were not entirely sufficient. Joan was Elizabeth's confidante; on many occasions past she had enjoyed cordial relations with the Queen, and now their correspondence came to Gerald's attention. Whatever his shortcomings, he was an Irish chieftain; he would not be ruled by his wife, and he was outraged that she had the temerity to treat independently with his adversary. During his first detainment in London Elizabeth had written to Joan explaining why her husband was sequestered at the Lord Treasurer's house. The letter astonishes in its candor and familiarity; it is a cheerful note passed between knowing friends, between women, and with solemn irony assures the Countess of Desmond that her young, wayward lord is well and simply being taught an object lesson. His wife's intervention on his behalf was soon widely reported in England and Ireland, and on Gerald's return, he became convinced that the Butlers were laughing at him, that all Ireland believed he had hidden behind his wife's skirts.

Nothing more was needed to spark a flare-up, to break the fragile truce with his "stepson" Thomas Butler. Gerald flung himself out of Askeaton, Joan left behind, and on the move to Kilmallock began hosting the countryside, gathering his forces from Kerry and Cork, Limerick and Waterford. By early summer he had raised more than 2000 men-at-arms. Meanwhile, Black Tom levied his forces to meet Desmond, drawing men from Tipperary, Offaly, Kildare, and Kilkenny. The two sides met in July at the village of Bohermor on the Limerick-Tipperary border—more than 4000 foot, 750 horse, and several batteries of cannon—and while they faced each other, the Countess of Desmond rode between the camps begging them to refrain. For thirteen days Joan pleaded with her son and husband to avoid the collision, and for thirteen days the kern and gallowglass waited patiently, neither side much liking the idea of pitching into the other. On the fourteenth day, however, Gerald was persuaded to accept a new truce, and the Battle of Bohermor, for so the Irish still call the fight never fought, was over. What apologies were offered Gerald, or what concessions, is not known. It is virtually certain that both Earls feared Elizabeth's wrath, to say nothing of Joan's, and having saved face by their martial demonstrations went their own way without love or loss.

For the balance of her life the Countess of Desmond succeeded in keeping them from each other's throat. But Gerald was called to London again in 1562, and this time the charge of sundry aggressions was serious. He did not complain when Joan intervened, hoping to keep him out of the Tower, yet even her influence could not save him his first lengthy imprisonment. The great misfortune was that on his release two years later he returned to find Joan dying, and dying with her the real peace she had sustained in his absence. Gerald buried her in the friary at Askeaton and, mourning for all of three weeks, began a wild courtship of Eleanor Butler, Lord Dunboyne's daughter. The Kilkenny Butlers did not begrudge Gerald a new wife; they simply could not stomach the disrespect shown their mother, and in this regard Ireland sided with them. Still, the truce might have held if Gerald had not laid claim to the rents of the Decies and crossed into the Butler domains with a large army. The year was 1565, and he rode straight for Affane and total defeat at Ormond's hands. Worse, he had provoked Elizabeth for the last time, and carried from the battlefield, he was bound for seven years' bondage in England. So ended the Earl of Desmond's salad years.

At Askeaton in 1579 these events were far behind him. Gerald had aged; the feuding passion was extinct. Ormond was hardly a friend, but time had revealed their common interests, and Gerald was content to enjoy his own in Munster and let the world pass. A new war, should there be one, would be with England, and a war with Elizabeth could end only calamitously. The English presence in Munster, no matter how diminished, was still far greater than in the days of Affane, and Gerald had learned caution, if nothing more. As a consequence, Askeaton was gayer that New Year's than ever before. And the festivities were to be long remembered, committed to memory and then to lore. For the chieftains came with gold and harpers, the common people crowded into the courtyard for cakes and ale, and the rush torches lit the halls and chambers all through the nights. The chroniclers praise the munificence of the great Earl, the charm of his household, the beauty of his wife, but most of all

"Long dances danced in the garden, / Fiddle music and mirth among men." Desmond had brought weeping enough to Munster, and now at forty-six, graying and gaunt, he threw himself wholeheartedly into the celebrations. A song written by him in Gaelic is said to date from this period. "Against Blame of Women" is awkward and commonplace, yet there are phrases which might have expressed his mind:

> *Bloody treason, murderous acts*
> *Not by women are designed,*
> *Bells o'erthrown nor churches sacked.*
> *Speak not ill of womankind.*
>
> *Paunchy greybeards never more*
> *Hope to please a woman's mind.*
> *Poor young chieftains they adore.*
> *Speak not ill of womankind.*

New Year's, 1579, was the last festival celebrated at Askeaton. In England the Queen's government moved inexorably toward its decisive crisis, and at Rome James Fitzmaurice was granted his army.

James had applied to the Pontiff for 6000 armed soldiers and their pay for six months; 10 good Spanish or Italian officers; 6 heavy and 15 light cannon; 3000 stand of arms with powder and lead; three ships of 400, 50, and 30 tons respectively, three boats for crossing rivers, and a papal nuncio with 20 well-instructed priests. James was under no illusions about spring-time campaigning in Ireland; the land was a maze of swollen rivers and bogs, and boats with extra muskets and powder were a necessity. Even with these, he counted on widespread uprisings in Munster to supplement his small force and secure fords and river crossings. And to achieve this popular support, Fitzmaurice required a license from the Pope that all property taken from Geraldines during the warfare would remain in the family and that every Geraldine doing good service was to be confirmed by his Holiness and His Most Catholic Majesty of Spain in land and title. This document, which later fell into the hands of the English government, certainly suggests that James anticipated Gerald's support and that he was prepared to guarantee his jealous cousin the continuance of the Desmond earldom and prerogatives under Spanish rule. Fitzmaurice was by no means aware in 1579 of his cousin's mood; perhaps had he been, he would have proceeded differently.

For even his modest proposal of 6000 men, and 6000 to follow should the landing succeed, seemed at first beyond the capability or ambition of the Holy See. Philip II, for instance, favored the proposal and urged it on Gregory, but only because Philip was disconsolate over Elizabeth's intended French marriage and foresaw an alliance shaping between France and England against Spain. An invasion of Ireland might distract the English Court and, if successful, provide a base of operations against the new confederacy. As for France, where Fitzmaurice was always welcomed, his enterprise found wide encouragement but no support. So long as the French hoped to match Alençon with Elizabeth, they could not offer open assistance. It was intimated, however, that after the marriage had been consummated, reinforcements would be available. Consequently, the Irish party in Rome was thrown entirely upon the Pontiff, and Gregory faced the prospect of arming the insurgents at his own expense. He resolved to free 2000 troops for the venture, and no more. How slight was Gregory's grasp of the political and military realities surrounding the Irish question is apparent in the rhetoric of his grant: "If these men do not serve to go to England, and there unseat the heretic Queen, at least they will serve to go to Ireland, and there commence the attack, for the state of all Christendom dependeth upon the stout assailing of England." Notwithstanding the spell of her French suitor, Elizabeth was not about to be toppled by a handful of papal mercenaries.

To make good the shortfall in troops, Fitzmaurice was thrown upon his abundant ingenuity; he quickly improvised a solution. "At the time," wrote an Italian historian, "Italy was infested by certain bands of robbers, who used to lurk in woods and mountains, whence they descended by night to plunder the villages, and to spoil travellers on the highways." James implored the Pope to help the tottering Catholic Church in Ireland by pardoning these brigands if they would accompany him, and with his jailbirds, the expedition swelled to just under 4000 men. The desperadoes were formed into battalions and were commanded by a veteran Italian officer, one Hercules of Pisa, the entire force accompanied by Nicholas Sanders, the English Jesuit, and Cornelius O'Mulrian, Bishop of Killaloe. Such were the fortunes of war, however, that the efficacy of this force was never measured against English troops.

James determined early in 1578 to dispatch his ready battalions to Lisbon under the overall command of Thomas Stukeley. Later he proposed to join Stukeley with additional reinforcements at this staging point and sail with him for Munster. According to the plan, the old English renegade took command of 2000 men and left the port of Civitavecchia in early summer bound for Lisbon. Stukeley's stake in the expedition was more than sufficient to reward a soldier of fortune; Gregory bestowed on him the title Marquis of Leinster and pledged that if the English were driven out of Ireland, he would be addressed as "Knight, Baron Ross and Idrone, Viscount Murrows and Kinsella, Earl of Wexford and Carlow, and General of our Most Holy Father." Tom Stukeley drove a hard bargain. Unfortunately he was less persuasive with King Sebastian of Portugal. For no sooner had the Irish party arrived in Lisbon than Sebastian surrounded the ships and commandeered the lot. His intentions had nothing to do with Ireland; Sebastian had decided to invade Morocco with an army of Portuguese and German mercenaries, and to this end he impressed Stukeley's force. Neither Gregory nor Fitzmaurice learned of the development until much later, yet even had they known, they could not have forestalled the King of Portugal. The Italian brigands, with Stukeley at their head, were off to the African wars before they knew what had happened, and only Sanders, O'Mulrian, and a handful of officers made their way back to Rome.

Of all the events which whirl around the Irish issue during the sixteenth century, few are as bizarre as this adventure, more star-crossed. Suffice it to say that Stukeley disapproved of Sebastian's impetuous command from the first. He objected to landing and advancing forthrightly inland before his green soldiers had regained their marching legs. He scorned Sebastian's amateur preparations, his Portuguese pikemen, his grumbling mercenaries, his awkward tactics. But never once did he hang back or appear to remember his original mission. Another war, another opportunity, and Stukeley threw himself into the van of battle until on the ill-chosen field of Alcazar he fell leading his troops. Sebastian fell at Alcazar, the King of Morocco fell, the pretender to the throne of Morocco fell, and along with them, every one of Fitzmaurice's handpicked desperadoes. In one ill-fated and unscheduled engagement the invasion of Ireland was set back months. Not until Sanders and O'Mulrian reached Rome late in 1578 did James learn how little strength he could count on in the future. No one contends that Stukeley could have changed the course of Irish history, but his disaster represents a loss which should not be ignored. His Italian musketeers would be sorely needed at Monasternenagh the following year, and because they were not there, the Crown would be thankful. In fact, after Alcazar, an English agent was dispatched to Morocco. On his return he reported with solemn assurance that he had interrogated the new King of the Moslems and found him "an earnest Protestant . . . with great affection to God's true religion used in Her Highness's realm." Not likely, of course, but in this age of colliding ideologies *tout le monde à la bataille,* if the Moor was not for Rome, he must be for Canterbury.

In the early months of 1579 James apparently realized that his forces were dwindling rather than growing. Delays and mounting expenses quickly dissipated Gregory's largess, and the Pope was likely becoming restive. By February Fitzmaurice was convinced that he must either strike at once or wait for another year. From Paris he fetched his wife, son, and two daughters, said farewell to Gregory, and by mid-March had arrived at Madrid with Sanders. Fitzmaurice's family was close to penury, and Philip generously presented him with 1000 ducats for their maintenance, but neither men nor ships were forthcoming. James requested an audience with the King; he was denied, and shortly thereafter he wrote to Sanders in exasperation: "I care for no soldiers at all. You and I are enough; therefore let me go, for I know the minds of the noblemen in Ireland." How well Fitzmaurice knew anything of the kind is doubtful. Sanders, the treasurer of the expedition, was the Pope's nuncio; he had the last word as to readiness and was in regular communication with Jesuits in Munster. Everywhere in Ireland there was enthusiasm for the venture, though no firm commitments. Fitzmaurice broached his plan to Patrick Lumbarde, an Irish merchant in Spain, and Lumbarde wrote typically to his wife: "The men he say be willing; they want no treasure, they lack no furniture, and they have skillful leaders. To oppose the landing the Queen hath one ship in Ireland, and there be no means of fitting her out for sea." Nevertheless, Lumbarde found Fitzmaurice's preparations inadequate, "for that when the arms be occupied, he makes no account of the Queen's forces in Ireland."

By April Fitzmaurice had gathered his small fleet at Corunna, awaiting fair west breezes, and in the Channel the French privateer De la Roche stood out to seaward prepared to assist him. As near as can be estimated, James was accompanied by Sanders, Bishop O'Mulrian, and about 700 men —Italians, Spaniards, Portuguese, Flemings, Frenchmen, Irish, and a few English. The flagship of the expedition was of about 300 tons and carried most of the light artillery, muskets, and provisions for the expedition. The troops—the papal mercenaries, the few survivors of Stukeley's debacle, a contingent of twenty friars—all received two months' pay in advance and embarked on one of the six lighter craft gathered for transport. Thus, late in April the great adventure was set to begin, and in England and Ireland the Queen's government was either skeptical or preoccupied.

Some word of the preparations had reached Walsingham. At Leicester House the reports were greeted in grave silence; Sir Henry Sidney's words "If Fitzmaurice come back . . . he will have the whole country at his feet within the month" were not forgotten. But at Whitehall the threat was dismissed. The Archbishop of Canterbury, Matthew Parker, could not take Sanders seriously. Sanders had written a remarkably long and virulent treatise, *De Visibili Monarchia*, years before in Brussels. It had fallen to the Archbishop to answer the charges therein, and he had concluded that the task was impossible "not for the invincibleness of it, but for the huge volume." The author was characterized as mad, and any thought that he was now leading a serious invasion of Ireland was greeted with derision. So it happened that the Crown was not impressed with Fitzmaurice's progress. A Bristol ship discovered the storm-tossed armada in April, but the merchantman was quickly taken and its crew thrown overboard. Other ships were overtaken and boarded soon after, their English crew put to death, their French set ashore at St. Malo, and finally by May word reached London that a landing was soon to occur. Receipt of this intelligence alarmed the puritan faction most, especially Walsingham. But Cecil and the Court faction refused to credit exaggerated estimates of Fitzmaurice's strength and argued that the Queen's loyal lords and garrisons in Ireland were sufficient to meet the threat. By way of refutation, Sir Francis introduced Sidney's testimony and stolen documents corroborating the extent of the forces requested from Pope Gregory. Though temporarily in disfavor, Walsingham moved through friends at Court in persuading Elizabeth at least to release her ships at Dartmouth Harbor for interception. Her permission came too late; Humphrey Gilbert, in command of the squadron, passed to the southwestward of Fitzmaurice and, coming about on the wrong tack, was several days' voyage from the armada by the time it made land. Subsequently the English squadron was so battered by gales that it was driven into the Bay of Biscay and only limped into port weeks later, unable to continue on station. Indeed, as James approached the Irish coast, his success or failure rested principally in his cousin's hands.

The first word of the landing was passed by James Golde, Attorney General for Munster, to the Mayor of Limerick on July 22. Golde witnessed the coming ashore at Dingle Bay and, fleeing, paused only long enough to write from Tralee: "The traitor upon Saturday last came out of his ship. Two friars were his ensign-bearers, and they went before with two ensigns. A bishop, with a crozier-staff and his mitre, was next the friars. After came the traitor himself at the head of his company, about 100, and went to seek for flesh and kine, which they found, and so returned to his ships." After the long sea journey the armada put ashore to find fresh provisions. The standard-bearers of whom Golde wrote carried no ordinary ensign; on leaving Rome, the expedition had been entrusted with a papal banner, blessed for the occasion and embroidered with the head of Christ encircled by thorns. The sacred banner was brought ashore first, and under it prayers of thanksgiving were raised for safe arrival. Yet somehow the town of Dingle managed to be set aflame, and after summary looting, the fleet weighed anchor and sailed out of Dingle Bay, around Blasket Island, and into Smerwick Harbor on the other side of the peninsula. Here the force disembarked and, establishing a headquarters in the village, at once began digging those breastworks overlooking the harbor which in time would be called Fort Del Oro.

How Gerald came to hear of his cousin's arrival is told in the Irish

Chronicle: "At this time the Earl of Desmond was encamped at Cuilleann-O'gCuanach [Cullen], where he had begun to erect a castle; and, having heard by messenger of the arrival of the fleet in Kerry, he went to see it. The chief marshal of the two provinces of Munster, Arthur Carter by name, Master Davells, and all the Queen's people in Munster, set out to meet the same fleet, as did also the kinsmen of the Earl of Desmond, John and James." That Gerald knew of the armada's arrival in Spain is generally conceded, for Father Allen, in close attendance on him, had received messages from Corunna. Yet there is no indication that Gerald knew precisely when the fleet sailed or that he offered any assurances of aid. Quite the contrary, he now acted in ways which suggested his disapproval. From Cullen he wrote to Sir William Drury, acting Lord Deputy at Cork, that "I and my own are ready to venture our lives in this Her Majesty's quarrel . . . that we may prevent the traitorous attempts of the said James." Gerald rode toward Dingle to see for himself the magnitude of his cousin's efforts, and his brothers, John and James, did not travel with him; they rode south to serve other purposes.

To some historians Gerald's protestations of loyalty are suspect; his duplicity on so many occasions is well established; but never has there been the slightest proof that he did not mean what he wrote to Drury— at least in July. At the onset of the Second Desmond War, the Earl had more reason to fear and envy James than he had to welcome him. Fitzmaurice must have anticipated this response, for on landing he sent forth proclamations declaring that he had been appointed general only in the absence of more worthy leaders at Rome and that he intended to act by the advice of the Irish prelates, princes, and lords "whom I hold to be in greater part my betters." His appeal for support ended with an avowal of principle above any personal gain or ambition: "This one thing I will say, which I wish to be imprinted on all our hearts, if all we that are indeed of a good mind would openly and speedily pass our faith by resorting to his Holiness' banner, and by commanding your people and countries to keep no other but the Catholic faith, you should not only deliver your country from heresy and tyranny, but also do that most godly and noble act without any danger at all, because there is no foreign power that would or durst go about to assault so universal a consent of this country. . . . His Holiness' army means not to prejudice any nobleman in his own dominion or lands, which he otherwise rightfully possesseth, unless he be found to fight, or to aid them that do fight, against the Cross of Christ and his Holiness' banner, for both which I, as well as all other Christians, ought to spend our blood."

There is no doubt that James believed in the rightness of his cause; his credo had not changed since the First Desmond War, only his style. But if the proclamations which reached the lords of Ireland in the early summer of 1579 are signed *in omni tribulatione spes mea Jesus et Maria, James Geraldyne,* they were more likely written by Father Sanders. And Sanders brought to the Irish cause an intellectual and spiritual respectability which it had not hitherto possessed. His lengthy discourses are characterized by the dialectic of the Counter-Reformation and the attitudes of thought associated with the Counter-Reformation's militant arm, the Society of Jesus. In a letter to Gerald, Sanders outlined the obligation laid upon all true Christians: "A just war requires three conditions—a just cause, a lawful power, and the means of carrying on lawful war. It shall be made clear that all three conditions are fulfilled and that the cause of this war in Ireland is God's glory.... Furthermore, the power of this war is derived first from natural, and then from evangelical, law. For natural law empowers us to defend ourselves against the very manifest tyranny of heretics, who, against the law of nature, force us, under pain of death to abjure our first faith in the primacy of the Roman Pontiff, and profess a plainly contrary religion. And evangelical law empowers us to defend ourselves against those who belie the glory of Christ by denying that his sacraments confer grace and the truth of the Scriptures." Much more remains of Sanders' sermon, but no reply from Gerald to explain how he received this new light of doctrine. The dialectic of the Counter-Reformation had become a conservative force, even an incentive to inquisition, on the Continent, but in Ireland it appeared dynamic and revolutionary. Curiously, as the Irish wars grew more frequent and more intense, a doctrinal stridency manifests itself on both sides. While a distinct logic and rhetoric distinguish the pronouncements of Sanders and the devoted rebels, the distinctly Protestant logic of Pierre de La Ramée, an anti-Aristotelian killed in the St. Bartholomew's Day Massacre, distinguishes English judgments and policies. The point is of interest only because it is likely that such subtleties flew well over the head of Gerald Fitzgerald. War he certainly understood, but war for power and possessions, and in 1579 he was not about to hazard everything he owned because a theologian had landed at Dingle with 700 soldiers.

Because the Earl of Desmond favored an invasion in 1575 is hardly reason to assume that he favored an invasion four years later. In the best of times Gerald changed his mind frequently, and that July palpable power appears to have outweighed the Catholic cause in his thoughts. Come the worst, Fitzmaurice stood to lose his life, but the Earl of Desmond, at peace with the English, stood to lose life, land, and his family's future. He therefore ingratiated himself with Drury during the weeks following the landing. Drury, however, was not certain that he possessed the power to control Gerald. The unreadiness of the Crown's forces was proverbial. At the base of the Dingle Peninsula stood Castlemaine, the Crown's forward position in Kerry, and the constable of the castle reported that he had only five hogsheads of wheat, two tuns of wine, three hogsheads of salmon, and some malt to support his twenty-four troopers; for meat he was dependent on "such bruised reeds" as Desmond and Clancar. From the start the English understandably distrusted Gerald, and having given the dog a bad name, they were not going to wait for him to bite. Drury might have had Gerald's support, but he discounted it out of hand. And since he commanded virtually nothing to stop the invasion, he sent emissaries into the West to negotiate while he called down Whitehall on the Geraldine heads.

His emissaries, Arthur Carter and Sir Henry Davells, were no ordinary officials. Both were old Irish hands, well known to the Geraldines and well versed in the intricate politics of Munster's clans. In theory they were safe riding to find Gerald, his brothers, or even Fitzmaurice. And their mission was to bluff, to remind Gerald of his pledges to the Queen. How little chance of success they were given is apparent in Drury's letters to Walsingham. But Davells carried great prestige in the country. He had lived in Munster for twenty years; he had befriended Carew in time to argue against his follies; and he was known to be on close terms with Sir John of Desmond. In fact, so far as Sir John was concerned, Davells had acted as his surrogate father on many occasions, advising him, easing his difficulties with Dublin and London. Hooker testified to Sir Henry's excellent character and the affection felt toward him by the Irish on account of his honesty and goodwill: "If any of them had spoken the word, which was assuredly looked to be performed, they would say Davells hath said it, as who saith 'Davells' saith 'It shall be performed.' For the nature of the Irishman is, that albeit he keepeth faith, for the most part, with nobody, yet will he have no man break with him." Objective Hooker certainly was not, but his witness is verified by Irish sources. Besides being a byword for straight dealing, Davells' name would secure for an English traveler free passage and hospitality anywhere in Munster or Leinster. Carter, Davells, and their small party therefore found no difficulty in overtaking Gerald on the road to Dingle. Desmond, it is said, accepted the Englishmen graciously and rode with them to inspect the fortifications above the town at Smerwick. Whether Sir John and Sir James were part of this contingent is not known for certain.

What was discovered at Smerwick were half-built breastworks, under construction by English prisoners and manned by fifty or sixty regular infantry. Davells immediately judged that the fortifications were ripe for assault, and he urged Gerald to lend him a company of gallowglass and sixty musketeers. Drury had employed an English sea dog by the name of Thomas Courtenay to make up the lack of a fleet in Irish waters, and while

90

Davells bickered with Gerald, Courtenay stood out to sea ready to attack the few remaining Spanish vessels at anchorage. Three of Fitzmaurice's larger ships had already put to sea, but the pinnaces which remained were still essential to his expedition. Gerald, however, was unwilling to commit himself; he replied that his musketeers were "more fitted to shoot at water-fowls than at a strong place," and that gallowglass were "good against gallowglass but no match for trained soldiery." Almost at once the frustration of the Queen's men vented itself in ugly rumors about Desmond's loyalty. An English officer present wrote to Drury that "sixty resolute men might by now have taken Smerwick from the rebels but for the Earl's timidity." And Thomas Courtenay, unimpressed by the quality of Fitzmaurice's naval support, wrote boastfully: "James Fitzmaurice and his company have lost a piece of the Pope's blessing, for they be now altogether destitute of any ship to ease and relieve themselves by the seas, what need soever should happen." Smerwick could have been taken easily; because it was not, Gerald was blamed, and in a letter to Burghley, Drury clearly discounted the Earl as an ally when he wrote: "Stand stoutly to the helm, for now at hand is a great storm of rebellion and infamy."

Desmond conceivably had no intention of hindering James; his presence at Dingle might have been a firsthand reconnaissance or even an attempt to shield the rebels' base. Yet on the other hand, Gerald was aware that James had moved inland, for he wrote to the Archbishop of Cashel at this time: "On Saturday the last, the rebels burned Dingle, spoiled my tenants, and doth not now spare none of her Majesty's subjects. Having all my force, I hope soon with the hand of God to expel this traitor." As survivors of the First Desmond War knew, few men were as familiar with the terrain of Kerry as James Fitzmaurice, and while Gerald argued with Davells, James was riding roughshod not through the Queen's lands but through his. If Gerald did not act valiantly before Smerwick, he at least did not make the error of thinking the rebellion a small venture to be snuffed out with a handful of gallowglass. For all he foresaw, Ireland might yet rise to Fitzmaurice's cause; the Geraldines themselves might yet be constrained to join James; and surely, when the decision was made, it would be made inland, not on the sea. At this time it was much that Gerald was not forceably aiding his cousin; it was perhaps too much to request that he take up arms against him. Within a few days Desmond departed Dingle for Askeaton, and pressed by Davells, he promised to provide gallowglass for Drury's forthcoming expedition against Fitzmaurice. So matters were left, and after a few days of inconsequential skirmishing around Smerwick, Carter and Davells fell back to Tralee to await reinforcements.

They took up residence at one William Rice's house, a "victualling-place and wine-tavern" by reputation, where they were confident no harm would come to them. Their decision to stay in Kerry was fateful, for on a quiet night at the end of July Sir John of Desmond and Sir James surrounded the tavern and, bribing the porter to open the gates, surprised Davells and Carter asleep. The episode is captured in a contemporary print which depicts Davells and Carter asleep in a common bed, Nicholas Sanders and the rebel army drawn up outside. Except for this last detail, the print is unusually accurate. When Davells saw Sir John entering the room with a drawn sword, he is reported to have cried out, "What, son! what is the matter?" John is said to have replied, "No more son, nor no more father. Make thyself ready, for die thou shalt." Davells' page threw himself between the men, but Sir John, holding off the page with one hand, ran Davells through with the other. Simultaneously, James cut Carter's throat, slew the page, and signaled from the window. In a rush Sir John's men broke into the tavern and put to death most of the English party before they were awake to danger. Several accounts relate that the bodies were mutilated after death. And the Irish Chronicle, though conflating several events, corroborates that Davells and Carter were beheaded: "John and James were in confederacy with James, son of Maurice; and they made an attack by night upon the Marshal and Master David, at Tralee, where they beheaded them while asleep in their beds and couches. They then brought James on shore, and all repaired to the woods of Clonlish and Kilmore. James went forth from these woods thereafter on his first expedition, with all his cavalry and infantry, through the middle of Hy-Connel-Gaura and Clann-William, and they proceeded to plunder the country as they passed along."

Notwithstanding chronicle and print, there is no evidence that Fitzmaurice or Sanders ordered the assassination of Davells and Carter; on the contrary, the act was distinctly out of character with Fitzmaurice's usual means. Camden asserts that Sanders lauded the murders with "suave Deo sacrificium," but while Sanders may have stirred Sir John and James to their deed with inflammatory rhetoric, he was certainly not in the neighborhood of Tralee when the killings took place. John could have acted on his own. He was by far the more fearless and bloody-minded of the brothers, and if he had resolved to join the rebellion, he might have sought to burn his last bridge, to make his decision visible, irreversibly, on his enemies. Precisely this attitude is expressed in the O'Daly chronicle: "Sir John killed an avowed enemy who sought to crush the cause of liberty." Though John was a firebrand who in war matured into a determined leader, he was never to escape the stigma of Tralee, except in the eyes of extremists like the O'Dalys. He had been befriended and sheltered by Davells, and now much of the country was outraged at his wanton treachery. Understandably the murders became a *cause célèbre* not only in Ireland, but also in England and on the Continent, and few were disposed to accept them at face value. Before long the finger of accusation pointed beyond John, beyond Sanders, to Desmond and a dark conspiracy.

Gerald did not help matters by refusing to break off with his brothers. Only a week after the massacre he presented a silver bowl to his brother James, and this gift, supposedly innocent, gave rise to the rumor that he had paid for Davells and Carter to be slain. Drury, Walsingham, Sir Nicholas Maltby, the senior soldier in Munster, all believed that Gerald paid for the murders with this silver bowl and, moreover, that he ordered the crime because Davells had uncovered his part in the invasion plan. Gerald was assuredly not above assassination, he had argued with Davells at Dingle, and Davells had expressed suspicion about his refusal to assault Smerwick. Still, the fact remains that Gerald could have gained nothing by Davells' death. If he needed time to decide on a course, his need was best served by an appearance of loyalty, and if he was indeed a party to the rebellion, his advantage lay in obscuring discovery for as long as possible. By the time of the murders Davells had had ample opportunity to acquaint Drury with all that he had learned. The argument can be made that Gerald was notoriously petty and vindictive, that he may have had Davells murdered on some minor pretext. Yet Desmond acted with exceptional control and coolness throughout that difficult summer, and it is unlikely that he would have jeopardized his position by savageries such as befell at Tralee. He protested to those who would listen that he had nothing to do with John's deed, and in retrospect, he likely spoke the truth. What cannot be doubted, however, is that the majority of the Desmond Fitzgeralds favored war. John and James not only rode off to join Fitzmaurice, but brought from Imokilly and Muskerry their share of bonaghts and clansmen. Before July the Earl of Desmond commanded between 1000 and 2000 gallowglass; after July the English grew aware that his personal force had dwindled to under 100. The balance of Gerald's might had simply dissipated, either with his consent or without it, and his gallowglass were now in the forests and bogs with Sir John and the Captain of Desmond. Immovable, Gerald remained at Askeaton, but the astonishing disappearance of his army was the last provocation required to turn the English against him.

From Cork and Dublin a flurry of communiqués went out to Cecil and Walsingham, calling for arms and reinforcements, begging for ships, striving to impress on Whitehall the gravity of the situation. Sir Edward Waterhouse, Chief Secretary, wrote to Walsingham apprising him of the latest developments: "This rebellion is the most perilous that ever was begun in Ireland. . . . Foreign help in multitudes is looked for presently. . . . Sir John of Desmond is more dangerous than the archrebel Fitzmaurice both for his credit and his bloody-mind, and but the Queen look now to the safety of her realm, the same is like to be carried away in the storm at hand. . . . The Earl of Kildare dealeth honourably with the Crown. . . . The Earl of Desmond doth not, for of the 1200 gallowglass that were late with him, not 60 are left." Appended to this message is an urgent request for the men and horses required to march inland from the coast. There is an account of the sad defenses of the Queen's towns and a closing malediction on the murderers of Davells and Carter. Walsingham did not need to be told that the Irish situation was becoming desperate; his problem was to persuade Cecil and the Queen that the rebellion was outreaching the ability of the loyal lords, such as Ormond and Kildare, to deal with it. Burghley appears to have placed his faith in diplomatic initiatives, believing perhaps that diplomacy could stem the flow of aid to Fitzmaurice more effectively than all the Queen's troops. His position was not without merit, but Walsingham and the party at Leicester House were confronting the military developments at hand, and they called for the immediate return of John Perrot and a younger and more forceful replacement for Drury. Chance, however, was about to upset the best laid plans of both sides.

An Irish historian has written that "landed gentlemen have molar teeth, and are destitute of the carnivorous and incisive jaws of political adventurers. The Munster proprietors held aloof with the Earl of Desmond, while the landless men followed his bolder and more unscrupulous brother." Here is a reason why many of Gerald's men deserted Askeaton for the camps of the rebels and certainly a reason for James Fitzmaurice's violent disagreements with Sir John. Waterhouse, in his letter to Walsingham, is conscious of a distinction between the archrebel James and the demagogue John. Fitzmaurice and Sanders had called out for men of conscience; in reply they received every scoundrel and land-hungry deloney between Kinsale and Killarney. And this rabble, gathering around their banner, had as little respect for the lives and property of devout Catholics as for Protestant Englishmen. No direct evidence proves that Sir John, a younger brother, appealed to the destitute with promises of land reform and egalitarianism; he is only said to have done so; but by his actions he unquestionably politicized the rebellion beyond limits acceptable to Fitzmaurice. Nevertheless, their dispute might have waited had Sir John not lent his sanction to behavior James could not countenance. The occasion of their final parting came about over the rape and murder of a common camp follower by one of John's men. When James learned of the offense, he ordered the offender hanged out of hand, and John refused, "little regarding the Pope's commission, and not respecting murder or rape." James was a severe commander, no less disciplined than devout, and it had always been his practice on campaigns to punish wrongdoers swiftly and harshly. Now, as John blocked his way, James evidently concluded that he could no longer tolerate a joint command with Desmond. He broke out of Sir John's camp in Kilmore with a handful of followers, and possibly intending to join with Sanders, who had ridden ahead into Connaught, he set out for Holy Cross Abbey.

His route led him to the northeast of Limerick, and after hard riding the small party came within vicinity of Castle Connell. Near Barrington Bridge, or *Beal Antha an Bhorin*, their trace horses apparently gave out, and James ordered his men to scour the neighborhood for fresh draft animals. In a nearby field they came on a peasant plowing his field, and unharnessing his plow horse, they returned with it to a temporary encampment below the bridge. Pursuing these soldiers, the outraged churl is said to have confronted James and to have been told that a horse was the least he could give for his country and his faith. Religion and politics mattered to the lords of Ireland; they did not matter a whit to the peasants. Theft concerned the simple people more. And now this churl ran to his lord, Theobald Burke at Castle Connell, and acquainted him that his horse had been stolen by the Pope's men encamped under Barrington Bridge. Burke was thus made aware that Fitzmaurice had strayed onto his lands, and since Burke was a Protestant and an Anglophile, he was one of the few lords in the South unequivocally opposed to the rebel. Gathering arms and a few retainers, he set off for the bridge to intercept Fitzmaurice before he could escape.

The meeting of Fitzmaurice and Burke is one of the remarkable accidents in Irish history. In detail the encounter is heroic melodrama, ageless, Irish; the fight is over a horse, the combat takes place at a ford, and the chance at arms suddenly and unaccountably alters history. At the water's edge, Burke could identify Fitzmaurice by the bright yellow tunic he was wearing, and advancing into the stream, Theobald made ready to attack the camp. By then Fitzmaurice had seen him and was mounted. He now rode halfway down the stream bank opposite to be in hailing distance of Burke. All indications are that James preferred parley to fight. Raising his banner over his head, he cried at the men facing him, "Papa a boo," or "for the Pope," the cry as much a question as a challenge. And Burke, it is reputed, yelled back, "God save the Queen and devil take James Fitzmaurice." With that, the musketeer at Burke's side fired a shot into the yellow tunic. James crumpled in the saddle, but he was evidently moving forward already, and impetus plunged him into the stream and across. He rode headlong for Burke and, closing with him, quickly turned aside his guard. He drove his sword through Burke's collar and into his neck, killing him instantly. Then, as Theobald toppled from his horse into the stream, James fell wounded from his onto the bank. In the melee which followed, a

Geraldine named Gibbon Duff was severely wounded, but his fellows seem to have succeeded in either killing Burke's party or driving it off. Barrington Bridge was an empty victory. James Fitzmaurice lay dying on the bank, a ball lodged in his lung. Now, strength failing, he commanded his men to take his head from his body. He feared that if the English found his grave, they would make a trophy of him. And in accord with his request, after his death, his head was severed and carried away, his body hidden in the trunk of a hollow tree to keep his death a secret from the enemy as long as possible. James was not mistaken. On August 22, three or four days after he fell, English troops did discover his body. It was taken in triumphant procession to Limerick and hung in the marketplace in front of the cathedral. During the tedious maneuvers of the next few months the idle English amused themselves by shooting at the carcass with calivers and crossbows until it fell to pieces.

James Fitzmaurice had plagued Elizabeth for more than ten years; he had cost her lives and treasury; he had foiled her colonization of Munster and turned her commanders into laughingstocks. And before his end, he had done far worse; he had opened Ireland to foreign intervention. The English Court had reason to rejoice at his death; the marvel is that it did not. For once the realm had escaped a grave threat, yet since there was slight understanding, there was less thankfulness. Absorbed with Alençon, Elizabeth paused long enough to express satisfaction at the traitor's timely decease. And now what Waterhouse might have feared came to pass. Sir John of Desmond inherited a full-blown rebellion—more than 3000 men, a papal nuncio, and the authority to prosecute a holy war against England. But while Sir John could command a rebel army in the field, he could not bring all Munster and Ireland together under one flag. Only Gerald Fitzgerald possessed the power, wealth, and prestige to carry on Fitzmaurice's crusade, and he was not seeking a rebellion. Therefore, the rebellion came seeking him, and he was alternately drawn and driven into a role he had not sought.

YOUGHAL, 1579

Resolution

Before news of James Fitzmaurice's death reached London, preparations had been made to muster 1000 troops in Wales, 300 at Berwick, and an indeterminate number at Holyhead, Tavistock, and Bristol. Money and provisions were promised. Sir John Perrot received a commission to cruise off the coast of Ireland with five ships and 2000 men, his purpose to intercept and destroy any foreign reinforcements attempting to reach Fitzmaurice in the West. Yet no sooner did word of Barrington Bridge break than all preparations ceased and the troops gathering at Bristol for embarkation were discharged. Evidently a logistic muddle resulted from these contradictory instructions; the soldiers, many actually paupers and vagrants of Somersetshire, had no means of leaving Bristol and, milling about in the port city, became a threat to civil order. Finally, in early September, they were each awarded a halfpenny a mile to disband and find their way back to their place of conscription.

In Ireland the state of readiness also suffered. The Lord Chancellor and Council of Ireland had commanded all men between the ages of sixteen and sixty and living within the Dublin Pale to prepare for active service in the Queen's forces. Since there was fear in Dublin that the O'Neills might join Fitzmaurice to harry Ulster and the city, extraordinary measures were passed to contain the Gaelic or "mere" Irish element: "the leaders of blind folks, harpers, bards, rhymers, and loose and idle people having no master are to be now executed by martial law." After August 22 little came of this ruthless edict, for like London, Dublin lapsed into complacency with the news from Barrington Bridge.

Drury grew heartsick as he surveyed the latest ravages of Elizabeth's parsimony. His state of mind was not improved by the lingering symptoms of Irish fever which had afflicted him in the previous winter and undermined his health. Depressed, not confident of his ability to outface John's large army, he feared the worst for Munster and wrote desperately to Walsingham: "The traitor that remaineth, John of Desmond, is not slightly to be regarded. His credit is universal with all the ill men of Ireland. The Earl of Desmond, Clancar, Barry, Roche, Richard Burke, called 'Richard-in-iron,' and Edward Fitzgibbon, called 'the White Knight,' be suspect of consorting with him. Everywhere is to be seen nought except extreme negligence of Queen's officers, who have left this realm without munition or powder." Sir Nicholas Maltby, Drury's principal field commander, shared his superior's view, and having fewer illusions about Gerald's goodwill than even the Lord Justice, he demanded forthright renewal of the Crown's original commitment of men and ships. During these weeks Maltby was the steady rock around which the English in Ireland rallied. He was an uncomplicated soldier; for him there were only friends and enemies, loyal servants or traitors, and he was not given to weighing distinctions. In letters to Walsingham he found conspiracies springing up on every side: "Connaught hath not swerved yet from obedience. They have supplied 600 English and Irish well furnished, and had 1000 more ready to come with the MacWilliam. Let this be remembrance therefore to have a settled government and stout governor in each country. . . . The Earl of Desmond hath given great advantage to the rebels in protecting them and their goods. These several rebellions now begun across the realm are concluded on by secret meetings held everywhere and the last at Holy Cross Abbey. In Munster, distrust all; none but Sir Cormac MacTeige in Cork and Theobald Burke's sept in Limerick will do ought against the rebels." Maltby had reason to call Connaught to Walsingham's attention; a few months before Fitzmaurice landed, Sir Nicholas razed the countryside in one of the most brutal punitive expeditions in Irish experience. Now he obviously felt that his handiwork was paying dividends. Curiously, although both Drury and Maltby were Cecil's men, they wrote to Walsingham when in need of military support. Only when Drury had to plead for personal favors and remuneration were his letters addressed to Burghley.

Lord Justice Drury had served the Crown long and well in Scottish affairs before being posted to Ireland; he had compelled the surrender of Edinburgh Castle in 1573, and from his letters to Cecil on this occasion, posterity has learned much of the Scottish political climate. Inexplicably, his reward for success was the most difficult and perilous governorship in Her Majesty's gift—Lord Justice of Ireland. And now having survived a difficult apprenticeship, Drury discovered, as Sidney and Perrot before him, that he had spent much of his own fortune to sustain the Queen's administration. On top of his money, he had also lost his health and reputation. For Waterhouse, with whom he was apt to disagree violently, had written disparagingly of him to Cecil, claiming that before Davells' murder, Drury had intended to pay Sir John a royal pension for loyalty and good service. The charge is accurate, but then Drury was not the only English official taken in by John; Davells and Carter were also. Whichever way he turned that summer Drury met pitfalls. He wrote to his patron that he would "like to taste the Queen's bounty"; he was conscious of his physical decline and feared for his wife's welfare should the worst happen. Cecil consented to help lift the burden of state expenses from his shoulders; he circumvented Elizabeth and imparted 4000 pounds to one Richard Coleman for transport to Drury. By September the money was already gone. In the meanwhile, the cry for Drury's replacement had grown louder at Leicester House, and even as Coleman carried funds to the Lord Justice, Sir William Pelham was prepared to supplant him.

The Lord Justice had at his disposal 400 foot, many of whom were in garrison but were at least commanded by seasoned captains, and perhaps 200 horse. Maltby commanded Irish provisionals, but his reputation for discipline was so awesome that his 600 foot were exceptionally reliable. Beyond these companies, the Crown had neither men nor arms in Ireland. And those Irish lords who wavered during 1579 never lost sight of the fact that the rebels outnumbered the Crown three to one. But now a stroke of good fortune befell Drury. The Earl of Kildare, Gerald's uncle, grew incensed with Sir John's actions. Ten years before he had supported Fitzmaurice against the Munster planters, but Sir John lacked a worthy objective, and Kildare could find no good in his uprising. Consequently he eased Drury's way among the more influential lords, sent men and munitions to the army at Cork, and finally convinced Gerald to meet with Drury at Kilmallock. Desmond was still protesting his innocence, and it was the measure of Drury's need that he muzzled Maltby and journeyed to Kilmallock to hear Gerald's side of the story.

The forty miles to Kilmallock in heavy rains and wind did nothing to improve Drury's weakened constitution; he was fifty-four years old; observers thought he looked a hundred, and the belief persists that Gerald took advantage of his condition. Nothing could be further from the fact.

Desmond rode into the lion's mouth at Kilmallock, and once there, he was held in custody for more than a week. Drury had arrived with his entire marching force; Gerald came alone. What was actually said at Kilmallock is obscure; there are no reliable records. But doubtless Drury upbraided Gerald for his delays and timidity; doubtless Gerald protested that his lands were in jeopardy from both sides. Presumably neither could escape his position or his past sufficiently to speak candidly with the other, and the game was played out with profusions of loyalty on Desmond's side and assurances of immunity on Drury's. The results of the meeting were foreseeable from the start. Gerald vowed to aid Drury against his brothers if Drury would guarantee the inviolability of Desmond's lands. And by assenting to this proposal, the English party probably hoped to compromise Gerald in the eyes of the rebels or at least to neutralize him. For his part, Gerald probably hoped to stall, waiting to learn further how the Queen would act. Certainly his decision was influenced by the report that Sir John Perrot had just sailed into Baltimore Harbor in County Cork with four ships and several hundred men. Drury accepted Gerald's pledge, but after the previous months he was in no mood to turn Desmond loose without some palpable proof of his good intentions. Gerald consented, therefore, to send his son to Drury as a token hostage in exchange for Drury's assurances that no harm would come to the boy. Later Maltby claimed that Gerald also promised to provide intelligence and reconnaissance for the English forces and to throw open his strongholds as bases. Yet since Maltby eventually violated every agreement made at Kilmallock, his testimony is suspect. Once more blame is difficult to apportion. Gerald did send men, and he did surrender his son, but his men helped undo Drury, and his son was irrelevant to the issues at hand.

After Desmond had returned to Askeaton to ready his companies of gallowglass for service, the Lord Justice appears to have regained his confidence. Perrot's arrival surely helped, and word that Ormond had embarked for Ireland after three years in London also buoyed Drury's hopes. If nothing else, he would at least have Butlers to guard the strategic Aherlow Valley to the east of Kilmallock. The military situation was murky at best. Drury knew that Sir John and Sanders were hidden in Kilmore Wood with more than 3000 men, but Kilmore then touched the borders of three counties: Limerick, Tipperary, and Cork. Since the rebels dominated the West, they were expected to seek passage through one of several defiles into the East, and the Crown struggled during these days to shore up a line of defense across central Munster. In the center, astride the road from Cork to Limerick, lay Kilmallock; to the southwest, between the Ballyhoura Hills and the upper Blackwater River, lay the Barry stronghold of Liscarroll; and to the northeast, between Galtymore and Cashel, lay the notorious Aherlow, opening into the lush farmlands of the Golden

Vale. Maltby did not exaggerate when he stated that the English had no idea where Sir John might strike or where his forces might assemble, for during Gerald's years in Munster, English-born subjects had dwindled and the local Irish were silent as always. All that Drury and Maltby could tell in September was that Sir John was likely to threaten either Kilmallock or Aherlow or else swing southwest to flank the English fortresses and appear behind Drury at perhaps Mallow or Buttevant. Furthermore, no one was sure precisely what types of troops Sir John commanded. The loose folk and rabble were one element; trained Spanish and Italian infantry were another, and initial reports vastly overestimated the number of regular soldiers sent to Fitzmaurice after his landing. In late August, shortly before James' death, Gerald had at last leveled the breastworks at Smerwick. Yet oddly, the sixty men manning the position happened to escape, and while their escape was conceivably unavoidable, they also carried off with them their brass artillery—no mean feat for troops on the run. As a result of Gerald's incompetence or connivance, the Lord Justice and his commander now confronted a force not only larger than their own, but possibly better armed. And this army was deployed to slash at their supply lines wherever they chose to march.

In the light of these threats Drury's decision to split his force was risky but understandable. He could not hope to destroy Sir John en masse, and therefore, he counted on surprising the rebels piecemeal. To find the enemy's scattered elements in difficult terrain required aggressive patrolling. In order to cover more ground, Drury dispatched Maltby to the southwest with his cavalry, while he planned to sweep toward Limerick with 500 seasoned troops—right through the wastes and boglands of Kilmore. The English pikemen who filed out of Kilmallock that second week in September left to the beat of the marching drum and the skirl of bagpipes. For Gerald had sent his promised gallowglass, and since these knew Kilmore better than the English scouts, they led the columns of infantry, wagons, and light cannon forward into the shadow of the trees. Within a few hundred yards of Kilmallock, the forest swallowed the companies with hardly a trace. Kilmore was dense, crisscrossed by woody depressions, and during Drury's advance rain fell continually. Barring the Geraldines, his troops were a tough, disciplined lot, and they were led by three of Elizabeth's renowned fighting captains; still, their progress was excruciatingly slow. After three days they were only a few miles nearer Limerick than when they had started and had not yet caught sight of a rebel. The terrain separated the force into small parties; wagons mired up to their axles in mud; and powder and provisions were lost, discarded, or spoiled. Although no one is sure, the suspicion remains that Drury marched in circles.

He emerged through the worst of Kilmore's rocky outcroppings somewhere between Kilfrush Crossroads and present-day Herbertstown, and turning northwest toward Lough Gur, he plunged into a country of wooded ravines. Within a few miles he was clear of even these obstacles and had entered gently rolling meadows. Here the advance stopped not far from a place the English have called Springfield, the Irish *Gort-na-tiobrad*, or field of the spring. If John had wanted an ambush, he could have attacked Drury's men within the forest. Instead, he let Kilmore wear them down, scatter and exhaust them, and then as they emerged with relief into the open, he struck them full force, their backs against a wall of trees and undergrowth. No eyewitnesses have left an account of the Battle of Springfield; most of the English died there or under the forest eaves, and the hundred or so who escaped were private soldiers, not dispatch writers. Gallowglass rose out of the fields of grass at Gort-na-tiobrad to charge fiercely into the enemy with spears and battle-axes. Spanish musketeers were there, and they must have volleyed into the English ranks before they broke. From terse communiqués sent Whitehall in the aftermath, it is assumed that Captains Herbert, Price, and Eustace fought to rally their companies, but all three captains were slain on the field, their seventy years of combined fighting experience in continental wars useless in this war. Their men simply ran. Arms and cannon were abandoned, and the best infantry in Munster was reduced to a handful of desperate survivors. Drury, ill and exhausted, could not stand the shock; he collapsed in the confusion and was somehow carried to safety by unknown hands. For hours he lay hidden in the woods or perhaps in a ruined peel tower on the edge of the battlefield, and during the night he was smuggled back to Kilmallock on an improvised litter. If Springfield was like other Irish victories, John's men probably ran amok, stripping the dead, cutting the throats of the wounded, pilfering the English baggage. In their haste they missed the biggest prize of all: the Lord Justice of Ireland and acting President of Munster.

Drury's health now broke completely. Back at Kilmallock, he was taken by a severe fever. For several days he was delirious, and when at last he recovered his senses, he was overwhelmed by the shame of his defeat. He told Maltby that "he could not get any spiall [reconnaissance] while in the field," and he blamed his ignominy on treachery and surprise. Any soldier could see that the cause of disaster at Springfield was a failure of reconnaissance, and Drury's reconnaissance had been Geraldine gallow-glass. Whether they were McSheehys, McSweenys, or O'Flahertys is of no consequence; their clansmen were also at Springfield—with Sir John. If Drury surmised treachery, Maltby as usual was certain of it, and without further proof he resolved to revenge Springfield on Gerald. Assuming temporary command at Kilmallock, he wrote to Walsingham: "I will follow this service with severity. I request that Her Majesty acquaint me how I shall deal with this mad-brained Earl, the only archtraitor in all Ireland." One inestimable advantage had been achieved by Springfield; at least Maltby knew now where to find Sir John, and before he could come to grips with the "mad-brained Earl," he first had to destroy the army shielding Askeaton.

While Maltby gathered strength at Kilmallock, virtually assuming the entire administration of Munster, the Lord Justice departed by cart for Waterford. His wife was to attend him there, and the government persisted in the fiction that he was on temporary sick leave. In reality, Ireland had almost finished with Drury. As his cart jounced over the stony track between Kilmallock and Waterford, he performed his last duty. The Countess of Desmond overtook him on the road and in the middle of the way surrendered her son James into his keeping. Gerald had kept his final promise, but he turned the boy over after Drury had ceased to look for him. It was a rare and moving encounter, this meeting between Eleanor and the Lord Justice, for tradition holds that she beheld him with unaccountable gentleness and took pity on him in parting.

Eleanor had borne James in English captivity, in the humiliation of St. Leger's ramshackled household, and she had watched her husband badgered and bullied by Whitehall for more than ten years. She had ample reason to despise his enemies. Because of them, she had betrayed her own people and murdered hospitality. For a few days after Springfield, Desmond replied to the charge that he harbored rebels by throwing Bishop O'Healy and Owen O'Rourke as a sop to the English. O'Rourke had come from Spain with Fitzmaurice, and he and O'Healy had stopped at Askeaton as Gerald's guests. The Countess was forced to beguile them to save her husband, and entertaining them lavishly, she informed the enemy of their whereabouts as soon as they had left. Both men were taken and eventually hanged. The price of Eleanor's loyalty was the blood on her hands, and it was not Gerald who was to blame but the English, hounding them incessantly, driving them against their own. And now they demanded her son. If true, it is remarkable that this woman found any compassion at all for her adversary. Yet perhaps she and Drury shared one thing in common: they both loathed Ireland, and they were Ireland's casualties, people caught up in a catastrophe they never sought and could not control. Neither could feel pride in what they had done to survive. Drury had been a harsh governor, a flail to Connaught's Burkes; not a man without innocent blood on his hands, too, and now Eleanor overtook him on the road, wasted and frail. Some few figures in the long course of the Irish wars seem to rise above the parochial claims of sides and issues, to sense the awesome cruelty of the land, its chaos, its treacheries. Eleanor is perhaps one, for knowing that she too was tied to Fortune's wheel, she found the will to be kind. With her own hands she made him comfortable in the cart, arranging his bedclothes, slaking his fever with drafts from her own flask. "She spake softly to him and bid him be of good cheer," and along with her son, she sent her own escort to bring him safely into the town. Eleanor's generosity to a desolate enemy is a last act of grace; the like would not be seen again in Munster for many years to come.

Drury reached Waterford on September 30, and by October 2 he was dead. On the day he died, Thomas Butler arrived in Ireland, and shortly after, Ormond wrote thanking Elizabeth for her letter to the late Lord Justice. The Queen was beginning to heed the warning signs in Ireland, and she had tried to encourage and console Drury in his decline. Nowhere in the official record, however, is the cause of Drury's end mentioned. Springfield is passed over in silence, and the Lord Treasurer of Ireland explained to Walsingham: "The Lord Justice having been dangerously ill 15 days is still in a very doubtful state. The want of the money detained by [Sir Edward] Fitton troubled the Lord Justice and caused his sickness. The 4000 pounds brought by Coleman is gone." Money surely added to Drury's anxieties, but even a Lord Treasurer could not seriously believe that want of money killed him. More likely the record has been edited to assuage alarm. For in early October Cecil was still counseling Elizabeth: "You must conciliate Ireland; allow the chiefs to continue their ancient greatness, take away the fear of conquest lately grafted in the wild Irish, and wink at disorders which do not offend the Crown." The fate of Fitzmaurice had perhaps suggested to Cecil that Ireland had the means within itself to settle rebellion. His theory, unfortunately, was not to be put to the proof.

Maltby waited for no instructions. Reinforced by 600 English pikemen in early October, he struck out for Lough Gur and the rebel army. And he was in no mood to negotiate with fence sitters. Simple countrymen gave information or information was rung from them by headband and thumbscrew. Along his route of march Maltby left more than 200 Irish hanged, and his flying squadrons scoured the countryside, searching out rebel sympathizers. When they were found, it went hard on captured rebels; Bishop O'Healy, for instance, had his tongue loosened by having his feet roasted in iron boots. Other captives experienced a variety of portable torture devices. But by far the worst vengeance was wreaked on the defenseless villages. These were fired into, plundered, and burned, and from them survivors fled by the hundreds to Sir John's camp. Maltby knew what he was doing: if Sir John did not move into the open now to intercept the English, he would lose the support of his embattled peasantry. Somewhere between Kilmallock and Limerick, Sir Nicholas counted on flushing out the rebel army, and he advanced purposely through open country to bait them into a full-scale engagement.

From various estimates it is believed that Maltby probably commanded about 1000 troops in the field—only half the strength of the Irish army—but more than 600 of the English were "halberdiers, cabiners and pikemen in blockish bands." That is to say that the companies were trained and armed to form the Spanish square in battle. This tactic of the infantry square was to work terrible effect on the Irish, for the formation consisted of pikemen several ranks deep with musketeers clustered in each of the square's four angles. Under attack, the musketeers enfiladed an approaching enemy, while the pikemen forced them back at close quarters. Impervious to frontal assault, the square could be shattered only by accurate cannonade or musketry, and Irish gunners seldom had enough ball and powder to become proficient. From the start Maltby appears to have been confident that he could revenge Drury's defeat and disperse the rebels. He got his chance a few miles outside Limerick. Word was brought to him that Sir John had left Kilmore Wood and that his army was encamped and waiting along the Maigue River. Between Bruff and Croom stood the ruined monastery of Monasternenagh, and nearby the Desmond clans were drawn up for battle in full regalia. Sanders and Allen were with John, and Maltby's informers reported that on the previous evening the Earl of Desmond had visited his brother's camp. On the outskirts of Limerick the English force wheeled around and headed south immediately toward Croom, the ancient and abandoned seat of the first Irish Fitzgeralds. And a few miles beyond Croom, along the banks of the deep Maigue, they pitched their bivouac, expecting to fight in the morning. The ground in the area has not changed much; it is still as flat and empty as when the English soldiers looked out and saw clearly to the verge of the woods several hundred yards away. Their commander had chosen his terrain carefully. Before nightfall Maltby's pickets detected movement through the trees. Beyond the woods the main body of the Irish force waited to attack at daylight and drive the English into the Maigue. For Maltby had made sure that his men would stand and fight; the river was to their backs, and there was nowhere to run.

On the evening before the Battle of Monaster, a middle-aged captain named Barnabe Rich found his way into the English camp with a letter of introduction for Maltby. He had arrived at Cork only two days before and had ridden hard to reach the army. Rich wanted a command; the letter he brought from Francis Walsingham requested that he be given one, and

Maltby did not need to be told twice. He needed all the men he could find, and the following day Captain Rich, pikeman, took his place in the line beside everyone else. Walsingham no doubt had hoped to promote the career of an experienced officer; inadvertently he managed to turn loose on the English army in Ireland a fervent reformer and voluminous writer. Through the eyes of Barnabe Rich many Elizabethans were to see Ireland for the first time and to realize at last the pitiful state of their army. Rich got his first taste of Irish warfare in the smoke and clamor of Monaster, and weeks after, when the shock of the first charge had worn off, he would recall the experience in an account which still remains a model of war reporting. Rich pursued an odd career. He would serve for many years in Ireland; he would write more about that country and military life than any other Elizabethan, but long after the great soldiers of his day were gone, he would still be a captain, the oldest in King James's army. On October 3, near the ruined Abbey of Monasternenagh, he watched the Irish cut down in windrows, saw the McSheehys throw themselves screaming over the English pikes until the pikemen's hands ran red with blood. And from where he stood, Rich would believe always that the English had the better of the day.

Sir William Stanley found himself elsewhere on the field, and he felt the full, awesome madness of the gallowglass. He wrote afterward that "these rebels came as resolutely to fight as the best soldiers in Europe could." Once having dodged their swords and axes, Stanley filled with admiration for the gallowglass who crashed through the English ranks around him. Where he fought, the effect of the musketry must have been minimal, for the Irish pressed to close quarters. In the morning mist the collision was blind and ferocious. In places the Irish seemed to carry the battle, in other places to lose heavily. The engagement, it appears, was a confusing, headlong affair, and somewhere between Rich's account of a complete triumph, Stanley's tale of a near defeat, and O'Daly's insistence on an Irish victory lies the truth of Monasternenagh.

The battle began before either side could see the other. At daybreak the English camp was shrouded in river mist, and the Irish debouched from the treeline under its cover. Time was needed to raise the clans to fighting pitch, and the preparations lasted nearly an hour. According to a French account: "The papal standard was displayed; and Allen, the Irish Jesuit, went busily through the ranks, distributing his benedictions and assuring them of victory. Their dispositions were made by the direction of the Spanish officers among them, with an address and regularity unusual to the wild, pagan Irish." All the while, according to Rich, shouts were heard drifting through the mist in Irish and Spanish, and the screeching of the war pipes grew progressively louder. English drums beat the troops to quarter; pikemen formed their dense squares; and gunners set their sights through gaps in the mist, yet nothing could make them forget the waiting or the noise. Rich described the Desmond battle cry as a long, swelling moan—"Ooboo Ooboo," he writes—and in Anglicizing the sound, he coined the word "hubbub." The hubbub at Monaster reached its peak moments before the gray mass of the clans moved into the open and began their attack. At first they advanced slowly, hooting, waving their weapons over their heads, their officers steadying the ranks, and then the gallowglass began to charge. Many were slain outright as they came within range of the English muskets or the calivers firing loads of nails, but the survivors carried forward into the pikes or even beyond them. A sixteenth-century pike measured from fourteen to eighteen feet in length. The gallowglass who got in among the thrusting steel had literally to chop their way through a hedge of shafts to reach the enemy. Some did; many more died on the pikes. Some drew back to regroup. Others joined fresh waves of axmen to plunge into the wavering lines again. The English lines did waver and break in places, and wherever they did, the defenders were often worsted in the savage hand-to-hand fighting. But raw courage and individual prowess could never make up for the lack of firearms. On the morning of October 3 the full meaning of Stukeley's destruction became clear, for at Alcazar he threw away the Italian musketeers who might have tipped the balance at Monasternenagh. Against Maltby's disciplined, though terrified, infantry the Irish exhausted themselves. Rich observed justly that "the service of gallowglass in the field was neither good against horsemen, nor able to endure an encounter of pikes." For as Sir John committed his last reserves, Maltby loosed his small body of cavalry on the Irish flank and rear, and cut off from the forest, the gallowglass withdrew hastily, fighting through the horsemen and resisting the advancing squares of pikemen on their front.

The Irish Chronicle tells of the outcome: "And on the same day that the younger sons of the Earl of Desmond came to look for fight or prey in the country of Limerick, they and Captain Maltby met face to face, although they could have shunned and avoided him. A battle was bravely fought between them, in which the Irish army were so resolutely encountered and pressed by the Captain's forces, that they were finally routed, with the loss of Thomas, the son of John Oge, son of John, son of Thomas, son of the Earl and Owen, the son of Edmond Oge, son of Edmond, son of Tirlogh MacSheehy; and a great number of the constables of the Clann-Sheehy, with a great many people of the sons of the Earl. Great spoils, consisting of weapons and military attire, were left on this occasion to Captain Maltby's people." The Irish Chronicle normally shows extraordinary interest in spoils, but the debris of war left on the field at Monaster was as nothing compared to the forfeitures. On October 12 Sir William Stanley wrote to Walsingham from Abbey Adare begging to be remembered in the sharing of forfeitures, for the sons of many Irish magnates died at Monaster. They were attainted posthumously, and either their lands confiscated or their shares fined. The Earl of Clancar, MacCarthy More, may have lost a legitimate heir at Monaster and a bastard son; Sir John lost one son; Tirlogh MacSheehy another. Beneath the piles of slain, the English also discovered the body of Father Allen, sword in hand, and John Hooker, who remained in Ireland and possibly accompanied Maltby, wrote enthusiastically of Allen's end, likening his death to the fall of the prophets of Baal. As for Sanders and the Desmonds, they escaped into the woods along the Maigue, and Maltby wrote to Walsingham with some satisfaction: "The two brothers escaped by the speed of their horses and bore off the consecrated banner, which I believe, was anew scratched about the face, for they carried it through the woods and thorns in post haste." The face of Christ embroidered on the papal banner might have been torn by thorns, but significantly it was not captured. The gold reliquaries and crucifixes taken on the field were melted down and divided among the victorious captains; the great prize, though, had eluded them.

The exact casualties for the Battle of Monaster are not known. Likely, Sir John lost about a quarter of his 2000 men, for many of his wounded, hidden in the ruined abbey, were found and put to death by the English. Maltby's casualties were not as severe, but then Monaster was not the end of war, only the beginning, and many of the English troops were already tired and sick. The autumn rains fell relentlessly on Maltby's columns, and where he looked for food and forage, he found only burned earth. The retreating rebels spared nothing. Maltby's victory, however, cannot be measured in Irish dead or countryside conquered. For a short while he had cleared Limerick of rebels, and there was time enough for him to set his army on the road to Askeaton and to a final reckoning with Gerald.

Maltby clung tenaciously to the notion that the Earl of Desmond was the archtraitor behind the rebellion. Since he believed as much, time was everything to him in October. His authority was expiring. Sir William Pelham had arrived in Dublin and would soon be invested with Drury's offices. And no one could vouch for Pelham's allegiances. The English camp was still deeply divided between the servants of Walsingham and those of Cecil, and while Walsingham agreed with Maltby that Gerald had to be eliminated, the Queen had as yet issued no orders for the Earl's arrest. Cecil continued to believe that Desmond needed time to prove his loyalty, Ormond supported him in this opinion, and together they had easily persuaded a hesitant Queen. Influence with Elizabeth, however, was not a decisive factor at this juncture; control of the English army in the field was, and here Walsingham had a distinct advantage. Sir Nicholas Maltby was a patriot and a puritan, and he was endowed with a narrow righteousness which complemented his military instincts and made him remarkably insensitive to political realities. Maltby wanted Gerald, and he was willing to disregard legal technicalities in rooting him out of Askeaton. The evidence on which he acted was circumstantial and hearsay, but then he was caught in a spreading conflagration, a civil war more violent than Whitehall seemed willing to recognize. On march with a weary, dwindling force, perhaps Maltby had reason to move with uncalled-for severity. In any event he violated the assurances made to Gerald at Kilmallock; between October 6 and 10 the English army marched from Adare through the Earl's fortress towns of Rathkeale and Rathmore, and although the Earl's wardens offered no resistance, the castles were stormed, and their inhabitants put to the sword. Wherever the English found them along the road, the liveried servants of the Earl of Desmond were hanged, until in the countryside it became perilous to whisper Gerald's name.

The case against Gerald is worth restating. He was accused of conspiring with Fitzmaurice in the invasion of Kerry. He was blamed for failing to destroy Smerwick at once and for eventually permitting the garrison to escape with their arms. He was suspected of abetting the rebellion of his brothers, of instigating the murders of Davells and Carter, and of supplying the rebels with men and supplies. Maltby was also convinced that Gerald's aid to Drury had led the Lord Justice into ambush and defeat at Springfield and, further, that Gerald had often visited the camp of the rebels before Monaster. In support of these charges there was little hard evidence. On the contrary, the Earl of Desmond had met each accusation with concession; he had surrendered his son as a hostage; he had surrendered his countrymen where he dared; and most of all, he had declined to leave Askeaton. Even as Maltby advanced across his lands, murdering his people and destroying his castles, Gerald would not come out against him. Whether this inaction was owing to restraint or loss of nerve, Desmond voluntarily sacrificed the respect of friends and enemies. If he had not rushed to Bohermor and Affane fifteen years before, it would perhaps be possible to dismiss his behavior as simple cowardice. But Desmond had never before turned the other cheek; that he chose to begin now argues for reasons beyond fear of physical harm. The humiliation heaped on him would have tried a man more patient than the Earl of Desmond. Maltby suspected, for instance, that Sanders had sought refuge at Askeaton in the wake of Monaster, and perhaps Sanders had. But what Maltby could not know was Gerald's bearing toward the rebels. As they flocked to him for shelter, he admitted them to the safety of his courtyard, but when they stood outside his windows, challenging him to join them, he suffered their

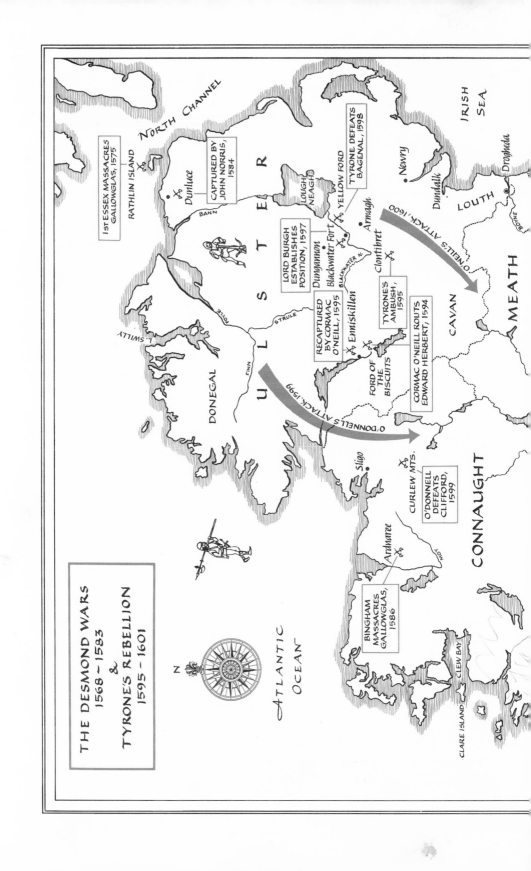

THE DESMOND WARS
1568 – 1583
&
TYRONE'S REBELLION
1595 – 1601

ATLANTIC OCEAN

N

NORTH CHANNEL

IRISH SEA

1ST ESSEX MASSACRES GALLOWGLAS, 1575

RATHLIN ISLAND

CAPTURED BY JOHN NORRIS, 1584

Dunluce

U L S T E R

BANN

LOUGH NEAGH

TYRONE DEFEATS BAGENAL, 1598

YELLOW FORD

Newry

Armagh

Dundalk

LOUTH

Drogheda

BOYNE

LORD BURGH ESTABLISHES POSITION, 1597

Dungannon
Blackwater Fort

BLACKWATER N.

Clontibret

O'NEILL'S ATTACK, 1600

MEATH

RECAPTURED BY CORMAC O'NEILL, 1595

Enniskillen

TYRONE'S AMBUSH, 1595

CAVAN

FORD OF THE BISCUITS

CORMAC O'NEILL ROUTS EDWARD HERBERT, 1594

STRULE

FINN

L. SWILLY

FOYLE

DONEGAL

O'DONNELL'S ATTACK, 1599

Sligo

CURLEW MTS.

O'DONNELL DEFEATS CLIFFORD, 1599

CONNAUGHT

Ardnaree

MOY

BINGHAM MASSACRES GALLOWGLAS, 1586

CLARE ISLAND

CLEW BAY

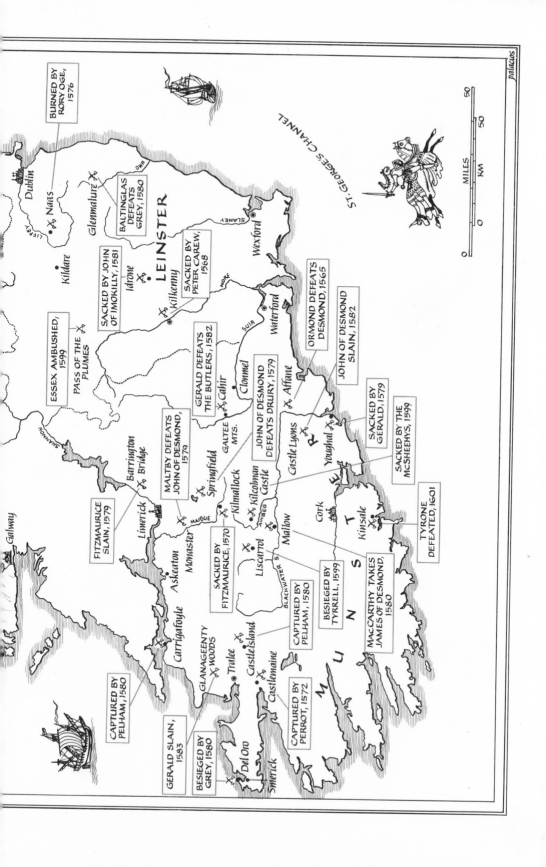

palacios

BURNED BY RORY OGE, 1576

Dublin

Naas

Liffey

Glenmalure

BALTINGLAS DEFEATS GREY, 1580

Owr

LEINSTER

Kildare

SACKED BY JOHN OF IMOKILLY, 1581

Idrone

SACKED BY PETER CAREW, 1568

SLANEY

Kilkenny

Wexford

NORE

ST. GEORGE'S CHANNEL

ESSEX AMBUSHED, 1599

PASS OF THE PLUMES

GERALD DEFEATS THE BUTLERS, 1582

Cahir

Clonmel

SUIR

Waterford

ORMOND DEFEATS DESMOND, 1565

JOHN OF DESMOND SLAIN, 1582

SHANNON

Barrington Bridge

MALTBY DEFEATS JOHN OF DESMOND, 1579

GALTEE MTS.

Springfield

JOHN OF DESMOND DEFEATS DRURY, 1579

Affane

Castle Lyons

SACKED BY GERALD, 1579

FITZMAURICE SLAIN, 1579

Limerick

MAIGUE

Kilmallock

Kilcolman Castle

AWBEG

Youghal

SACKED BY THE McSHEEHYS, 1599

Galway

Monaster

Askeaton

SACKED BY FITZMAURICE, 1570

Liscarrol

Mallow

BLACKWATER

Cork

Kinsale

TYRONE DEFEATED, 1601

CAPTURED BY PELHAM, 1580

Carrigafoyle

GLANAGENTY WOODS

Tralee

Castleisland

CAPTURED BY PELHAM, 1580

BESIEGED BY TYRRELL, 1599

MacCARTHY TAKES JAMES OF DESMOND, 1580

M
U
N
S
T
E
R

GERALD SLAIN, 1583

BESIEGED BY GREY, 1580

Del Oro

Smerick

Castlemaine

CAPTURED BY PERROT, 1572

MILES

KM

50

50

0

0

contempt for refusing. He did not deny his brothers succor, but he did deny their cause, and it is questionable whether the Crown could have asked more.

Of course, Gerald gave aid to the rebels; the fact, and it is paramount, is that he did not give his prestige. He temporized with both sides, not from weakness so much as from a sense of opposing interests. Behind the clash at Monaster were aligned the forces of English nationalism and Irish egalitarianism; the Second Desmond War would be fought on a loftier ideological plain than the first, and yet whichever triumphed would be inimical to Gerald. Therefore, surrendering to neither side, he struggled for a reasonable alternative, and for once he must have believed that Cecil appreciated his dilemma.

Cecil did, but the situation in England and Ireland had passed beyond reasonable. In the fall of 1579 the Elizabethan regime was in crisis; its neutral policies were challenged at home and abroad; its people were restless over the Queen's intended marriage and the arrest of Stubbs. The causes of this unrest were likewise overtaking Desmond. Maltby, descending on him, had become the instrument of the puritan will in Ireland. He represented those who in their determination to found an imperial state could no longer tolerate independent Irish chieftains or their subject Gaels. And besetting Desmond within his own domains were the partisans of the other revolution, the Counter-Reformation, no less determined to change Ireland in order to free it. Gerald was caught in a historical crux. He hoped to remain Irish, while an English peer, Catholic, while loyal to a Protestant Queen, and in the bipolar world of the late sixteenth century, these terms had grown self-excluding. It is the great irony of Irish history that when Gerald Fitzgerald finally achieved mature moderation, moderation no longer mattered. He could not turn against Ireland, for his home and loyalties were there, and he could not join the rebellion against England, for from England he derived his rule and authority. And so Gerald sat at Askeaton, while Maltby and his band marched right up to his gates. The outrage done Gerald was a dreadful and tragic mistake, but in 1579 the wrath of the English nation-state turned less against visible enemies than hidden, and among those most suspect were the symbols of an older world, the hereditary lords.

"He is in deeply," Maltby wrote to Walsingham. "I have received letters from the Mayor of Limerick which now declare that the Earl of Desmond has joined the traitors." The announcement was premature, yet Sir Nicholas believed it, and his subsequent letters to the Secretary are posted from points along the road to Askeaton. Exchanges between Maltby and Gerald should be read in precise order; they are as important for what they imply as for what they say.

The first letter from the acting President to the Earl precedes Monaster; it was dated September 28, Limerick: "The Lord Deputy in his sickness hath made choice of me to prosecute the traitors. . . . I desire your assistance with forces and advice in council . . . and do hereby send into your keeping a proclamation against the traitors to be posted by you in all your countries." Sir Nicholas is reminding Gerald of the Kilmallock accords; the proclamation is meant to force his hand. Gerald replies: "My plot regarding the prosecution of war against the rebels ought to have been followed. . . . I remind you that the army is not to spoil my tenants. . . . My service against the traitors will be more available than my presence." Gerald disapproved of Maltby's forthright march into the West; he had advised against scorching the earth out of fear for his own lands. Now he tried to impress on Maltby the difficulty of his position; he pledged to send aid, but he refused to come himself. Maltby would not accept his excuse, and arguing that he was only carrying out Pelham's orders and the Council's, he pressed for Gerald's presence: "Your presence would more avail her Majesty's service than your absence can do. . . . I cannot depart from my charge without the sanction of the Lord Justice and Council, and hereby insist that the proclamation sent unto you be posted in declaration of your intentions." Gerald answered from Askeaton on October 3; he turned a deaf ear to Maltby's instructions and informed him of Sir John's inconsequential doings in the neighborhood of Ballygillacan. On the third, the date of Monaster, Maltby hardly needed to be told of Sir John's whereabouts. Then on the fourth, Gerald, who had meanwhile learned of the battle, wrote exuberantly: "I have heard sure news of your victory over the traitors. . . . Send to me details of the same. . . . I hope to light on the residue that are fled." Desmond apparently thought that he was rid of Maltby for the moment, and he was extravagant in his offers of aid. For his part, Sir Nicholas needed Desmond's help in pursuing the rebels, and therefore he wrote to him now, promising great honors and the Queen's favor "If you will but get that papistical arrogant traitor Sanders, who deceiveth with false lies, to be arrested." Over the next few days there were no communications. By then Maltby was aware that many of the rebels had fled toward Askeaton. He was in hot pursuit across Gerald's lands. Finally, on October 6 Gerald became alarmed. Sir Nicholas was putting his estates to the sword, and the Earl protested, "I marvel that you should destroy my poor tenants." Maltby's curt reply was dated October 7 from Rathkeale: "Your presence is requisite to show your obedience." Desmond must either come out and join the English or the force invading his domains will march to his doorstep and drag him out. At Rathkeale, Gerald's retainers were forced to defend themselves; several of the Queen's men were slain. Solicitations now broke off completely; Maltby continued down the rainswept road to Askeaton, and Gerald withdrew into his castle. The last letter exchanged between these men is dated October 8 from Askeaton Abbey, and it contained Maltby's ultimate demand that a conference be called. Curiously, the letter was addressed "to the Earl of Desmond, or the Countess, or Maurice McSheehy, the Constable of Askeaton." Maltby was unable to raise any reply from within the walls.

What happened subsequently is largely surmised from the legends of Gerald Fitzgerald, the Rebel Earl, and from scanty reports entered in the *State Papers*. From the ramparts of Askeaton, Gerald marked the progress of Maltby's soldiers across his lands by the pyres of smoke along the roadway. In the dampness, the homesteads and hamlets smoldered for days, clouds of white smoke hanging over them, but the Earl of Desmond did nothing. Askeaton, on its island in the middle of the Deel, was impregnable against all but siege artillery, and Maltby did not have siege guns. Within the walls were certainly some of the wounded from Monaster, possibly Sanders himself, and the weary remnants of Clan McSheehy. Gerald had no choice but to allow Maltby to march unopposed into the village of Askeaton and to occupy the friary across from the castle. He hardly had the means to resist effectively. But Maltby also could do little, except vent his wrath on what came to hand. The commander was sick of the rain and mud; he had come down with the ague, and nearly 20 percent of his several hundred men were sick or bedridden. For one entire day his musketeers fired at the walls of the castle, trusting to hit someone in their barrage of shot, but beyond nuisance attacks and a general blockade of the approach ways, they achieved nothing. Maltby's force was clearly inadequate to the task, and as the days dragged by without reinforcements or the appearance of Perrot's heavy guns, the English force grew restless. Frustration is the only explanation for what they now did.

The friary or Abbey of Askeaton, as it was known, had been abandoned at the approach of the English, but the vessels of service and the rich vestments of the Abbot had been left behind. The English troops broke into the church and desecrated the altar, defaced the statues, and smashed the finest stained glass in the West of Ireland. It was all to be expected, this zealous destruction of Papist idols and art. But Maltby went further. He ordered his men to break open the tombs of the Desmonds and scatter the remains of the dead along the riverbank, where they could be seen from the walls of the castle, and he tore open the late Countess of Desmond's grave and had Joan's bones flung out with the rest. The savagery lasted an afternoon, and by the following morning, probably October 10, the English had left. They withdrew to Limerick to replenish their stores and await reinforcements.

In the aftermath of the atrocity Gerald's letters grew shrill and excited. He wrote to Ormond at Kilkenny, furious that the Crown should send a man "who hath always hated my family and done us disservice" to enforce his loyalty. "Maltby hath done no less than treat me as an enemy," he explained, "and most maliciously hath defaced the old monument of my ancestors, fired both the abbey, and the whole town, and all the corn thereabouts, and ceased not to shoot at my men within Askeaton Castle." Desmond held back the full truth for last: "He hath also most spitefully broken and burned your mother's grave . . . and he hath performed these acts of an enemy without authority, which I beg you to consider on my behalf." Ormond had a great deal to consider. But meanwhile, Gerald wrote as well to Sir Henry Sidney, from whom he had always received just treatment, and in his letter enumerated the points of service done the Crown and the wrongs received. He reminded Sidney how he had resisted Fitzmaurice; how he had handed over a Bishop and two scholars who had accompanied the invasion; how he had resisted the Clan O'Flaherty for joining with James. In return Maltby had killed his retainers, Rory Ny Dillon and Kuagery Okyne, "hath spoiled Rathmore Castle and murdered the keeper, spoiled Rathkelly, defaced and burnt the town and abbey of Askeaton." Gerald desired Sidney, "as he is a gentleman, to certify Her Majesty and the Council of these doings." And it is likely that Sir Henry did no less, for within a few weeks there were repercussions. Cecil wrote angrily to Pelham and for his benefit emphasized the fact that Gerald was not yet a declared traitor. The Queen's displeasure apparently reached her Irish officials but did not hinder them. Shortly after, Vice Treasurer Wallop wrote to Walsingham assuring him that Sir William Pelham was more than fit to be Lord Justice and insinuating that Gerald was only up to his old tricks. "It is merely his practice," Wallop confided, "to charge Maltby with driving him into rebellion when he has long been a party to the treason." In the eyes of Elizabeth's officials, Gerald was guilty beyond doubt, and her distraction and hesitation only hardened their resolve to prosecute matters as they stood.

Thomas Butler knew better, but he was confounded by a rebellion in his lands seemingly far greater than the one Carew had provoked ten years before. Once again he had rushed home from England to do his cousin's bidding, and in his own words he discovered a country "all bent to the popish religion and making no reckoning of perjury." Butler was a Protestant and, next to Gerald, the largest landholder in the South. He must have appreciated Gerald's plight more than most, but self-interest strangled his natural sympathy; from the start Ormond belonged to the other camp, firmly committed to the policies of Cecil, if not Walsingham. More than the desecration of his mother's tomb was required to sway his allegiance, and he subsequently passed Gerald's letters along to Pelham. Possibly Ormond believed that negotiation was the only means by which Desmond could save himself and his earldom, and by enlisting Pelham, Butler might have hoped to forestall the worst. If true, he misjudged the gravity of the situation. Pelham invited Gerald to meet with him on neutral ground, somewhere between Limerick and the Rock of Cashel. Gerald replied that he had met with the previous Lord Justice at Kilmallock and had promptly been arrested; he declined to appear. Behind his answer was partly a reaction to Pelham's extraordinary arrogance; the Lord Justice had instructed him not to lose time, for he was exceptionally busy and determined not to lie idle.

At this juncture Ormond volunteered to meet with Gerald in place of Pelham and to discuss the Crown's terms. These were little less than surrender of Askeaton and Carrigafoyle Castle, prosecution of his own brothers, and capture of Sanders. Negotiation was out of the question. The penalty for refusing was to be the charge of high treason against Gerald. Desmond argued that he was loyal, that he was more wronged than otherwise, that his brothers had murdered Davells against his advice and threatened the life of his own son if he did not support them. Finally, he agreed to hunt down Sanders as a token of his sincerity. But Ormond was not empowered to accept any terms except Pelham's. As he left Gerald for the last time, he was appalled by the signs of physical and nervous collapse visible in the Earl; the two had not met for several years, and Gerald was now only the shadow of Butler's old antagonist.

Gerald's ordeal, however, was only beginning. Next, Pelham wrote to him ordering that he appear in Dublin within three days or be proclaimed a traitor; the struggle had become a war of nerves, and the Lord Justice added that the proclamation was drawn up and ready. Gerald did not respond and did not come. On October 30, meeting with Ormond, the Earl of Desmond had crawled for the last time. Pelham warned him on November 2 that he would be given only one more chance; the Council and the Lord Justice of Ireland demanded that he meet with them at eight the next morning, or the proclamation would be published. Should Gerald comply, he would have license to go to England and live at peace beyond the turmoil of Munster, Pelham promised. But Gerald had been to England long before Pelham had ever set foot in Ireland, and he was now determined to die in Ireland if he could not live. Not only did he not come to Dublin and not meet with the Lord Justice, but on November 3, the day he was published a traitor, the day incidentally that John Stubbs went to the scaffold in London, Gerald was carried out of Askeaton and placed on

a white charger. He could barely sit a saddle, all agree that his limbs shook
with palsy; but into his hands was placed the sword of the Desmonds, and
to the cheering of the kern and the battle cries of the McSheehys, the Earl
of Desmond rode out to war. By no choice of his own he had been declared
a traitor, and now a traitor he would be, under Sanders' banner, Spain's,
or need be his own.

In the weeks immediately following, the Earl of Desmond disappeared from sight in the mountains of Kerry. The entire country was
aware by now that he had joined the rebels, and an ominous quiet fell upon
Munster, Leinster, Limerick, and even the Dublin Pale. During these
weeks the *State Papers* are filled with sinister rumors: "Spanish conquistadores at Askeaton"; "Papal troops ashore on the coast of Kerry"; the
imminent revolt of Lords Baltinglas, Barry, Roche, Sir Cormac MacTeige.
Along with Gerald, the West rose almost to a man, and the sudden appearance of the clans O'Sullivan, McSweeny, and Finnin MacCarthy in arms
terrified the English towns. In the Wicklow Mountains, barring the overland passage from Waterford to Dublin, the Kavanaughs also rose in sympathy, sweeping down from the mountains against Idrone and their own
family. At Limerick the Queen's garrison withdrew for safety into the
castle, mobs roamed the city's streets, and Maltby reported to Walsingham:
"On this 27th of November, the bark I have had for service on the Shannon
River hath been assaulted and taken by the townsmen . . . with the murder
of Francis Shirley, the captain, in the presence of the Mayor [of Limerick].
Clinton, the new captain of the bark, come then to Shirley, was drowned
by the townsmen along with the master gunner and most of the crew."
Apparently the Mayor was a prisoner of the rebels; the great English base
in the West was eroding from within. Meanwhile, Sir John of Desmond,
with Spanish troops, had marched through Kerry and Killarney, burning
Tralee and plundering the larger landholdings. They "preyed" the property of James Rowley and left him nailed to his tower door, dead; they
burned Dengill and Ludenbege; they overtook a company of Maltby's
infantry, commanded by one Captain Apsley, and wiped them out to the
last man. Stanley, in the vicinity of Adare, executed forty rebels in reprisal
for this exploit, but by then Sir John had swung through the lake country
of Killarney and was threatening Kinsale and Cork in the East. Everywhere that Pelham looked after his ill-timed proclamation, Ireland was in
arms against him.

In the North the Scots poured into Ulster, in the South foreign troops
were aiding Gerald, and within the Dublin Pale the Lord Justice's orders
were ignored with impunity. Sir Henry Wallop bemoaned the fact to
Burghley: "The Pale will not bear its charges; our nation is misliked and
the Spanish much affected. . . . The Irish do not care what we say." Now

not only was Sanders loose and preaching religious war, but the Earl of Desmond was moving through the land at will, distributing Her Majesty's property. Pelham complained to Walsingham: "He doth distribute Her Majesty's lands in Munster, which Doctor Sanders confirmeth, reserving some tribute to the See Apostolic and certain duties to legates that shall yet arrive. The Queen must maintain her army and force the surrounding country to contribute to her strength." Once he had joined the rebels, Gerald never hesitated to pledge land reform or to reapportion property to his hungry peasantry. As for the spiritual welfare of his charges, Sanders promised a papal dispensation to all who murdered Englishmen in the cause of Irish liberty.

The situation was at its darkest in November and December. At one point, Edward Waterhouse wrote to Sir William Gerard, Lord Chancellor of Ireland, virtually suggesting that he pack his bags: "The Earl of Clancar and Sir John of Desmond have burned Kinsale and are marching on Cork. . . . Turlogh Luineach is promised the principality of Ulster by the King of Spain, and the Earl of Desmond that of Munster, by the Pope. . . . An Italian legate is coming. . . . An exceeding great army is preparing in Italy to come over, and there be indication how the popish faction in England will soon be in arms against the Queen. Mr. William Norris, with his troop of horse, is delayed at Bristol by contrary winds." Remarkable though it seems, there are indications that many Irish officials doubted the stability of the monarchy. Reports of imminent rebellion at home, of rioting in London, of an uprising of English Catholics reached many of them that fall. Unfortunately Cecil was grievously ill during this period, and Walsingham was still immersed in the marriage controversy. There was no one to quiet their fears.

Plans to crush the rebellion passed regularly from Ireland to Whitehall, but while there was never any question that measures might be taken, there was seldom any means. Maltby envisioned a defense based on a triangular cordon of strongpoints. "I recommend a plot to govern Ireland," he wrote to the Queen's Council, "with only 2000 men; placing 400 at Coleraine and 400 on the Blackwater, which forces may meet in less than 8 or 10 hours." Sir Nicholas appreciated the peculiar exigencies of guerrilla warfare; his proposal for interlocking fire bases was both novel and ingenious, but in all Ireland the Crown could not muster 2000 regular soldiers. Sir Warham St. Leger, the battle horse of the previous rebellion, emerged from retirement to recommend defoliation of the forests: "All the Geraldines have risen . . . and the traitors burn all the corn they may get and demolish all castles. No doubt they will have foreign aid soon, and the scope of their range includes the Great Wood, Aherlow Forest, Dromfinyne Forest, Glanmoire, and Glanfriske, which are their chief and near impregnable fortresses. We must plot to employ a force of soldiers large enough to protect laborers while they cut and burn the woods. Ormond has a force sufficient to front the enemy, but it would require above 4000 English to assail them on three or four sides, destroy their forests, and effect their defeat. Clanricard's sons are in arms against the rebels, but they are insufficient. The North is on the verge of rising. Sir William Morgan has arrived with some soldiers. But more forces are needed and must be despatched soon if Ireland is not to be lost."

St. Leger's letters read much like his communiqués of ten years earlier; if anything, he has only grown fiercer in his hatred for the Gaels. Nevertheless, his advice is sound; soon Ormond would raise his voice demanding similar solutions, and both men would discover that the Queen was unprepared to support them. Throughout the *State Papers* for November and December runs pathetic evidence of unreadiness and penury. Drury's widow, for instance, the Lady of Thame, was caught by a storm in St. George's Channel and driven back to Cork by adverse winds. She had been trying to reach home; she was bankrupt and must now throw herself on the generosity of Vice Treasurer Wallop. He, like her late husband, had already spent 1000 pounds of his own income in the Queen's cause, and he wrote to Burghley requesting the means to make the Lady of Thame a decent pension. Storms kept supplies from reaching Ireland; the grainhouses of Munster had gone up in smoke; and Ormond begged for 2500 pounds of biscuit to feed his men. At one time nearly all of Pelham's field commanders were down with the Irish fever: Maltby, Sir John Zouche, Sir William Norris. Norris, an especially popular captain, was killed fighting in the North a few weeks later. Captain Fisher, a hero of Monaster, died in Limerick of infected wounds and mistreatment. And in December, Wallop wrote gravely to Burghley: "Ormond's journey against the rebels in Kerry has endured for twenty days, but his soldiers had bread but for five days and no drink at all. They passed rivers, wading to the stomach, seven times a day, and then lodged abroad without tent, house or cabin. It is easier to talk at home of Irish Wars than to be in them. We must pay the men. Captain Secomb, quartermaster, is young and unskillful and he forces the men to eat spoiled beef, new salted. The beer is deficient in every hoghead, and so dead it cannot be drunk without new brewing. We must have aid or more forces."

The slow reinforcement of the Queen's garrisons did continue through November and December. A bright spot was the nearly complete control of the sea by the ships of Sir Humphrey Gilbert and Thomas Courtenay. Gilbert, however, again proved a doubtful asset. In October he put into Cobh, the port of Cork, with the *Anne Archer*, the *Relief*, and the *Squirrel*; he had been on station since mid-August and his crews were given the liberty of the town. Within a fortnight Gilbert was himself in serious trouble, and the townspeople were clamoring for his arrest. The explanation appears in a letter from Sir Owen O'Sullivan to the Earl of Leicester, protesting Gilbert's behavior. According to O'Sullivan, who was vouched for by Captain Yorke of the pinnace *Foresight,* Gilbert challenged his loyalty to the Crown and assailed him in a tavern, beating him terribly about the head with his sword. Far worse, on putting back to sea, Gilbert also argued with a merchant of Cork and in his rage slew the man on the dockside. Leicester made no reply to the letter. As usual, the Queen's forces lived at arm's length from the Irish, and even in the secure city of Cork, there was widespread suspicion and dissension.

Perhaps nothing more infuriated the English officials in Ireland or at home than the ease with which the Irish abandoned English ways and turned to Spain. The merchants of Cork and Dublin passed Spanish wine to the rebels and Munster grain to the Spanish right under Pelham's nose. The red Spanish wine came to be called "the King of Spain's Daughter" by the Gaels, and certainly they were enamored of her. Fynes Moryson described the typical courtship: "The Irish, when they come to any market town to sell a cow or a horse, never return home, till they have drunk the price in Spanish wine . . . and till they have out-slept two or three days' drunkenness." Moryson had a jaundiced view of the Irish, and their affectation of Spanish speech and customs did not please him: "The chief inclination of these people is to be robbers . . . for if the people in one village become aware that in another there are cattle or other effects, they immediately come armed in the night, and go 'Santiago,' as they say, or kill one another in their madness." From the day that Gerald Fitzgerald rode out of Askeaton until the time of the Spanish Armada, rebel Ireland looked increasingly to Spain for all manner of help. No one has ever been certain how many soldiers Philip II landed in Kerry or how many Spanish ships reached Irish ports. The best and most energetic leaders in Ireland hungered for Spanish intervention, and Spain sent a few ships and a handful of men. Thereby Philip lost his great opportunity. Perhaps in hindsight he realized how Ireland had been his only chance of tearing England away from the Netherlands, of canceling its influence among European Protestants, and of sailing the invincible Armada up St. George's Channel as well as the English Channel. But Elizabeth, too, lost an opportunity. Walsingham complained to Maltby throughout October and November of the Queen's "French Cause," and surely in Elizabeth's inattention to Ireland at this juncture lay the seeds of vast future distress. The war was allowed to flare up during this period, fed by the impolitic perceptions of Pelham and Maltby. Between September and November the Desmond Rebellion evolved from a revolt into a civil war, and it was soon to become a great conflagration in which approximately a half million people were to perish.

Thomas Butler could read the danger signs: the wanton destruction of food reserves by both sides; the diminished harvest; the wholesale murder of peasants and townspeople; the flight of merchants and tradesmen; the depopulation of whole neighborhoods. The sensitive balance between commerce and the backward agriculture of the land was being lost, and along with it the annual income on which the lords of Ireland relied. Ormond was in the field; he watched his men suffering from want of food, sickness, and shortage of arms. He also understood the leverage that Gerald brought to a war for religious freedom. And he wrote bitterly to the Queen's Council, his letter intended for her eyes as well as theirs: "I require to be victualled, that I might bestow the captains and soldiers under my leading in such places as I knew to be fitted for the service, and most among the rebels. I was answered there was none. I required the ordnance for batteries many times and could have none, nor cannot as yet, for my Lord Justice sayeth to me, it is not in the land. Money I required for the army to supply necessary wants, and could have but 200 pounds, a bare proportion for to leave with an army. Now what any man can do with these wants I leave to your judgment. I hear the Queen mislikes that her service has gone no faster forward, but she suffereth all things needful to be supplied, to want. I would to God I could feed soldiers with the air, and throw down castles with my breath, and furnish naked men with a wish, and if these things might be done the service should on as fast as her Highness would have it. This is the second time that I have been suffered to want all these things, having the like charge that now I have, but there shall not be a third; for I protest I will sooner be committed as a prisoner by the heels than to be thus dealt with again; taking charge of service upon me."

This time Butler's complaints did not fail to reach Elizabeth. It is known that she was genuinely concerned for his success and safety, that Cecil and Walsingham both supported his expedition. Furthermore, when in December this letter reached the Queen, she was already reconsidering the French alliance, her French courtship, and Philip's maneuvers. Pelham and Maltby were to soon come under severe questioning, and gradually, very gradually, England was to commit itself to an all-out war in Ireland. Ormond's letter had much to do with this change in policy, but by far the greatest provocation came from Gerald himself. In the last days of November Gerald struck at the Queen with a fury and vengeance at which all Europe marveled. He had been weeks in waiting, and now everyone in Ireland at last knew where he was.

◆

The town of Youghal is built on the estuary of the Blackwater River, about twenty miles up the coast from Cork and forty miles down from Waterford. Today it is a modest seaside resort, and even in Elizabeth's time it was famed for its wide, curving strand and fine seascape. Here, on the day that Gerald Fitzgerald was proclaimed a traitor, a coincidence took place which is at once embarrassingly flamboyant and indisputably factual. Almost to the hour of the proclamation, a large section of the defensive wall of Youghal fell down; it was not pushed; it collapsed of neglect and its own weight. The City Corporation grew uneasy over this evidence of their decayed defenses, but since the town had always been under the patronage of the Desmonds and since a large Jesuit school flourished surreptitiously there, they were convinced that they had nothing to fear from the rebels. A messenger was sent nevertheless to fetch powder from Cork. And Sir Warham St. Leger, who had been acting as Provost Marshal of Munster since Carter's death, gave powder and good advice. He suggested that one of Sir Humphrey Gilbert's well-armed ships be dispatched to cover the collapsed wall; the section affected stood on the south side of the town, perpendicular to the strand and within the range of naval guns. The Corporation, however, was unwilling to pay the support of Gilbert's sailors or Ormond's soldiers and, declining the offer, made no preparation for defense at all. Perhaps its decision seemed justified at first. Desmond's growing army was believed to be gathering in the Knockmealdown Mountains, twenty miles up the Blackwater. Everyone expected them to march on Cork and to join with Sir John's forces then besieging Kinsale, south of Cork. The thought that they might come to Youghal seems never to have occurred, possibly because the town favored the Geraldines and possibly because the Earls of Desmond had built and endowed the port.

No alarm was heard, therefore, when toward the end of the month a contingent of rebels camped on the south side of the town, near a Franciscan priory founded by Gerald's ancestors. The rebels did not interfere with the life of Youghal, and their only request was that the Mayor supply them with wine. To this end they requested, and the citizens of Youghal granted, the only ferry connecting the town with the Waterford side of the Blackwater. It was agreed that the rebels would transport two tuns of wine in the vessel and then depart. But during the transaction Gerald's captains found an opportunity to converse with the citizens, and apparently they learned from them of the town's unpreparedness. The ferry was not returned, for on the following morning the rebels had vanished without a trace. In Youghal it was generally assumed that the vanguard of Desmond's army would soon be seen outside Cork; they never suspected that Gerald was headed for them.

The rebel army waited a few miles north of Cappoquin, in a bend of the Blackwater River, until the weather grew stormy. On November 24 there were snow squalls and heavy rain, and masked by storm, the rebels crossed the Blackwater by Lismore and proceeded downriver. They reached the south wall of the town late on the twenty-fourth and, forming along the beach, moved into range of the remaining wall. What happened next is known from an inquiry conducted by the Lord Justice and from eyewitness accounts. In the round tower which commanded the seaward landing the gunners were commanded by the Mayor not to fire first, although they had a "saker charged with a round shot, a square shot, and a handspike an ell long, wherewith they were like to have spoiled many of the rebels." One elderly member of the guards "commanded not to shoot off lest the rebels would be angry therewith, and threatened to kill the gunner if he would give fire." Other sympathizers had already carried out ladders and hung ropes over the walls. The Queen's men in Youghal were powerless to restrain the Geraldine supporters, and without the ferry, they could neither flee toward Waterford nor summon help. Consequently, at low tide and in the midst of a great thunderstorm, Desmond's followers advanced over the strand and stormed through the hole in the wall into the town. The melee which ensued was both terrifying and confused. Bolts of lightning lit the sky and the gallowglass setting about them with swords among the townspeople. Many of the inhabitants helped the carnage, widening the breach in the defenses, throwing the Queen's few soldiers over the walls into the waiting arms of the kern. Often sympathizers were themselves slain in the bloody fury of the sack. Within an hour, the town was in Gerald's hands, the defenders dead, the English officials dragged out of their houses and hanged, their womenfolk ravished. Desmond was not done with Youghal, however; he intended to make it an object lesson to the citizens of Cork and Waterford. For the next three days his men methodically stripped every household of plate, furnishing, and other valuables. The Irish Chronicle describes how "the Geraldines seized upon all the riches they found in this town, excepting such gold and silver as the merchants and burgesses had sent away in ships before the town was taken. Many a poor, indigent person became rich and affluent by the spoils of this town. The Geraldines levelled the wall of the town, and broke down its courts and castles, and its buildings of stone and wood, so that it was not habitable for some time afterwards."

Youghal appears not to have followed the grim course of other more conventional sackings. The blood spilled copiously was soon forgotten, and Gerald's men, with the surviving townsmen, threw themselves into a wild celebration. "The inhabitants joined with them," it is recorded, "notwithstanding that they saw the Earl and Sir James, the Seneschal of Imokilly, and divers others draw down in the court-house of the town her Majesty's arms, and most despitefully with their daggers cut it and thrust it through, and notwithstanding that they saw the ravishing of their women, the spoiling of their goods and burning of their houses." Dermot O'Sullivan's son recorded that as one of Desmond's followers filled his pouch with gold and silver from a broken chest, he said to his master that the thing was very pleasant, if not a dream. O'Sullivan stood by and warned the Earl that the sweetest dreams might be but a mockery.

By November 28 the Geraldines had pulled down most of the walls of Youghal, burned most of the public buildings, and divided the women of the town into lots, each assigned to a clan or company. Weighed down with booty, the town burning behind them, they abandoned Youghal en route to Sir John's army in the South. Behind them they left clear evidence that Fitzmaurice's war had become the Earl of Desmond's, and Gerald, who had once been "the mad-brained Earl" had at last become "the Great Rebel Earl" of Irish legend. But by way of showing Elizabeth the power of his displeasure, he had sacked his own city. The wreckage was appalling. When Ormond entered Youghal a few weeks later, he found the ruins in the sole possession of a friar, whom he spared for his humanity in securing Christian burial for Henry Davells. On the other hand, the Mayor of Youghal was caught and hanged at his own door for gross negligence. Thereafter Ormond never again referred to Gerald with sympathy; he was ever after to Butler that "cankered and alienated heart." Assuredly no hope of pardon remained for the Earl of Desmond after Youghal, but whether Whitehall possessed the wit to catch him was a question still to be settled.

KILMORE, 1580

Pursuit

In January, 1580, William Cecil conceded defeat. Elizabeth had turned against his plan for a French marriage, Walsingham and Leicester had returned to Court no longer in disfavor, and in Ireland Desmond had sacked Youghal. On January 26 Burghley apologized to Ormond "that for lack of furnishments you should have suffered such indignities committed by the rebels." Then, speaking as one who had counselled conciliation, he admitted "the Queen has yielded to your wish; money is sent; munition is in lading, and so is victualling for 2,000 men for three months, and there are now to be more men serving under the Queen's pay than ever there were in Ireland in all these hundreds of years." For his part, Cecil concluded: "So must I now merely say with others *Butler a boo*, against all that cry as I hear in a new language *Papa a boo*. God send you your heart's desire, which I know is agreeable to mine, to banish or vanquish those cankered Desmonds and to plant again the Queen Majesty's honour and reputation."

Elizabeth had finally turned her gaze to Ireland, and in the wake of disasters at Youghal, Kinsale, and Tralee, she began to question the worthiness of her officials. The government at Dublin was rife with recriminations. Maltby had fallen out with Pelham, Pelham with Ormond, and the Queen's shrewd inquiries aggravated the situation. "Why," she wanted to know, "was Desmond proclaimed a traitor before he was in hand?" Common sense argued that he be caught before attainting, not left free to raise the countryside. Maltby had driven Gerald into rebellion, but now Pelham took the blame. He was also accused of dispensing pensions and knighthoods to the Irish at great cost to the Crown, these gifts intended to buy the loyalty of the smaller lords and chieftains. Elizabeth utterly rejected all attempts to inflate the English knighthood, and now she demanded that Pelham rescind the honors and recall the pensions he had given prodigally. But the Lord Justice argued that if the Irish were not to be bought off, then the means must be found to convince them that Elizabeth would win in Ireland and that her goodwill might be worth their lives. He needed assurance from Elizabeth that no pardon would be given the Desmonds and that no lord supporting the Queen would ever have to fear reprisals from them. To his credit, he told Elizabeth what she did not wish to hear: that she must either act boldly or return to appeasement. And backing his argument with an offer to resign, he insisted that only total measures could save Ireland for the Crown. Within a week Pelham had his answer from Burghley: "I and others have persuaded her Majesty that you may have authority to reclaim by offer of pardon all such as have offended, saving the Earl and his brothers, and such as murdered Davells, and such as have come from foreign parts to stir up rebellion, among which I mean Sanders, that cipher, whom of all others the Queen's Majesty is most desirous that you could take hold of." Pensions and titles were out, but Pelham had wrested the authority to wage war fully and to exact in turn a high price for the Crown's pardon. In effect, the Desmonds were condemned irrevocably, and in the future their followers would be allowed to purchase mercy only by betraying them.

In practice, "Pelham's pardon," as the new measure became known, was enforced ruthlessly. Burghley certainly could not have foreseen Pelham's interpretation, for now wherever English troops penetrated, persons implicated in the rebellion were permitted to surrender only by bringing forth evidence of having slain another rebel of higher rank than themselves. Rory McSheehy, for example, was told that he could have a pardon if he gave up Sanders alive. And while Rory deliberated, Maurice McSheehy was led to understand that he would be granted a pardon if he gave up Rory alive. Almost from the start of the Great Desmond War, Gerald's forces were compromised from within; his leaders increasingly grew to distrust one another, and with defeat and discouragement, rebels sometimes brought Desmond heads by the basketful into English camps as the price of pardon. These grisly trophies were the putative heads of fellow rebels; more often they were not, for Pelham's pardon worked a monstrous injustice on the innocent people of Ireland. Yet if his harshness did incalculable damage by turning Irish against Irish and weakening traditional Gaelic ties, it accomplished a military aim. No matter where he turned, the Earl of Desmond could never feel safe, and following his victory at Youghal he withdrew unexpectedly into the fastness of Aherlow Forest rather than press his advantage against the English. Gerald's fateful decision to fall back on the West Country can be traced to his usual hesitance, but Pelham's pardon undoubtedly contributed to his anxieties. Thereafter the Earl dealt openly with few but his closest lieutenants. He ravaged Munster indiscriminately, extending mercy to neither friends nor enemies. Pelham succeeded in undermining Gerald's confidence, but he did so at a terrible cost to Ireland's stability. During the Second Desmond Rebellion, sides would shift continuously, families would turn against themselves, and towns would change allegiances from day to day. Finally, when the last vestiges of Irish self-respect and cohesiveness were gone, individuals would be left to survive as best they could, alone in a devastated countryside.

It is difficult to appreciate how much more ferocious the Second Desmond War was than the First, for the fighting was often sporadic and local in nature, and even now many of the actions are obscure. Yet in the memory of the Irish people the war has passed down linked with such national catastrophes as Cromwell's invasion and the Great Potato Famine. The English, too, found Gerald's rebellion a watershed, and horror at the destructive finality of the war fills many of their records and personal accounts. One explanation for the unusual duration and savagery of the war is not difficult to discover: formidable European forces converged on Ireland to fan the rebellion and sustain it. But Gerald himself was responsible for much of the blind fury, and never more than when most indecisive. From the start his leadership was crippled by contradictions: a man of slight religion, he inherited a holy crusade; a great landlord, he commanded landless vagrants and younger sons; a weak tactician, he was pitted against England's most resourceful commanders. After Youghal, when Desmond might have seized the initiative and driven the English out of Cork, his actions instead became hesitant and almost frivolous. He turned his bonaghts loose on the English settlements in Imokilly, but just as St. Leger was writing that all was lost, that "no messenger can depart half a quarter of a mile out of Cork without danger of his life," Desmond vanished suddenly into the West. His destination was Adare, and while Adare was worth half his army to get and hold, his stratagem for forcing the castle was small and sordid: "Under the walls, the garrison being hungry, he did order to be driven cattle that they might be lured out, but this failing, he sent a fair young harlot as a present to the constable, by whose means he hoped to get the house; but the constable, learning from whence she came, threw her with a stone about her neck into the river." Because it stood midway between Limerick and Askeaton, Adare was critically important to the security of Kerry and Desmond's estates. But where James Fitzmaurice might have stormed the castle and overpowered the starving garrison, his cousin wheedled and bribed. When his bait was cast into the moat, he not only failed to attack but retired farther south to Carrigafoyle and the safety of its Spanish garrison.

Between November and February Gerald traveled virtually the length and breadth of the South; he was tracked to Aherlow after Youghal, he appeared at Adare in December, at Carrigafoyle in January, and within a few weeks had fled that fortress island for the traditional Desmond refuge of Castlemaine. The point is that Gerald apparently did everything within his power to avoid engaging Ormond. Ten years before, James Fitzmaurice had fallen back upon the same mountainous region, but the Captain of Desmond retreated to catch his breath; Gerald had not even begun to fight. The conclusion is inescapable that having once revenged his honor on Elizabeth at Youghal, he was done and had become again the reluctant rebel of a few months before. Desmond now awaited one of two developments: either the English would seek terms or Spain would send men. Outside these two possibilities, he believed his cause lost; he was content consequently to delay and gather strength in the most inaccessible reaches of his domain.

A case can be made for Desmond's strategy. Without significant foreign aid, his army, hardly an improvement on Fitzmaurice's force of ten years earlier, probably could not have carried Limerick or Cork. Therefore, he chose to withdraw into a ring of strong defenses guarding the neck of the Dingle Peninsula: Castlemaine, Castleisland, Tralee, and Carrigafoyle. Dingle was then a convenient landfall for ships bound from Spain; Fitzmaurice had landed there, and the survivors of his expedition garrisoned the strongpoints of the area. Whatever Desmond might have lacked in tactical ability he made up for in his intimate knowledge of Kerry and a fine eye for terrain. Dingle is a bottle-shaped peninsula jutting into the Atlantic from the mainland, and stopping the neck of the bottle are the Slieve Mish or Phantom Mountains, a series of sharp-backed ridges. In the glens of Slieve Mish Perrot had been fought to a standstill ten years before. And even to reach the mountains, an English force had to capture Castlemaine to the south, Tralee to the north, and Castleisland directly to the east. Once again the Castlemaine redoubt would become the killing ground of the Irish wars.

But while Desmond secured the coast, he threw open the fertile heart of Munster. This great larder of cattle and grain, the foundation of the Fitzgeralds' power, was there for taking. Askeaton and the line of castles along the Shannon were jeopardized, and many of the peasants and towns-people, who openly supported the rebellion, were abandoned to the enemy. How vain Gerald's sacrifice proved became clear in February, when a single Spanish ship sailed into Tralee Bay. The captain of the vessel inquired of local inhabitants if any Fitzgerald was still alive. Not only was no help under way, but the King of Spain had given up the struggle.

The ship's officers were rushed to Castleisland to be introduced to the Earl, his brothers, and, of course, Sanders. The captain recalled how he there observed a lengthy ceremony performed between Gerald and Clan-car, each pledging his undying support to the other, "which oath was solemnized by Dr. Sanders, having a mass-book under their feet and a cloth spread over their heads." Evidently every effort was made to impress on the Spanish sailors the continuing vitality of the rebellion and the determi-nation of its leaders. Sanders apparently reviled them "for not performing their promises to perfect Christians," entrusted them with many letters for Philip, and saw that they sailed immediately on the next tide. Sanders had been promising Gerald great stores of arms and powder, a papal army, and ships from Spain. Now that Gerald knew the truth, he placed Sanders under close guard, a hostage for his promises. Yet within weeks reports informed Whitehall that 20,000 men were gathering in Spain for Ireland, that France was ready to help, and that the Geraldines were themselves on the threshold of victory. To read English accounts for the same period is to believe that Spanish conquistadores lurked behind every stone and tree; the panic is real and accounts for the Crown's severe countermeas-ures. It must have galled Elizabeth to see how quickly her erstwhile suitors celebrated her reversals in Ireland. She loosened her purse strings, she gave orders, and early in the new year, Pelham and Ormond were ready to march into exposed Munster.

They came together at Clonmel, early in March, and there, in Pel-ham's words, they decided to make Munster "as bare a country as ever Spaniard set his foot in." At Rathkeale, on March 10, they met again to agree how the destruction would be distributed. Ormond was to take the Shannon side; the Lord Justice the inland, and they were to rejoin near Killarney fifty miles away. The country between them was to be scoured and left dead; no one was to be spared, no living thing, and every few leagues garrisons were to be planted to consume the land and fatten on Desmond's cattle. Along the coast, meanwhile, Admiral Sir William Win-ter was to sail with a flotilla to Valencia Island, at the mouth of Dingle Bay, and he was expected to provide the heavy guns required to reduce Askea-ton, Carrigafoyle, and Castlemaine. The expedition cost a fortune. It did not wait for clement weather but set out in rain and snow to make an immediate example of rebellious subjects.

The account of the Irish Chronicle is not disputed; it records that "the Lord Justice proceeded with all his forces to Limerick; and although it was at that time cold spring weather, he delayed in that town only a week, to furnish his soldiers with arms and provisions there. Thence he proceeded southwest, by Deis-beag, and along the salmon-full Maigue, and pitched his camp in Hy-Connello. He sent forth loose marauding parties into Kilmore, into the woods of Claenglaise, and into the wilds of Delge. These, wheresoever they passed, showed mercy neither to the strong nor the weak. It was not wonderful that they should kill men fit for action, but they killed blind and feeble men, women, boys and girls, sick persons, idiots, and old people. They carried their cattle and other property to the Lord Justice's camp; but great numbers of the English were slain by the plundered parties, who followed in pursuit of the preys." Pelham himself admitted that "we consumed with fire all inhabitants and executed the people wherever we found them."

What was novel to Munster was not the raiding or pillaging—these were always present—but the massacre of people regardless of service or loyalty. Just to be Irish was a sentence of death. Pelham had little use for the scruples or compunctions of his predecessors. He clung obsessively to the view that Ireland could be saved only through the wholesale destruction of the Geraldines, and in his eyes every Irishman had become a Geraldine. Never once during his whirlwind campaign across Munster and Kerry did he relent until his dispatches grew monotonous with self-congratulation. "My manner of prosecuting," he wrote to the Queen, "is thus: I give the rebels no breath to relieve themselves, but by one of your garrisons or other they be continually hunted. I keep them from their harvest, and have taken great preys of cattle from them, by which it seemeth the poor people that lived only upon labor, and fed by their milch cows, are so distressed as they follow their goods and offer themselves with their wives and children rather to be slain by the army than to suffer the famine that now in extremity beginneth to pinch them." In a countryside stripped and consumed, death becomes the final favor. Pelham never ventured to guess how many people were put to the sword, but the estimates of Ormond and his lieutenants approached 10,000. No effort was made to distinguish "the poor people that lived only upon labor" from bona fide rebels; Butler, who had more of an eye for these distinctions, boasted that during the campaign he had put to death 46 rebel officers, 800 "notorious traitors," and somewhere between 4000 and 5000 other people. He was Irish himself, and upright, yet along the banks of the Shannon he exterminated as methodically as the Lord Justice.

In the valley of the Maine the English discovered 1500 head of cattle, 2000 sheep, and the Clan O'Callaghan. The herd was the property of the

Earl of Desmond; it had been hidden by the O'Callaghans along the upper reaches of the Blackwater, and in one afternoon both men and livestock were ridden down and slaughtered in the fields. For years to come their bones lay bleaching in the meadows beside the river. Thousands of pounds of beef and mutton were sent by Pelham to the southern ports, to feed the English fleet, to be barreled in brine and fed to English soldiers during the spring. But the herds of Munster were fat and plentiful; there was more meat than the army could consume, and it was burned in heaps to keep it from the starving population.

The Desmond clans must have fought the incursions where they could. In addition to the O'Callaghans, the O'Keefes, MacAuliffes, and O'Donughues were mentioned frequently in English communiqués. There is evidence of some slight casualties among Pelham's patrols, of small retaliations and ambushes, of atrocities committed against captive soldiers. Yet on the whole, there was little resistance in Munster. Neither Pelham nor Ormond fought one pitched battle with the Geraldines or one engagement with the Spanish. They found them in their castle strong-holds, seldom in the open. Not a sign appeared of Desmond's 600 gallow-glass, 2000 kern, cavalry, or musketeers. And the neutral lords, who might have helped their tenants, usually declined. Lord Roche, for example, offended the English by offering them scant provisions when they marched into Buttevant, but he withdrew compliantly into his castle while they scoured his estates. Among the Barrys, Fitzgibbons, and Fitzmaurices it was much the same. The conclusion is inescapable that the Irish lords consented in the destruction of their own peasants.

Mass execution was difficult during the sixteenth century. Occur-rences were most common in the confines of city districts and walled towns. Only in land overrun by the Turks was anything like a thorough destruction of countryside seen. Swords and halberds were then cast of softer metals; they dulled quickly on bone and gristle, and no army ever possessed enough powder and ball to execute neighborhoods efficiently. Therefore, Pelham relied wherever possible on hanging. Hanging worked well among compliant victims, and in Munster the common people appear to have cooperated. Hanging trees, great oaks of many branches, were seen festooned with this grisly fruit months after the Crown's forces had passed through. For all in all, Pelham and Ormond needed eight or nine months to destroy Munster, and their handiwork remained in evidence long after.

In 1581 Edward Fenton was surprised at the beauty of the landscape as he traveled from Cork to Limerick. He had an eye for scenery rare in those days, but he was astonished and then shocked to find the countryside empty, totally devoid of men. The explanation greeted him as he traveled farther and saw the remains of herds and herders blanketing the fields and meadows. Sir Nicholas White joined Ormond at Cashel toward the end of the campaign, and traveling from Kilkenny to the Rock of Cashel, he too was overwhelmed by the realization that "her Majesty had many countries forsaken of people, but well stocked with hares." In fact, coursing hares became the principal sport of Elizabeth's soldiers in Ireland, and several wrote home that since the people were gone, the animals multiplied mightily.

What happened to the peasants of Munster was hardly concealed. Some years later Raphael Holinshed, Shakespeare's historian, recorded the horrors of war in Ireland; as a consequence, this edition of his work was called in and destroyed by the authorities. Camden also knew about the extent of the devastation, but he did not record the details until after the Queen's death. And Edmund Spenser, who never forgot what he saw while marching south with Lord Grey in 1580, left his experiences unpublished. His account was still circulating in manuscript after his death and poses a central question: "Notwithstanding that Munster was a most rich and plentiful country, full of corn and cattle, so that you would have thought they would have been able to stand long, yet ere one year and a half they were brought to such wretchedness as that any stony heart would have pitied them. Out of every corner of the woods and glens they came creeping forth upon their hands, for their legs could not bear them; they looked like anatomies of death, they spake like ghosts crying out of their graves; they did eat of the dead carrion, happy were they if they could find them, yea, and one another soon after, insomuch as the very carcasses they spared not to scrape out of their graves; and if they found a plot of watercresses or shamrocks, there they flocked as to a feast for the time, yet not able long to continue there withal; that in short space there were none almost left, and a most populous and plentiful country suddenly made void of man and beast." How a land as rich and fertile as Munster could be reduced and depopulated so quickly remains puzzling. Within a remarkably short time, some of the inhabitants had turned from herding to cannibalism; they lurked in the woods like hungry wolves, and by the next winter they were gone. Famine caused more death by far than Pelham's rope, yet Munster should have had reserves of grain and livestock. Admittedly, from 1579 to 1581, several armies overran the land: Fitzmaurice's; Sir John's; Maltby's; Pelham and Ormond's; and finally, Lord Grey's. But Munster had been laid waste on many occasions before without succumbing. Why the inhabitants perished this time, why the land died in a season, can only be appreciated by looking at the precarious economy of Desmond Ireland.

Pelham was an angry and bitter man, but he had no intimate knowledge of Ireland. He was a creature of Whitehall, a typical servant of the state, raised to high office by a despotic bureaucracy. It was rather Thomas Butler who understood the country, who realized how its slender advantages could be used against it and who most likely conceived the campaign of 1580. As his old adversary, Butler naturally harbored no illusions about Gerald's revolutionary fire. The Great Rebellion was not planned and incited by him; the uprising was indigenous and only found its symbolic leadership in the Earl of Desmond. Strike against the people, their homes, their herds, Ormond suggested, and they will turn against themselves and their leader. Destroy the slight agriculture of Munster, and those few peasants who survive the ensuing famine will bring Gerald in of their own accord.

Munster was indeed a beautiful and fertile land, but by virtue of fine meadows, ample water, and an underlying formation of limestone, it had always been grazing land little farmed by the Irish. Even in Elizabeth's day the Anglo-Norman lords with their tenant farmers and villages were but a small part of Munster's economy. The vast substrata of "mere" Irish lived as they had always—beyond the Common Law and outside the reach of English-speaking cities and government. Their wealth was measured in horses and cattle, not gold, and the rhythms of herding were deeply set in their life and culture. Each summer they drove their herds up into the mountains to graze on the freshest grass, and each autumn down onto the plains. As a result, they tilled the soil seldom. They lived in temporary shelters, usually wattle huts, and were bound more by tribal compunctions than familial ones. Their ancient ways explain the lingering habit of cattle raiding in Ireland and the reflex defense of river fords and passages. Cultivation was slightest in Desmond Munster, most extensive within the English pale and Butler's Tipperary, and where herding remained the support of the people, there English customs held the least sway. This was the Gaelic world that Peter Carew penetrated and despised, that Sidney hoped to convert to agriculture, that Perrot tried to civilize, that Ormond now realized was at the heart of the Desmond Rebellion. Oats and milk, these were the foodstuffs on which Desmond's revolt could feed, and by invading Munster during March, when the herds were turned out onto the plains and the few plowmen were just breaking the earth, Butler disrupted the livelihood of the province for years to come. Munster was inured to clan warfare, but it had never experienced total and methodical devastation. It possessed no reserves of grain or meat and was far more vulnerable than it appeared to English observers.

The history of Elizabethan Ireland is largely a record of Irish lords and English governors; the "mere" Irish are usually little noticed. They have left few records of their own, yet they suffered in extreme the fluctuating policies of their own chieftains and overlords. Ormond could declare gallantly that he slew 46 rebel officers and cite each by name and title, but nothing is known about the 4000 or 5000 simple Irish he put to death. To this time there is no account of their passing. The silence is sometimes broken by the Irish Chronicle, occasionally by an English official unnerved and haunted by his experience. But where descriptions of the "mere" Irish remain, these are often tinged with contempt. Desmond's Ireland was a primitive land. It was harshly judged by Renaissance Englishmen, and only one among them, Edmund Spenser, had the temerity to suggest that "one time England was very like to Ireland as now it stands."

Barnabe Rich observed the country life of Munster at close quarters during his service with Maltby. His conclusions are inevitable: "the Irish would rather still retain themselves in their sluttishness, in their uncleanliness, in their rudeness . . . than they would take any example from the English, either of civility, humanity or any manner of decency." All over Ireland people "had no other means to draw the plow but every ox by his own tail, until when the hair of the tail was rubbed so short it could no longer be tied, the plow stood still." Rich noted the sod-and-wattle hutments of the common Irish; he could scarcely stand to enter them, for "their dwellings were rather swine-sties than houses . . . the chiefest cause of the Irishman's beastly manner of life and savage condition is his lying and living together with his beast in one house, in one room, in one bed." Poverty was, of course, to blame, but most Elizabethans also agreed that if the Irish were not so lazy and cultivated their land better, it would sustain more of them. Complaints about laziness and superstitiousness are proverbial. The Irish held it unlucky to keep their milking vessels clean, and Rich reported: "I myself have seen that vessel which they hold under the cow to be furred half an inch thick with filth. Dublin is served with the loathsome butter of this milk." Concerning feminine hygiene, he hesitated: "I will not speak of those affairs belonging to child-bearing women, that are no less uncivil than uncleanly in many of their demeanors belonging to those businesses." That is to say: "I myself have seen a woman sitting with a mustard quern between her bare thighs grinding oatmeal; I think a man would have little list to eat of that bread. But of this meal as ill in complexion to look upon as a little dirt under a man's feet they make their cakes, for other bread they have none and it is but seldom when they have this." Barnabe's comments reveal almost as much about him as the country Irish. He was not alone in his fastidiousness, however; descriptions such as Fynes Moryson's expanded ad nauseam: "The wild, and as I may say, 'mere' Irish, inhabiting many and large provinces, are barbarous and most filthy in their diet. They scum the seething pot with a handful of straw, and strain their milk taken from the cow through a like handful of straw, none of the cleanest, and so defile the pot and milk. They devour great morsels of meat unsalted, and they eat commonly swine's flesh, seldom mutton, and all these pieces of flesh . . . they seethe in a hollow tree, lapped in a raw cow's hide, and so set over the fire, and therewith swallow whole lumps of filthy butter. . . . They do not thresh their oats, but burn them from the straw, and so make cakes thereof, yet they seldom eat this bread, much less any better kind. . . . They willingly eat the herb Shamrock, being of a sharp taste, which as they run and are chased to and fro, they snatch like beasts out of the ditches."

It is an irony of fashion and taste that an age much given to idealizing pastoral life should be thoroughly repelled by it in the flesh. Moryson and Rich could take pleasure in the idylls of *The Shepheardes Calendar,* yet cooperate in eradicating the model. The people they disdained were rural folk, hardy and primitive, and centuries behind their European observers. They subsisted from season to season on the bounty of a few cows. They ate little beef, and in the North they commonly made meat from the drawn blood of living cattle, as the Scythians did of old or the herders of Uganda do today. If they had not even approached the threshold of modern civilization in 1580, they were still secure in the changeless patterns of tribal life. They took more than sustenance from their herds; they drew solace and meaning from the perennial wanderings of their cattle. Their language was rich in images of earth and sky, and their songs celebrated nature with an immediacy seldom met in Elizabethan verse. No matter how degenerate they might appear to English travelers, a noble vision of man impelled these people. Through their legends of kings and cattle raids pass the warriors of a heroic age: Cuchulain, Conchobar, Fergus, Ferdiad. Their pride was all in individual prowess and valor, in the exploits of wandering heroes; their understanding was bounded by the grasslands and forests of their island world. From the beginning these people were supremely unsuited to throw back Elizabeth's iron armies. The loss of their herds, and consequently their freedom, was an ultimate catastrophe. And in the aftermath of Pelham's invasion many did not find the will to endure.

The necessity of the invasion is explained by military expediency and the exigencies of war in an undeveloped land. But the day-to-day ferocity of the campaign is not as easily dismissed. A rage seemed to grip the English forces; they struck at the poor peasantry as if to punish them for gross and carnal amusements. The Irish were spoken of repeatedly as children or beasts; there was little sense of their individualness or claim to humanity. Time and again their destruction was justified by references to uncleanliness and incivility, and more underlies these charges than housing and sanitation. The pastoral customs of the common Irish encouraged a family life alien to decent Englishmen; on this point all agreed. The women were blamed for their nakedness, for "only chemise or loose linen shirts do they wear for wantonness and bravery," and they are "well-favored, clear-colored, fair, big and large." Marriage vows were honored mostly in the breach, and on one observation both Captain Barnabe Rich and Captain Don Francisco Cuellar are in accord: there was a frank and uncompromising sensuality between families and relations. Both captains intimate that the high rate of defection from English and Spanish camps was owing directly to the beauty and looseness of Irish women. Legitimacy was of little consequence; the children of the septs ran freely and were reared in common. Chastity was held of no account, and if this notably outraged Don Francisco, Rich was more offended by the confused lines of parentage within the clans.

Across Irish society the sacred tie of communal life was as often fosterage as parentage. Among the simple people it was not uncommon for male children to be adopted and reared outside their own homes. In the noble families the custom reinforced Norman practice, and the honor so bestowed on sons and daughters was never taken lightly. Fosterage was generally misunderstood by the Elizabethans, who themselves had pronounced views on the rearing of children, and English observers are frequently astonished by the strength of the custom. Just how deeply the sentiments ran between a foster son and mother was witnessed by Edmund Spenser during a mission to Limerick in 1577. He had just come ashore from his ship anchored in the Shannon when he was drawn along by the crowds to the execution of a local renegade. The man had been hanged and disemboweled, and the quartering of his body was about to begin. "The traitor was called Murrogh O'Brien," Spenser wrote. "And I saw an old woman who was his foster mother take up his head whilst he was quartered and suck up all the blood running thereout, saying that the earth was not worthy to drink it and therewith also steeping her face, and breast, and torn hair, crying and shrieking out most terribly." This scene was the poet's introduction to Ireland. It would be repeated on all the battlefields of the Desmond War and fill honest and devout Elizabethans with unaccountable anger and dismay. Such glimpses of native life emphasized the irreconcilable, the differences no longer to be tolerated in one realm.

The Desmonds stood for all that the Elizabethans had grown to hate in Irish life, and if Gerald believed that he could hide from their wrath in the Slieve Mish, he was deluded. Pelham grew stronger as he marched through Munster. Although he detached Maltby into Connaught to secure his rear, he replaced Maltby's 600 troopers with Winter's seaborne soldiers, augmenting his army with their naval cannon and fleet gunners. By April he had already arrived before Carrigafoyle Castle with the largest English force ever seen in the West. The stronghold was the keystone of Gerald's defenses, and Pelham and Ormond were determined to crack it.

———✦———

Carrigafoyle lies just within the mouth of the Shannon estuary, perhaps a hundred yards from shore. Even today it looks formidable, a windswept jumble of rocks rising sheer out of the sea. To Gerald's mind Carrigafoyle was an impregnable fortress, and by the usual standards of Irish campaigning he was undoubtedly right. Many of the Spanish and Italian troops who had sailed with Fitzmaurice found refuge in Carrigafoyle. They had months to perfect its defenses, and their efforts were directed by an excellent Italian engineer, Captain Julian, acting on the instructions of the Countess of Desmond. Julian filled every chink in the island's precipitous face with bricks and mortar. He shored up the castle's weathered battlements and towers, piled the great keep eighty-six feet into the air, and brought every piece of Desmond's artillery to bear on the channel below. On the landward side he threw up outworks: glacis, barricades, casements, with a walled landing encircling all and capable of accommodating a 100-ton ship. Carrigafoyle was to be Gerald's only concession to the new technology of war. He spared no expense in rushing the work to completion, and either he or Eleanor personally supervised the site during the long construction. For Carrigafoyle was much more than just another castle. It was the fabled Carraic-an-phuill of the ancient Irish writers, the sacred island of the pagan Celts, the "Rock of the Hole" to local fishermen who believed it guarded the mysterious deeps of the tidal Shannon. If anything, its symbolic value was greater than its military, and Desmond probably surmised that its loss would be sufficient to shatter the fragile alliance of the Geraldine chiefs. At Carrigafoyle neither side could afford to lose. To assault the castle, Pelham had summoned the Royal Navy and the largest standing army in Irish history; if he failed, his beaten force would be deep within hostile country, cut off from the sea. To fortify the castle, Gerald had bought time with the lives of his peasants; if Carrigafoyle fell, he would have sacrificed them in vain. He would be penned against the mountains of Kerry, without food or popular support.

Pelham went forward to reconnoiter the position as soon as he arrived. His guns were being landed, and his siege lines laid. As he approached the water's edge, his party was swept by a volley of musketry, and the Lord Justice was struck down by a ricocheting ball. He was uninjured, but shaken, and as the firing ceased, the Spanish jeered at him from the walls. No quarter would be given by either side during the siege, nor rank respected. "The villainous Spaniards and traitors," wrote Ormond, "railed like themselves at Her Majesty, especially the Spanish, who named the King of Spain to be King of Ireland, which ere it be long and God willing, they shall pay for dearly." Elizabeth was branded the usual:

bastard whore; heretic; she-devil witch. The oaths were Spanish, for there were few Irish in the castle except camp followers. This was the first time since the Great Desmond War had begun that English soldiers were pitted against Spanish, and the encounter was destined to win wide notoriety in European circles.

The answer to the Spaniards' challenge began after a few hours, when Pelham had sited his three demi-cannon, a saker, and a culverin. His culverin, great by Irish standards, was more effective as a naval gun than as a siege weapon. It could be as much as fourteen feet long, five to six inches in bore, and weigh four thousand pounds. But as a siege gun it threw a small projectile and could hardly accomplish the wonders attributed to it by the Irish Chronicle. The Irish who crept out of hiding to watch this miracle of war claimed that "there was not a solitude or wilderness, a declivity or woody vale, from the Carn of Breas in the southwest of the province of Clann-Deirgthine to Cnoc-Meadha-Siuil in Connaught, in which the sound and roar of these unknown and wonderful cannon were not heard. The western side of Carraic-an-phuill was at length broken from the top to the foundations, and the warders were crushed to death by its fall." The guns were awesome to the local inhabitants, but hardly miracle weapons. The effectiveness of the cannonade was increased by Gerald's folly. Demi-cannon were effective against stone only if permitted to fire unhindered. But since Gerald placed all his trust in the walls of Carrigafoyle, he never once attempted to lift the siege or disrupt the bombardment.

After hours of relentless cannonading, the brick and mortar of Julian's carapace began to crumble, and at this point Pelham ordered an attack. His troops, crammed into ships' boats, crossed the narrow channel and landed against the seawall. Coming across, they were raked by musketry; boulders hurled from the battlements crushed their boats; and Spanish halberdiers pushed their crowded assault ladders clear of the walls and into the sea. Watching the landing, Ormond saw the narrow channel fill up with floating wreckage, noticed the rocks of the island slippery with blood. Yet somehow survivors of the landing clung to the slippery glacis, digging into crevices for shelter, hiding under overturned boats, while all the while the bombardment continued over their heads. For two more days the English guns shot repeatedly at the walls, finally toppling battlements, holing towers, and slowly chipping an opening through the smooth base of the castle. The decimated landing party was reinforced each night and on the third day of the attack could report some progress through ruined portions of the fortress. From the seaward side Winter may have attempted a landing of his own; he most likely lost heavily, for his account of the action is more sober than Pelham's. The Lord Justice found Carrigafoyle easier than he had thought. His artillery annihilated counterfire; it pummeled the walls until clouds of stone dust rose over the island, and never once did Gerald interfere. Desmond was, in fact, forty miles away, at Castleisland, lapped in luxury and never more confident.

The final assault on Carrigafoyle was led by Captains Humfrey Mackworth and John Zouche. They and their men were halted by only one tower, the farthest from the guns, in which the dwindling garrison had taken shelter. Three or four hits, however, were sufficient to break open the tower and dislodge the defenders, of whom Zouche says that "there escaped not one, neither man, woman, nor child." Those who swam were shot in the water; others were put to the sword; and a few who surrendered, including one woman, were hanged in the English camp. Julian fell into Pelham's hands, and for some days the Lord Justice toyed with the notion of putting him to work on English fortifications. The Italian's skills were much admired. But because either he proved intractable or Pelham implacable, Julian was hanged in the English camp three days after the fall.

The example made of impregnable Carrigafoyle was not lost on the defenders of Desmond's other strongholds. Within a week Pelham's artillery was before Askeaton. The Spanish garrison defending the castle departed by the back door, running a trail of gunpowder to the magazine. The explosion left the towers of Askeaton standing but demolished most of the walls and buildings. Without a single shot the proud home of the Fitzgeralds was turned into a deserted ruin. Newcastle and Balliloghan, Rathkeale and Ballyduff were abandoned, until the road lay open to Tralee and Castlemaine. Gerald paid for his indolence by losing the confidence of his countrymen. Everywhere in Munster and Kerry the simple people cursed him for the miseries he had brought upon them. The clans balked at his command, and worst of all, MacCarthy More, Earl of Clancar, sued for the Queen's pardon. Only a few months before, Clancar had knelt by Gerald's side, his hand on Sanders' prayerbook, his head covered by a holy kerchief, to swear before the Holy Ghost to uphold Desmond until the English were driven out of Ireland. MacCarthy had cause to reflect: the Spanish had not come in strength; the Holy See had sent no aid, and Desmond was inept. He turned, therefore, and with him turned the great subject clans of the South, deserting Gerald in his need and marching on Cork to surrender. In a few short weeks Pelham had broken the Desmonds' defenses, driven a wedge into the rebel confederacy, and recaptured most of Kerry. There was fierce fighting, to be sure. The McSheehys fell on the English columns in the Slieve Mish, the O'Flahertys came down from Ballincollig Hill and attacked Ormond's rear, Piers Grace led his marauders against isolated English garrisons, and in Connaught Maltby methodically reduced the insurgent Burkes. There were marches and countermarches, as Pelham's force grew divided in the mountains, and there was great hardship in the bogs and forests. But in the end Tralee fell, Castlemaine and Castleisland fell. In the account left by Nicholas White there is a description of the sack of Castleisland: "The island, and the ruins attest it, is a huge, monstrous castle of many rooms, but very filthy and full of cowdung." Desmond and Sanders had just time to escape, and White told how the Earl's store of whiskey, the Countess' "kerchers," and certain sacerdotal vestments, which Pelham called "masking furniture," fell into the soldiers' hands. White stole the Sanctus bell from the chapel, the cruciform lectern, and the cover of a chalice. "Never," he wrote, "was the bad Earl and his legate *a latere* so bested in his own privy chamber and county palatine of Kerry." The bell and the lectern went to his patron, Burghley, "with remainder to Mrs. Blanche as toys."

So Kerry yielded souvenirs to the English; they repeated the extermination they had begun in central Munster, and while Gerald fled from mountain to mountain, they burned out the country around Killarney and sent flying patrols to scour the woods for him. Dispatches at this time were heady with the feeling of victory; the rebellion was broken, Pelham stated, and he went aboard Winter's flagship at Dingle to feast and celebrate. It was only a matter of time, Ormond believed, and he retired to Kilkenny in a triumphant procession. To confirm their optimism, the neutral lords of Munster came forward for the Crown: Lords Dunboyne and Power; Sir James Fitzmaurice of Decies; Lord Roche and his son Maurice; Lord Barry and Sir Cormac MacTeige MacCarthy joined together at Castle Connell to witness the investment of Sir William Burke by the Lord Justice. Sir William was the father of Theobald, who lost his life at Barrington Bridge, and now in a show of gratitude the Crown granted to Burke the barony of Connell. To divide and conquer remained Pelham's foremost policy, but the ceremonies at Castle Connell had an unforeseen outcome. "The poor old gentleman," wrote Nicholas White, "made many grateful speeches in his own language, and afterwards, partly from joy at his own promotion, partly from some natural remembrance of his child, and partly from the unwonted straitness of his new robes, fell suddenly in a swoon at the Lord Justice's table, so as he was like to have been made and unmade all in a day." Burke's near-fatal seizure amused the Geraldines; Pelham's promotions seemed as punishing as his enmity.

But Gerald, John, Father Sanders, and Eleanor had little else to amuse them. After their narrow escape at Castleisland they fled over the Mullaghareirk Mountains toward Kilmallock. But egress from Great Kilmore was difficult; Kerry was overrun; County Cork was crisscrossed with garrisons. The party was flushed like partridges from hiding place after hiding place. Gerald worked his way westward toward Adare. Nearby he collided in the

dark with Captain Walker's pikemen and was routed after a fierce engagement. Along the Maigue, Sir George Bourchier surprised John of Desmond and killed sixty of his followers. Captain Dowall tracked Gerald's
gallowglass into Tipperary and, losing them in the Aherlow Valley, garrisoned the Rock of Cashel with 300 men to deny any retreat to the north.
By late May Gerald had been baffled; he was safe in the deep forests but
could hardly venture out for a day without being seen. Most of Munster
was looking for him, and everywhere his own people were prepared to
hand him over to the English in order to stop the slaughter and misery of
the war.

Sir John was in the vicinity of Kilmallock when Bourchier jumped
him once more. Eleanor and Sanders accompanied him, and while the
party hid from the English cavalry in a wooded hollow, John toyed with
the idea of betraying Sanders. The Jesuit was a thorn in everyone's side;
he had promised aid which never came; he was more a wanted man than
any Geraldine. It is said that only Eleanor's pleading dissuaded John from
trading him to Bourchier for a few hours' head start. Evidently the confederacy was under great strain. Even in Gerald's company Sanders was
never entirely secure. Pelham had intelligence that Gerald distrusted the
Jesuit and would not let him out of his sight for fear that he would abandon
Ireland. On the other hand, it was assumed generally that Sanders had
misgivings about the Irish, that he had lost faith in Gerald's ability to lead.
Nothing would have been more convenient for the Crown during these
weeks than a mutual double-cross. Pelham shared this hope on several
occasions with Whitehall.

That Gerald could have saved his life by capitulating seems likely
despite all the the efforts of Ormond and the Lord Justice. The Crown
would have accepted his submission rather than spend gold hunting him.
He had lost his castles, his allies, his loyal gallowglass. Not so much as a
whisper of encouragement came from Spain. Eleanor was sick and in rags,
and the Earl could barely walk because of the pain in his hip. He was, for
all that was told of him, only another hungry vagabond in a land of
vagabonds. But although he despised Sanders, he never deserted him. It is
not difficult to imagine the company they must have kept in the filthy huts
and dank caves of Kilmore: Sanders preaching; Gerald swilling whiskey
to dull his pain; the old broken promises gone into again and again. Desmond was not a believer. Sanders' vows had never moved him; his cousin's
fanaticism had left him cold. Yet he had become a party to their self-
delusions, and if he could not share their faith, he would not betray it.
When the horses died, therefore, his servants carried him on their shoulders through the bogs. When four Geraldines weakened and applied for
pardon, Gerald found them and dragged them out of their cabins. By the

law of blood and clan he judged them and, finding them traitors, had them stripped naked and slashed to death by their kinsmen. "Every sword in this band shall partake in their deaths," he commanded, "for so shall every Geraldine be served who will not follow me." But very few followed Gerald after Carrigafoyle; his entourage shrank to under a dozen gallow-glass by June, and on several occasions he and Eleanor wandered the mountainsides alone. Had Gerald surrendered then, Ireland might yet have bound up its wounds. But he refused to die, and his detractors hold that cowardice, not patriotism, kept him alive. He endured privations, crawling out of the forests to steal cattle and horses, falling upon small encampments of English like a common renegade, and this, according to his critics, because he feared the gallows. From this viewpoint Gerald's survival was a burden his land and his people could ill afford. But when had he ever fought for land or people? In the end he resisted because he was the Desmond. It was not fear of the gallows which kept Gerald alive in the Galtee Mountains or which drove him to fend off capture. And it was not hope of Spanish aid or devotion to the Counter-Reformation which fed him. Rather the abasement, the self-negation, demanded by Elizabeth was not in him.

Certainly he tried to go back. In June Eleanor left his side and entered Kilmallock under a guarantee of safe-conduct. Before Pelham, weeping and on her knees, she begged for her husband's pardon, and the Lord Justice refused her except on one condition: Desmond had to give up Sanders and throw himself on the mercy of the Crown. These terms Desmond dismissed out of hand, and considering his slender alternatives, the decision is remarkable. He had certainly betrayed men with less provocation; it is a matter of record that he had no use for Sanders, yet at the crucial moment he declined to purchase his life with the Jesuit's. Nor is it that suffering ennobled Gerald, made him generous; his utterances are as crabbed and violent as before. Honor does not concern him, nor tenuous notions of right and wrong. Instead, what most likely saved Sanders' life was the enormity of destruction in Munster. Virtually an entire nation had perished in Sanders' cause, and that cause had become the sole, rational explanation for their sacrifice. Gerald was thrown on the mercy of his people as never before, and to them the Jesuit was the holy man in the mountains, an incarnate Christ, scourged, despised, and driven as they were. Naturally Whitehall wanted Sanders more than Desmond. But Gerald could no more surrender him than surrender his own title and the power for which it stood. Circumstance had thrust him into the midst of his people, and wandering in the Galtee Mountains after Carrigafoyle, he became one of them. During the ensuing months he drew courage from their will to resist, casting off the Desmond earldom, becoming by slow degrees the Fitzgerald chieftain. When his feudal levies fell away, he took refuge in tribal loyalty, and loyalty was to override his keen sense of self-preservation. Desmond was never to be more Irish than when most desperate. Before he vanished into the hills, and into the legends of the land, he offered a glimpse of what he had become. He replied to Pelham's proposal with an insolent letter to the Queen: "I understand that the Earl of Ormond giveth forth that I should submit myself before him as attorney and come before your Majesty, but know that I shall never stoop to a Butler, whose blood I would drink like milk but for your English churls."

Much remains to be told about the Earl of Desmond's adventures. For three years more he haunted the hillsides of Munster and occasionally dealt sharp blows to his enemies. But the chronicle of Gerald effectively ends in 1580; thereafter his legend grows paramount and the facts indistinguishable from the fiction. No man ever brought more suffering to Ireland than Gerald Fitzgerald. No leader ever showed more callous disregard for his people. He was a blundering general and a woefully inept politician. Yet he was destined to become a hero to his countrymen. Stories of his exploits persist in Munster to this day, and proud memories overlie the stark facts. For when Elizabeth declared the war won, many of Munster's better folk deserted Gerald; Irish and English alike hunted him for the bounty on his head and, not finding him, slaughtered his followers instead.

In June the Queen decided not to renew Pelham's commission. By then the Lord Justice was racing back from Limerick to meet a fresh rebellion threatening Dublin from the Midlands. England's Sisyphus had rolled his stone to the hilltop again only to watch it careen down the other side, and Pelham now paid the price for his excellent service in Kerry. The new revolt rose in the Wicklow Mountains, a nearly inaccessible region, directly south of Dublin and several days' march from the West. At first the onslaught met no check as it swept through Leix, then through Kildare, Offaly, and the Dublin Pale itself. The Crown's forces were still concentrated in the West, and there was even question whether they could reach Dublin before the city was enveloped.

Suddenly Pelham's prodigious accomplishments appeared in a different light; he had denuded two-thirds of Ireland to subdue Kerry and had walked open-eyed into the colonial governor's worst dilemma. His strength was not where he needed it. All at once Gerald Fitzgerald was forgotten. The Queen's principal Irish city was in danger, and Whitehall had begun to suspect that a more powerful lord and administrator was required than Sir William Pelham. Writing from Dublin, Lodowick Bryskett painted a terrifying picture of Ireland for his patron Walsingham. In both Connaught and the pale, he said, the rebels were held in check only by the watchfulness of Maltby and Captain Mackworth. In Munster Ormond, for all his professions of "exceeding toil and travail," had achieved little of lasting value. In Ulster Turlough Luineach O'Neill presented a friendly front while privately sowing seeds of revolt over the whole realm. Never, declared Bryskett, since the Norman Conquest, had Ireland been in so perilous a state, and unless the fire was extinguished, it was likely "to burst out into greater flames than ever before." Pelham had hammered the Irish mercilessly but, in doing so, had overextended himself. Now he would be superseded like Perrot and Drury before him and, like them, would be poorer in purse for all his triumphs. The bitterness of unexpected defeat broke his constitution, but not his hold over the army. Exhausted and ill, he trooped toward Dublin, prosecuting the rebels with unabating fury, upholding the Queen's law until he could relinquish the sword of office to his replacement. Pelham was never troubled by misgivings; he continued to believe in the efficacy of his Irish solution long after he had departed from power. Only Black Tom survived the crisis, for he was too near the hub of the great turning wheel to experience more than a few weeks of disfavor.

The revolt which toppled Pelham's government was led by James Eustace, Viscount Baltinglas, a most unlikely rebel. Eustace had only just assumed his father's title in 1580, and though he had annoyed the Crown on several occasions with his enthusiastic Catholicism, he was trusted to abide within the law. He had little in common with the roughneck Desmonds and, beyond an acquaintance with Sanders, had no significant contact with the Geraldines before 1580. At home on his Ballymore estate in County Kildare, he lived at the center of a respected group of Anglo-Irish gentry: Plunkets; Dillons; Aylmers; Brabazons; Nugents—all devoutly Catholic, all loyal subjects. Eustace had never been a man to hide his convictions; no sooner had he returned from an extended visit to Rome in 1575 than he acquainted England's highest cleric in Ireland, Adam Loftus, Archbishop of Dublin, with his spiritual state. Loftus understandably took offense and apprised Sir Henry Sidney of the young lord's lapse. Sidney, in turn, replied archly that he himself had always been "unable to countenance papistry and abolished religion." And since the land was as Catholic as ever and since the Archbishop had made so little progress against idolatry, he recommended a small fine and a night in jail. Eustace, therefore, spent all of twenty-four hours in prison and, on signing a bond, was released with a sermon and a reprimand. Such was the extent of his early indiscretions. James Eustace went about his life undeterred by the stirring of passions in Munster or the rumors of James Fitzmaurice's expedition. The government believed that Sanders had introduced Eustace to Pope Gregory in Rome, that the Jesuit still communicated with him, that the Viscount Baltinglas bore watching, but Ormond and the Earl of Kildare felt secure in his peaceful nature. The first indication that they might have been wrong occurred after Fitzmaurice's death. Baltinglas wrote to a Waterford merchant: "I mean now to take this holy enterprise in hand by the authority of the Supreme Head of the Church." His messenger was ambushed, as it happened, by Butler's men; his letter was forwarded to London, and the bearer was hung in chains by the roadside as an object lesson. Eustace was no doubt sincerely concerned for the church in Ireland; he despised Loftus and was prepared to fight for his faith. But Thomas Butler was no mean adversary, and between his threats and Kildare's cautions, Baltinglas somehow contrived to swallow his fervor for the time being.

Like many of his station, he hedged when Desmond revolted. Possibly he waited for a sign, victory or a strong Spanish show, but he was as likely offended by Gerald's cynicism and the atrocities committed in his name. It is difficult to blame Eustace for not joining the rebellion sooner. For the Geraldines were habitually in arms, and whether Sanders condoned their acts or not, the suspicion that their hosting was a private affair may have lingered. Eustace appears to have taken no part in Gerald's fight until the Desmonds were all but crushed. Why he joined sides with a cause already lost remains a principal question. Certainly there was little to inspire confidence in the defense of Carrigafoyle, Castleisland, or Askeaton. And the answer is more likely found in Pelham's actions. Long before Whitehall knew of the annihilation in Munster, Baltinglas saw the effect in refugees trampling his crops and choking his roads. They appeared everywhere, fleeing for their lives, slaughtering cattle and horses for food, stripping the land and terrorizing the villages. From the South, they brought accounts of vast death and devastation, rumors of churches and friaries leveled, clerics put to the sword. If the misery of the people did not move Eustace, the destruction of the Roman Church in Munster must have, and between the promptings of his own considerable ego and the inveiglings of Sanders, he threw off restraint. When Ormond heard rumors and rode to Ballymore to demand his intentions, Eustace delayed. Several days later he wrote his declaration, scorning Elizabeth as the head of the Established Church of England and denouncing her before God for her injustice to the people of Ireland. Butler, in the fashion of the day, had assumed a fabulous genealogy, and in an aside Baltinglas mocked his pretense to descent from Thomas Becket: "Questionless it is a great want of knowledge and more of grace to think and believe that a woman incapable of all holy orders should be the supreme governor of Christ's Church; a thing that Christ did not grant unto his own mother. If the Queen's pleasure be, as you allege, to minister justice, it were time to begin; for in this twenty years' part of her reign, we have seen more damnable doctrine maintained, more oppressing of poor subjects under pretence of justice, than ever we read or heard within this land. . . . If Thomas Becket, the Bishop of Canterbury, had never suffered death in the defence of the Church, Thomas Butler, alias Becket, had never been Earl of Ormond." This reply fairly did it; Ormond was instructed to give Eustace one more chance to retract his statements. He received a polite but firm answer: "Sir, I pray you tell her Majesty that I will remain constant in the true faith, whoever follow the Pope and do the contrary, and that neither Becket nor Canterbury shall alter me."

Thus began Baltinglas's holy crusade, undertaken in the spirit of the Christian warrior and soon to devolve into the throat-cutting skirmishes of a larger enterprise—the Earl of Desmond's struggle for survival. Alone, with the Dillons and Nugents, the Plunkets and Aylmers, Eustace could not have raised a company, but he found the muscle where he needed it, among the clans of the Wicklow Range. The O'Byrnes and the O'Tooles were to make up the backbone of his small army, and from the mountains they brought the Kavanaughs, who had lost their lands to Carew ten years before. The O'Mores joined him, and the veteran renegades of Piers Grace, and all this while Kildare, entrusted with maintaining the peace, trimmed and equivocated.

Widespread confusion preceded the first actions of the uprising, and the story is told of Adam Loftus and the Earl of Kildare surrounded in the dark by Kildare's own rebellious companies. The Archbishop of Dublin met Kildare on the legendary hill of Tara. Baltinglas was only two miles away and in charge of the Earl's own troops. "The first exploit they will do," Kildare told Loftus, "will be to kill you and me; you, for the envy they bear to your religion, and me, for that being taken away, they think there is no one to make head against them." Loftus pressed the Earl to arrest Baltinglas before it was too late, but Kildare was content to skulk around in the dark, going from one camp to the other, and he answered Loftus' request characteristically: "I should heap to myself universally the hatred and ill will of my countrymen, and pull down upon my house and posterity for ever the blame." If Kildare would not aid the Crown, he also refused to aid the rebels. Baltinglas requested an interview with him at the bridge of Ballymore Eustace. Kildare did not appear. Finally, he was sent the message: "I trust therefore the day shall never come that strangers shall say that when Christ's banner was in the field on the one side, and the banner of heresy on the other side, that the Earl of Kildare's forces were openly seen to stand under the heretical banner." There was never a reply to this letter, but neither then did Kildare interfere to stop the rampaging clans that overran the Midlands and broke in a furious wave against the Dublin Pale itself. By early August, 1580, Eustace had set the English villages within the pale aflame, and English refugees mingled with the Irish fleeing before Pelham's advance.

One has the feeling that all Ireland was in frantic motion by the summer of 1580; the forces of both sides were cut off and surrounded momentarily; the peasants were on the roads or hiding in the forests, and from east to west the Queen's army struggled to rejoin itself like a severed and writhing snake. By August the war had degenerated to chaos, and bands of troops and rebels wandered aimlessly across the countryside, foraging in the ruins, colliding in numerous and nameless clashes. A sharp action occurred ten miles from Idrone. Sir Peter Carew, the younger, with his kinsman George, found themselves cut off and ambushed by Fiach MacHugh O'Byrne and a party of vengeful Kavanaughs. Carew's party was driven into a nearby glade, and while George was able to fight his way out of the encirclement, Sir Peter was taken and murdered. Ten years after his father had robbed the Kavanaughs of their land, the "Geraldine" Kava-naughs killed his only heir. Within a few days more they had penetrated to Idrone itself and, after burning the manor house, executed those Kava-naughs who had remained docile under Carew's rule. In the South, along the road from Cork to Youghal, Carew's cousin Sir Walter Raleigh hanged an Irish peasant. He found the man scavenging willow branches near his camp and, inquiring what he wanted the branches for, was told "to hang English churls therewith." Raleigh had the man strung up on the spot, remarking that the branches would serve just as well to hang an insolent Irishman. This time of confusion also saw the death of Gerald's youngest brother, James. He had raided into Muskerry with Rory McSheehy's bands and, after driving off 1200 head of cattle, blundered headlong into the Sheriff of Cork, Sir Cormac MacTeige MacCarthy. Cormac had only re-cently come over to the Crown and, in order to make good his pledge, had departed westward from Cork with 150 English pikemen under Captains Apsley and Dering. On a dusty road not far from Mallow ford he met James and cut his raiding party to pieces. Three English pikemen were killed in the skirmish, and a score of McSheehys, but James fell into Cormac's hands wounded and was dragged in chains to Blarney Castle and then to Cork. After months, during which time he gave his earnest atten-tion to religion, he was hanged, drawn, and quartered under the supervi-sion of Sir Warham St. Leger and Raleigh. The Irish Chronicle claims that he was "cut into little pieces while alive, yet died a fervent Catholic." Even his enemies admitted that "he yielded to Godward a better end than otherwise he would have done if he had not died the death." But the relentless Hooker was not to be blinded by his demeanor. Bitter against Desmond to the end, he observed that "the pestilent hydra hath lost another of his heads."

Strictly speaking, the death of James of Desmond did not injure the Geraldine cause; that cause was already lost, and Gerald escaped his brother's fate only through good chance. On the eve of Eustace's rebellion Desmond began a long trek into the north on Baltinglas' invitation. Ostensibly they were to join forces; in reality, Gerald had no forces left to dispose. Alone with Eleanor and Sanders, he dodged from one forest cabin to another, slowly making his way toward Wicklow and the rebel camp. On one occasion he and the Countess were asleep in a woodsman's hut when English troops, directed to the place by a spy, surrounded them. Gerald heard the soldiers' footsteps approaching and, rushing out with Eleanor, flung himself into a stream beside the cabin. While the troops ransacked the hut and stabbed at the warm bed where they had been sleeping, the Earl and his Countess escaped their attention by keeping their faces just above the surface of the water. If there were numerous close scrapes, there were also moments when Gerald struck back—and savagely. His few remaining gallowglass, raiding out of the Aherlow, surprised and captured six English soldiers in the vicinity of Youghal. These were dragged before Desmond, and he himself, knocking off their morions and grabbing a halberd, bashed out the brains of five of them. The ensign in charge was spared temporarily; later he was flayed alive and left tied to a tree. With the increase of mindless butchery in Ireland, flayings and quarterings increased alarmingly. The opposing sides were no longer content only to kill; they vented their contempt for each other in mutilation and torture. Flaying was the Irish answer to the Crown's block and knife and demanded in practice a terrible indifference to mortal agony. Pulled out of his skin, the victim died slowly under the rays of the sun or under the lacerating impact of wind and rain. Torture was women's work, and in the Irish encampments it was frequently the widows and orphaned daughters who revenged their grief on the captive enemy.

Trading atrocity for atrocity, Gerald was nevertheless driven northward and eastward before Pelham's army, seeking Eustace but often traveling in circles. In the waning days of his commission Pelham scoured the land for Desmond, but the Earl eluded every trap, every ambush with uncanny instinct. One escape in particular has remained a part of the Earl's legend, and even Pelham, witness to the event, admitted it to be "passing strange." Along with twenty-five followers, Desmond and Sanders crossed Tipperary into Carlow in mid-August. They were guided to the Wicklow border by the O'Mores, and there the O'Byrnes were expected to meet them. But before they could reach the foothills of the mountains, they were overtaken on the road by Ormond, and Edmund Butler called out, warning them that they were in a net. Just short of their refuge Pelham had at last got his quarry in sight, yet luck was not on his side this day. An unknown Catholic writer speaks in awe of how a great wonder befell, how "a sudden tempest arose on a fine day—whether at Doctor Sanders' prayers, or not, God knows—and the rains were so thick that the Earl of Ormond, with the ministers of Satan, could not advance against the Catholics, nor even hold up their heads for a whole hour." The fugitives, presumably with the wind at their backs, jettisoned their baggage and vanished into the mountain defiles. Gerald's hagiography suggests that a miracle occurred on the slopes of the Wicklows, that his deliverance was an act of Divine Providence. But whether heavenly intervention or just a quirk of the Irish climate, the wind which blew Gerald to safety blew victory out of Pelham's grasp. His exhausted forces could expect to meet the fresh bands of James Eustace in Wicklow, and Pelham wisely chose to seek shelter in Waterford, instead, and await his successor. It was apparent that the issues of the Desmond War were being decided elsewhere: in London, where Walsingham reported that a Spanish fleet had departed Corunna in August bound for Dingle Bay, a coast deserted now by Pelham's precipitous march eastward; and in Rome, where the mere fact of Gerald's survival was cause for optimism. A papal nuncio in France reported to the Vatican: "Yesterday by letters from friends I had more certain confirmation of the affairs of Ireland, that the Catholic party there is equal in strength to the enemy, and very constant: and with them is joined an English lord called Valtinglas [*sic*] and one they call the great Onello [O'Neill] has finally taken up arms on the side of good."

It was now as if the terrible campaigns of Pelham and Ormond had never been. After a year of burning and killing, the religious conflict was only then being joined, and Ireland could scarcely stand more. Those English who had ridiculed Alençon the year before, and who had demanded a strenuous Protestantism, a blow to antichrist and the whore of Babylon, were having their way. Few knew the real state of Ireland or seemed to care. One who did, Edmund Spenser, was to restate the question facing Elizabeth in 1580 many years later, and he was to frame the answer in form of a Platonic dialogue. Spenser made his speaker ask a question as old as war—"why must it go on?"—and then offered a reply Elizabeth herself seemed to have found—"because it has already gone too far." Elizabeth decided to send Lord Grey to Ireland with a larger force than even Pelham had commanded. The vanguard of the new army began to arrive at Dublin in August; by September the war had begun again.

SMERWICK, 1580

Siege

The final phase of the Great Desmond War commenced with a swelling of popular support. In London preparations were apparent by early June, and throughout the summer excitement mounted, stirred by public prayers and martial displays. The puritan clergy thundered from the pulpits and drew comfort from the God of the Old Testament. Typical of the mood is *A Prayer for the Troops* published by Christopher Barker, printer to Her Majesty the Queen. "We pray for the good success of Her Majesties forces in Ireland," the prayer begins, and asserts that "Almighty God by his holy Word declareth himself to be the first ordainer and continual upholder of Princes' power and right." Jehovah could never befriend revolutionaries, Barker claimed, "Having manifest to the whole world by his terrible judgements how much he hatest all resistance against Princely power and right." He is summoned: "Be thou to our armies a Captain, Leader, and Defender," and the single foe against whom heaven is invoked is Gerald Fitzgerald—master then of woods, caves, and a small company of gallowglass. Nine months after Stubbs's public reprimand his spirit and doctrine had become official policy.

While divines urged their congregations to war with biblical exhortations, London's scribblers crowded the bookstalls of St. Paul's churchyard with rhymes for the occasion. Humphrey Gifford's jangling lyrics were especially popular. "For Soldiers" appeared in *A Posie of Gilloflowers*, and before long town wags had retitled the collection "A Posie of Gallowflowers." Gifford never volunteered himself, but he was forward in volunteering others:

> *Ye curious carpet knights, that spend the time in sport and play,*
> *Abroad and see new sights! your country's cause calls you away!*
> *Do not, to make your ladies' game, bring blemish to your worthy name!*
> *Away to field and win renown, with courage beat your enemies down.*
> *Stout hearts gain praise, when dastards sail in Slander's seas.*
> *Hap what hap shall, we sure shall die but once for all.*

And 1580 was the year in which a "new northern ditty" became the rage of the city, and by summer the balladeers had set political lyrics to this tune of "Greensleeves":

> *You traitors all that do devise*
> *To hurt our Queen in treacherous wise,*
> *And in your hearts do still surmise*
> *Which way to hurt our England;*
> *Consider what the end will be*
> *Of traitors all in their degree:*
> *Hanging is still their destiny*
> > *That trouble the peace of England.*

Now was by all accounts a time to lionize soldiers, to sharpen swords, and Spenser expressed the highest esteem for the profession when he wrote in *Mother Hubberds Tale* that "it is that which is the noblest mystery." Although a state of virtual war had existed for a decade, the attention of ordinary Elizabethans had been bent on peace. Ireland changed that. The Desmond Rebellion, the looming war on the Continent, the undeclared war at sea were beginning to draw forth the entire nation, not just the dregs of the shires or a few soldier adventurers. Gifford's prating of honorable death was the first note in a rising chorus. And while there would be much death, Ireland would supply little honor. For a few weeks, however, during the golden summer of 1580—and the weather was splendid—ordinary subjects were conscious of great stirrings. Later a few were to know how poorly the rhetoric of the moment served them.

For the enemy in Ireland was never to be the legions of Spain or the Holy See; rebels themselves were scarce, and the cold and sickness would take a higher toll. Official indifference, greed, and corruption were the only "mysteries" Spenser would experience in Ireland. One Irish hand tried to tell young men what to expect; he wrote too much, too quickly, and was not heeded. Thomas Churchyard was a rough and unlearned versifier who had spent his youth as a common trooper in Ireland. If his lines lack grace, authority is their virtue. His reply to would-be heroes is the timeless "never volunteer":

> *You ward the day and watch the winter's night,*
> *In frost, in cold, in sun and heat also;*
> *You are so bent that labor seemeth light*
> *And in the stead of joy you welcome woe.*
> *Who bides the brunt, or who bears off the blows*
> *But you alone? Yea, who doth show his face*
> *In time of need, among our foreign foes,*
> *Or boldly saith, "Let me supply your place"?*
> *Tush! that's a tale was never heard no seen,—*
> *That anyone, to serve a king or Queen,*
> *Did strive with you, or offered half so much*
> *For fame.*

Falstaff would concur, but his creation was a decade away; the Elizabethan stage had not yet matured, and outside Rich and Churchyard, war was more frequently allegorized than depicted. Nor would the philosophy of the Irish conquest be propounded seriously until Spenser wrote from Kilcolman in the wake of fresh confiscations and colonization. Lord Grey's army would arrive in Dublin as Sidney's, Perrot's, Drury's, and Pelham's had before: ill-assorted and ignorant. From the start of her Irish difficulties, the Queen's army, the main instrument of her will, proved a slender reed. Mismanagement, graft, gross negligence were endemic to all her expeditionary forces. She knew as much, condemned the abuses, and profited from them. In the final analysis, her greatest resource was a rapacious people eager for new opportunity and wealth. As for plans, few lasted; she had attempted restraint in Ireland; she had attempted conquest; she had treated and quibbled. Now the issue drifted beyond her grasp again, and as England invaded Ireland in earnest, the war raced ahead of anyone's ability to explain, justify, or direct it.

If the public mood was savored anywhere, it was at Leicester House. The recommendation of Arthur Grey, Baron de Wilton, to lead the Crown's Irish armies was first made there, and the influence of Leicester, Walsingham, and Sir Henry Sidney is apparent in his nomination. Perrot was available, but Perrot was unpredictable, as likely to negotiate with Desmond and Baltinglas as to fight. William Russell, Richard Bingham, and Roger Williams were sound professionals; each was to serve a turn in the Irish wars, but the crisis of 1580 demanded unusual qualifications. Grey combined these to his advantage. He was the unanimous favorite of the puritan faction, as much for integrity and patriotism as for religious zeal. He was the favorite of the Dudleys, who remembered that his father had supported Lady Jane Grey at their side. Finally, Grey had woven about himself a reputation for infallibility and courage. His father, William, had commanded the Queen's armies in Scotland and France. He was Elizabeth's first general, and perhaps her worst, but time and a vindicating biography by his son, Arthur, had done much to repair his reputation. Men were inclined to forget William's bungled siege of Leith in 1560 and his son's foolhardy charge at the head of the demilances. Even Cecil, who bore no love for the family, dismissed the old grudge with a kindly apothegm: "the adventures of war have many hidden fortunes, which neither the counsel nor courage of men can assure." His was an important concession, for Cecil salvaged at the negotiating table the victory the elder Grey had squandered in the field. Essential to understanding Arthur is the fact that following his father's last campaign into Scotland, an acrimonious inquiry was held into the reasons for his disastrous defeat. Arthur had been severely wounded at Leith, but he was present to hear the Duke of Norfolk say of his father before the Privy Council that "every man that can lead a band of horsemen is not for so great an enterprise as command." The incident can only have scarred him; it contributed to his efforts to refurbish his father's memory in *A Commentary of the Services and Charges of William, Lord Grey de Wilton,* and it inspired his lifelong study of military matters. Cecil observed of the elder Grey that "he was a noble, valiant, painful and careful gentleman," which was to say he was "indecisive." His son was to be the opposite: precipitous in action. Writing of him in 1580, Sir Henry Sidney said that sending instructions of a military nature to Grey was like a scholar offering to read *De Arte Militari* to Hannibal. The compliment is sincere; Lord Grey seemed everything a commander should be: tall; imposing; austere. He was adept with siege artillery, an uncompromising disciplinarian, and a fair administrator. He was inured to the horrors of war and had himself described how at the siege of Guisnes, when sent out as a hostage during a truce, he had to cross a bulwark on naked and new slain bodies, some still sprawling and groaning under his feet.

The weaknesses were not apparent from the exterior. Grey would be haunted most of his life by Leith, and in Ireland the nightmare would repeat itself, provoking measures even his friends could not accept. There was also the matter of his personal fortune. He had sold the ancestral castle at Wilton-upon-Wye to ransom his father twenty years before, and no Lord Deputy of Ireland ever avoided crushing personal expenses. Grey could ill afford the Queen's favor. His readiness was no less questionable; he was forty-four and had not seen active field service for two decades. His grasp of tactics and techniques might have been put to best use in the Netherlands, but Ireland, more than any other theater of war, required experience and flexibility. Drury had lacked it; Perrot came to it naturally; Arthur Grey would carry off his campaign by preconceived plan, seldom suiting his actions to the peculiarities of the country. In fairness, Grey had never sought or desired the generalship of Ireland. On June 29 he wrote ruefully to Sussex that he had just arrived in London and had been commanded to be ready to depart for Ireland in ten days. Elizabeth required months to reach decisions; she then demanded results within days.

In effect, Grey received two sets of orders: one from Whitehall and one from Leicester House. The plight of Protestant subjects in Ireland occupied Leicester's circle, and Grey was not gone a week before Sir Henry Sidney was writing to him: "As I know you are religious, so I wish your lordship to frequent sermons and prayer in public places; it would comfort the few Protestants you have there. . . ." Elizabeth did not share Sidney's concern; privately she warned Grey not to be overzealous in religious matters, for she was convinced that more harm had been done in Ireland through meddling in religion than through all of the Crown's actions taken together. Cecil's belief that reform of law must precede reform of faith is strongly reflected in her opinion. But while Elizabeth wanted the rebels prosecuted harshly, she also wanted peace and war at the same time. Troubling her most were charges that she was methodically exterminating her Irish subjects; her instructions to Grey commanded him, therefore, to punish outrages committed by his troops severely, officers not to be exempted, and to suppress the rebellion as swiftly as possible to spare the charges. Grey was being pushed and pulled in every direction, for while the Queen ordered him to refrain from pardoning transgressors easily, she also instructed him confidentially to handle Desmond with care. This was not the understanding at Leicester House; they wanted Grey because they expected him to bring back the heads of Gerald, John, Sanders, and Baltinglas. As usual, there is a dreamlike quality to London's instructions and expectations. Once in Ireland, Grey would have to decide for himself, and the confusing claims made upon him only reinforced the confusion within him.

Everything went wrong from the start. Grey was delayed at Beaumaris on the island of Anglesey for ten days by contrary winds. His raw Welsh companies were not ready for transport, his Berwick regiment had not even begun its march from the Tweed, and the gentlemen who had traveled 225 miles with him from London were already complaining about provisions. The families of the troops frequently sailed with them, and on Anglesey there was barely shelter for the men, to say nothing of the women and children. The ships loaded slowly, there were lading errors, and more than a month elapsed before Grey was able to cross St. George's Channel and arrive in Dublin.

At dawn on Friday, August 12, the *Handmaid* on which Grey sailed with his staff and two secretaries, Edmund Spenser and Timothy Reynolds, arrived at the peninsula of Howth in the port of Dublin. Friday was judged a day of bad omen by Elizabethans, and even amid the celebrants greeting Grey's arrival on the quays there was grumbling and doomsaying. Pelham had not yet reached Dublin with the sword of state; his army was not even on the road, and the green troops Grey brought with him provoked more mirth than respect among the Irish townspeople. Even then Dublin was a town of great charm; on the hills overlooking the bay stood substantial dwellings, and the country penetrated almost to the heart of the city. The problem in Dublin was always security. Secrets were difficult, if not impossible, to keep, and the traffic between the townsfolk and the rebels lurking in the hills was never broken for long. The town was divided and treacherous, and quarrels could break out at any moment with fatal results. Barnabe Rich tells of an adventure he experienced. The causes of the dispute involving him are obscure, the results instructive. "The very next day being Wednesday the 14 June about 6 o'clock in the evening, as I was passing along the high street of Dublin there were six [Irish] that were laid there to murder me, three hid behind a conduit with their swords ready drawn, and another three a little distance from them in the house of one Kelly, a surgeon. I, coming along the street passing towards my lodging accompanied by one Albany Clearke, who had neither sword nor dagger about him, was not aware of this ambush, till all three of them started out hewing at me with their swords. I having no leisure to draw my own sword, but only a cudgel that by chance I carried in my hand, was driven to ward and bear their blows, they driving me thus down the street before them, until my foot failing me in a broken gutter, I was overthrown. One of them, pressing hard upon me fell with me, a second striking at me when I was down. I bare his blow with my cudgel, which was cut clean asunder so that I had not scarce half of it left in my hand. The third of this company likewise when I was down struck a full blow at my head, but there came in a young man, whom being a stranger and who never knew me, nor I him, brake that blow with his sword from me. By this time I was rising on my knees, and one of them thinking to have run me through with his sword, there stood by a merchant of Chester called by the name of

Thornton, who throwing his cloak on the thrust as it was aimed, by that means it missed me.... And I upon my feet, and seeing where a door stood open, escaped safe into a house.... The Lord Chancellor being given to understand all that had passed, would yet take no part in the matter, till shortly thereafter I was forced to flee into the country for the safeguard of my life."

So delicate were the relations between Irish Dubliners, English Dubliners, and the occupying forces that Grey took no chances with his men; they were accommodated where space permitted within the strong walls of Dublin Castle, and there in the square northeast tower, known as Storehouse Tower, the Lord Deputy set up his headquarters. Presumably Spenser lived and worked there; at one point Barnabe Rich commanded the guard there, and in and out passed the entire muster of the Queen's government in Ireland. The fighting captains came: Raleigh, Mackworth, Zouche, Christopher Carleill, and Thomas Norris. The provincial Presidents were summoned—Maltby from Connaught and Perrot from Munster—and in the New Year the lords of the Irish Parliament gathered there to greet Grey on his return from the field. Ireland did not attract the galaxy of wealthy young aristocrats such as went with Leicester to the Netherlands a few years later. But among the civil servants at Dublin Castle were several prominent intellectuals, gentry by birth or merchant class, without worthwhile prospects at home. Spenser, Geoffrey Fenton, Barnabe Googe, and Lodowick Bryskett were among the poets and translators who found places in Grey's establishment. In fact, as the original documents prove, most of the Lord Deputy's dispatches to London were written or transcribed by them. Dependent on him for advancement, these men were counted discreet, and all were vouched for by either Sir Henry Sidney or his son, Sir Philip. Ireland seasoned them, stripping them of ideals they were educated to uphold, and consequently, their response to the harsh experiences of war is of more than passing interest.

Grey's ordeal commenced with unprecedented ceremony; his induction as Lord Deputy occurred in St. Patrick's Cathedral on September 7, with Lord Justice Pelham and the peers and councilors of the realm in attendance. Nicholas White, Master of the Rolls, solemnly read the Queen's letters patent, and Grey received the sword of state and took the oath of office. Official Ireland spared nothing; Grey was ritually draped in the armor of justice and righteousness, and all the splendor of the chivalric past was evoked to consecrate his mission. The cathedral was filled to overflowing with worshipers, heralds, rabble, and clergy, and amid prayers for success and hymns of thanksgiving, he was sent forth at the government's darkest hour to save Elizabeth's investment. The medieval circumstances of Grey's induction left a lasting impression on Spenser, who doted on armor, heraldry, and military display. In his "Book of Justice" he would eventually idealize the moment, mythologize it, discovering in Grey's vestiture the dawn of a new order. But from another point of view, Geoffrey Fenton's, the show at St. Patrick's was a last ceremony of innocence, an anthem for doomed youth. Days later, in the narrow defiles of the Wicklow Mountains, there would be no trumpets and precious little order.

James Eustace and Fiach MacHugh O'Byrne knew of course of Grey's arrival. What they did not know was how close the Spanish fleet was to Ireland. For the time being they had the English where they wanted them. Grey could not march south into Munster without exposing his rear to the rebels hiding in the Wicklow glens, Butler was occupied just sealing off the corridors into the mountains and screening the adjacent counties from their encroachments, and Pelham's force was held on the coast, warding against a breakout toward Cork. Eustace could survive in the mountains indefinitely, with any attempts to root him out too costly to consider. In effect, the Spanish had all Munster in which to land and a grateful Earl of Desmond eagerly awaiting their arrival.

Grey was not blind to this situation in his planning. During August and September his letters paint a gloomy picture. He is worried about the pressure of invading Scots gallowglass on Maltby in Connaught, he suspects treachery from the O'Neills along the Ulster frontier, and he is apprehensive about the strength of the Spanish force approaching the coast. To make matters worse, Admiral Winter had withdrawn from Irish waters to careen his ships, their bottoms fouled by long duty off the coast of Kerry. Grey solved his problem in a manner characteristic of all his campaigns: he refused to wait for Pelham's veterans from the South; he formed his green troops into marching formation and launched his attack headfirst into the Wicklows.

Every old hand in the Irish service warned Grey against this course of action. In the steep wooded glens his army would lose all advantages over the rebels; they would be consistently outfought in the rugged terrain, a lesson Perrot and Drury had learned to their sorrow. No hope of surprise existed. Well-trained regiments could march fifteen miles in a day; Grey's men could hardly cover ten, and by the time they had reached Enniskerry, twelve miles from Dublin Castle and in the foothills of the Wicklows, every O'Byrne and O'Toole within a fifty-mile radius knew they were coming. In fact, Eustace was not even in the mountains; he was at Ballymore in Kildare when the word reached him of Grey's approach, and he rode day and night to reach his kern in the highlands. The Crown would always attribute its total defeat at Glenmalure to the deeds of traitors, the hired Irish accompanying Grey and the information given to Fiach MacHugh by a defector, Gerard Fitzmaurice. But Fiach surely needed no spies to tell him the enemy's line of march. He could hear them coming miles away and from the heights of Lugnaquilla see their progress by the bright red and blue of their coats. There was time enough to position his kern and gallowglass along the wooded slopes of Glenmalure, their wheel locks and crossbows trained on the muddy bottom of the glen where the Oure River flowed in and out between the rocks.

Within the Queen's Irish army, Grey's brazen advance into the rebel stronghold was seen for what it was—"knight errantry"—making a name for himself. The Lord Deputy never hesitated to invite along on his attack virtually the entire corps of officers serving Her Majesty in Ireland. Sir Henry Bagenal, Sir William Stanley, Colonel George Moore, and Sir George Carew were in the attack, while Maltby, on leave from Connaught, watched the engagement from Grey's side. Pelham and Ormond were notably absent, and Perrot declined to come. On the first anniversary of Drury's lamentable defeat at Springfield, Grey was again about to prove Barnabe Rich's favorite maxim: "The inexpert captain, and the unlearned physician, do buy their experience at too dear a rate, for it is still purchased with the price of men's lives."

By no estimation was Grey an incompetent, but he was a driven man and habitually showed a distressing disregard for the lives of his men. Behind his decision to penetrate the Wicklows lay a sound strategic objective: the need to remove this canker from the vicinity of his most vulnerable cities. But his tactics were owed elsewhere. The memory of his father in Scotland must have come to mind. William Grey had dawdled just over the border, allowing opportunities to escape him, until finally he was forced by circumstance into the disastrous siege of Leith. After, he blamed the cowardice of his men for his defeat, and the charge was returned that he had delayed action until Leith out of cowardice and ineptness. His son would never make the same mistake. Trusting in the natural superiority of English pikemen over Irish rabble, he gambled everything in the Wicklows, aware perhaps that Whitehall, like Athens in the Peloponnesian War, always distrusted a general moderate in the field.

It is not difficult to follow the route of the English march. The final advance staged forward from Naas to the present hamlet of Laragh, passing between Camaderry Mountain and Tonelagee. The route can be traveled today, and it is immediately evident how grueling the climb must have been for English soldiers weighed down by body armor and heavy pikes. Francis Cosby, general of the Queen's loyal kern, was appalled by the task facing his men, and Cosby was known throughout Ireland for his unrivaled experience and extraordinary personal courage. He had dire reservations about Grey's plan to flush the rebels from their cover, so that they might be shot or ridden down on the open hillside. He said as much, was not listened to, and went into the battle believing it to mean his certain death. He was not mistaken. Jacques Wingfield, the Master of the Ordinance, was present with two nephews, Sir George Carew and his brother, another Sir Peter. He tried vainly to dissuade them from risking their lives together, arguing, "If I lose one, yet will I keep the other," and in the end George remained at his side during the battle, while Peter advanced into the glen in a full suit of armor. From Laragh, Grey's progress led him southward toward the modern village of Aghavannagh, crossing the headwaters of the Oure just to the northeast of Lugnaquilla. He entered Glenmalure from above, and his companies advanced in battle formation, wherever possible, down through the glen. Sir William Stanley, who brought up the rear, best described the order of battle and the ensuing results:

When we entered the foresaid glen, we were forced to slide sometimes three or four fathoms ere we could stay our feet. The glen was in depth at least a mile, full of slippery rocks, stones, bogs, and wood; in the bottom a river full of loose stones meandered, which we were driven to cross divers times in our descent. So long as our leaders kept the bottom, the odds were on our side. But our Colonel, being a corpulent man [Moore], before we were half through the glen, being four miles in length, led us up the hill that was a long mile in height; it was so steep that we were forced to use our hands as well to climb as our feet, and the vanward being gone up the hill, we must of necessity follow. . . . It was the hottest piece of service for the time that ever I saw in any place. I was in the rearward, and with me twenty-eight soldiers of mine, whereof were slain eight, and hurt ten. I had with me my drum, whom I caused to sound many alarms, which was well answered by them that was in the rearward, which stayed them from pulling us down by the heels. But I lost divers of my dear friends. They [the Irish] were laid all along the woods as we should pass, behind trees, rocks, crags, bogs, and in covert. Yet so long as we kept the bottom we lost never a man, till we were drawn up the hill by our leaders, where we could observe no order; we could have no sight of them, but were fain only to beat the places where we saw the smoke of their pieces; but the hazard of myself and the loss of my company was the safeguard of many others. . . . Were a man never so slightly hurt, he was lost, because no man was able to help him up the hill. Some died, being so out of breath that they were able to go no further, being not hurt at all.

What actually happened in Glenmalure is that the vanguard of the army, led by Moore, Peter Carew, and Captain Audley, was peppered descending into the glen. Stanley did not feel the brunt so long as his company remained in the rear. But when Moore recognized that to continue the advance would result in the annihilation of his command, he began to claw his way out of the glen over the slope closest to Lugnaquilla. Stanley covered the retreat, or rout, though no one ran quickly, and at times his men were shoulder to shoulder with the rebels hidden in the undergrowth. A contradiction appears in Stanley's account; he claims in his letter to Walsingham to have lost only eight men slain, but elsewhere he admits that his entire company was destroyed—a number upwards of 100 men. Casualties sustained in Irish victories are usually difficult to ascertain. Then, as in all wars since, those in command found ways to juggle the figures.

One fact emerges from the varied accounts of Glenmalure: Grey's troops were less than well led and panicked in a tight spot. Before they descended into the glen, Peter Carew and Captain Audley had a loud dispute which echoed back through the ranks. The reason for the argument is obscure, but the loud talk of these two usually quiet and modest officers had a bad effect on their men. The soldiers in the lead companies were freshly arrived from England, poorly trained, and not very steady on their feet after their arduous climb to the head of the glen. As could be expected, they were thrown into confusion by an unseen enemy, by the bloodcurdling war cries of the Irish, and by the scene below, as they struggled out of the glen, of gallowglass chopping their dead and wounded to pieces with battle-axes.

Maltby, the victor of Monasternenagh a year before, stood by Grey's side and was outraged at the folly of what he saw. He and Spenser watched the troops picked off on the open slope and roll down into the swampy river. It was a sight the poet never forgot; in later years he described how the river ran red with blood and clogged with bodies. Maltby knew what he was watching, however, and his description of the battle was accusatory. "The strangeness of the fight," he observed, "is such to the new-come ignorant men that at the first brunt they stand all amazed, or rather give their backs to the enemy. . . . Their coats stand them in no stead, neither in fashion nor in giving them any succor to their bodies. Let the coat-money be given to some person of credit, with which, and with that which is lavished on their colored hose, they may be clothed here in Ireland with jerkins and hose of frieze, and with the same money bring them every man an Irish mantle which shall serve him for his bedding and thereby shall not be otherwise known to the rebels than the old soldiers be. . . . The recruits wavered, the kern ran away to the enemy, and so the gentlemen were lost." The bright scarlet and blue doublets of Grey's men, and their white kersey hose, made them clear targets. Maltby was groping toward the idea of camouflage, and after several years of tough campaigning in Ireland, he knew of what he spoke. Grey's debut was a crushing defeat for reasons that would obtain in later colonial wars. His army suffered for the same reasons Braddock failed on the road to Pittsburgh and Abercrombie before the French Line at Ticonderoga: officers were overconfident, and men undertrained. Sir Peter Carew is a case in point. He went into battle clad in complete armor, which proved even more fatal than a red coat.

Suffocated from running up hill in his iron suit, he was forced to lie down to catch his breath. He was captured flat on his back, and Hooker, another witness to the event, recalled how "one villain, most butcherly, as soon as he was disarmed, with a sword slaughtered and killed him."

Cosby, Audley, and Moore were killed at Glenmalure; Bagenal, Wingfield, and Lieutenant Parker were wounded; and somewhere on the order of 500 soldiers perished in the glen. This figure is a high approximation, but given that whole companies were decimated or worse, it is a reasonable guess. After the defeat Grey withdrew to Dublin under a continual harassing fire. No account survives of this bitter retreat or the extent of its damages. All that mattered in the aftermath was disguising the fact that English arms had suffered the worst defeat to date in Ireland. And covering up the truth was not easy. Word spread quickly through Ireland, buoying the hopes of the rebels to be sure, but also intimating to uncommitted and war-weary Irish that a break in the Desmond War might be at hand. Maltby rushed back to the West, anticipating trouble, and in Leitrim he found it. He had been building a castle with the forced labor of the O'Rourkes and O'Donnells. The news of Glenmalure reached them before he did, and on arriving, he found them dismantling the walls. Months would pass before Maltby could set Leitrim to rights again, rebuild his castle, subdue the clans, and in the meantime, Grey would receive no help from him. Matters were hardly better in the North. Turlough O'Neill swept around the lower end of Lough Neagh, routed the forces of the loyal Sir Hugh Magennis, and let Glenmalure signal his demand for expanded rights and privileges. Turlough commanded a private force estimated at 5000 strong, and Grey risked a general attack on the Dublin Pale by ignoring him. Consequently, in late September, he rushed north to Drogheda to begin negotiations. The substance of his talks is not clear, but one interview with O'Neill was apparently sufficient to relieve his worst apprehensions. Turlough was deep in his cups; he was grown much debilitated through drink, and the abstemious Grey wrote contemptuously of him to Elizabeth: "As toys please children, so to Bacchus' knights the lick of grapes is liking, of which crew this is a royal fellow. If Her Majesty would give him a butt or two of sack, it might, for the moment, make him forget to urge inadmissible claims." As a token of his low esteem, Grey left the Earl of Kildare behind to continue negotiations and turned south to more serious challenges.

John of Desmond had besieged Maryborough, Baltinglas was burning villages outside Kilkenny, and the O'Connors had risen afresh, murdering the family and supporters of loyal Ross MacGeohegan. The garrison at

Cork did not learn of Glenmalure until two weeks after the defeat. As a result, the countryside was aflame before Pelham's men could be put on their guard. The first parties venturing out of the city were greeted with news that the rebels were moving southwest in droves on the road to Kerry. Reports reached them of a Spanish landing near Dingle, and rumors were abroad that within a fortnight more than 1000 foreign troops would be ashore. The long-awaited Spanish aid was arriving, and the first parties had moved into James Fitzmaurice's old breastworks at Smerwick, Fort Del Oro. Desmond was in Tralee, where he had begun, and Spanish ships lay anchored in Dingle Bay, where Winter's squadron was supposed to be harboring. The climax of the rebellion appeared to be at hand. Desmond and Baltinglas traveled wherever they pleased and were greeted with an enthusiasm not seen since the days of the Captain of Desmond. By then James Fitzmaurice had been dead more than a year. The counties on which he had drawn for support had been depopulated by the war. And now as Sanders' pledge of foreign aid was about to be redeemed, no one was certain whether the remaining rebels could exploit the opportunity before the Crown gathered together its scattered forces.

Grey had been briefed by Walsingham concerning Spanish ships departing Corunna, and there is no reason to believe that the landing at Smerwick caught him by surprise. He was under express orders to repel any foreign invasion at once, and thus, from the moment the first papal soldier stepped ashore at Dingle Bay, the full weight of the English presence in Ireland was directed at Smerwick. In the confusion Desmond and Baltinglas were forgotten. The unconquered Wicklows were left behind, and the pale was stripped of available defenses. The entire English army was ordered to converge on the West, the English squadron put to sea again unfit, and Ormond was instructed to bring in 1000 head of Munster beef to feed the advancing regiments. It is said that he laughed at the request. Munster had been reduced so thoroughly by war that in the entire province Butler found no more than 300 head of cattle, and as the cold autumn rains began, he retired to his home at Kilkenny without authorized leave. Ormond had led a flying column to Smerwick to inspect the Spaniards. He had skirmished with the invaders just out of range of their artillery in Fort Del Oro, and he had found that Sanders' "Spaniards" were in fact Basques and Italians, ill trained and poorly equipped for Irish warfare. Not only did he attach no particular importance to their fortifications, but in a letter to a Spanish friend, the Count de Lerma, he offered a prediction: "As for the foreigners, this much I will assure you, that they already curse the Pope and as many as sent them, and they shall shortly have still better cause to do so." Butler was appalled by now at the duration of the war. He no longer had any wish to join Grey in its prolongation or in the anticipated assault on Fort Del Oro. From this time forth he left

Kilkenny Castle only reluctantly, thereby earning Grey's lasting enmity.

Fort Del Oro was built on a barren, windswept point of land jutting into the Atlantic. It stood near the tip of Europe's most westerly peninsula, and even now, with the ocean smashing at the rocks below and the mists swirling in from the North Atlantic, Del Oro can seem the very edge of the world. Fitzmaurice first raised the fort and called it "Del Oro," and the name held a special significance for him. At the base of the cliffs lay a fragment of Elizabeth's vainglory, the carcass of an English ship. She had been one of Martin Frobisher's bullion fleet, returning from Newfoundland in 1577, when she was driven ashore at Smerwick in a gale. And out of her broken sides had poured the seeming riches of the New World, Frobisher's ore, the black rocks in which Elizabeth saw her own Peru and in which the high lords of England invested their hopes and capital. Frobisher's discovery of gold in the icy wastes of North America had caused an outbreak of prospecting fever in London the year before, and thousands of pounds were subscribed for his second voyage before assayers agreed that his samples were only pyrite, fool's gold, with a particle of silver. The truth came too late; by then Frobisher was returning from Newfoundland a second time with tons of his black rock, and a portion of this "treasure" never passed Ireland. There it washed ashore in shoals to become a symbol for Fitzmaurice of Elizabeth's greed. In the name "Del Oro" he hoped to memorialize her embarrassment lastingly.

But if the place is one of Ireland's most famous battlegrounds, it is also one of its saddest. The trenches and earthworks of the decayed fort can still be traced, and no feat of imagination is needed to see the difficulties the papal troops faced. The rocky promontory appears formidable indeed until it is recalled that the nearest supply of fresh water is a half mile away. Along with the bitter cold and chilling fogs, thirst—the most unlikely enemy in Ireland—was to assail the besieged and weaken their determination. Fitzmaurice had raised the fort as a depot, a base of operations; he had never intended it to withstand siege. And after the disaster at Carrigafoyle, there is difficulty believing anyone did. Yet no sooner had the papal forces come ashore then they planted themselves in Del Oro. They strengthened the breastworks, mounted fourteen sakers, or medium-size culverins, in the earthwork embrasures, and raised a platform and redoubt of timbers and stone. The enclosure was 350 feet in length and about 100 feet wide, and since more than 700 men were crowded into Del Oro, no more than 50 square feet remained for each. Overcrowded and exposed to the elements, its earth and stone shoveled together quickly by forced labor, Del Oro was hardly a propitious spot to begin the liberation of Ireland. By the end of October, 1580, the chill weather had begun to tell on the Italians. Even before Grey arrived, they had begun to curse Ireland and die.

The Irish called them "brave Romans" and tried where possible to ease their condition. But all the problems of an international command plagued the effort; few of the soldiers could speak English or Gaelic, and for their part the local rebels refused to be cooped up inside the palisades. Oliver Plunket was an exception; he and William Walsh, Sanders' English secretary, entered the fort and remained as interpreters. A few Irish-women familiar with the rebels preferred to take their chances in the fort rather than the woods, and they were accompanied by an Irish friar named Moore. No notable rebels joined the garrison besides these. Conferences were held during October between Gerald, James Eustace, and Sebastiano di San Joseppi, the Bolognese in command of the expedition, and their resolve was to separate the commands entirely. Gerald suggested a tactic reminiscent of the Carrigafoyle campaign. He would wait in the surrounding hills with all of 4000 men, and as Del Oro drew the besiegers' attention, he would fall on their rear and drive them into the sea. An elaborate system of signals was arranged. San Joseppi was to raise a black and a white flag when he felt his garrison in need, and the signal was to indicate the start of Desmond's attack. Anyone but a newcomer to Ireland might have thought to ask where Desmond expected to find 4000 able men or how he proposed to offset Grey's undisputed control of the sea. But San Joseppi trusted in his allies; outside of a few skirmishes in the neighborhood, including one with Ormond, he was content to sit in Del Oro and await Grey.

In the English accounts there is no consensus on the quality of the troops landed at Smerwick. Ormond found the garrison inexperienced but combative. According to him, he might have assaulted the fort's landward glacis had it not been for the volume and accuracy of the artillery fire. Richard Bingham, on the contrary, found the Italians "as poor rascals as I have ever met with." He arrived before Grey or Winter, and commanding the *Swiftsure*, Her Majesty's slowest man-of-war, drove the few remaining Spanish vessels inshore without the slightest show of resistance. Concerning the garrison at Del Oro, Grey was to have the last word; he later called them "as gallant and as goodly personages as ever I have seen," but then he had a motive for making them seem better. In likelihood the arrival of San Joseppi's men was a result as much of Drake's piracy and Philip's desire for revenge as of the pleadings of Irish expatriots in Rome and Madrid. The 700 troops who came ashore were not invincible conquistadores; they had been recruited especially for the expedition in Genoa, Florence, Naples, and Bilbao. There is no evidence that they were jailbirds, like Stukeley's companies, and still less that they were professional soldiers. They came ashore with a barrel of gold reals, which fell into Gerald's hands, some artillery, and enough muskets, powder, and ball to supply an army. But they were at least a year too late. At Monaster,

Carrigafoyle, or any of a dozen fields they might have tipped the scale, but the popular rebellion in Munster was dead. There was no unified effort to direct them, few gallowglass to teach them the hard-learned lessons of the war, no experienced officers to command them. For lack of a better deployment, they sat huddled in Del Oro, homesick and despondent, scarcely aware of the cause which had brought them to Ireland. San Joseppi's men grew to believe that they were only the stepchildren of Spain and the Catholic Mediterranean, flung ashore in the North to be forgotten. And their suspicion was well founded.

Grey drove his army hard to reach them. By late October he had left Dublin with an army of nearly 1000 men, the survivors of Glenmalure and fresh reinforcements. From Cork in the south the remnants of Pelham's army advanced toward Smerwick more than 1000 strong, and at Askeaton another 1000 English troops previously assigned to Butler awaited Grey's arrival. Winter's squadron transported 1000 more and all the siege artillery Grey would require to reduce Del Oro. As Irish armies went, Grey's was the largest, and the cost of maintaining it was frightful. No less frightful was service under Grey. He drove his regiments relentlessly, through some of the worst rains in memory, and along the way executed several sergeants and a score of private soldiers for unauthorized foraging. His route is known from Spenser, who traveled with him and who consequently fared better than most. Even at that, the long hours in the saddle, subsistence on spoiled food, and ceaseless vigil came as a revelation to him. Ireland had few remaining bridges, and as the army made its way south, it forded the fast-flowing Liffey, Barrow, and Nore in freezing rain and darkness. Where roads had been untraveled during the war, they had become overgrown with brush and hedge, and where armies had passed months earlier, the rutted lanes were a sea of mud. Along the way stood burned peel towers and devastated villages. Corpses moldered in the fields and ditches, and at the edge of the forests were caught glimpses of frightened and starving peasants. Spenser corroborates the account of the Irish Chronicle: "At this time not the lowing of a cow, or the voice of a ploughman, could be heard from Dunqueen in Kerry to Cashel in Munster." The full horror of the Irish war came home to him during this march, and with utter astonishment he entered the civilized world of Butler's Kilkenny. Years later he paid compliments to Ormond and his establishment. By then, however, all resentment against Black Tom for not joining the expedition to Del Oro had been forgotten. The Countess of Ormond Spenser called the nymph of the River Suir. Her Ladies-in-Waiting were remembered as the "delight of learned wits," and inside Kilkenny's "brave mansion" grace and courtesy reigned eternal. Outside "the savage soil is left almost waste through long wars, and a brutish barbarism has spread over a fair land," but at Kilkenny there was laughter and art. Spenser would never forget the countryside beyond Kilkenny; in his masterpiece *The Faerie Queene*, he repeatedly contrasts empty, brooding landscapes, where travelers are suddenly beset, with the cloistered civility of the isolated and barricaded home. Plot and character are frequently of Italian origin, but the caves and forests are inimitably Irish, and the fragility of civilization a lasting theme.

Grey did not pause long at Kilkenny. There is no record of his conversation with Butler or his dispute. It is known that by the last week in October he had crossed the Golden Vale of Tipperary and had begun to descend the Dead River toward Limerick. During this time he was deep in Desmond Munster, and his long, straggling column was exposed to attack. But while Gerald and James Eustace probably appreciated the need to strike the English army before its pieces united, neither commanded sufficient men in Munster to meet Grey in the open field or ambush the column moving westward from Cork. Once more the principal Irish lords turned to their favorite ploy. Those who remained strong waited to see whether Pope or Queen carried the day at Del Oro before they committed their kern to one side or the other. Consequently, Desmond never had the men to harass Grey or the companies to support San Joseppi. The Lord Deputy crossed Ireland with hardly a shot fired and, in a field just beyond the walls of Limerick, united his forces.

On Saturday, November 5, Admiral Winter arrived off Smerwick and began his blockade of the peninsula. On the following day Grey's reconnaissance pushed to within gunshot of the walls and exchanged insults with the garrison. Captain John Zouche, veteran of Carrigafoyle, led the advance party and was wounded slightly in the leg. He reported how the enemy's gunnery was exceptionally bad; for all of 600 rounds fired, they were able only to break the skin of Zouche's right calf. If the initial resistance was inept, however, it was also spirited. As Grey came up, he was saluted with cannon shot; the Pope's banner was hung out over the walls, and a skirmishing party of thirty sallied out to drive him back.

That Sunday the Lord Deputy studied the ground. He strolled upright to within a few hundred yards of the embrasures with Bingham and Winter at his side, the picture of perfect composure under fire. Unfortunately a shot meant for him struck Jacques Wingfield, Master of the Ordinance, and thereafter Admiral Winter himself would have to lay the English artillery. Grey pitched his tent near the fort and resolved to dig trenches forward during the night. His letters to Walsingham provide many details of the siege of Smerwick; they were most likely written by his secretary, Spenser, and reveal an almost clinical efficiency on Grey's part. The Lord Deputy was an ardent student of siege warfare, and his inspection of Del Oro evidently convinced him that the defenders' position was hopeless. Thereafter he conducted his maneuvers with a rapidity and grasp rarely seen in the Irish service. San Joseppi had presented him with an unhoped-for opportunity, precisely the sort of tactical problem he excelled at solving. Sunday night, under cover of darkness, Winter's sailors dug a trench to within 240 yards of the earthworks. They manhandled two of the *Swiftsure*'s largest guns up the slope of the promontory and brought them to bear on Del Oro's seaward embrasures. Meanwhile, as the main body of the English came up from Dingle, sappers began digging zigzag trenches to within 120 yards of the landward walls. Grey was ready for sallies against the sappers, and both Captain Zouche and Captain Walter Raleigh warded the trenches against light attacks. By Monday morning Grey had mounted his four heaviest cannon within range of Del Oro, had sighted them against the enemy's smaller artillery, and was prepared to reduce the fortifications preparatory to a general assault. It was Grey's belief that 1500 rebels lurked in the hills around Smerwick, and though this was most likely an overestimation, he detached infantry to form a tight defensive cordon around his operations. As events would prove, much of this infantry would never see action, for unlike the Irish, Grey observed maximum economy of force, never permitting his numerical superiority to confuse the direction of his attack.

The bombardment of Del Oro commenced at dawn on November 7 and was accompanied from both sides by great, crashing exchanges of musketry. Within an hour the smoke of battle hung low over the trenches, but by then many of San Joseppi's guns were already out of action. His artillery was poorly sited, and only two of the sakers were able to bring the English under fire. By two o'clock in the afternoon these had been silenced by Grey's demi-cannon. By three o'clock segments of the earthworks had collapsed into the garrison's trenches, and thereafter Del Oro's only answer to Grey's relentless cannonade was from harquebuses, heavy muskets fired from rests. One of these pieces probably inflicted the only notable casualty among the English attackers during the siege. A young soldier who had joined Grey only several days before was struck in the head by a ball somewhere in the forward trenches and killed instantly. He was John Cheke, William Cecil's nephew and son of the famous humanist. His late father had been renowned as "England's Exchequer of Eloquence," the first Regius professor of Greek at Cambridge, tutor to Elizabeth herself. But "good young John," as Grey called the son, "had inherited a most scholarlylike poverty." Evidently the boy had grown tired of living as a dependent on his uncle's favor and, drawn to the one place his guardian did not wish him to go, borrowed a horse from Cecil's stables and departed for Ireland. He reached Smerwick after a breakneck ride from

Cork and was not in the lines more than a few minutes before he was killed. In the confusion of battle no one noticed; he raised his head incautiously, it was smashed by a ball, and without uttering a word, he died. Grey, as if sensing the magnitude of this singular casualty, praised Cheke's death-bed oratory at great length in a letter to the Queen. "Young John," he wrote, "made so divine a confession of his faith, as all divines in either of your Majesty's realms could not have passed, if matched, it; so wrought in him God's spirit, plainly declaring him a child of His elected." To a Calvinist such as Grey, deathbed professions were of special moment. At home Burghley was made desolate by the loss of his sister's son; he blamed himself for acceding to a war in Ireland, for not preventing his nephew from joining Grey. The Lord Deputy's distortion of the truth was there-fore meant to console the uncle while disarming the politician. Young Cheke's time had come; God summoned him to his elect, and a Spanish harquebus was the means of conveyance. The lie was both politic and humane; it was only the first of many more lies to grow up around the siege of Smerwick.

Tradition holds that Grey observed the volley which killed Cheke coming from under a wooden platform and, pointing out the spot to Winter, aided him in laying a gun on this target. Several shots were fired before the musketeers were driven out, and on the fourth salvo, which happened also to collapse the platform in an avalanche of earth and timber, San Joseppi hoisted the black and white banners intended to alert Des-mond. The signal caught the Irish in the hills by surprise. Battle had just been joined when Del Oro appeared to be calling for a supportive attack. And inside there was good reason for alarm. Panic broke out as the wooden platform collapsed. The constant cannonade was demolishing the earthen embrasures, striking down gunners, driving infantry under cover of the crumbling breastworks. By late Monday the garrison's water was gone, the fort was invested on all sides, and trenches had been pushed to within pistol range of the walls. By the practice of war an assault was imminent, and because San Joseppi had no confidence he could withstand a storming, he signaled the Geraldines prematurely. As a consequence, Madrid would eventually accuse him and his garrison of cowardice. Cowards or not, they were penned like cattle inside their enclosure, and as the walls began to give, Grey slaughtered them at his leisure. Conceivably they should have held out longer. Yet the suspicion was among them that their mission was hopeless, and this suspicion grew after their distress signal received no answer from the surrounding hills.

Desmond's critics charge that he deserted San Joseppi much as he deserted Captain Julian at Carrigafoyle. The view is supported by certain English dispatches mentioning a large Irish force in the neighborhood of

Smerwick. Gerald is believed to have had the strength to aid Del Oro and did not. No one is sure of his whereabouts on November 7, but tradition has it that he and James Eustace, John of Desmond, and Sanders were in the vicinity. The problem with the English dispatches, however, is that they were issued to justify Grey's later actions and tend to exaggerate the danger to the English force. It is notable that during both the approach to Smerwick and the withdrawal no large party of Irish was actually seen or engaged. Irish accounts state that Gerald found no means to help the Spanish, and in all likelihood they are correct. At Carrigafoyle he had commanded an army; in the hills around Smerwick, a band. Had he there-fore tried to lift the siege, his small force would have been destroyed. Gerald had waited a whole year for the Spanish to arrive only to watch them break in an afternoon. Del Oro never allowed him time to raise men in Grey's rear or to keep his promise to San Joseppi. In fact, disaster overtook the garrison so rapidly that the Irish were unable to participate, and in the subsequent controversy over the siege Desmond's allies never once accused him of desertion. If Gerald was culpable at all, it was in allowing the foreigners to fortify Del Oro in the first place. He had had ample experience of English siege guns and the inadequacies of Irish defenses. But the man who lost Askeaton, Castlemaine, Carrigafoyle, and Castleisland was not one to admit and learn from past mistakes. He had a habit of responding to dangers, never foreseeing them, and in the end San Joseppi was on his own, at the mercy of Grey and his captains.

The first truce party came into the English lines shortly after dark. As they made their way toward the trenches, they were silhouetted by flames, Grey's gunners having succeeded in setting the fort afire with heated shot. This first party was apparently intended to test the temper of the English, for they brought with them no terms but a valuable prisoner to be exchanged. Sir James of Decies had been captured by the Geraldines, and Desmond had given him to San Joseppi to be ransomed for 1000 pounds if the opportunity arose. Now the commander gave him back in exchange for a glimpse at his enemy's preparations. So formidable did these appear that a path was virtually beaten to the English trenches during the night by other delegations. The struggle for Del Oro was over; the struggle to surrender had begun.

The next party to enter the lines was led by a Florentine campmaster, Alexander Bartoni, who tried to soften Grey's heart by claiming that the Italians had been lured to Ireland by false representations. He insisted that they had no quarrel with Queen Elizabeth and were ready to depart as they had come. Bartoni laid blame for the expedition on the Pontiff and a mistaken desire to defend the *Cattolica fede* in Ireland. By implication the Florentine disassociated himself from his Irish allies, who now appeared in a fresh light as mere rebels against their Queen and questionable Christians. The Lord Deputy's reply to this speech is memorable. The enemy was clearly at his mercy, and Grey took the occasion to lecture: "His Holiness was a detestable shaveling, the right Antichrist and general ambitious tyrant over all right principalities, and patron of the *diabolica fede.*" All conditions were refused.

By late Monday night San Joseppi began to realize that Grey offered no terms of surrender. The two parties which entered the English camp had been sent back without guarantees or conditions. A new tack was called for, and since Bartoni had failed with a political summary of the situation, San Joseppi sent a Spanish captain to argue the military situation. This man was brought before Grey sometime after midnight and, speaking through an interpreter, flatly stated the garrison's desire to surrender. Del Oro was an untenable position; the expedition had fought by the rules of war and was entitled to honorable terms. According to witnesses, Grey listened and understood the significance of the captain's proposal, but before he would answer he provoked a confession from the man that no one higher than Recalde, the governor of Bilboa, had authorized the expedition, that the captain had no knowledge of patents from King Philip or the Pope. The admittance was fatal. Grey was not constrained by honor to recognize Recalde or the Pope; only service under the royal banner of Spain could entitle Del Oro's garrison to honorable conditions, and insofar as Philip had not authorized the landing, it was construed as piratical lawlessness. Grey adhered strictly to this line, and because the Spanish captain was probably proscribed from implicating Philip, he was returned into Del Oro with no conditions and no agreement to truce beyond morning.

The negotiations surrounding the surrender of Fort Del Oro have always raised questions. On this subject there are no impartial historians, only fierce partisans of one side or the other. By their very nature the events at Smerwick were to grow in significance as Elizabeth's reign continued and to become charged with more meaning than a minor siege and its aftermath would suggest. Despite Grey's adamance, both sides doubtless knew why they were there and who had sent them. Not an English officer who left comment on the battle failed to recognize that the fight was with Imperial Spain, Rome, and the Counter-Reformation. Desmond and the Irish were secondary, for the issues being decided at Del Oro were the major issues of English foreign policy. San Joseppi's men were, of course, no more piratical adventurers than Grey's and in all probability infinitely more honorable than Drake's sailors who had burned Cádiz and pillaged New Spain. But for militant Protestants such as the Lord Deputy, who had long waited for a chance to strike out at Catholic hegemony, the opportunity found was not to be squandered. The victory at Smerwick was to mean something. Here was none of the indecisiveness of the siege of Leith, none of the ritual war of Guisnes. The army would remember the fate of Protestant women and children in Paris on St. Bartholomew's Day. Justice was to be meted out in strict measure, and forgotten in the process was the disheveled, pathetic remnant of a not very effective adversary. There is the suspicion that in this moment of triumph the defeated garrison ceased to be human and became for Grey a symbol of the irremediable error his life had been a preparation to meet. In any event he did not lose his head at Smerwick; he acted with cool deliberation, and the question has never been why he settled Del Oro as he did, but how.

In the early hours of Tuesday, November 8, San Joseppi himself came to Grey. By then it was clear to the Italian that no quarter would be promised and that at dawn the bombardment would commence again. With San Joseppi came Oliver Plunket, his interpreter, and to English witnesses Plunket seemed unusually reluctant to be a party to negotiations. The Irish in the fort were under no illusions about their fate if the garrison surrendered, and so long as English lives could be taken, they had little interest in saving Italian. Plunket was disposed to fight to the last; he had made a shrewd appraisal of Grey, and as a consequence, it is wondered whether he did his offices in good faith. The conversations between the two commanders are recorded nowhere. Spenser claims to have "been as near them as any," and he bears out Bingham, Hooker, indeed Grey himself in stating that no guarantees were offered San Joseppi. The garrison was to surrender only at discretion, which in the parlance of war left the question of quarter or mercy to the victor's judgment. Perhaps Grey implied mercy; perhaps Plunket misinterpreted, or conceivably Signor Sebastian misunderstood. The meeting was a heated exchange, embarrassing, a marketplace haggle. At one point San Joseppi is said to have begged Grey on his knees to spare his troops; at another, to have hurled the worst imprecations at his enemy. Who can say what either heard or thought he heard in the babble of English and Italian? San Joseppi was accompanied by his principal officers—Stephen San Josepho; Hercules Pisano; the Duke of Biscay—and together during the parley they outraced Plunket's ability to translate. On the English side there was confusion, too, and from among the contradictory reports of English witnesses, the historian Camden chose to believe that Grey, weeping to be sure, left the cruel decision up to his officers. The facts belie Camden. On only one point is there unanimity: Grey, with or without tears, personally refused to grant safe-conduct to the Italians. According to his own testimony, he stuck to the view that the expedition was uncommissioned and, therefore, unentitled. According to the Irish, Grey falsely promised quarter in order to lure the garrison out and then reneged. According to the Italians, Grey seemed to suggest the possibility of mercy but evidently changed his mind in the morning. Beyond these assertions it is difficult to go. Posterity has tended to credit Grey's uprightness, if little else, and to discount the Irish version. Plunket, the only Irish witness, did not outlive the morrow, while the Italians, who had acted none too valorously, later made excuses for losing their command. Probably no one will ever be certain what passed between San Joseppi and the Lord Deputy. Blame enough attaches to all the participants in the Smerwick affair to allow for misunderstanding on the evening of November 7. What happened in the morning, however, was not open to interpretation. It was an unequivocal act of cold-blooded murder.

At dawn the English renewed their bombardment of Del Oro and were answered by a desultory fire. By approximately seven o'clock even this slight fire had ceased, and as the English captains readied their men for an assault on the breastworks, a white flag of surrender was hoisted above the fort. There was a cheering in the English lines, and the cannonade stopped. On either side of the gates infantry formed file to receive prisoners. San Joseppi was capitulating without assurances. And in the silence that had fallen over the battlefield the English could hear men clamoring to unbar the gates and get out. The Italians left Del Oro, dragging their banners in front of them and crying *misericordia*. In their exit they mingled with the victors. They were still armed but begging water, for most had had nothing to drink in the last forty-eight hours. The surrender was virtually accomplished before Grey took charge of the situation and ordered Captain Wingfield to disarm the men and herd them back into the fort. The prisoners were rounded up from within the English trenches, their pikes, swords, and muskets were collected in piles beside the gates, and they were led back into the enclosure. Wingfield ordered them to strip off their helmets and corselets, and the body armor was carried outside to be shared among the English infantry.

In the meanwhile, soldiers had searched the fort and dragged out Plunket, William Walsh, Father Lawrence Moore, and a crowd of Irishwomen. The Irish had no appetite for surrender. San Joseppi and his principal officers were safe, officers without commission but gentlemen. The Irish were rebels; as such they never doubted the fate awaiting them. And Grey did not hold them long in suspense. While the Italians were pushed back into the fort, he ordered gallows erected outside the walls. There followed that ghastly scene so often repeated in Ireland during the wars. Women pleaded their bellies, and Grey's troops strung them up, nevertheless, with requisite speed and efficiency. The plea, truthful or not, had grown customary, and in Ireland no one took time to examine for evidence. The women hanged at Del Oro fared better than the men. A special end was reserved for Plunket, Walsh, and Moore. According to Nicholas Sanders, they were led in chains to the blacksmith of Smerwick Village. On the smith's forge their arms and legs were broken in three places each. They were allowed to suffer without food and water in a shed for two days before they were carted back up the hill to the English encampment and hanged, drawn, and quartered. They had trusted in the puissance of Spain, and their long dying was intended as an example to the local Irish. After, when the English were gone, the people of Smerwick buried them, raised a cross to their memory, and resigned themselves to undying hatred.

Concerning the Italian captives, the record is also clear. The Lord Deputy summoned his officers of the day, or warders, and instructed them to enter the fort with a company of men. They were to dispatch the prisoners as quickly as possible, each soldier to account for approximately three foreigners by sword or pike. The officers of the day turned out to be Captain Mackworth, one of Pelham's trusted veterans, and Captain Walter Raleigh, conscientious and forward. Together they would lead nearly 200 troops into the fort and begin the slaughter, and to them would fall the duty of inspecting the bodies and dispatching the wounded. Richard Bingham noted in his account of Smerwick that Winter's sailors, afraid that plunder would pass entirely to the army, climbed over the walls unordered and joined in the killing. And later, when recrimination started, some would blame the seamen for the massacre since they were notoriously ill disciplined and cruel. The explanation satisfied many, but Grey himself never shirked responsibility for the decision; in his November 12 letter to Walsingham and the Queen he appended the following to his report of the surrender: "And then put I in certain bands, who straight fell to execution. There were 600 slain." No mention is made of plunder-crazed sailors. The executions were carried out by his commissioned officers and their soldiers, and Grey had reason to know the final body count: he himself counted the corpses.

What happened inside Del Oro that morning is described as "hewing and paunching," for a cut to the neck or a stab to the belly was the prescribed practice of mass execution. The prisoners had already been stripped of their armor; they were defenseless against pike thrusts, and those who dodged the long poles were slashed by the swordsmen. As could be expected, the killing was heavy work; the prisoners clung to one another in a corner of the enclosure and had to be dragged free. An English soldier complained: "Never since I was a man of war, was I so weary with killing of men, for I protest to God, for as fast as I could I did hew them and paunch them, because they did run as we did break them, and so in less space than an hour this whole and good field was done." The pleas and cries of the victims fell on deaf ears inside and outside Del Oro. While Mackworth and Raleigh carried out their assignment, others tallied the spoils found in the fort—food and provender for three months; powder and arms for 6000 men—and then stripped the dead of all valuables, including their clothing. The bodies were carried to the sea face, flung over the wall, and allowed to roll down onto the narrow beach below. It was easiest to dig mass graves in the soft sand at the base of the cliff, and there, as he walked among the naked and mutilated bodies, Grey made his comment on the worthiness of San Joseppi's troops: "Here lay as gallant and as goodly personages as ever I have seen." The dead of Del Oro had been rabble and scum while alive; slaughtered, they became gallant foe. Perhaps this change of mind is a part of all war, the inevitable aftermath of hatred; yet it is not the victor suddenly pitying the vanquished which disturbs in this scene. Grey speaks as though his enemy were slain in defeat, where, in fact, his enemy was murdered in surrender.

The grim particulars of the Smerwick massacre are described in order that the close and personal nature of such things be understood. Atrocities are the property of no one age, but in the period of the Irish wars they required an intimacy with the victims which later progress has made unnecessary. Raleigh's troops, for instance, came out of the abattoir dazed and blood-splattered; the metal of their blades had been turned and dulled by bone and gristle; the blood of their victims had streamed in their faces; the screams had been in their ears. The whole of the next day they spent sharpening their steel and scrubbing their gear. Raleigh never mentioned Smerwick thereafter. In the months immediately following he wrote contemptuously of Grey; he grew to despise his misrule and doctrine, and the Lord Deputy returned his scorn. But the terrible events of November 8 were never recalled. Only many years later, when Elizabeth was gone and Raleigh himself had landed in the Tower, did the theme of man's cruelty to man suddenly obsess him and fill his vast *History of the World*. The book, some of his biographers have claimed, was atonement for a ruthless, ambitious youth. It also signifies how deeply Del Oro had moved his conscience. Worse atrocities occurred during the sixteenth century, worse massacres occurred in Ireland alone, yet of all the arguments summoned to dismiss or justify Smerwick, none seems more patently false than the broad historical, the view that such things were less objectionable to an earlier and more barbaric age. To say that mercy or compassion had a different value for Elizabethans, that they found the slaughter of prisoners more congenial, is to miss their shame and horror. The controversy which at once sprang up around Smerwick inspired attempts to cover the truth, to rationalize, to pardon. Twenty years after, the participants would still be arguing the merits of Grey's decision, and their memory of that awful day would remain clear and vivid. Smerwick was undoubtedly a turning point in the relations between the realm and its rebellious Irish subjects. Unquestionably it confirmed England's drift toward war with Spain. In political importance, therefore, Smerwick counts for more than a sum of life lost. But the price of Grey's decisiveness was high. Behind him the nation grew divided between those who argued expediency and those who argued honor. The varied responses to his deed do not reveal a nation confirmed in cruelty. Those who sent him to Ireland did not fail to stand up for him, but beyond official gratitude, a shadow of controversy attached to his name and limited his usefulness in the future.

Elizabeth wrote to her Lord Deputy at Christmastide in her own hand: "The mighty hand of the Almighty's power hath showed manifestly the force of his strength in the weakness of the feeblest sex and mind this year, to make men ashamed ever hereafter to disdain us. In which action I joy that you have been chosen the instrument of his glory, which I mean to give you no cause to forethink." Her letter was in a vein assuring; Grey had done God's work, he had aided a poor and helpless woman, and Elizabeth would have him feel no regret. She went on to suggest that perhaps he was too diffident in sparing the principals when slaying the accessories. The officers, too, should have been put to the sword. But publicly the Queen expressed regret at the duty forced upon her commander. She granted an audience to Mendoza and heard out Spain's charges of perfidy and dishonor. In Spain and Italy the massacre received less censure than the rumor that Grey had gone back on his word to San Joseppi. Elizabeth vehemently denied the accusation on Grey's behalf, but she could not forestall his growing notoriety. While the affair at Smerwick remained news, the byword for treachery in Catholic Europe was *Graia fides*, Grey's promise, and in Ireland, where memory is exceedingly long, the phrase has endured to this day. The only Irish witnesses to the fate of Del Oro did not survive to leave an account, but this did not keep Irish historians of the next generation, Philip O'Sullivan Beare and O'Daly, from lengthening the siege of the fort to forty days and further exaggerating Grey's shame. Among contemporaries, Grey found little support from Cecil or Sussex. Both were disturbed by the evident rift between him and Ormond, an indication that the Irish government was shifting its trust from loyal Irish lords to English military governors. Sussex fastened onto Smerwick to denounce Grey's inflexibility; it was one thing to massacre insurgent Irish, another to dispatch honest soldiers, and Smerwick had, in fact, done nothing to bring the Earl of Desmond and his followers to justice.

A veritable chorus was raised in Grey's favor. Bingham, as noted, placed the blame for the slaughter on Winter's sailors. Hooker claimed that the enemy needed to be taught a lesson. Geoffrey Fenton found the proceedings repellent but unavoidable. And Edmund Spenser defended his employer by explaining that if the troops had been spared, they might have joined with the Irish; that their destruction was a warning to rebels who had been heartened by thoughts of foreign assistance; and that in general, "there was no other way but to make that short end of them which was made." Objections were raised that Grey had no means of feeding the prisoners, no means of transporting them, and that he was surrounded by a large, hostile Irish force. These claims are not borne out by the facts, but they became a part of the historical justification and were still being urged in 1600.

Camden's version of the siege must be considered as near an official version as was achieved. The year before his death William Cecil made his voluminous papers available to the historian, and from Burghley's correspondence, government records, and accepted tradition, Camden creates his account. Truth and distortion are caught up indistinguishably in the *Annales*, and what remains unsaid is perhaps what Elizabethans found most difficult to admit. The length of the siege was given incorrectly, the dangers and inconveniences to Grey were overestimated, and the final responsibility for the killing was parceled out among the officers: "The Lord Deputy consulted his officers what should be done with them. But since those who had given themselves up were as many as the English, and there was danger from the rebels who were at hand more than 1,500 strong, and the English were so destitute of food and clothing that they would have mutinied if they had not been relieved out of the spoil taken from the enemy's fort, and there were no ships to carry the enemy away, this was their conclusion (against the will of the Deputy, who wept thereat) that the leaders should be saved and all the rest put to the sword for an example, and that the Irish should be hanged; which was presently done."

Elizabeth had been badly frightened by the landing of foreign troops at Smerwick, and she was willing to countenance any ferocity to remove the source of her worry. But as the English came to protest their innocence, the Irish naturally came to protest their guilt, and Grey learned before long that his problems in the country had only just begun.

SLIEVE MISH, 1583

Ruin

The traitor Earl has but a company of rascals, four Spaniards, and a drum to make men think he leads a great number," Ormond wrote to Grey in the aftermath of Smerwick. The rebellion is done, Ormond argued; foreign intervention is forestalled; English arms vindicated, and the time has come to pardon offenders and knit up the peace. He bade gallantly for an end to the war, and for a short time his points seemed well taken. As a consequence of Del Oro, Maltby had routed the Burkes and O'Rourkes in Connaught; Kildare had reluctantly chased Fiach MacHugh back into the Wicklows; and Turlough O'Neill had drawn back from the border of the pale. But Butler's wish to cap the triumph at Smerwick with a speedy settlement was spoiled by bad news. Early in December the town of Youghal reported that rebels had cut the upland road and that Desmond had appeared outside the fallen walls on a white charger. No one had counted on Gerald's perseverance. Suddenly he was in the East, carrying the war forward against all hope. And Thomas Butler, who would have led both sides to peace, was discharged by the Lord Deputy in the New Year, suspected of disloyalty.

Butler's reasoning was not wrong: Irish lords defeated in rebellion customarily fled to the Continent, and Desmond had certainly been defeated. James Eustace, Viscount Baltinglas, slipped into Ulster in March, took boat for Scotland, and was in France by late spring. At home, Grey hanged the male Eustaces and sent their heads to Dublin Castle, but in Irish eyes no dishonor attached to the Viscount. He had lost his gamble to free Ireland, and thereby forfeited his land. He would spend the last years of his life in Rome. The choice was also Gerald's, and Ormond expected him to seize it. That he did not was a measure of his newfound determination. The Earl of Desmond would not be parted from Munster. No good would ever come from his decision to stay, but the decision was the bravest he would make.

Between the East Coast and the West ran a highroad and a low. As Grey drove his army through the valleys, over rutted wagon trails, Gerald rode eastward through the forests, over the hills. And while Grey lay only a few miles outside Limerick, Desmond was murdering his own cousin Thomas near Cashel and burning villages in County Cork. The disaster in Kerry had swung many Geraldines to the government's side; Thomas of Desmond was one, and Gerald made an example of him. At Youghal, Ross, and Killarney the lesson was brought home to other supporters. So long as there were Desmonds, there would be no surrender. Villages which treated with the conqueror were put to the torch by Gerald, and villages which harbored rebels were put to the sword by Grey. In a word, Smerwick had forewarned Catholic Europe against interfering but had settled nothing in Ireland.

There was no pattern to the fighting. The killing was wanton, attributed to Gerald or John of Desmond or even to bands of marauding English troops. Grey struck into the Wicklows, but Fiach MacHugh slipped behind him and arbitrarily burned Rathcoole, ten miles outside Dublin. Captain Zouche played hide-and-seek with Gerald in Kilmore Wood, but when Zouche's companies were reviewed at Cork in March, fewer than 100 men remained out of 400. The rest were accounted for by sickness, desertion, or enemy action. Ormond's efforts brought him only greater calumny; he was so unsuccessful that Walsingham declared Butler had never killed more than three rebels. Ormond protests that he had killed thousands, but Warham St. Leger, Marshal for Munster, reviewed his company musters and wrote: "The Earl hath lost twenty Englishmen killed for every one of the rebels." Doubtless St. Leger exaggerated, but the attrition was appalling nonetheless. The suspicion lingered that upward of a third of Grey's army deserted after Smerwick. "The soldiers," said Sir William Stanley, "are so ill chosen in England that few are able or willing to do any service, but run away with our furnishings, and when they come into England there is no punishment for them, by means whereof we can hardly keep any." Those few private soldiers who slipped home were to be congratulated. In the West Country, and in Wales especially, their experiences became litany: atrocious climate; evil food; endless vigilance; unceasing marches; chaotic hostilities; and, worst of all, no pay and slight plunder. The Irish could not live, and the ordinary English could not prosper. Everyone was sick of the fighting. As many of his countrymen hated Gerald for prolonging the war as hated Grey for failing to end it, and still nothing changed. Against this backdrop of pitiless guerrilla warfare, the English now fell out among themselves.

From the Irish viewpoint it is difficult to sympathize with Ormond. He was forever on the Queen's side; he hammered Munster relentlessly with never a care for its starving people. But it may also be argued that Butler was never against the country, only against Desmond, and that he was quick to save Irish lives when his interests permitted. Now that he saw the waste and confusion of Munster encroaching year by year onto his own lands, he hastened to suggest a truce. And in that moment, when his employers were concerned only with dividing their Irish spoils, he suddenly became as Irish as Gerald Fitzgerald in their eyes. Ormond would survive the comparison, but for several months in 1581 he must have felt what it was like to be the Earl of Desmond. In the storm which now broke he was shielded by his cousin Elizabeth, and except for her, he, like the Earl of Kildare, might have been sent to London in chains.

Besides attacks on his military abilities, Ormond came under scrutiny for his management of government money. Through all his campaigns in Munster, Butler complained of inadequate pay and provisions; he was shocked, therefore, to learn of his alleged misappropriations and wrote to the Queen: "I know it is sour speech to speak of money; I know it will be also wondered at how victuals should want. . . . I never had for me and my companies one hundred pounds worth of victual, and this being true, I can avow that some have told lies at Court to some of your councillors —yea, not only in this, but in many other things." In reply, English officials maintained that Ormond had shown himself unfit to conduct the war. One writer estimated his emoluments at 215 pounds a month, and another at 3677 pounds a year, and the first result of a peace would be to deprive him of these comfortable subsidies. He was mixed up with Irish families and Irish lawsuits and could not have a single eye to the public service. He owed the Queen more than 3000 pounds in rents, and the war was an excuse for not paying. Finally, his system of warfare did not seem calculated to end a rebellion but rather to continue it. St. Leger charged: "He followeth his enemy with a running host, which is to no end but only wearing out and consuming of men by travel, for I can compare the difference between our footmen and the traitors to a mastiff and a greyhound." According to St. Leger, Ormond was generally disliked, and those whom he was set over would "rather be hanged than follow him, finding their travel and great pains altogether in vain."

What happened was that the Crown's auditors had finally been turned on Butler. The one-column ledgers of Elizabethan accounting showed expenditures against his name; what the accounts did not show, however, was the final destination of money and supplies meant for him. The glorious adventure which had been launched from London in the summer of 1580 was also to be a glorious windfall for corrupt captains and sutlers. No one, now or then, can really be certain what became of the Queen's Irish appropriations. Even the Vice Treasurer in Dublin was forced to conclude: "Ireland would always be what it long hath been—the sink of the treasure of England." Ormond could defend himself against charges of graft as well as anyone. Furthermore, his long service in the field gave him sufficient distinction to meet St. Leger's accusations. But where he was truly vulnerable no argument would suffice. Behind the dispute lay the nature of Ormond's power and influence in Ireland. In default of Gerald Fitzgerald he was among the last of the great Irish magnates. Suddenly he was required to forget his lineage, to put aside his feudal privileges, to become with Grey, Maltby, and their sort just another servant of the Crown. Thomas Butler had fought the Queen's wars in order to end forever the violence and disorder of the Desmond dynasty. Never once does he appear to have suspected that Gerald's demise might also mean the demise of an entire order. Butler had been in London when Peter Carew, the elder, crossed into Kilkenny and ravaged his estates. He attributed that outbreak to the instigation of his brothers, Edmund and Edward, and not to the insatiable hunger for land among English adventurers and upstarts. Now he was hard pressed to hold his own. Along the northwest border of his properties he seized the lands of the Baron of Upper Ossory, who had connived with the Geraldines. But the English reaction was swift and unequivocal. Vice Treasurer Wallop accused him of coveting his neighbor's lands, being "so imperious as he can abide none near him that dependeth not on him." Wallop's sentiments are proof that official Ireland could neither sanction nor tolerate Ormond's pride. The worst was to come. Grey's army was full of untitled gentlemen who by the sole virtue of English birth were preparing to dislodge the noblest Irish. Walter Raleigh, for instance, had not done Grey's bidding without hope of reward; he now claimed his share of the conquest and in the process encroached on Butler.

Early in 1581 Raleigh was the talk of the army. He had been ambushed near Ballinacurra on the road from Youghal to Cork and alone in the middle of a ford had fought back the henchmen of Eustace FitzEdmond. This gallant action was to shape his future. Because of it, he would lay claim to lands within the Earl of Ormond's seigniory, and because of it, Elizabeth would hear of his heroism from Burghley. The skirmish occurred on a dark afternoon in February as Raleigh, carrying dispatches

from Dublin to Cork, tried to reach the shelter of Ballivodig Castle. He and
his companion, Henry Moile, had ridden ahead of their party in the company of an Irish guide when, not far from the ruined castle, their guide
deserted them. Raleigh decided to continue anyway, and crossing a fast-
flowing stream, he and Moile suddenly came under fire from both banks.
Moile's horse collapsed under him, and he was thrown wounded and
bleeding into midstream. Raleigh, who had reached the cover of the opposite bank, could not desert him and, plunging back into the water, tried
to help Moile remount. With his kern, FitzEdmond charged into the water
after them, and Raleigh held off the rebels with a pistol and staff. Moile
was dragged clear of the stream by his horse and pitched headlong into a
bog, but Raleigh drew the Irish after him and, managing to get his back
to a tree, wounded several. FitzEdmond crossed swords with him along the
muddy bank, and the kern had almost pinioned him when his party finally
reached the ford and drove the Irish back. Raleigh's leather jerkin had been
cut and slashed by arrows, but he was unscathed. According to the various
accounts of his adventure, he had faced from a dozen to two dozen rebels
alone and in the end had held them—surely no mean feat.

But the fight had taken place on the lands of Lord Barrymore, who
held his estate and privileges in turn from Ormond. Within a few days
David Barry, Lord Barrymore, compounded matters by revolting against
the Crown. He and FitzEdmond were confederates under Sir John of
Desmond, and Raleigh subsequently thought to petition Grey for custody
of Barrymore Court, the ancestral home of the Barrys on Queenstown
Island. Grey could find no reason not to reward a good soldier at the
expense of rebels, and disregarding Ormond's right, he consented to the
grant. By his signature passed into the hands of a then obscure English
captain the island on which now stands Cobh, the port of Cork. Raleigh
tried to take possession at once, but Ormond interposed delays. Raleigh
repaired a castle on one side of the island narrows, but Butler drove him
out and seized "the fruit of his trouble and expense." Finally, Raleigh
traveled to meet Butler at his camp near Kilkenny and there among English troops also met FitzEdmond—in the service of the Earl of Ormond.
Outraged, Raleigh demanded the immediate arrest of FitzEdmond, and
reluctantly, Ormond complied.

But in regard to Barrymore Court, Butler did not give an inch. These
men, one the son of a ninth Earl, the other the son of a Devonshire tenant
farmer, would never agree, not then or in later years, after Elizabeth had
knighted Raleigh and raised him to one of the wealthiest men in the realm.
Ormond had driven his vassal, David Barry, out of Barrymore, but he
would as soon return the property to an Irish traitor as an English upstart.
He did not care about Grey or his grants, Raleigh or his petitions, and at

Barrymore Court he drew a line over which he would not be pulled. Raleigh wrote to Burghley, Ormond to the Queen, and in time the issue was allowed to lapse. Yet Raleigh's headstrong letter to Cecil is evidence of the insolence Ormond experienced and the growing distaste for loyal Irishmen. "When," Raleigh wrote, "my Lord Deputy came, and Barry had burned all the rest, Ormond, either meaning to keep it for himself, or else unwilling any Englishman should have anything, stayed the taking thereof. . . . I pray God her Majesty do not find, that—with the defence of his own country assaulted on all sides, what with the bearing and forebearing of his kindred, as all these traitors of this new rebellion are his own cousins-germane, what by reason of the incomparable hatred between him and the Geraldines, who will die a thousand deaths, enter into a million of mischiefs, and seek succour of all nations, rather than they will ever be subdued by a Butler—that after her Majesty hath spent a hundred thousand pounds more she shall at last be driven by too dear experience to send an English President to follow these malicious traitors with fire and sword, neither respecting the alliance nor the nation of Irishmen. . . . This man having been Lord General of Munster now about two years, there are at this instant a thousand traitors more than there were the first day. Would God the service of Sir Humphrey Gilbert might be rightly looked into; who, with the third part of the garrison now in Ireland, ended a rebellion not much inferior to this in two months."

Humphrey Gilbert, Raleigh's half brother, had, of course, not ended a rebellion; he had pacified a neighborhood by depopulating it. Harking back to Gilbert's example, Raleigh was searching for that simple, elusive answer which was often sought and never found. Inevitably, he underestimated the complexities of Ireland. He believed Ormond stood in the way of a settlement with the Desmonds, he believed Ormond to be continuing the war for his own profit, and he saw in Grey the type of ironbound commander ineffectual against the swift and secretive rebels. In effect, Raleigh advised the uprooting of all Irish aristocracy and privilege. What Cecil made of Raleigh's proposal is difficult to tell. The high lords of Ireland were responsible for the war, but without them, Ireland might descend to total chaos. Cecil refused to turn against Ormond, whom he preferred to Grey. In time Cecil would even be pleased to see the Queen lavish Irish lands on Raleigh and elevate him as a counterpoise to her old favorite Robert Dudley, Earl of Leicester. But neither he nor the Queen ever intended to supplant the aristocracy of Ireland. Nevertheless, the popular outcry against Ormond became too strong. The Irish war was over and not over, and Elizabeth, caught in that familiar condition, finally yielded to pressure. She ordered Grey to tell Ormond that his authority as Lord Lieutenant of Munster was at an end. She wished no measures taken against Butler but this, and he, relieved to be beyond backbiting and reproach, submitted cheerfully. His parting letter reminded Elizabeth how much of his property was wasted in her service, how much the loss of his salary would impoverish him. His last remark, however, is the most significant: "Men do now talk of pardons to be granted freely; had I known of such pardons, I would have brought in every rebel in Munster."

General pardon, the answer Pelham had made the Crown promise to forgo, was the last means open to the Queen to end the fighting. She was prepared to pardon every rebel except Gerald, John, Father Sanders, and Eleanor, Countess of Desmond. The subject broached in Dublin brought a furious reply. Grey asked to be recalled. "Fear and not dandling," he wrote, "must bring them to the bias of obedience. . . . it is a pity that the resolutions in England should be so uncertain. . . . You ask me what I do? If taking of cows, killing of their kern and churls had been thought worth the advertising, I could have had every day to trouble your Highness. . . . He that today seems a dutiful subject, let him for any crimes be tomorrow called upon to come and answer, straightway a pardon is demanded and in the meanwhile he will be upon safe-keeping, which in plain English is none other than a traitor that will forcibly defend his cause and not answer to justice. . . . Beggars fall to pride, rail at your Majesty, and rely only upon the Pope, and that pardons shall in the end free them." Waterhouse wrote to Walsingham: "I will hear your honour's opinion whether her Majesty will be content to have her great expenses answered out of the livings of the conspirators, and to use a sharp and severe course without respect of any man's greatness, wheresoever law will catch hold, or whether all faults must be lapped in lenity with pardons, protections, and fair semblances, as in times past; if severity, then is there hope enough of good reformation; if mildness, then discharge the army and officers, and leave this nation to themselves, for sure the mean course will do no good. We must embrace one of these extremities."

Elizabeth clearly favored pardon or, as the Lord Deputy put it, "leaving the Irish to tumble to their own sensual government." But for once she listened to her officials. The argument which appears to have won her was Waterhouse's: by confiscating the land and properties of rebels, she could repair her treasury and make good her great expenses. From this moment forward no Irish lord with so much as the rumor of suspicion about him was safe. For his lenience in dealing with the Eustace rebellion, the Earl of Kildare was sent to the Tower; for his failure to keep Connaught free of rebels, the Earl of Clanricarde watched his son executed; and for his failure to apprehend his old enemies, the Earl of Ormond was confined to his lands. Where Desmond had ruled, land passed to the Crown. But the Desmonds alone were free and still defiant, and in the immemorial way of Ireland, unity came too late. Gerald had been at war for two years when a number of his noble countrymen finally began to grasp the meaning of his resistance. An Englishman wrote to Walsingham at this time: "If hell were opened and all the evil spirits abroad, they would never be worse than these Irish rogues, rather dogs, and worse than dogs, for dogs do but after their kind, and the Irish race degenerates all humanity." The question was no longer whether Gerald Fitzgerald could save his earldom; it was whether any Irishman could save his life holdings in the face of such implacable hatred.

The practice of amnesty, as prescribed by the Crown, turned out almost worse than open warfare. The land had been so stripped and ravaged, its institutions and structures so thoroughly leveled during the Desmond Wars, that nothing remained to restrain the worst tendencies of its people. During Grey's government Irishmen betrayed Irishmen as seldom before; head money was commonly paid in towns, and the traffic between informers and officials grew more lucrative than ever. Of the beaten men of Desmond's army, one official wrote to Cecil: "If they meet an Englishman or two walking the streets, they shake their heads, they rouse themselves in their lousy mantles, and advance on tiptoe, as if to say 'We are those who have done your mischief, what say ye to us?' These creatures are captains who carry in their fists sackfuls of their brothers' heads." Grey's enforcement encouraged extremities; his zealous puritanism, his antipathy for the race of Irish led his followers to encroach on the last vestiges of stability left the nation: its lordships and family prerogatives. Ormond was almost ruined by suspicion and slander, and Ormond had been Ireland's great compromise, the Crown's oldest and firmest ally. No wonder that long after the Desmond cause was doomed at Del Oro, Irish lords persisted in rebelling. Lord Barry, Lord Roche, the Baron of Lixnaw, James Fitzjohn of Strancally—all joined Gerald at the ebb of his cause, and all joined him regardless—to fight was enough. Grey had succeeded in isolating the Irish war from European support, but his overweening nationalism prevented him from ending it.

If Raleigh was disappointed in his quest for Barrymore, he was shortly thereafter recompensed by the gift of Lismore Castle and several thousand acres along the upper Blackwater. It was in the Lord Deputy's power to reward his followers with gifts of land taken from felons and traitors. Grey exercised this privilege sufficiently that cries of angry expostulation reached Elizabeth from Waterhouse and Wallop. She was soon made to see that property revenues assured her were being squandered through the generosity of her commander. Cecil wrote to Grey, the Exchequer brought pressure to bear, and before long another scandal threatened to rack the English government in Dublin. However much the situation in Ireland was of Grey's own making, his predicament was truly pitiable. To the problems of rebellion, social disintegration, economic collapse, famine he now had to add royal meddling. What Elizabeth and her advisors did not understand was that life in Her Majesty's Irish provinces was so brutal, so uncertain, that good and loyal men had to be bribed to stay. John Zouche, Thomas Norris, Sir William Stanley, and many more were not given the lands of rebels merely because Grey desired to bankrupt the Crown or humiliate Irish families. By no other means could he keep them. Perhaps the best documented case of favor granting concerns Edmund Spenser.

In 1581 Spenser was granted a lease for properties at Enniscorthy. The gift included the site of a friary, with mill and orchard; a manor, ruined castle, an old weir; and farmlands. Spenser held the property for only three days. Enniscorthy lay on the other side of the Wicklows from his residence in Dublin; perhaps he had little desire for an estate in Wexford, but more likely he needed cash. In any event he sold his leasehold to Richard Synnot, an English gentleman of some consequence in the neighborhood, for an indeterminate amount of silver. A few days later he was recorded as purchasing land at New Ross, even farther south in Wexford, from Lord Mountgarret, an impoverished Irish noble. He held the New Ross property until 1584, when he finally sold the lease to Sir Anthony Colclough, another English settler, for a substantial profit on his earlier investment. Spenser had arrived in Ireland with hardly a penny. In the windfall days of the early eighties, he rushed to make himself self-sufficient. On August 24, 1582, he leased "the site of the house of friars called the New Abbey, County Kildare, with appurtenances; also an old waste town adjoining, and its appurtenances, in the Queen's disposition by the rebellion of James Eustace." In other words, Spenser's "old waste town" and "house of friars" were not archaeological relics; they had been living institutions under Baltinglas and had passed into the Crown's hands after his flight. Standing by the Liffey in a country of green rolling hills, a day's ride from Dublin Castle, New Abbey was presumably a pleasant spot. Spenser chose to live there for more than a year, until the misfortunes of John of Desmond presented a new opportunity.

While land changed hands and the government grew in confusion, the Geraldines found the respite they needed. Younger sons of lords and chieftains, none of whom would have been permitted to embroil themselves previously in a Desmond quarrel, now flocked into the woods to join him. The Earl of Desmond rose from his nadir through their efforts, and he flung them into a running cavalry battle for County Cork. His maneuvers are difficult to trace; there are few firsthand accounts; at best a scattering of English reports tell his whereabouts. The fighting seems to have centered on a triangle of towns formed by Fermoy, Mallow, and Buttevant. It cut the Cork-Limerick road, transversed Kilmore, and led as always into the fastnesses of the Aherlow Valley. To this day the countryside recalls Gerald; the Desmond Caves at Mitchelstown, the Glen of the Awbeg at Castletownroche were his hiding places. From there he sent his renegades against the loyalist families of the neighborhood in what became increasingly a civil war. This was the country of the Roches, the Fitzgibbons, the Barrys, the Muskerry Burkes. For more than a hundred years the pasturage to the east of the ruined town of Buttevant had belonged to McSheehy gallowglass, and Buttevant and the river town of Mallow were in the domain of Sir John of Desmond. The area now caught fire as family met family and divided within itself.

The English did not interfere; they could not. With Ormond's retirement they lost all control over the internecine conflicts of the South. The great intermediary was gone, the interpreter of local quarrels, and the nobility of Munster tore itself apart in feuding skirmishes. They clashed on horseback in desolate fields and fire-blackened villages, and littering the ground over which they fought lay the bones of their tenants—killed the year before by Pelham or Grey. Glimpses remain of the fighting's ferocity. The Irish Chronicle remarks that when Grace MacBrien, the wife of Theobald Roche, "saw her husband mangled, and mutilated, and disfigured, she shrieked extremely dreadfully, so that she died that night alongside the body of her husband, and both were buried together." Gerald has been blamed for such atrocities, for the torture and disfigurement of prisoners. He appeared in the countryside on a white charger, his crippled body wrapped in a black, silken cloak, and he became an image of terror never to be wholly forgotten. But Gerald also moved through a world deeply corrupted by war. On every side he feared treachery, Grey's agents, Grey's silver. He had endured long enough to watch friends turn enemies for gain or pardon, and he believed in making examples. The war had reached a pass where no quarter was expected. For the likes of Desmond, expediency was survival, and he never hesitated to mutilate his enemies or abandon his friends.

During the spring of 1581, while Gerald scourged County Cork, Father Nicholas Sanders died of starvation and dysentery in the depths of Kilmore. It is believed that the fall of Del Oro broke him, that he wandered in the forests for weeks, alone, delirious, unable to feed or care for himself. Sanders claimed from the start to be the soul of the Irish rebellion. Until the catastrophe at Smerwick he had endured failure: Stukeley's destruction; Fitzmaurice's death; collapse and flight in the West. But when his sustaining hope for Spanish aid, for a papal Ireland, for a land holy and cleansed of heresy was brought to nothing, his grip loosened perceptibly. From the moment Sanders advertised his presence in Ireland, with the wanton murders of Davells and Carter, he strove to enlist the Irish in a cause greater than themselves. His efforts were in vain. Eventually privation and defeat modified his zeal, softened his determination. Yet even at the end there is no indication that he grasped the essence of the Irish conflict. In the name of the Church he pitted a tribal people against a cohesive nation, and they were easily divided and overcome. He held out hope for a Spanish Prince in Ireland, for just Christian rule, but never for an Ireland ruled by Irishmen. Inadvertently Sanders helped awaken the vague stirrings of nationhood, but he did not exploit these possibilities in his struggle to restore religion to Ireland. If in time the simple people came to view him as their martyr, their Christ in the wilderness, the measure of their devotion was not that they followed him, but that they did not sell him. Long before Smerwick the pinch of hunger and exposure overtook him, and although he begged bread and shelter up and down the land, even Ormond's informers could never pry loose his whereabouts.

Father Sanders died in April, 1581; Ormond did not learn of his end until June. Fifty years later no one knew precisely how he had died, until the historian O'Sullivan Beare revealed the secret his father had passed on to him. Sanders' companion at the last was Cornelius Ryan, the papal Bishop of Killaloe, and according to O'Sullivan the following scene took place: "In the beginning of the night, Dr. Sanders, whose naturally strong frame was worn out by dysentery, thus addressed the Bishop of Killaloe, 'Anoint me, illustrious lord, with extreme unction, for my Creator calls me, and I shall die tonight.' 'You are wrong,' answered the bishop, 'and your case is not bad, and I think that there will be no dying or anointing just now.' Nevertheless, he grew worse, and was anointed at midnight, and at cockcrow resigned his spirit to the Lord, and the following night he was secretly buried by priests, and borne to the grave by four Irish knights, of which my father, Dermot, was one. Others were forbidden to attend, lest the English should then or later find the body, and make their usual cruel spectacle of the dead."

The section of Kilmore where Sanders was buried was called Clonlish Wood. Today it has vanished, and with it his grave. His legend lives on, however. Gerald might have disliked his company and distrusted his intentions, but Sanders is remembered as the priest of the Desmonds and in the popular mind remains a token of Holy Church's compassion for her persecuted children in that time. Although the Crown could never produce his corpse, they benefited from rumors of his death. Sanders' presence in

Ireland had consecrated the Desmond cause, and without him, the Earl and his followers grew to seem mere outlaws in the eyes of some their countrymen.

In the summer and fall of 1581 Gerald's adherents won several victories, but a slow attrition had also begun to reduce them. On Bantry Bay, David Barry destroyed an English detachment under Captain Apsley. When Apsley attempted to cross the bay at Bearhaven, trying to reach the cover of Bantry Abbey, he and his men were butchered on leaving their boats. The *Calendar of State Papers* records concern for his widow and offers the eyewitness account of James Fenton, Spenser's acquaintance, the only survivor of the ambush. Months later the fighting went on. Captain Ascham and a score of his men were killed, and his company besieged in Ardfert Abbey. Finally, Zouche came to their rescue; he lost half his command but killed 100 of Barry's kern and took the rebel prisoner. On Zouche's return toward Cork he was ambushed by the Kerry McSwineys, but an Irish traitor stabbed the McSwiney chieftain in the throat and his men were routed before they overcame the English party or rescued Barry. Zouche entered Cork through the Shandon Gate, with Barry tied to his saddle by a halter and the Great McSwiney's head in a sack.

Of all the English captains who fought in Ireland during these years, none appears more often in dispatches than John Zouche. In action at Carrigafoyle, at Glenmalure, at Del Oro his bravery was apparent; he was in the field continually and was wounded several times. While Raleigh and others were bickering with Grey over preferment, it was Zouche who opened the roads and relieved the garrisons of Munster. He was tireless in pursuit of Gerald, and his companies suffered the highest casualties. In 1581 he begged Grey for reinforcements, but the Queen was determined to reduce her Irish expenses, and the Lord Deputy was powerless to find him men. Zouche was not discouraged, however; he followed every lead, every report brought to him, and because of his perseverance the Crown finally triumphed over its inveterate enemy, Sir John of Desmond.

If any Geraldine possessed the fury and ruthlessness to bring order to the Irish cause, John did. Those chieftains who grudgingly provided the Earl with men and food were won to him by John, for Gerald was often too proud and aloof to assure their allegiance for long. It was John who reconciled feuding clans, who blackmailed subject chieftains into support, and who either by eloquence or example brought out the kern and gallowglass through defeat after defeat. Only certain facts are known about him. He was the first Desmond to join Fitzmaurice in arms; he murdered Davells in cold blood; he, not Gerald, drove the Desmond levies through the harrowing baptism of Monaster. What John believed in, however, is more difficult to tell than what he did. Early in the uprising he seemed to promise land reform, a division of Crown lands, and he is perhaps the prototype of that Giant of Equality overcome by Artegall (Grey) in Spenser's *Faerie Queene*. At Sanders' instigation he killed his friend Davells to token his independence from the English. At Fitzmaurice's death he inherited the generalship of papal forces, slim though these were. Yet nothing kept him from eventually becoming Sanders' adversary and antagonist, a priest baiter, an opponent of all foreign schemes to interfere in Ireland. He made no attempt to secure his property but threw everything into the cause. He was the one leading rebel who never flirted with flight or pardon. And the reasonable conclusion is that he was by far the most political of the Desmonds. Encumbered by few of Gerald's feudal pretenses, he was the one pure nationalist to emerge among the Geraldines. So much for glimpses of his mind; in action he was visceral, a war lover, cruel even in the eyes of his own. In the end he was not betrayed or even overwhelmed. He fell in a chance collision on a dusty road and was gone before anyone even realized.

On January 2, 1582, a spy came to Zouche with information that James Fitzjohn had been seen in the vicinity of Castlelyons. Fitzjohn was hardly the most important rebel, but a rebel nonetheless, and at nine o'clock that evening Zouche left Cork with fifty horsemen in pursuit of him. The chase was routine; it was to conclude, however, in a singular triumph. What had happened was that Sir John Fitzedmund Fitzgerald, the Seneschal of Imokilly, Gerald's faithful retainer and kinsman, was at odds with the rebel Barrys and Patrick Condon. The dispute bade to split the Munster Geraldines irrevocably, and to help compose their differences, Gerald dispatched Sir John toward Castlelyons. John, traveling from the Aherlow, where Desmond lay hidden, had no reason to believe that the English were out in strength, and he and his party rode without body armor on light ponies. Toward daybreak, as they neared their destination, they galloped headlong into Zouche. Neither side was ready for the other. Zouche's men dressed their lances; John's tried to break their line in a rush and, in passing, a trooper lanced John through the side. Most of the Irish carried through the enemy and made their getaway, but a onetime servant of Sir John's, an Irishman enlisted with Zouche, fired a pistol into his neck point-blank and toppled him from his saddle. Fitzjohn, who had joined the party, tried to shield him but was overwhelmed and taken prisoner. Shortly after, the serving man confirmed the identity of Sir John.

Before he lost consciousness, John is purported to have said that had he lived longer he would have done more mischief to the English and that Davells was never really his friend. The version has most likely been sanitized for the record. What is virtually certain is that John was thrown over the back of a mule alive and during the journey to Cork bled to death.

Some of his men tracked the English company as far as they could by his blood left in the dust.

As a New Year's gift Grey received Sir John's head from the Mayor and Corporation of Cork. The trophy was spiked on the walls of Dublin Castle alongside many others. John's body was hung in chains from the great portal at Cork and remained there for four years until a great wind blew it into the river. A turquoise set in gold was found on his body and was sent to the Queen; his Agnus Dei, with its glass and gold frame, was presented as a gift to the Earl of Bedford. More important to the future of Ireland was the disposition of his lands. Captain Thomas Norris was eventually to receive John's great castle at Mallow, a thousand or so of his acres on the Blackwater were awarded to Raleigh, and Edmund Spenser was granted his castle and plowlands at Kilcolman. Since the Norman Conquest, Mallow, Kilcolman, and the ancient town of Buttevant had been in the gift of the Fitzgeralds and never again would be. Where the Desmond gallowglass, the McSheehys, had once grazed cattle, a new nation of Anglo-Irish was to take root and has remained until the present.

As for James Fitzjohn of Strancally, he confessed under torture to aiding and abetting his cousin Gerald; according to him, the Earl was in desperate straits and "lived only by eating at night the cows that he had killed in the day." The news was tonic to Grey, who, after hanging Fitzjohn, ordered Zouche to press Desmond harder than before. Again, English troops scoured the Valley of the Aherlow, yet whenever they caught sight of Gerald, he managed to elude them. On one occasion Zouche surprised Lady Desmond's baggage train and Ladies-in-Waiting before they could flee. In a swoop he gathered in the wives and daughters of several noblemen, but before he could overtake the Countess, she had vanished into the Galtee Mountains. The Fitzgeralds had grown used to life in the woods, and if Eleanor sometimes slept on silk after her husband's successes, she was reconciled to bedding on straw after his defeats. Zouche chased her over difficult terrain, never caught her, and in the meantime, Gerald slipped unnoticed into Tipperary. The death of Sir John was a grave blow to the Geraldines, but try as he would, Grey was unable to profit from it.

In Dublin his government was unraveling. Elizabeth had become visibly disturbed by his lack of progress, and through the offices of Wallop and Waterhouse she moved to reduce his expenditures unaccountably. Lord Deputies did not receive moneys unless they were successful, yet without moneys they could not succeed. The old conundrum remained insoluble as always, and like his predecessors, Grey drew on his private means to fulfill his public duties. Reward was slight, and recompense unlikely. By early 1582 he had begun to welcome his impending recall. Cecil was convinced that he was completely unsuited to Irish government. He was too much the soldier, too much the puritan to accommodate himself to the realities of the country. Supporting this view were letters from Grey's own secretary, Geoffrey Fenton. "Where," wrote Fenton, "there is so great an antipathy and dissimilitude of humour and manners between a people and their governor, then the government cannot be carried in just rule and frame no more than a wound can be healed which is plied with medicine contrary to its proper cure." Apparently the Lord Deputy had begun to lose the confidence of his staff. His young secretaries argued fiercely over his mission. Fenton reflected on the debacle at Glenmalure, the wanton bloodshed at Smerwick, the terrible suffering in the countryside, and was disposed to denounce Grey's methods. His brother had narrowly escaped death with Captain Apsley's party, and Fenton had grown depressed with the spectacle of wasted lives and devastation. Spenser admitted that Grey was thought "a bloody man, who regarded not the life of her Majesty's subjects," but he refused to make Grey a scapegoat for all that had happened. The enemy was still Rome, the perpetrator of the great lie, and to him the Western world appeared in the grip of a mighty crisis. Civilization retreated, as everywhere strong appetites overwhelmed moderate in pursuit of gratification. Short of divine intervention, a day of apocalypse, no man could hope to stand against the storm indefinitely. Spenser recognized Grey's shortcomings; he recorded them in *The Faerie Queene* in his allegory of Justice, but he clung to the authority the Lord Deputy represented as the only stay against a universal darkness.

Indeed, conditions warranted his worst apprehensions. What befell Munster late in 1581 was probably beyond the control of any human agent. The imbalance created by war and depopulation now resulted in a monstrous famine and all-devouring plague. In six months preceding March, 1582, 30,000 people died of hunger and sickness in County Cork alone, perhaps a third of the inhabitants. The city of Cork, population about 10,000, registered an average of 70 deaths a day. In the countryside loyalist landlords reported that 90 percent of their tenants were gone. An earth which might have fed Ireland and most of England could not support a handful of men and cattle. So dreadful was the state of Munster in early 1582 that Elizabeth heard rumors from European capitals and, conscience-stricken by what she learned, turned her blame on Grey. Even St. Leger, who admired the Lord Deputy as much as he despised the Geraldines, could not deny that the only inhabitants of Munster in anything nearing satisfactory condition were the rebels themselves, who stole liberally and escaped disease "by enjoying continually the wholesome air of the fields." Laughable though this last charge seems, the Desmonds indeed did not die of hunger or plague. They were never penned in towns or villages; they seized the food they needed, and in his great pride, Gerald exploited churls and tenantry without compunction. Spenser's claim that only the English army stood between the oppressed Irish and their wolfish lords contained a germ of truth. The knowledgeable men in Grey's entourage—Spenser; Fenton; Bryskett; Norris—did not agree on philosophy, but they did concur on the necessity of destroying the Earl of Desmond quickly. Practical soldiers like Raleigh had never doubted this necessity, and therefore, they lobbied incessantly for a less orthodox commander than Grey. Encouraged by the spread of his reputation, Raleigh became more of a thorn in the Lord Deputy's side than ever. "I like not his carriage or company," Grey complained, "and he has nothing to expect from me." But Raleigh had won Cecil's ear and, having reversed his thinking, was urging that Ormond be recalled from retirement to replace Grey. By early 1582 the bickering had led to paralysis; Dublin Castle, the seat of government, had internalized the chaos of Ireland.

What now happened to add to the confusion of Grey's administration was totally unexpected. During the first week in May, when even Ireland gave hope of renewing life, a woman arrived at Dublin Castle, demanding an immediate audience with the Lord Deputy. Drawn and haggard from hunger and exposure, wrapped in a gray threadbare mantle, she looked like the other ruined gentry then thronging into Cork or Dublin from the countryside. She was turned away several times from Storehouse Tower and was finally admitted into Grey's audience chamber only with a company of ragged supplicants. Once in his presence, though, she stepped forward and identified herself as Eleanor, Countess of Desmond, and, before the astonished assembly, threw herself on the mercy of the Crown. Grey, stunned, treated her with all courtesy; the amenities of Dublin Castle were put at her disposal, and no questions raised of arraignment or trial.

Three years before, the Countess of Desmond had met Lord Justice Drury on the road to Waterford, a dying and defeated man. She pitied him and entrusted her son to his care. Now she had come to his successor worn out and vulnerable. By entering Dublin, she placed herself in great jeopardy. Eleanor had been proclaimed a cardinal rebel, her head carried a price as surely as her husband's, and there were those who believed that no rebellion lasted long in Ireland without a woman to stir the coals of hatred and sedition. Persuaded that Gerald must grow weaker with her loss, they advised that the Countess receive the full and awful measure of the law. Given her circumstances, she inspired an unaccountable fear. Among the common soldiery she was a she-devil, treacherous, licentious, and their stories about her are clearly an amalgam of folklore and propaganda. Eleanor was a fine horsewoman, she had proved an elusive foe, but she was hardly the termagant of rumor, much less an active combatant. Her reputation may have owed to the notion that Irishwomen were forward in war and excessively cruel. The Gaelic virago was legend shared by both sides. In the thirteenth century Red Eva McMurrough, for instance, was said to have wound iron bars in her long red braids before battle; in the fifteenth century Marra Kerrigan was believed never to have spared a man overthrown in battle, and even in Elizabeth's reign the flamboyant Grace O'Malley terrorized Galway with her Connemara pirates. The Countess of Desmond was viewed in this tradition, and while Grey treated her with the utmost diffidence, public opinion grew outraged at his misplaced chivalry. No one appears to have understood the reasons for Eleanor's sudden surrender, and in the poisoned atmosphere of Dublin Castle the worst was always suspected. Spenser, in his allegory of Justice, censures Grey for his courtesy. Here Eleanor becomes the grotesque amazon Radigund and because Grey, in the person of Artegall, spares her on the battlefield, she is able to imprison him in her dungeon dressed in woman's clothing. Only Elizabeth, represented by the poet's Britomart, is finally capable of setting Grey free and destroying Radigund's power over him.

Concerning the Countess of Desmond's surrender, several explanations are offered. To the South, Zouche was pressing the Earl harder than ever; English troops were everywhere, and in only a matter of time they might have trapped the Countess. In late April they almost took her husband. Gerald was camped with eighty gallowglass near Kilfinnane when, in the midst of preparing a horse for dinner, they were suddenly surprised. A brief fight left half his troops dead, and he escaped Zouche across a bog, carried out of the engagement in a blanket by four men. The dampness of the spring had paralyzed his hip; he was hardly able to walk or sit a horse, and again the McSheehy gallowglass paid for his freedom with their lives. In these conditions Eleanor was a liability, and Gerald probably dispatched her to Grey under the pretext of discussing surrender. She had fulfilled a similar mission to Pelham once before, and though the offer was not genuine, she would be safer in Dublin than in Great Kilmore. During the winter Zouche let it be known that Desmond would be received honorably if he capitulated. Here at least were grounds for negotiation, and Gerald was shrewd enough to realize that Grey would have to consult Whitehall on a question of this magnitude. In the meantime, the pressure would ease, good weather would bring reinforcements, the loyal septs would send men as they had every spring since 1579, and with new strength Gerald might conceivably stalemate the English for another season.

Eleanor was again a willing pawn in her husband's struggle for survival. She dwelt at Dublin Castle with all the honors accorded a woman of her rank, and while Grey awaited Whitehall's decision, he treated her more as an emissary than a rebel. To the hard-bitten officers of his army, he had fallen for a ruse. He was enthralled by a powerful traitor, emasculated, more prisoner than she. They had chased her into the plashings of rebel ambushes, had lost men because of her in the bogs and glens of the South, and for them war was war. Grey was playing for a quick settlement to a struggle he could not win, and they were aware all this time of Desmond's increasing strength. Eleanor, however, was beyond their grasp, sheltered by Grey's old-fashioned courtesy and the reluctance of the Queen to punish a loyal wife for the misdeeds of her husband. As a consequence, Eleanor bought Gerald the time he needed, and yet from her letters it is clear that she was in Dublin for purposes of her own.

Her son, the one she had given up to the Crown when the war began, was back in Dublin Castle. She saw him for the first time in three years, and her fear that he would be used to trap his father was put to rest. What she soon realized was that the boy had grown into a man and that his education had been sadly neglected. Her letters are to William Cecil, who, if understanding of the Desmond plight, was also a renowned advocate of education. "Why," Eleanor asks Burghley, "hath he remained in the castle of Dublin, without any kind of learning or bringing up, or any to attend on him?" Far better, she argues, "that he be sent again into England . . . the lesser evil of the two." The Countess of Desmond was a true Irishwoman, yet she had no illusions about the salutary effects of her country on young men. The inevitable outcome of the Desmond War was clear to her; she and her husband were finished, and a desire to remove her son out of the way of disaster, as much as the excellence of London tutors, prompted her request. Elizabeth was not unsympathetic; she appreciated the difficult position of Irish noblewomen; the Countess of Kildare, for instance, was her dear friend, while the Earl of Kildare was restrained in the Tower of London. In accord with Eleanor's request, her son was sent to London; thereafter he was cloistered in the Tower, more resident than prisoner, and if his education had been neglected at first, English tutors now enforced study and celibacy. Sixteen years later, when the Queen sent him back to Munster in the middle of another war, he was too unnerved by scholarship, confinement, and sexual repression to survive for long.

While Whitehall pondered the possibilities of negotiating with Gerald, he for his part launched the most devastating attack of the entire war. In the first weeks of a lovely summer, dry and warm, the long oppression bore its fruit. From every hidden corner of Kerry and Cork, Kildare and

Tipperary, the Irish kern poured into Desmond's camp in the middle of the Aherlow. Almost at once Zouche's patrols ran into difficulty; the Crown was without eyes; it became worth a soldier's life to wander in Kilmore. Gerald broke out of the Aherlow near Bansha. With almost 1000 men he streamed into the Golden Vale, foraging the grain and cattle he needed to sustain his drive. Tipperary fell to the Geraldines, and the sacred Rock of Cashel. Clonmel, in the shadow of the Comeragh Mountains, was occupied, and the roads to Fortress Cahir cut. As far south as the Knock-mealdown Mountains and as far north as the Slieveardagh Hills rebels plundered garrison towns and castles. Pelham at Cork and Grey at Dublin were stunned by the suddenness of the attack, and while they shifted forces to meet it, Edmund and Edward Butler were persuaded to fall on Gerald from Kilkenny. Day by day it grew clearer that the Crown could not hold Ireland without the Butlers.

But for once, Gerald handily defeated them. By Cahir, along the head waters of the Suir River, stood a key fortress. To this day it looms over the river gorge as formidable as ever, and beneath its walls Desmond led his followers to their greatest triumph over the ancient enemy. With fewer men and no artillery he captured the castle, routed Edmund and Edward, and put more Butlers to the sword "than ever they had Desmonds at bloody Affane." Gerald was not like himself; he had begun to fight as his cousin Fitzmaurice had and, refusing to fall back on his victory, pressed his enemy along the length of the Suir. The Seneschal of Imokilly was out in strength. He pillaged and burned Black Tom's house at Carrick-on-Suir. He next appeared at Fermoy, some twenty-five miles from Cork, where he annihilated an English garrison and put the neighborhood to the sword. By late June he was as strong in the vicinity of Cork as ever he had been, and reports reached Grey and Pelham regularly of Gerald's progress toward Waterford. Three years into the war the military situation was as perilous as when Fitzmaurice had landed. The Geraldines had driven a wedge into the coastal counties. A triangle of destruction lay between Fermoy, Tipperary, and Waterford. Gerald stopped short of entering Waterford, but for the moment Grey was powerless to reverse the tide. He sat in Dublin, aware that this latest outbreak assured his removal. Communications with Cork were disrupted; Fiach MacHugh had seized the opportunity to infiltrate the pale, and in Offaly the O'Connors were rampaging. Grey's worst nightmares had probably come true, and at Dublin Castle his officers blamed defeat on his dealings with the Countess of Desmond.

But in regard to her, a decision had been reached: if her husband would not consent to unconditional surrender, Elizabeth ordered that she be sent back to him. Gerald could ill afford to be burdened by his Countess, but he also would not surrender. Now he wrote to the Queen that he would never trade victory for vague assurances. And thereby he sealed his wife's fate, for in the months to come she would be tied inseparably to him, her last refuge lost. When she came to Dublin next, she would be in rags and ill, and she would bear no messages, only a request for shelter and clemency. As Eleanor left the city, escorted south under guard toward the rebel hills, the last chance passed for a negotiated settlement to the war. So, at least, runs the Irish interpretation. From another point of view, Grey was at last freed from Radigund by the Queen's intervention. His own better nature had worked against him, his sentimental attachment to chivalry, and now he was to recognize that survival in Ireland called for more than martial prowess and noblesse. To his credit, he wanted no more; this was not the land for an English Hannibal, and he conspired as much for his recall as Burghley.

As the war dragged on into the summer, first favoring one side and then the other, Grey appeared perplexed by his own ill success. The fault with his policy was deeply rooted in the man. He had lived his life in the shadow of his father's military botches and, to do him justice, did not repeat them. With the exception of Glenmalure, he suffered no personal defeats. He canceled the Spanish presence in Ireland; he subjugated more of the country than any predecessor and ultimately made possible more acreage under English tillage than even Sir Henry Sidney had thought feasible. Yet what Grey could not accomplish was a permanent cessation of hostilities, and his failure was in the final analysis more political than military. He viewed his adversaries as a threat to the survival of a central-ized and legitimate state and, therefore, as a threat to the civilization for which the Tudor state stood. He could not see beyond the religious and ideological challenges to the root cause of the Irish upheaval, the endless, shifting struggle for baronial preeminence and security. To a man better grounded in history, Ireland in the throes of the Desmond War might have appeared comparable to England in the throes of the War of the Roses a century before. To be sure, the analogy was complicated by cultural differ-ences, but the way toward settlement required a similar compromise and allowance for time. Above all, it was essential to isolate the Irish lords from their people, not to destroy the people and the fabric of their society to topple the lords. The process was slow, and Grey impatient. In common with other governors ordered to Ireland, he had no wish to remain. Glory and renown were to be his rewards, compensation for an earlier stain to his family's honor. As a consequence of his attitude, he was soon crossed and bewildered at every turn, for in his high-minded devotion to duty, he generally mistook the more material motives of men. St. Leger, who had toiled in Ireland since the First Munster Plantation, who had known

Gerald in London, who alone among Grey's advisors was a true pioneer, never doubted the reason for the fighting. He explained: "It is death to all the Irish lords and chieftains of whatever faction to have English government be established here, and their Irish exactions laid aground; the which to forgo they had as leave die, such is their devilish consciences." For St. Leger, "Irish conscience" was made of land and money, the concrete personal worth no lord or chieftain would ever exchange for the intangible benefits of nationhood. Such was their distrust of political abstractions and their intense individualism that they were not ready for the choice Grey gave them.

It was only to be expected that Sir Warham would attempt to break the impasse by methods of his own. While Grey remained in Dublin, baffled and frustrated, St. Leger kidnapped the seven-year-old son of the Seneschal of Imokilly. The boy, he wrote, "is as like his father as if he had spit him out of his mouth," and Sir Warham proposed to hang the child if the Seneschal and Gerald did not surrender. Here was the kind of entreaty the Irish understood, not Her Highness demands this and Her Highness demands that. For his initiative St. Leger was authorized by the Queen to offer Gerald his life, restraint without imprisonment somewhere in England or Ireland, and hope of further mercy for himself and his heir. Restoration to his title, however, was out of the question. The terms were probably the best Desmond could have expected, but for some reason the Countess disliked the arrangement. She suspected a trap, and since Gerald was still optimistic about foreign intervention, she persuaded him not to answer St. Leger. The indications are that she was right; Sir Warham was angling only to get Desmond into his hands. As for the Seneschal, he was desperate to save his son, and he conceded at last to remain in his own territory and outside the general warfare being waged in County Cork. Not unexpectedly Sir Warham let the boy go. He had got all that he could, more certainly than Grey had, and after all, he intended to live in the country win who would. Sir Warham, like Perrot, committed his bloodiest thoughts to paper but in action was often moderate and even humane. He clearly knew the nature of the men he was fighting and could distinguish the effective limits of a plan. He had seen them all come and go, all the Queen's Deputies and Justices, all the rebel lords, and he outlived most of them, fuming and fretting all the while. He and his kind, settled in the neighborhood of Cork, Waterford, or Dublin, were the bedrock of English Ireland, the Crown's real hope.

If Grey did not always understand St. Leger, neither did his entourage. The young men who had followed the Lord Deputy to Ireland were slow to comprehend the attitude of the old hands. And their understanding was hampered as much by their idealism as by any lack of experience.

Through them, Dublin experienced its first intellectual foment in generations, and the learned atmosphere which they encouraged within the government and the Church of England eventually persuaded Elizabeth to endow Trinity College. Lodowick Bryskett's cottage is traditionally associated with this society. There, from 1582 to 1584, the elite of the English administration, church, and army frequently gathered. The topics of conversation ranged from Plato's *Republic* to Castiglione's *Courtier*, from Greek studies to English sonnets, and underlying and unifying these concerns was the absence of Renaissance civilization in Ireland.

In a book appropriately titled *A Discourse of Civil Life*, Bryskett suggests a typical meeting. He is taking physic for a few days in the spring at his cottage, "somewhat more than a mile from Dublin," when he is visited by a troop of his friends: John Long, Archbishop of Armagh; Chief Justice Sir Robert Dillon; Sir Warham St. Leger; Captains Thomas Norris and Christopher Carleill; Edmund Spenser; and a Dublin apothecary. Ostensibly they have come to inquire why Bryskett resigned his post as Clerk of Munster, and they are told that he has had more satisfaction in this short period of leisure with his books than in all his years of service to the state. Bryskett's book is, in fact, a translation of Giraldi Cintio's treatise on the education of gentlemen, and the visit is only an excuse for introducing the text. In place of the Italian's speakers, Bryskett's dialogue substitutes his friends, and the point of the exercise is to assert that self-enlightenment and service to the state must go hand in hand. From *A Discourse* it is learned that Spenser is at work on his *Faerie Queene*, a heroical poem about the moral virtues, that Ireland is quieter because Grey "has plowed and harrowed the rough ground," and that a new nation is soon to be raised there by men educated in moral and natural philosophy. Where the soldier has stopped, the poet will now begin. The dialogue, unconstrained by the wild Celtic Wicklows visible in the South, transplants Florentine Neoplatonism to Ireland. As might be expected, the one member of the party who shows signs of discomfort, who often veers toward skepticism, is St. Leger. The scene is fictionalized, of course, but it presents an ideal of life, a belief in knowledge, rational discourse, and public service, which each of the guests would pursue in his own way. For all were to remain in Ireland, the beneficiaries of the Second Munster Plantation, and most were actively to replace the soldiers and adventurers of previous regimes.

To each of them, with the exception of Sir Warham, Grey had been either patron or mentor. They were his true legacy. He had chosen them and rewarded them and was in turn influenced by them. As Lord Deputy he might have guessed how brittle their ideals would prove, how great was the gulf between their conception of an ordered, rational universe and the mutable world of the Irish. This awareness played no small part in his own debilitation and final paralysis. Desperation is heard in his insistent pleas for recall, the desperation of a man who can no longer perceive a coherent and divine intention behind the accidents of experience. No venture into the countryside was ever more brutal or futile than Grey's last. Spenser and Bryskett accompanied him and discovered first hand just how implacable savage man could be. The cause of the expedition was a few scraps of flesh and bone found tied to a tree in Offaly. These were the remains of Captain Mackworth; the O'Connors had captured him, mutilated and flayed him alive. Mackworth had overseen the execution of prisoners in Del Oro, and the O'Connors, knowing him and waiting their opportunity, had made his end as frightful as possible. But their revenge was not the ultimate horror; it was rather the price they were willing to pay for satisfaction. By murdering Mackworth, they left their women and children open to reprisal, and they were prepared to lose heavily. While the O'Connor kern took to the bogs, Grey's horse soldiers ferreted out their families and, after riding them down as far as Tullamore, burned most of their homes behind them. His column returned to Dublin with a prize of fifty heads. Yet he had been defeated. The women and children did not matter; the O'Connors would be back, and the struggle for Offaly, like the struggle for Kerry, Limerick, or Tipperary, would begin again. These future wars the Lord Deputy left to the gentlemen in Bryskett's cottage.

In August Elizabeth summoned Grey to a conference in London. The meeting was a guise for removing the Lord Deputy without unduly embarrassing him, and shortly after he sailed with his wife, his sword of state was returned to the repository at St. Patrick's Cathedral. He never came again to Ireland, and in order to spare his reputation, the Crown refrained from immediately naming a successor. Arthur, Lord Grey de Wilton, had ten years of life left, and he spent that time largely in retirement. No offices were thereafter extended to him, and from the decayed state of his fortune, it is unlikely he could have afforded them. Eventually he consented to join the commission trying Mary, Queen of Scots, and after her execution he zealously defended William Davison's initiative in communicating her sentence. From his speech on behalf of Davison, it is apparent that his temperament had not changed. In 1588, during the summer of the Armada, he hobbled out of retirement to take part in preparations for the defense of England; he had been among the first to fight Spaniards in Ireland, and he deemed it fitting that he should fight them in England if the need arose. Yet despite his valor, a suspicion of fanaticism clung to his name. Elizabeth used him sparingly. His fervor at Smerwick and his depopulation of Munster did not suggest a man sensible to nuance. By all indication, Grey's reputation died a casualty of the Irish wars.

———◆———

Between his departure and Ormond's reinstatement as Lord General of Munster, the Desmond War continued, repetitious as ever. The *State Papers* cite the same places, the same officers and rebels, repeatedly. Youghal was besieged again; this was the fourth time, and the Geraldines, who had once taken it and twice lost it, were narrowly kept out. Under attack, Youghal sent as usual to Cork for aid and as usual was refused. Outside Cork the rebels had "come up to the very walls of the city and have carried off the linen which was drying on the hedges"; the Mayor could not spare men or munitions. Youghal sent to Waterford for help, but the dispatch riders did not get through; that town was invested by a ravenous army of beggars, who slew the riders and ate their horses. Finally, Ormond marched south in the last weeks of 1582 and succeeded in driving off the Seneschal of Imokilly and the Earl his cousin, who lost sixty gallowglass in the withdrawal. Ormond proceeded to relieve the coastal cities, by now a *pro forma* maneuver and, by reinforcing Kilmallock and Carrigafoyle, hoped to pen Desmond in Kerry for the fifth time since the war began. Famine was most acute in the West, and Butler calculated that Gerald's forces might starve there. He reestablished communications between Cork and Dublin, drove the rebels out of the Aherlow and Kilmore, and reinforced the garrison towns along the Blackwater River. Ormond was successful as usual, but there were no celebrations, no enthusiasm; the rite had been performed too many times before.

The only change in Ireland following Grey's removal was in the extent of suffering. Famine and pestilence, once confined to the South, spread now into Tipperary, Kildare, Offaly, right up to the gates of Dublin. There was a common saying in the city: "The wolf and the best rebel lodge in one inn, with one diet and one kind of bedding." Indeed, during January, 1583, wolves were seen in the streets, even in the vicinity of Dublin Castle. They entered Dublin in a heavy snowfall and subsisted through the winter on domestic animals and the unburied dead. The city was crowded with refugees, and no food surplus remained to support them. When a stable by Dublin Castle caught fire, Geoffrey Fenton's horse was burned, and before his eyes it was pulled from the flames by the people and eaten "before it was half-roasted." Vice Treasurer Wallop's horse died of sickness in the winter, and before the carcass could be removed, "it was devoured, entrails and all, without any preparation." While the populace suffered, scarcity also appeared to have affected the members of the government for the first time. Horse meat became a common staple until the discovery was made that English troops were selling their mounts to Irish butchers, who in turn fed them to the troopers' officers. Ormond was to be hampered for months by a shortage of decent cavalry mounts. Finally, it fell to the most powerful man left in Dublin to reason with the Crown. In eloquent Latin, Archbishop Loftus, the highest prelate in Ireland, wrote to Burghley advising the Queen to pardon Desmond. There might, he said, be some question of the Queen's honor if the war of Ireland was like other wars, between one prince and another, but this was against a subject, bare, rude, and savage. The only honor to be had was by healing the sores of the poor subjects. Loftus now saw the nature of the war at close hand; he was horrified, repelled, full of censure for Grey, but he was too late. Once loose, famine could not be contained easily. Years before, it had been initiated by Pelham and Ormond as a weapon of war; it was continued as such by Grey, and by now the economy of the land was irrevocably upset. The famine would continue until the population was reduced to within the limits of the food supply.

Under these conditions neither side could launch a large expedition to annihilate the other. Gerald was hard pressed to feed his family, let alone his men, and Ormond gave up all thought of pursuing him into the Mountains of Kerry. Instead, Butler took to pardoning Irishmen wherever he went. The government in Dublin argued for justice and retribution, but in the field he resorted to bribery. Purchasing loyalty invariably proved more expeditious than forcing it, and in accord with his instructions from London, he also overlooked all but the most flagrant cases of treason. As could be expected, his actions outraged English officialdom. When St. Leger learned that Ormond contemplated pardoning Desmond, he wrote expressly to the Queen, broaching his own plan for luring Gerald into the English camp, provoking him to new treasons, and beheading him. "I dare adventure the loss of one of my arms," he wrote, "which I would not willingly lose for all the lands and livings that ever Desmond had, he will, within one quarter of a year after he is so received (if the matter be well and politically handled), be wrought to enter into new treasons, and thereby apprehended, and his head cut off according to his due deserts." Due deserts or not, Elizabeth never heard of the proposal. Burghley now stood firmly behind Ormond and, knowing that he could not succeed under the aegis of Dublin, sheltered him from all meddling, intercepting the more inflammatory protests sent to the Queen. Cecil was prepared to countenance any measure, honorable or not, by which the war could be ended, but Ormond's policy of isolating Gerald from his countrymen was infinitely safer than St. Leger's scheme.

By May, 1583, Butler's patience and craft were about to bear fruit. Gerald was sealed up in Kerry; the Geraldines had endured the greatest privation for more than six months, and their confederation had begun to crack. In March Patrick Condon and more than 300 of his followers had come forward to receive pardon and protection. They were an army of scarecrows, no longer fit to fight and ready to murder their own officers rather than serve longer. Behind them came the Baron of Lixnaw with his men, Gerald MacThomas with his, and Tirlogh MacSheehy with his clan, a certain sign of collapse. All received the Queen's pardon from Butler and restoration of their properties, for the time being. Then, in late April, the Countess of Desmond obtained a twenty days' protection from Ormond. She came to negotiate her husband's surrender, but learning that no terms were to be offered him, she could not bring herself to return to the misery of his camp. She was half starved and feverish. The strain of the winter still told in her face, and those who had heard of her beauty were surprised at how old and gray she appeared. Her pride broke at last, and she surrendered in her own right to the man she likely hated above all others, her kinsman the Earl of Ormond. Nor was she ever accused of disloyalty. From their days together in St. Leger's crowded tenement to their final years in the wilderness, Eleanor endured her husband's misfortunes. It was obvious to all that she could no longer help him. The last of the Geraldine leaders probably shared her apprehension. In the first week of June the Seneschal of Imokilly came to capitulate. He had been with Gerald since the sack of Youghal in 1579; he could not longer share his cousin's faith in an imminent foreign deliverance and saved his life by a timely obeisance. John Fitzedmund Fitzgerald was the most sought-after rebel in Ireland, after Gerald, and if he could find a pardon, anyone could. Following him came an army of repenters: Lord Roche and Lord Barrymore; Thomas of Desmond; Owen MacCarthy; Owen O'Sullivan; Cormac MacDermot; the clan chieftains O'Keefe, MacAuliffe, O'Callaghan, O'Donughue, MacCarthy, MacFynnyne; the rhymer Donogh MacCrag; 100 kern; and an uncertain number of horseboys. Not all of Gerald's followers surrendered, to be sure. Goran McSweeny, the last of his gallowglass captains, would not leave him and was slaughtered as a consequence by his own men as they deserted en masse to the English. Gerald's ruin was irrevocable; too many erstwhile compatriots had joined the enemy. By July they were scouring the fastnesses they knew intimately in search of him, and the wonder is that he eluded them.

How he avoided capture during the summer or stretched his luck into the fall is not understood. Ormond was at Kilkenny, but Castlemaine, Tralee, Castleisland—the Kerry triangle—were in English hands, and week by week a net was drawn closer around Desmond. For a short time men believed he had fled to Scotland or France; that alternative was always open, but in September he descended out of the Slieve Mish—the Phantom Mountains—and pillaged the neighborhood of Ardfert. Immediately the chase was on again, until Gerald, like a wounded stag, became the sport of every peasant plowboy. Nowhere was he safe. Many times during the last four years he had purchased freedom at the expense of his tenants, and they, while no friends to the English, no longer held him in awe. As Ormond surmised, Desmond was now in more danger from simple churls and peasant opportunists than from English troops. His very need for food could trap him. Sooner or later some countryman's hunger for gold might overpower his fear, or some farmer's indignation at losing a sheep yield information. The finest of the Geraldines, James Fitzmaurice, died at Barrington Bridge because he stole a peasant's horse; his cousin, the Great Rebel Earl, was to fall because he stole a cow and a basket of clothes.

On November 9 Gerald dispatched a small party of his followers to the southern shore of Tralee Bay. They were instructed to scour the neighborhood for cattle and food and to steal what woolens they could find against the onset of winter. Desmond remained behind, hidden in the Glanageenty Woods, his joints swollen with dampness and cold. The party made their way to the house of a small farmer, Maurice O'Moriarty, and, breaking down his door in his absence, despoiled his house, his wife and children, and his stable. In an affidavit filled out before English officials the following morning, O'Moriarty claimed the loss of several cows, sundry housewares, and all the clothing belonging to his family. He was especially outraged that his wife was left naked by the robbers, though there was no mention that she was molested. The Clan O'Moriarty was never faithful to Gerald, and now with the permission of Sir William Stanley at Castlemaine, Maurice led a score of kern and a half dozen soldiers in pursuit of the thieves. More than a lost cow must have led the O'Moriartys into the Slieve Mish; in the heart of those treacherous mountains lay a fortune in head money, and Maurice probably resolved to have it before the English.

The Slieve Mish Mountains are famous for thick mists. At all seasons of the year the mists swirl inland from the Atlantic to fill the deep glens and marshy bottoms. Fogbound and labyrinthine, the hills still have about them a curious insubstantiality. From time immemorial the Phantom Mountains were considered the refuge of gods and heroes; they had been sacred to the ancient Celts, and if they were peopled by ghosts during Gerald's age, they were also filled with very real desperadoes. O'Moriarty would not have entered them without a large company of his family, and even at that, his men were visibly nervous. Throughout November 10 they climbed the wooded slopes, while storm clouds seemed to hover just over their heads. The weather changed quickly from a warm humidity to a chilling dankness, until around midnight the rain stopped and the air grew clear and icy. By then they were in the lee of Caherconree Mountain and

Baurtregaum, in the Glanageenty Woods, all told perhaps six miles from Tralee. O'Moriarty climbed to the top of a rise ahead of his men and, looking down into a glen, spied a cabin and the embers of a campfire. He had found Desmond's last hiding place.

The party surrounded the cabin during the night. At first light they rushed the hut and, breaking through the door, took everyone inside unawares. It was still dark inside, however, and in the confused struggle, several persons escaped, including a priest. When candles were finally lit, the hut contained only a woman, a child, and an old man, half awake and terrified. It seems they were not sure who the Earl of Desmond was. The old man, crippled, his black hair almost gray, cowered in a corner, and Daniel O'Kelly, trying to make him speak, broke his arm with the flat of his sword. All at once the man cried, "I am the Earl of Desmond. Save my life!" "Thou hast killed thyself long ago," Owen O'Moriarty replied, "and now thou shalt be prisoner to the Queen's Majesty and the Earl of Ormond." The exchange is recorded in virtually all contemporary accounts. Yet whether the O'Moriartys or Daniel O'Kelly were responsible for what now followed is still questioned. As they dragged Desmond out of the hut, the glen seemed preternaturally quiet. They had no way of knowing how many servants the Earl had or how soon his friends might return to free him. Gerald could not walk, his arm was smashed and bleeding, and the O'Moriartys would have to carry him down the steep slopes. And so in fear at what they had done and remembering the dogged devotion of Geraldines to their leader, either O'Kelly or Owen O'Moriarty cut off Desmond's head on the spot and, leaving the bleeding trunk behind, carried it down through the woods to Castlemaine.

On behalf of Her Majesty's government, Sir William Stanley accepted the trophy and paid out 1000 pounds in silver to Maurice O'Moriarty. Maurice was to live out his life surrounded by cattle, but his family has borne the disgrace of his act to this day. The head itself was sent from Castlemaine to Kilkenny, for the Earl of Ormond's viewing, and from there it was forwarded to London and the Queen. Legend holds that she spent the morning sitting quietly and looking at it, before having it impaled on London Bridge. Gerald's body, however, was never found. Cork prepared to receive and display it, but friendly hands hid it away and eventually deposited it in a nearby chapel where only Fitzgeralds are thought to lie. As for those Geraldines who remained, most found their way home, for the Desmond Wars were over at last.

Surely there was mourning for the passing of the Earl, but such grief showed itself in secret. Publicly there was celebration. At Cork, in January, 1584, the populace still gave thanks for Gerald's end. In Dublin, Waterford, Limerick, and Galway municipal ceremonies commemorated the

Queen's triumph, and contemporary letters and statements make clear that most civilized men, English or Irish, were glad of Desmond's death. The Geraldines had kept Ireland in a state of war and disorder for more than twenty-five years; they had brought untold suffering to thousands by imposing the worst devastation in Ireland's history. Those citizens of Munster who had survived famine and plague, the battles and years of civil war had no choice but to pin their hopes on Elizabeth and on "the swelling act of her imperial theme."

But in the years of peace which followed, and then in the aftermath of the next great uprising, Gerald's place among his people was recognized. The great lords of the North had stood by indifferently during his struggle; soon they were to inherit his cause and discover in their defeat how his death was also theirs. Gerald was already obsolete by the time of his murder; the Ireland he had fought to preserve was already dead. Celtic society in the South had been destroyed; the Norman lords who had been the mainstays of this world were now gone. There might be small risings and intermittent outbreaks during the next few decades, but Munster would never again, in the sixteenth century or any other, seriously threaten the Crown.

The legends of the Earl of Desmond do not belong to the healing years immediately following his defeat. They were heard in the next century, from the next generation, and they are part of a litany of resistance still heard in the country. Father Dominicus De Rosario O'Daly, the son of that O'Daly who long served Gerald, was to write Desmond's threnody a half century later in Lisbon. As a historian of fact, O'Daly is among the worst, but feeling the passion of those Geraldines of whom he writes, his was the last voice of the rebels: "God, who knows my heart, now sees that I cannot speak of the ruin which came upon them without tears and groans. For, let me ask, who is there—a true Irishman—who can listen to the story of their destruction, or mention it, without bitter grief? Ever were the Geraldines loved in Ireland, and venerated for their devotion to the faith; but particularly by those who value their religion and country. And how could I, who am an Irishman—and the son of that Irishman, who, leaving all that he held dear, even from his boyhood, sat by the hearth of these Desmonds, and when he grew up was made a depository of their confidence, held command under them in their last wars, and saw the slain Geraldines with his own eyes—how, I say, can I, the son of such a father, commemorate them without sigh and groan, unless I be lost to all honourable sensibility."

Gerald became at last a patriot to his people, an early fighter for liberty and nationhood. But the other Earl of Desmond, the romantic rebel, the magnanimous lord, lived on as long. In 1926 a folklorist recorded among the peasants of Kerry a curious belief: if on a dark night in November, in the glen below Slew-Logher, a peasant should be given the sight, he will see a company of silver horsemen galloping through the night. At their head rides the Great Rebel Earl himself, garbed all in silver brocade and astride a mighty white horse. And should he pass the man and should the man ask to shoe his horse, the Earl will laugh his laugh and throw him a gorgeous purse. In the purse will be found 1000 silver pieces, the price Sir William Stanley paid to Maurice O'Moriarty, and when the vision is gone, the money will remain.

KILCOLMAN, 1588

The Broken Land

From the crest of the Ballyhoura Hills it is possible to see for miles across the fields of central Munster. Southward the Nagle Mountains appear in clear relief, and on the plain below, the River Awbeg winds through meadows and villages to a confluence with the Blackwater a few miles below Mallow. In 1583 the meadows were empty, and the villages ruined. Since the plain lay astride the main route from Cork to Limerick, it had been the site of fierce fighting. A prospect of utter desolation in the aftermath of the wars, the Vale of the Awbeg was still fertile farmland. Its potential in grain alone was valued by the government at several thousand pounds per annum, for all that the ground had never seen a plow. For three generations the Clan McSheehy had herded cattle beside the rivers and hunted in the forests. They had tilled the soil indifferently. Now as their remnants found a way home after defeat, they were shut out of the vale. The McSheehys, who had held their land from the Earls of Desmond for 100 years, spent the harsh winter of 1583 shivering in the Ballyhouras and watching English surveyors at work on the plain below.

Elsewhere in Munster the scene was repeated. For as the Earl of Desmond's vast palatinate passed to the Crown, there was need to survey his property and reapportion it. The Desmond Wars had cost Elizabeth a half million pounds. If she were to recoup her losses in taxable income, Desmond's domains would have to be resettled with English families. Reliable Irish families were out of the question; in Munster too few remained to restore the land to either pasturage or tillage. In Counties Limerick, Cork, and Kerry many estates were escheated, the male line dead or attainted, and even in areas peripheral to the rebellion large tracts lay waste. The Second Munster Plantation, as the solution became known, was not born of aggression like the First. The scheme was a tacit admission that victory had been bought too dear. So far as she was able, the Queen hoped to make amends to her Irish subjects. Her intention was to rebuild the towns and villages and to restore the economy of the land. Ormond, Kildare, the hereditary lords opposed her in this; so within their power did the evicted Geraldines, and yet from place to place her colonies took root. The most famous colony flourished in the Vale of the Awbeg and along the Blackwater River, and there among disgruntled Fitzgibbons and Roches, dispossessed gallowglass and churls, the future of English Munster was decided over the next two decades.

At the moment of Gerald's death, no Lord Deputy was in Ireland. As early as 1582, men spoke of Perrot as a likely nominee, not least because he liked the Irish and knew them well. But between Desmond's fall and Perrot's arrival, it fell to Wallop and Archbishop Loftus to begin the reconstruction of the South. Prelate and financier confronted two difficulties: neither had possessed the temerity to go into the countryside for years, and neither had been apprised which Irish were pardoned and which not. Eleanor, Countess of Desmond, was resettled near Dublin on a small pension, there to await the Queen's further pleasure. The Seneschal of Imokilly was allowed his terms, so were the Barrys, but old reprobates like Patrick Condon escaped the gallows only through Ormond's intercession with Wallop and Loftus. As for the McSweenys and McSheehys, they were conspicuously missing from the lists of the forgiven. Allowed to sink into the sea of "mere" Irish spreading across the land in search of food, these gallowglass families suffered most for Desmond's defeat. In 1584 Irish policy was being made in London, not Dublin, and although reports concerning the devastation in Ireland were embarrassing, constructive proposals for alleviating the misery were tempered by a lasting fear of gallowglass and Gaelic savagery. Ten years later the word "gallowglass" was still synonymous with ferocity. The poet Michael Drayton, praising Irish bards, claims for them the power to "Call back the stiff-neck'd rebels from exile, / And mollify the slaught'ring gallowglass." Twenty years later the image still works its terror; Shakespeare's Macbeth begins his bloody rise with victory over a gallowglass captain, who ". . . from the western isles / Of Kerns and Gallowglasses is supplied; /

And Fortune, on his damned quarrel smiling, / Show'd like a rebel's whore." Memory of the Desmond gallowglass faded slowly; they were to frighten children for generations, their name invoked in soldier stories and old wives' tales. The lords and chieftains of Munster found pardon; their soldiers did not.

Prejudice played no small part in Whitehall's proscription of the gallowglass, but in Dublin, where enforcement began, more cogent reasons were found for their suppression. Gallowglass and kern constituted the marshal class of Gaelic Ireland and, because they lived principally for war, tended to consume the substance of the land without contribution. Twenty years of strife had offered them ample scope for their profession, and by now many were unsuited to other livelihoods. They excelled at raiding, were maintained by coyne and livery in the interim, and, war failing, resorted to extortion. The practice of coynage set them on the necks of the peasantry, who were made responsible for boarding their men and stabling their animals without recompense. And though any petty chieftain could field a force by this means, his land was stripped of its produce and eaten up in the process. The English profited from the system more than they cared to admit; Ormond's Irish companies were supported by the method. But in peacetime the government was understandably determined to abolish coynage and the warrior caste it sustained. Unfortunately, by banishing the gallowglass to the woods and mountains, it also banished the most enterprising Irish.

Argument was made that the McSheehys and McSweenys were not typical gallowglass, that they were respectable Irish families, only gallowglass in their origin. Since they had served the Desmonds for generations, they had long ago put aside Highland manners and become landholders in their own right. In his travels, Vice Treasurer Wallop observed that much of the Awbeg Valley belonged legitimately to the McSheehys, while the depopulated condition of Kerry reflected high mortality among the McSweenys. Nonetheless, the government saw a principle at stake. The suppression of these families was intended to be symbolic, a lesson to all mercenaries who had fattened on the wars in the South. When the government's surveyors found their way into the Vale of the Awbeg, they drove Tirlogh MacSheehy and his people out of Mallow and into the hills. When Murrogh McSheehy descended to raid a supply convoy near the town a few months later, he was captured and given a life sentence in Dublin Castle. Simultaneously, the few McSweenys remaining in Kerry were driven into Connaught. And there, in 1586, Richard Bingham, Maltby's successor, slaughtered 1000 Scots gallowglass who had ventured into Ireland for the spring fighting. This massacre, among the worst during Elizabeth's reign, was carried out with such cold-blooded thoroughness among men, women, and children that Scots gallowglass were not seen again in Ireland for many seasons. Even his own countrymen decried Bingham's act. Detractors compared him with the sadistic first Earl of Essex, who, ten years before, annihilated gallowglass on Rathlin Island amid circumstances of peculiar horror. But Bingham was not without defense. In his own cause he argued: "The people of Connaught, for every small trifle, are daily suggesting that they are intolerably oppressed and extorted upon. . . . By degrees they must be raised from want, and by the rigor of her Majesty's rule also held to the course, so that by having too little, the country be not waste, and by having too much, the people may not rebel. My meaning in all that I do is rather to better their estate than to make it worse." Bingham was an effective, though brutal, governor, and a strong case was made for his methods. Mercenaries were a perennial scourge; their infiltration was difficult to deter, and their incursions were more often halted by gold than by battle. As Lord President of Connaught, Bingham had to choose between meeting their extortion or meeting them in the field. And by striking them as hard as he could, he bought time to return his devastated province to order. Wallop, the pragmatist, approved his determination; Loftus, the moralist, endorsed it, and on this single point of agreement—an end to coynage and all vestiges of heroic society in Munster—the foundation was laid for the Second Plantation.

That plantation would endure, and even in some respects succeed, but the Irish displaced by its founding would nurse their grievances in the hiding places of the South. During the next fifteen years their shadow fell frequently on the rebuilt towns and villages. Their story, obscure in detail, underlies that of the Munster settlers. They are the muted background against which English life appears, the hostile setting, the vague threat. In the Valley of the Awbeg, Spenser was to be crossed by the McSheehys several times. He learned to fear them as he feared the wolves of Kilmore and to watch for them along the borders of his fields. Thomas Norris, his friend and neighbor, found his cattle rustled by them, his servants abused and intimidated. From Killarney to Youghal, virtually the entire length of the Blackwater, settlers grew inured to such harassment. Perpetual apprehension came to be the price paid for life in Munster, yet none appreciated at the time how truly grave the peril would become. In 1584, as the Crown dismembered and distributed the worldly possessions of the Rebel Earl, few looked for danger. Sir Edward Fitton, destined to be a settler, rode with the surveyors and sounded the first of many warnings to go unheeded. "The country is generally wasted," he wrote, "but yet not a pile or castle is found in any place but what is full of the poorest creatures that ever I saw, so lean for want of food as wonderful, and yet so idle that they will not work, because they are descended either of kern, horsemen, or gallowglass, all three the very subversion of this land." If the English government had sought to suppress warrior society in Ireland, it had only managed to submerge it in a sea of Gaelic indigence. Upheaval thereby became inevitable, and in the last years of Elizabeth's reign, when the storm broke, settlers like Spenser and Norris were suddenly amazed to see armed men spring up out of their plowlands of golden wheat.

Wallop and Loftus, however, could not concern themselves with distant threats. In the days between Desmond's death and Perrot's arrival they were fortunate to hold the government together at all. Their first priority was to ascertain the true dimensions of Gerald's property. Each of his castles, homes, and villages stood in need of appraisal; benefices within his gift were counted and reverted to the Crown with their fees, and almost everywhere the legal grounds for his ownership remained to be demonstrated. Three years would pass before the Earl of Desmond could be formally attainted and his lands escheated by act of Parliament, and during that period the litigation never ceased. Fortunes were made at law before any English undertaker occupied a square yard of forfeited seigniory. The victors had not intended to forgo the spoils, but Gerald's domains were a patchwork of ancient grants and recent confiscations. Survivors of the First Munster Plantation, Carew's followers, had lost heavily and were entitled to restitution. Loyal Irish, who had fled their lands and could not be denied under the law, contested thousands of acres, while Ormond, Kildare, and Tyrone demanded large tracts for services rendered. Most of the decade would be spent untangling these claims, for the courts were slow, and Elizabeth involved herself deeply in the details of substance and revenue. The government had little wish to expedite settlements which might alter the balance of power among the great lords or the surviving chieftaincies. Therefore, as late as 1590 grants of Desmond property were still being made to settlers and claimants.

Wallop was well qualified to administer matters of property. During his interregnum the surveying went forward, and more than 100 suits were adjudicated. For himself he contrived to be awarded the barony of Coshma, including the venerable Desmond seats of Askeaton, Croom, and Adare, and on many of Grey's adherents he settled favorable awards. Bryskett fared handsomely with grants in the vicinity of Enniscorthy; Sir William Stanley received several thousand acres in the vicinity of Tralee; Spenser acquired the prebendary of Effin near Kilfinnane; and Bingham, in addition to the presidency of Connaught, was presented properties in the neighborhood of Limerick. Where possible, the Vice Treasurer advanced those with experience, who would not shrink from stern measures. He had always preferred Grey's decisiveness to Ormond's equivocation and Perrot's leniency. And as a result, those like Geoffrey Fenton, who had dissented from Grey's policies, were settled in Ireland by Archbishop Loftus, not Wallop. There was more than enough to go around, however, and Wallop was constrained wherever the Queen interfered. On her instructions, Sir Walter Raleigh, newly knighted, was given the largest estate of all, initially 42,000 acres between Lismore and Youghal on the Blackwater River. Sir Christopher Hatton, who had never been in Ireland but had danced his way into the Queen's heart, received 12,000 acres between Dungarvan and Youghal. The boundaries of these estates were finally set in 1587, after Perrot's arrival, and it is known that the certifying parties were led by Sir John Norris, his brother Thomas, and Edmund Spenser.

By all accounts, Wallop was a meticulous administrator, a counting-house lawyer, experienced in the disposal of wealth. But as a Lord Justice, he set common law in Ireland back a hundred years. The case in point ranks among the most bizarre in English legal history; it is the last instance of trial by combat in the British Isles and violates every principle for which the English fought the Desmond War. The once-mighty tribe of the Leinster O'Connors had fallen very low, owing no doubt to Grey's efforts. Yet even in their reduced state, they fought among themselves, those who had remained marginally loyal to the Crown opposing those who had followed Baltinglas into revolt. Their disputes resulted in the famous trial. For Teig McGilpatrick, loyalist, was accused by Connor MacCormac, rebel, of murdering clansmen already granted protection by the government. Teig retorted that these men had begun plotting new rebellions as soon as they were pardoned. He declined to compensate their families. Ordinarily his decision would have resulted in feud, but since a violation of a government decretal was at issue, Connor resolved to test the law. He hauled his kinsman before Wallop and Loftus and accused him of violating the peace. What Connor could not have expected was bad faith. But no sooner had he arrived in Dublin than Sir Nicholas White persuaded him to charge Teig with high treason. Meanwhile, Wallop persuaded Teig to charge Connor with high treason. An appeal of treason was thus technically constituted, and for this, both men were told that trial by battle was the proper remedy. Not surprisingly the ardor of the litigants began to cool, and in order to hold them to their resolve, the combat was fixed for the next day.

Before Teig and Connor had time to withdraw their charges, they found themselves entering the lists. The inner yard of Dublin Castle was got up in medieval display for the occasion, and on a dais above the courtyard perched the Lords Justices. The galleries were packed with military officers, their wives, and leading citizens of Dublin. The combatants, who were stripped to their shirts, were allowed only sword, shield, and skullcap. They were led to stools on opposite sides of the lists and searched for hidden weapons by Secretary Fenton. They must have awakened suddenly to the gravity of the situation, for their protests were clearly heard in Gaelic. The tribunal, however, ignored them, and after Wallop apologized for the shortness of time, the pleadings were read, and the trumpets sounded. At first they circled each other warily. The crowd goaded them, sensing their hesitation. Then, after several minutes, Sir Lucas Dillon separated them and charged both with mocking the Queen's justice. Either they fought to the death to prove their innocence, or both would be punished as traitors. The struggle now became one of self-preservation, and both men fought in earnest. Connor, the smaller of the two, was wounded twice in the leg and once in the eye and, attempting to close, found his adversary too strong for him. Teig, who had held back as long as he could, was torn along the ribs, and as Connor pressed him back the length of the blood-soaked yard, he struck as hard as he could, tearing the sword out of his adversary's grip. Once having stunned and disarmed his accuser, Teig, hurt and blinded by fury, cut off Connor's head with his own sword and presented it on the point to the Lords Justices. The crowd cheered wildly at this proper Roman display, but Fenton, who sent the bloody sword as a souvenir to Leicester, expressed the government's true opinion: "Teig was wounded but not mortally, more's the pity . . . many wish her Majesty had the same end of all the O'Connors in Ireland as she has had of this Connor."

There are not many moments in the story of Elizabethan Ireland more shameful than the trial of Teig and Connor. Even Grey, despite his harshness, would not have countenanced this perversion of justice. And Perrot, who resorted often to questionable means, heard of the spectacle with disgust. Yet nothing better illustrates the moral ravages of the Irish war. Within the Dublin Pale, where memories of sickness and famine had not faded, the outlandish O'Connors were despised, and even moderates such as Fenton and Loftus were willing to warp all principles to be rid of them. Forgotten was the fact that Desmond would have settled the dispute just as they had.

Though Wallop looked forward to settling all disputes among the natives by similar trials, he was destined to disappointment. The Irish may have loved heroic combats among themselves, but no bards sang the contest between Teig and Connor; no genealogists glorified the line of McGilpatricks. Everywhere in the Gaelic world Teig and Connor were seen as dupes and reviled for their credulity in trusting Saxon justice. The fighting clans made no further representations before the Queen's Bench. In fact, they practically vanished from the government's sight.

Even Wallop knew by 1584 that Munster could not be ruled effectively from Dublin Castle. With the close of the war, Elizabeth had cut her garrisons in Ireland more than 50 percent. Government might go on regardless in Dublin, but little news was heard from the South or West. Loftus could not conveniently leave the city, and Wallop, burdened by age and infirmities, had no desire to travel South frequently. Communications with the countryside, even with parties of surveyors, were therefore tenuous, and the Lords Justices were urged by Whitehall to appoint a special traveling commissioner. Here Wallop called upon an old friend, an experienced Irish hand, Valentine Brown, to begin the labors. And had Brown not been an absurd choice, he would probably not be known now to history. The new commissioner weighed between twenty and twenty-two stone, or approximately 300 pounds. He could kill a good horse in a day's hard travel, and no axle in Dublin could stand both his weight and the terrible Irish roads. Mules were to be Valentine Brown's best mounts, and the sight of him mired in bogs and astride the backs of exhausted animals became the joke of the day. It may be said for Valentine that he reached the South and, with the help of Surveyor General Alford and auditors Jenyson and Peyton, began calculating revenues. He was a man of long experience in the English revenue business—one reason for his selection—and Wallop kindly overlooked his shortcomings. "He hath," wrote the Vice Treasurer, "been sundry times bogged, yet hath gone better through with it than might be imagined so corpulent a man of his years would have been able."

Brown was evidently a man of gargantuan appetite, hardly a welcome visitor to a land still in the grip of famine, and the growling of his belly is almost heard in his reports. Kerry, he wrote, was a vacant desert; nothing remained on which to found a colony, and new settlers would be required in wholesale lots. Killarney, though devastated, was a most rich and pleasing land. The Awbeg offered fine pasturage. Muskerry was in the grip of the scoundrel Cavanaughs and the delinquent White Knight, but application of English law might yet work wonders. Brown formulated his findings at great cost to himself, for everywhere he spread his tents and tables the Irish crawled out of hiding to beg his scraps, and he fed them. At one point more than 100 people supported themselves on his generosity and followed him everywhere. He was the representative of an oppressive regime, but no evidence lingers to prove him hardhearted.

Not only did Valentine Brown lay the foundations for the Munster Plantation, but his heirs continued to inhabit the land, becoming in their own right a dynasty. Almost a century later he was abused in the verses of the great Gaelic poet Egan O'Rahilly, who, seeking a cause for the long eclipse of Irish nobility, turned on Brown. Folk memory had doubtless exaggerated Brown's role, yet the bitterness of the confiscations is still fresh in the poet's comparison of the fat money-counter with the heroic Desmonds and Burkes:

> *That my old bitter heart was pierced in this black doom,*
> *That foreign devils have made our land a tomb,*
> *That the sun that was Munster's glory has gone down*
> *Has made me a beggar before you, Valentine Brown.*
> *That royal Cashel is bare of house and guest,*
> *That Brian's turreted home is the otter's nest,*
> *That the kings of the land have neither land nor crown*
> *Has made me a beggar before you, Valentine Brown.*

"Valentine Brown" is not one man, but several Valentines descended from the first. In O'Rahilly's eyes, they are a base and common line and have desecrated the home of Brian Boru. Closer to the actual moments of the Desmond disaster is the anguished cry of Fearflatha O'Gnive, greatest of the Desmond bards, who perished in the wilderness of Wallop's Munster:

> *The Gael cannot tell,*
> *In the uprooted wildwood*
> *And red ridgy dell,*
> *The old nurse of his childhood.*
> *The nurse of his youth*
> *Is in doubt as she views him,*
> *If the wan wretch, in truth,*
> *Be the child of her bosom.*
> *We starve by the board,*
> *And we thirst amid wassail—*
> *For the guest is the lord,*
> *And the host is the vassal.*
> *Through the woods let us roam,*
> *Through the wastes wild and barren;*
> *We are strangers at home!*
> *We are exiles in Erin!*

The lament was by no means novel in Irish verse; conquest and incursions had always given life to its conventions, but during the 1580s there was a truly unprecedented outpouring of indignation and sorrow. Conditions of life in Munster had never been worse, and Munster was the spiritual home of Irish bards. Yet what is heard in O'Gnive's poetry is the ritual strengthening of national awareness. If Gerald could not unify his people in their time of need, the depredations following his death did so.

Certainly Munster had become a political vacuum into which the Tudor imperium could expand at will. Scotland's turn would come later; Virginia's later still. The end of the war awakened long-dormant hopes of shireland in Ireland, and efforts were intensified to span St. George's Channel with one ruler and one law. Theoretically, Elizabeth ruled one domain; in actuality her territorial fortunes fluctuated. Not long after she ascended the throne, England lost Calais, its last possession in France. Subsequent fighting on the Continent was done in support of allies, not territorial aggrandizement. It was really not until 1584 that Elizabeth even began to grasp full control of her inherited possessions. English monarchs had styled themselves rulers of France and Ireland since the reign of Henry II; France was lost irrevocably, and only now could the title to Ireland be substantiated in revenues as well as heraldry. The Imperial Queen is worshiped during the 1580s as Gloriana, Empress of the West; Cynthia, Goddess of the Oceans; Astraea, Goddess of Justice—these are Elizabeth's symbolic persons, and about her is raised the myth of a new West, a counterbalance to Rome and its corrupted Empire. The conquest of Munster did not create these symbols; they were present from the first, inspired by the millenarianism of the extreme Protestants. For men of Stubbs's persuasion, Gerald's fall was more than a political development; it was a sign. The mishaps of the war were forgotten, and Spain's humiliation at Smerwick became confirmation of divine grace. For a short time the recalcitrant Celts were truly believed to have learned the errors of their ways, and the celebration of progress is never more gorgeous than in William Camden's commemoratory verses *Hibernia*, a Latin panegyric written expressly for Elizabeth. Ireland speaks:

> *The golden age of the primeval world is born again to me.*
> *I strip me of my forest ways and am no longer wild in my manners.*
> *Leinster claps her hands now that her farms are secure;*
> *And Connaught surrenders her swords to control of law;*
> *And joyful Munster beats her battle-axes into sickles;*
> *Shaggy-haired Ulster finally learns to become gentle;*
> *Meath runs riot throughout with welcome fruits for me.*
> *Keep you these things moving forward; do not let them slip back:*
> *Do not afflict us with envy in these increasing joys.*

Properly, the Queen answers in the persona of Jove: "Lay aside your fears conceived by a trembling mind; / Hold back now the tears, and expect deities favorable / Towards your pious prayers; for the coming day / And a happier hour will bring forth what you seek."

———◆———

What the Crown brought forth in Ireland was easily the most ambitious resettlement ever undertaken. Compared with Carew's halting and haphazard adventure, the Second Munster Plantation was to become a consuming mission, conceived in imperial might, and implemented by the full efforts of the English nation. The dissension of earlier years had vanished. Burghley no longer objected, as he had in 1579, that the Irish quagmire might swallow men and wealth. His fears had been justified; his worst predictions had come true. At issue now was not blame. The Desmonds were dead, and to question why they had been driven into revolt could not restore the land to self-sufficiency. Farsighted statesmen were convinced that Spain was arming an armada for a full-scale invasion of England. The time and circumstances of the attack were not yet clear, but England could not afford a hostile and undefended Ireland at its back. In a sense, events had overtaken Cecil; by 1584 his habits of mind were changing. Henceforth he voted with Walsingham and Leicester, conscious as they were of the growing danger and knowing that his friend Camden was right: "Keep you these things moving forward; do not let them slip back."

Over the next two years the Privy Council sent many letters into the shires advertising the benefits of transplantation. The appeals were directed especially at younger sons, gentlemen of good families, who might prosper through the large seigniories being dispensed by the Crown. A letter forwarded to certain Somersetshire gentlemen is typical: "Her Majesty has entered into consideration of some plot for the repeopling of such parts of Munster Ireland, as are now in her possession. The plot offers many advantages to the younger children, brethren and kinsfolk of gentlemen of good families, and those of inferior calling and degrees. We therefore have made choice of you to treat with such of that county of Somerset as you find able and willing to accept and undertake the same, and have given order to John Popham, Attorney-General of England, to confer with you therein." Appeal to the shires was only the start of the government's campaign to promote settlement in Ireland. Numerous tracts were commissioned to explain the advantages to interested parties, and not a few of these appear laughable in light of Irish realities. Robert Payne, who wrote the best-known *Brief Description of Munster,* praised the local Irish in a vein of naive optimism: "The better sort of Irish are very civil, hospitable and honestly given and bring up their children to learning. They keep faith, are quick-witted and of good bodily constitution, and form themselves daily more and more after English manners. Nothing is more pleasing to them than to hear of good Justices placed amongst them." As a description of Dublin's citizens, or Cork's, a case might be made for Payne's claims, but as an introduction to the redoubtable McSheehys, McSweenys, Cavanaughs, and O'Connors, nothing could have been more misleading. Payne is a reliable authority on many details of the Munster Plantation, but his inveterate hyperbole in selling the scheme to English yeomen and artisans resulted inevitably in disillusionment.

Payne's efforts were aimed at bringing bakers, brewers, carpenters, smiths, coopers, and masons into Ireland. Ordinary Englishmen were intended to form the bedrock of the colony and were promised handsome livings, while the landed classes were offered other incentives. "A Note of the Benefit that may grow in short time to the younger Houses of Gentlemen" advised on the subject of rents and export of surplus: "The gentleman undertaker to be the chief lord of so great a seigniory or parish, and to have the manrode [homage] of so many families, and the disposing of so many good holdings, as the greatest portion set down in her Majesty's plot doth offer, is a thing fit for gentlemen of good behavior and credit, and not for any man of inferior calling. To have the royalties and perquisites of courts within the whole, will be no doubt, a matter of good benefit to him in time to come, then to have 100 pounds per annum clear of revenue, to be paid yearly, as the Queen's Majesty's rent is paid, and yet with good content to the taker, is a thing very easy to be performed. . . . It is to be considered, the first year's charge overpassed, he may have the second year, corn and cattle sufficient for him and his family to spend, whereby he may be at no charge; and the third year, he will have to spare both corn, cattle, work, etc., which he may find a vent for at all times, either in England or other countries to his great benefit." Buried in the promises of this tract was the requirement that any gentleman availing himself of the Queen's offer pay to her an annual rent of 100 pounds, and although he must support himself during his first year, by the second his lands would sustain him, and by the third he would be clearing a tidy profit. What the Crown stood to gain by this arrangement was apparent: substantial rents; cheap imports; and an Anglicized Ireland. The society destined to take root in Munster was to be a mirror image of England's own.

Elizabeth played an active part in defining the organization and statutes of her new colony. First, she decreed "that all the lands within the Province of Munster which ought to come to her hands by forfeiture, escheat, or concealment, shall be divided into seigniories of 12,000, 8,000, 6,000 and 4,000 acres, according to the plots which shall be signed by her Majesty." The Queen herself would sign all titles to fee farm and seigniory. In view of the unusual devastation of some countryside, she established a schedule of varying rents: Limerick to pay 62 pounds per annum; Connello, 75 pounds; and Kerry and Desmond on account of their great fertility, 100 pounds. Concerning protection, she promised "that for seven years next coming the undertakers shall be defended with garrisons at her Majesty's charge, unless in the meantime it be thought fit by her Majesty or desired by the colonies to have them removed." Finally, to preserve the English nature and composition of the plantation, Elizabeth stipulated "that the heads of every family shall be born of English parents, and the heirs female, inheritable to any the same lands, shall marry with none but with persons born of English parents. . . . no mere Irish are to be permitted in any family there." Besides marriage with the Irish, it was also forbidden "to make any estate" to "mere" Irish, that is, to rent lands to them, employ them, or shelter them. The Munster Plantation was conceived as a racially exclusive colony.

Those English officials who had served in Ireland were, of course, the principal beneficiaries of the Queen's largess. They often remained in an official capacity and involved themselves in county life. Grandees who had never lived in Ireland and received large grants were almost invariably absentee landlords. But the English country gentleman, much sought, hardly came at all. So forbidding was Ireland's reputation and so widespread rumors of rebellion and racial discord that many younger sons would rather take their chances at home or on the Continent than lose everything in a vain gamble on Munster. Some few brave yeomen ventured over, but few stayed long. The upshot was that those English who stayed were compelled to employ the Irish. Elizabeth's statute against intermarriage was more honored in the breach than the keeping, and before the decade was out, many English manors were peopled with mixed families, even occasional gallowglass. Though mutual dependence was probably wholesome, the laws had not changed. Whitehall was to persist in the fiction that the English colony was self-reliant when, in fact, it was not and never would be. By 1592, at which time settlement had largely taken place, the list of active undertakers read like a roll call of Grey's army. Others had come and gone; official Ireland remained. In County Waterford, Raleigh and Hatton continued to hold the largest seigniories. In Kerry, Sir Edward Denny and Sir William Herbert dominated the scene. In Cork, Sir Warham St. Leger, Hugh Cuffe, Sir Thomas Norris, and Edmund Spenser were the principal settlers. In Limerick, Sir William Courtney, Francis Barkley, and the commandant of Kilmallock, Sir George Bourchier, led the county, while in Tipperary, the Earl of Ormond held everything. By then only 200,000 of Desmond's 800,000 acres had been resettled.

When Sir John Perrot arrived in Dublin on June 2, 1584, he brought many reservations concerning the Munster plan. Perrot was a logical choice for Lord Deputy; he had served as a Lord Justice before, he had been President of Munster most recently, and he was by far Elizabeth's most experienced Irish campaigner. He knew enough to anticipate resistance from the Irish, but he was also worried about the rapaciousness of his countrymen. To Perrot, with his affinity for the unexpected and unorthodox, Grey had been an inflexible ideologue and Wallop a mere functionary. So far as Perrot was concerned, the Irish stood more in need of protection than the English. The new Lord Deputy was as volatile as ever. Over sixty-five and long past rigorous service, he still loved a good fight. And he was to have one, not with the Irish, but with his own countrymen.

His first summer in Dublin saw the promulgation of new edicts. Those who recalled his proclamation of 1570, prohibiting bards, Brehons, native dress, and Gaelic, were amazed to learn that no peasant was henceforth to be called a churl, that no churl was to be a serf, or to receive unchristian punishment from his master. In the future the Irish peasant would be known as a husbandman or, where applicable, a franklin or yeoman. Not only was this sound English practice, fully consistent with an Anglicized Ireland, but it aimed to uproot an old oppression. Previous Lord Deputies had claimed to fight the Desmonds and their ilk in defense of the common people, but Perrot was the first to initiate reform. Moreover, he offered his new measures in a manner and setting flattering to the Irish. According to an ancient custom of Irish Kings, a general hosting of the countryside was held between August 10 and September 7 of every year, culminating at Tara in a meeting of all estates. In 1584 the Lords Tyrone, Ormond, Barrymore, and Mountgarret signed orders empowering Perrot to perform such a hosting, and in September at Tara he delivered his judgments to the people and formally assumed control of the government. Although Perrot's gesture was subsequent to his official installation at St. Patrick's Cathedral, many English were offended by the outlandishness of his behavior and its hint of "going native," or "degeneracy" as they called it. Archbishop Loftus smelled Popery or worse in his act, and to be sure, Perrot possessed an uncommon appreciation of pagan rites. But others saw positive aspects in the Lord Deputy's approach; Fenton wrote: "he is affable and pleasing, seeking by good means to recover the hearts of the people that were somewhat estranged, quick and industrious, careful of her Majesty's profit, sincere, just, and no respecter of persons." Indeed, Perrot was no respecter of persons or rank. This man who had pursued Fitzmaurice, fought John of Desmond and Imokilly, was not intimidated by clerics and clerks. Wallop was soon in despair over him, but recalling "the Deputy's passionate disposition," shrank from confrontation.

From the start of his administration Perrot was hard on the Munster settlers. He accused many of swindling, of confiscating land to which they had no right, and they rejoined that he did nothing to reform or civilize the country. Loftus charged him with ignoring religious policy; Perrot replied that religious policy had become an excuse for fraud. He blocked the settlers' legislation in Parliament, and they his. His opponents accused him of being soft on the Irish, and he used every underhanded means at his disposal to throttle their resistance. Fifteen years later Edmund Spenser would say that Perrot's conciliatory policies were the downfall of Anglo-Ireland, the beginning of the end of the Munster Plantation. But Spenser himself was a planter, with the viewpoint of a planter, and Perrot's actions were even more eccentric than he realized. No Lord Deputy, for example, ever played more scurvy tricks on the Irish or hammered harder at the privileges of the Celtic North. In method, Perrot resembled the irascible Warham St. Leger, and his tenacity and unscrupulousness also made him powerful enemies among the Irish. His defense of common Irishmen was balanced by his penchant for kidnapping, and his abduction of Red Hugh O'Donnell was not only the scandal of Ireland for a time but an incentive to rebellion in the North. Wherever he went in 1584 Sir John provoked controversy. Eventually the uproar was to overwhelm him and drive him out of the country in disgrace. But during the formative years of the Munster experiment his presence was continually felt.

Perrot, the commander who had once waited in the rain, in Irish dress, to fight James Fitzmaurice man to man, did not look sympathetically on the idealism of Bryskett or his friends. The tension between the two English views of Ireland is never plainer than when Bryskett explained to Walsingham his reasons for wanting to become a settler. By his own admittance he was lured into the countryside by the promise of pastoral pleasures heightened by danger and hardship: "I mean to make proof (God willing) whether the life of a borderer in this land be alike perilous unto all men, and to see if a just and honest simple life may not, even among the most barbarous people in the world, breed security to him that shall live near them or among them. There I mean to confine myself for a time, till God shall please to make my planet favorable to shine, having armed my mind aforehand to take any toil, any hazard, and any other inconvenience that this confused state shall breed, and being fully resolved to esteem the coarse and hard fare of a plowman void of indignities far sweeter than all the dainty dishes of princes' courts, where I think it easy for a man to fill his belly, and to be puffed up with vanities and never accomplished hopes and expectations, but very hard for an honest man to purchase the due reward of his service." If Bryskett's statement has roots more in pastoral poetry than pastoral reality, it also expresses the boundless optimism and determination of the best settlers. To be sure, he closed his letter with a request for fifty soldiers to accompany him into Waterford

—a request denied—but he went nonetheless, fully convinced that he had armed his mind for the worst. Perrot would probably have advised him to arm himself. He was bringing a fragile flower of the Renaissance to the embittered Kavanaughs, and the logical question was how long he would last.

Against all odds, many of the determined settlers succeeded. Even Bryskett, one of the least physical, managed to establish himself in Waterford, although doubtless he labored harder than he ever imagined with less to show for it. Whether driven by a passion to own or an ambition to rear their own squirearchy, many of the men who had once gathered at Bryskett's cottage appear to have prospered on the land. The obstacles facing them were certainly formidable: a long-neglected soil; hostile lords; recalcitrant natives; their own culture and education. When one recalls how little support they received from the Crown and the absolute loneliness they must have felt, it is difficult not to admire their resolution and courage. But through their endurance and sacrifice the countryside was made to respond. More than a decade before the Jamestown colony, thirty-five years before Plymouth, the Munster settlers were proving that "an honest life could breed security among the most barbarous people in the world." There were incidents and casualties, many immigrants left, unable to stand the lonely expanses of bog and sky, but in the vicinity of the English enclaves the land transformed slowly. Stone fences sprang up in the meadows, bogs were ditched and drained, and the cottages and enclosures which had stood ruined were rebuilt. The land was not a wilderness, but wild, and cultivation could drive back the encroaching forests. Hedges were planted and orchards, wild gorse was burned from the hillsides, and the plentiful timber felled for sale and export. Everywhere the choked roads were cleared, leveled, and filled until the English communities were knit together by a common network of roads and navigable rivers. Unlike the old settlers, the new did not live in penury; the peel towers which dotted the countryside were repaired and expanded to provide gentlemen's homes. A traveler's view of Munster after years of resettlement contrasts with previous descriptions of devastation: "Many gentlemen have castles built of freestone unpolished, and of flints, or little stones, and they are built strong for defense in times of rebellion, for which cause they have narrow stairs and little windows, and commonly they have a spacious hall joining to the castle and built of timber and clay, wherein they eat with their family." The colonists introduced gardens, fishponds, and even deer parks. At Mallow Castle, where the Norris family took up residence, the Queen sent them her white deer, and these still graze at Mallow on the property of their descendants.

By 1589 the condition of life in Munster was compared favorably to that in the English shires. Robert Payne reported: "There be great store of wild swans, cranes, pheasants, partridges, heathcocks . . . and all other fowls much more plentiful than in England. You may buy a dozen of quails for 3d., a dozen of woodcocks for 4d., and all other fowls ratably. . . . You may buy the best heifers there with calves at their feet for 20s. apiece, which are nothing inferior to the better sort of Lincolnshire breed. Their chief horses are of as great price as in England, but cart horses, mares, and little hackneys are of a very small price. . . . You may keep a better house in Ireland for 50 pounds a year than in England for 200. . . . One hundred pounds will buy 60 milch kine, 300 ewes, 20 swine, and a good team. The ground to keep these cattle and use this team on will be 400 acres at 10 pounds rent. . . . There is not a place in Ireland where any venomous thing will live. There is neither mole, pie, nor carrion crow; there is neither sheep dying of the rot nor beast of the murrain." Municipal expansion was fed by the renewal of the countryside, and in the 1590s a lively commerce sprang up between Cork and European ports. In fact, disaffected Irish imported powder and ball directly from Spain and paid for their purchases with Munster grain. Wealth filtered downward. Irish laborers were paid in the Queen's currency, and if little of the money found a way into the pockets of English merchants, it went to swell the growing trade in contraband carried on among the septs. Occasionally there is an ominous fact in the progress of Munster. When a bridge was finally built across the Blackwater at Mallow in 1587, the carters and masons were not English. McSheehys laid the foundations and set the stones. All along the Cork-Limerick road they bridged fords and strengthened defenses, until they knew the Munster colony better than the settlers themselves. Five years after the death of the Earl of Desmond it was not unusual to find his gallowglass serving in county militias. Their presence was often underwritten by the local barons and subsidized by the great lord in the North, the Earl of Tyrone.

The Second Munster Plantation imposed a shape on the Irish countryside which is still visible. The hedgerows have been continued, the forests have not crept back, and especially in County Cork the orderly abundance of the landscape recalls Somersetshire. Descendants of some of the original English families remain, citizens of the Irish Republic, and for all the passing of years, a mild estrangement still separates them from the Gaelic Irish. The works of the Second Munster Plantation became permanent, while the politics of the settlement did not outlive the century.

Of many agricultural advances, none is better remembered than Sir Walter Raleigh's potato. Tradition maintains that he first planted the Virginia root at Myrtle Grove in Youghal and later introduced it at Lismore, where, as he explained, the "easy" vegetable perfectly suited his "lazy" tenants. They had only to drop the plant in the ground for it to grow abundantly without tending. Raleigh also introduced tobacco to Ireland, and as often as he was to be condemned for that innovation, he was praised for supplying the poor with a cheap and plentiful food. Within fifty years Ireland was dependent on the potato as a mainstay of life; the plant quickly replaced grain crops, and only with the Great Famine of the nineteenth century did the consequences of a potato economy become apparent.

But by far the most interesting legacy of the plantation years is the poetry of Edmund Spenser. His work is a window through which the lives and actions of the first English colonists are seen. Because he lived and wrote at Kilcolman in the Vale of the Awbeg, he was part of the colonization and prepared to defend the Elizabethan conquest. His work was to exert a lasting influence on the development of English poetry, yet remarkably, more than half was completed in Munster, without benefit of universities, libraries, or even a community of common interest. Spenser is very much an Irish poet, but the Irish have never claimed him. He was a government official, an apologist and functionary, and this aspect of his life, most apparent in the prose, has been especially resented.

Unlike many professional poets, he was closely involved in the political controversies of his day. In 1579 he offended the Court Party and in 1580 found himself in Ireland. Once there, and hungry for advancement, he was not above telling Whitehall's representatives what they wished to hear. And what Whitehall's agents wished to hear was seldom flattering to the Irish. It is true that a number of Grey's communiqués were in Spenser's hand. There is little doubt that the poet supported Grey publicly and in Book V of *The Faerie Queene* argued Grey's cause immoderately. But if the "Book of Justice" is a tribute to Grey and his army, it is also a partisan tribute to the conquering spirit of the Reformation and is thus intentionally overstated. Elizabeth, Drake, the stalwart Dutch and French Protestants are each praised in a panorama of the Spanish Armada's defeat. As a political man Spenser was prepared to tolerate simplicities. Governments do not relish ambiguity, and the official poet is not necessarily the private poet. There are virtually two Spensers in Ireland: the servant of the state, who writes a terrifying treatise called *A View of the Present State of Ireland,* and the Munster gentleman, who celebrates his marriage in the imagery of the Awbeg Vale and imagines himself a shepherd on the slopes of the Ballyhouras.

Alone among the settlers he recognizes the ancient worth of Ireland, the vitality of its culture, the preeminence of the early Irish Church. The present condition of Ireland does not obscure for Spenser its glorious past. The island is not a backwater, outside history. It is rather a decayed garden corresponding to the first Eden. The reasons for the land's misfortune, for the curse it seems to bear, are rooted in human nature and are more universal than particular. In the poet's mind, the Munster Settlement did not ensue from the conquest of a nation so much as from an attempt to restore a lost possession, a place degraded by the brutal propensities of men. Munster engaged Spenser's imagination through his susceptibility to the past. Time is central to his vision, for through time and its record—history—man interprets his experience and discerns the divine intention. First, a lesson could be learned from Ireland's state past and present, and second, that lesson spoke eloquently to all men in all places. In the poet's work the Awbeg Vale and environs became the stage of conflicts far wider in significance than any dispute with the McSheehys or their like. The countryside is personified, allegorized, and, insofar as its topography becomes the material of verse, endowed with a veneer of classical civilization after the fashion of Roman Tuscany or Gaul. The effort is made at Kilcolman Castle, on the edge of the Kilmore, and this wild spot, once a Desmond lair, becomes the high-water mark of the European Renaissance in Ireland.

Spenser rode into the Awbeg Valley with a party of surveyors in the spring of 1585. He was at that moment a deputy to the Clerk of Munster, and the Clerk, ill disposed to make the journey, was his old friend Lodowick Bryskett. The deputyship was something of a political plum, for it led normally to the clerkship itself and a stipend of twenty pounds a year. Spenser thereby escaped Dublin, and Perrot, to serve under Sir John Norris, newly appointed President of Munster. Norris was under instructions to take up where Valentine Brown had left off and quickly divide the surveyed estates into actual farms. The Munster scheme was way behind schedule, and settlers who had come over early in the year had returned home in disgust because of delays. John Norris, Thomas Norris, Edmund Spenser, and a small party of English soldiers traveled the length and breadth of County Cork, and all that Sir John could report after several miserable, rainy weeks in the field was that the Crown had sent him to govern a graveyard. The surveying went forward, and at every bivouac droves of Irish came forward to be fed and pardoned. But this was not soldier's work, and John Norris was one of Elizabeth's ablest field officers. He spent much of his time arbitrating disputes among settlers and the "better" Irish, while Spenser and his brother carried out the actual measurements. By early summer Norris could hardly abide the wait for his reassignment.

No more reluctant official ever appeared in Elizabethan Ireland; no sooner was Sir John arrived and established at Cork then he requested recall. It was not that he could not stand Perrot, whom he liked well enough, but that the awesome emptiness of Ireland preyed on his nerves and filled him with futility. In a sense, he had appeared between acts, a veteran of the Netherland wars suddenly drawn into the wake of the Irish, and he neither knew what had preceded him nor cared what would follow. John Norris was to give substance to the Munster scheme during his short stay; he was also to be a great benefactor to his brother and Spenser, and if his heart was not often in his work, at least he brought a cool, appraising eye to the Munster scheme. Norris found himself divided between Perrot and Wallop, between the Irish barons and the undertakers, and, more significantly, between his desire to fulfill his duty and his ambition to succeed. Ireland was for him the nadir of a career. He spoke of "drowning in this forgetful corner" and yearned for a new command in the Netherlands. The contradictions underlying the Munster scheme apparently disturbed him, and he appears to have doubted the policy from the first. In Dublin, before the Parliament of 1585, he proclaimed "Ireland shall never be brought to obedience or good order but by the sword." Yet privately he wrote to Burghley that if hanging were the Queen's solution for disorder, then she had better hang the whole province and be done. Norris had a reputation to preserve, and official Dublin was favorably impressed with his soldierly bearing. Behind the scenes, however, in conversations with Perrot, he owned up to his confusion: he could not understand how the Crown proposed to turn the Irish off their lands and not feed the fire of rebellion. Against all expectations, Norris moved to conciliate the natives where possible, restraining his more rapacious countrymen, and in so doing bought relative peace and tolerance for several years.

John Norris was one of five brothers who chose to follow a military career in Ireland and elsewhere. They were the children of Baron Norris of Rycote, the grandchildren of Henry Norris, who in a cool and manly fashion had parted with his head as one of Anne Boleyn's alleged lovers. In memory of Henry, Elizabeth granted the family the barony of Rycote and ever after took an interest in the careers of the five Norris sons. She fondly nicknamed their mother "my black crow," and the sobriquet "black" appears to have clung to John on account of his dark complexion and black, grizzled hair. Three of the five brothers were to die violently in Ireland during the wars, but John, who was always in the forefront of a fight, survived.

To men like John Norris, solitary professionals without family, Ireland was always a dreaded station. Anything but a crusader or missionary, he desired one thing in life: to command regiments—not to compose disputes between ragamuffins and chase peasants through bogs. From the first he was an incongruity at the head of such troops as remained in Ireland by 1585. He was above average height, heavily built, and awesomely commanding. Like many of Elizabeth's best officers, he had learned his profession in the Lowland wars. At Malines in Flanders, before the entire English force, Norris scaled the walls of the town and strangled a Spanish friar who was rallying the defense. At Steenwijk he had three horses shot from under him in one day, and at Antwerp, unaided, he quelled an ugly pay riot among his troops. His memento of this mutiny was a flattened nose, still healing at the time of his arrival at Cork. His right hand, shattered by a musketball outside Nordhorn, grew arthritic in the dampness of Munster. His left thigh, hit at Malines, made sitting a saddle painful, and his eyes were troubling him. At thirty-nine John Norris was already too old and disabled for surveying in Munster.

No sooner had he arrived in the South than Perrot ordered him to Antrim in the North, there to meet an invasion of Scots led by Sorley Boy McDonnel. Sorley Boy was easily the most persistent and ingenious nuisance the English ever faced in Ireland, and though Norris chased him back to Scotland and captured Castle Dunluce near the Giant's Causeway, Sorley Boy would be back again the following year. Meanwhile, Thomas Norris and Edmund Spenser carried out the President's work in Munster. John had ordered a general strengthening of defenses, a response to the rumored Spanish Armada, and at Cork and Kilmallock his deputies oversaw the repair of walls and moats. During this time Spenser was granted the prebendary of Effin, a ruined parish near Kilfinnane, and while this gift from Loftus was probably meant to augment his income, it is also possible that he attempted to reestablish the church. Spenser had never taken holy orders, but the shortage of clerics was great in Ireland, and educated men were frequently pressed into the service of the Church of England. At Effin, Spenser moved among the Irish countryfolk freely. He administered to their spiritual needs but in all likelihood spent most of his time seeing that they were fed. In return, he acquired their legends and myths, a smattering of Gaelic, and a feeling for the countryside. He was not yet owner of Kilcolman, ten miles away, but he was already collecting the stories of the Galtee Mountains and the Ballyhouras. Concerning the country Irish, he recalled years later their abysmal ignorance of all religion —Catholic or Reformed. He experienced them as Erasmus had, a generation before, "ill-taught in holy scriptures as Saracens and Turks." The fault was not theirs; they were appallingly neglected, illiterate, and misled. Spenser blamed the English clergy for refusing to bring Christ's work into Ireland, and when he called down the curse of St. Patrick and Columba on lazy ministers, his puritan distaste for the clerical establishment was as great as it ever was in his first satire: "If the ancient godly fathers, which first converted them to the faith, were able to pull them from idolatry and paganism to the true belief in Christ, as St. Patrick and St. Columba did, how much more easily shall godly teachers bring them to a true understanding of that which they already profess. . . . It is a great wonder to see difference between the zeal of the popish priests and our ministers of the gospel, for the priests spare not to come out of Spain from Rome and from Rheims by long toil and dangerous travel hither to where they know peril of death awaiteth them and no reward or riches are to be found, and this only to draw the people unto the Church of Rome. Whereas our idle ministers, having a way for credit and estimation thereby opened unto them and having the livings of the Country offered them without pains or peril, will neither for the same nor for any love of God or zeal for religion, nor for all the good which they may do by winning of many souls to God, be drawn forth from their warm nests, and their sweet loves' sides, to look out into God's harvest, which is even ready for the sickle, and all the fields yellow long ago." Admiration is not withheld the martyred priests of Rome, yet even they, who inevitably were to win the Irish soul, made slow progress. A Christian overlay was evident in the Irish countryside, but underneath, observances could be unabashedly pagan. Camden and Spenser both testify that certain churls, when first seeing the moon after its change, commonly knelt and repeated the Lord's Prayer, addressing the goddess moon with these words: "Leave us whole and sound as thou hast found us." To Spenser's credit, he did not view the downtrodden peasant as irredeemable. He was among the few Elizabethans to venture a social as opposed to moral opinion: "the Irish were at that stage of development the English had been in Anglo-Saxon times." Once again his sense of history and change conditioned his judgment, and he held out hope in his most pessimistic writing for progress and enlightenment.

From 1585 through 1587 Spenser was in and out of County Cork many times. He accompanied John Norris to Dublin at the time of the Parliament; he was present with Thomas Norris at Mallow Castle; he attended assizes at Limerick and saw the first settlers take possession of their farms. The Kilcolman estate, which was to be his by autumn, 1588, was first granted to a settler by the name of Andrew Reade, a gentleman of means from Faccombe, Hampshire, who was held in esteem by the government. Spenser doubtless met Reade at Mallow and might have discussed the problems connected with his estate, for when Reade decided to give up at last and go home, he offered Spenser transfer of title. The principal problem connected with the property, as all were aware, was Maurice, Lord Roche, and Roche's servants, the McSheehys. They claimed that the Kilcolman plowlands, between 1600 and 2000 acres, lay across Roche's meadowland and blocked passage of cattle to the River Awbeg. Roche lacked influence to make good his claim—he had followed the Earl of Desmond and begged his pardon from Pelham—and over the next two years he and his tenants substituted molestation for litigation. All that is clear of the situation is that Reade eventually packed his belongings and left, while Spenser, who moved into the castle in 1588, was given lease until Whitsunday, 1589, after which if Reade had not reclaimed the property, it would pass entirely to him. By 1588 Spenser had the means to withstand Roche's actions; Sir Thomas Norris had been knighted by a new Lord Deputy and named Vice President of Munster, Spenser himself was the Clerk of Munster, and sufficient numbers of settlers had taken land in the neighborhood to withstand Roche. Maurice and the old Desmond retainers were not yet done, but for the moment they were contained.

It is clear that Spenser had little time for poetry or politics during this period. He had immersed himself in matters of the land, gradually becoming conversant with methods of farming and surveying, until by the close of the decade this son of a poor London tailor writes knowledgeably about plowlands and hides, virgates and oxgangs, all terms for the dividing of acreage. Meanwhile, he missed the worst political infighting Dublin had experienced since Grey. Perrot's administration succeeded in its goal of restoring peace throughout Ireland, but the price paid in political disunity was high. By 1587 the Lord Deputy was at feud with everyone. Wallop, Loftus, and Sir Richard Bingham were petitioning Whitehall for Perrot's recall, while Perrot did everything to favor the Irish and frustrate English resettlement. Spenser, buried in the Munster countryside, escaped an active role in these disputes. He was under the wing of Sir John Norris, and Norris was the only official acceptable to both sides. When Norris finally departed Ireland to join Leicester's expedition to the Netherlands in 1586, he left his brother and Spenser securely established in the South and beyond the reach of Perrot or his opponents. And by then the grave crisis foreseen in 1579 had overtaken England. Spanish forces were driving the Protestant coalition out of the Netherlands in the aftermath of William the Silent's assassination. There was certain knowledge that Spain was massing an armada for an invasion attempt on England. And as a consequence of mounting dangers, as well as plots to assassinate Elizabeth, Mary Stuart was executed at Fotheringay in 1586. While Spenser was absorbed in the tedious affairs of Munster, his world rushed headlong into a battle for survival and dominion. During his stay at Mallow Castle in September, 1586, his friend and patron Sir Philip Sidney was fatally wounded at Zutphen. Sir Henry Sidney, who had first arranged Spenser's post with Grey seven years before, had died of kidney stones the previous May, and Leicester, bogged down in the rain and mud of the Lowlands, was an unheroic failure. For the moment, Munster was at peace, although the world seemed to turn topsy-turvy around it, and this unnatural quiet encouraged homely, domestic ambitions.

The "manor, castle, and lands of Kylcolman," which passed formally on October 26, 1590, into the possession of "Edmund Spenser, gentleman," comprised 3000 acres according to the wording of his grant. Spenser was obliged to repair a manor house attached to the castle, and was permitted to impark 151 acres for horses and deer. From a survey of his seigniory made years later, the Kilcolman property appears to have contained "a great quantity of mountain, not capable of improvement, but little bog." The estate, therefore, extended well up the slopes of the Ballyhouras.

All that remains of Kilcolman Castle today is a three-story tower, ruined and covered with ivy. It stands beside a small crescent pond in the middle of the plain, and from its crumbled top the Ballyhouras are clearly visible in the north, the Nagles Mountains in the south. When Spenser took up residence there in 1588, a timber and stucco house was attached; most likely there were stables and smaller dwellings, and the path to the castle, now lost in underbrush, led directly to Buttevant and the Awbeg. The countryside is emptier today than it was then, a result of emigrations, and it is little traveled. But in Spenser's time the neighborhood sustained the remnants of Desmond's people, Lords Roche and Fitzgibbon with theirs, and several hundred English families. To the northwest of Kilcolman, Hugh Cuffe, with twenty-one families, was established on 11,000 acres, called Cuffe's Wood. To the southeast lay Thomas Norris' lands with several dozen families and 6000 acres surrounding Mallow Castle, and south along the Blackwater River Roger Keate and Arthur Hyde were established on 12,000 acres each.

The domestic lives of Elizabethans are notably difficult to reconstruct. Spenser's is no exception. Ordinarily, Elizabethan wives were diffident and Elizabethan children silent; the masculine cast of sixteenth-century society was seldom broken. Most of the Crown's officials brought families to Ireland, but little is known of the lives and the hardships they shared. Sir Walter Raleigh's mistress, Alice Goold, was delivered of a daughter at Lismore. One of Lord Grey's younger children died of typhus fever in Dublin during the terrible winter of 1582. Spenser, it is supposed, did not live at Kilcolman Castle alone. On the eve of his departure for Ireland he had married Machabyas Chylde at Westminster, and presumably she kept his houses at Dublin and New Abbey. But whether she ever lived at Kilcolman is questionable since she died sometime in 1588. The same year

Sarah Spenser, the poet's sister, is mentioned as living at Kilcolman with her brother. All that is certain about her is that she found a husband in the neighborhood and married him the following year. With his second marriage, Spenser made his wedding day the subject of poetry, conferring on Elizabeth Boyle, his bride, the attributes of Dante's Beatrice and Petrarch's Laura. The poem is ostensibly a wedding gift; it is sonorous and rich, filled with stylized details of life at Kilcolman. And because of *Epithalamion*, Elizabeth Boyle is remembered. Her letters are extant and convey a hint of personality; her place in Munster society is known, her burial place is recorded, and her children by Spenser are roughly identified. Yet her life with him remains in shadow.

While Spenser moved into his home at Kilcolman, a storm that soaked his carts and possessions and broke through the shingles of his house also drove the remnants of the Spanish Armada onto the rocky coasts of Ireland. The Armada, decimated and scattered in the Channel battles, had rounded the north of Scotland and been swept within a few miles of the Donegal shore by winds and heavy seas. Along the route from Donegal to Kerry, ships had sunk or been driven ashore. Where the O'Donnells or O'Neills could reach the wrecks, the Spaniards were helped, but where the northern chiefs could not, the local inhabitants often slaughtered the half-drowned sailors for valuables, to the immense delight of the English. Five years before, the Earl of Desmond had waited desperately for Spanish reinforcements. And King Philip had sent him handfuls of men and scant supplies. Now, amid scenes of awesome waste, an army was cast ashore. Near Sligo, on a sandy strip of beach, Geoffrey Fenton counted the bodies of 1100 drowned men. The piratical Dowdary O'Malleys caught Don Pedro de Mendoza's crew limping ashore, exhausted, near Clare Island and murdered them with clubs, "like seals" in the shallow shorewater. In Connaught, Sir Richard Bingham offered quarter to none. "My brother George," he wrote, "executed seven or eight hundred or upwards, first and last, one way or another." What Bingham meant was by hanging or by club. Several hundred survivors were formally executed at Galway. In Tralee, Thomas Norris, without means to imprison numerous castaways, hanged 120, and elsewhere along the West Coast English officers hanged sailors and plundered wrecks, if they could find them before the hungry Irish. All in all, nearly 10,000 Spanish soldiers and sailors are thought to have perished on the Irish coast at the hands of either their allies or their enemies. Even the O'Donnell, heartbroken because Perrot held his son imprisoned at Dublin, tried to barter thirty survivors for his boy's release and was only stopped by Hugh O'Neill. "We and our posterity," O'Neill told him, "might one day have to seek refuge in another country—as these castaways have done—and it would be a fitting revenge of Fate for betraying these poor creatures in their only refuge." Hugh O'Neill, the Earl of Tyrone, defied every caution in aiding the Spanish, and from this time forward dates his rising resistance to the English Crown. The bloody spectacle on the West Coast must have hardened his resolve, for in the years immediately following, his reach lengthened into the South, until it extended even into the secluded Awbeg Vale, to the McSheehys and Edmund Spenser.

The year of the Armada came and went without altering life at Kilcolman. Spenser played no role in the West Country defense, and his description of the victory in Book V of *The Faerie Queene* is allegorized without a trace of first hand experience. At most, he saw wagonloads of salvage passing down the Limerick road to Cork and England. Similarly, Perrot's dramatic departure that year left him unaffected. He was doubtless aware of the political crisis in Dublin but, secure in the South, was not a party to the events. Presumably he gave away his sister in marriage early the next year, possibly met and began his courtship of Elizabeth Boyle, and worked the land until its every characteristic became familiar to him. What Kilcolman now meant to him is learned from the first of three famous statements concerning his life in Ireland: *Colin Clouts Come Home Again*. This long, pastoral discourse is dated 1591 and recalls events of 1589 and 1590. It is famous in literary history for depicting the meeting at Kilcolman of Spenser and Raleigh, their subsequent journey to Whitehall, and the presentation to Elizabeth of *The Faerie Queene*. But *Colin Clouts* is also a poem of private resolve, containing Spenser's decision to remain in Ireland and sounding for the first time in English letters the colonialist's call to a simpler and more honest life overseas.

Colin Clouts begins with a recollection of Raleigh's visit to Kilcolman from his estate at Lismore, farther down the Blackwater. What brought Raleigh to Ireland from the English Court was a series of misunderstandings with Elizabeth and temporary banishment from London. From a simple soldier, Raleigh had risen in a few years to command Her Majesty's Guard, to become Lord of the Stannaries and Lieutenant of Cornwall and, as the Queen's favorite, potentially the richest man in the realm. He had no intention of remaining in disfavor and, fleeing to his Irish estates, sought the leisure to compose an epic poem praising Elizabeth. The project was worthy of him; he had distinguished himself as a soldier and sailor and was no mean writer. And behind his scheme lay the fact that England owned no master work of truly national significance. By the end of the sixteenth century Portugal boasted its *Lusiads;* France its *Franciad;* Italy its *Gerusalemme liberata;* but England had no epic poem, no compilation of its glories and achievements, no statement of values or national mission. *The Faerie Queene* was destined to fill this need, and legend has it that Raleigh, hearing of Spenser's work, rode into the peaceful Munster countryside to sample it for himself. "He pip'd, I sung; and when he sung, I piped," Spenser explains in the person of shepherd Colin. "By change of turns, each making the other merry, / Neither envying the other, nor envied, / So piped we, until we both were weary." Which was to say that Raleigh had the good taste and wit to recognize a masterpiece when he found one. His own plan to memorialize Elizabeth in heroic verse was forgotten; the Faerie Queene was Elizabeth; Spenser's antique world of knights and wonders was their world, veiled and allegorized. Raleigh now played impresario to genius and, fetching Spenser to London with him, presented the poet as a discovery to the Queen. For Spenser, it was his first visit to England since he had been sent away ten years before, and he returned in triumph.

According to tradition, Elizabeth invited Spenser to read to her from his poem. As Raleigh anticipated, she was flattered by her role in the romance and impressed with its scope and gravity. The Queen was as tightfisted as ever, yet either on impulse or out of genuine gratitude she awarded Spenser a pension of fifty pounds for life. At such rates, he would have been the best-paid poet in the realm, had Cecil not frustrated the payment of the gift. But in 1590 the poet at least saw his work published and acclaimed; he visited the English Court as heir to Philip Sidney, and was immediately swept up in the literary foment of London. *Colin Clouts* recalls this triumph, reflects on it, weighing its meaning in the setting of Ireland and Kilcolman. The poem is pastoral and, therefore, rude in style. Like much pastoral verse, it contrasts countryside with Court. But the comparison in the case of *Colin Clouts* is between savage Ireland and civilized England, between coarse country people and luminaries of the realm, between Munster's crude sureties and England's ambiguities. For the most part the comparison favors the mother country:

> *For there all happy peace and plenteous store*
> *Conspire in one to make contented bliss:*
> *No wailing there nor wretchedness is heard,*
> *No bloody issues nor no leprosies,*
> *No grisly famine, nor no raging sword,*
> *No nightly bordrags, nor no hue and cries;*
> *The shepherds there abroad may safely lie,*
> *On hills and downs, without dread or danger:*
> *No ravenous wolves the good man's hope destroy,*
> *Nor outlaws fell affray the forest ranger.*
> *There learned arts do flourish in great honor,*
> *And poets' wits are had in peerless price:*

Religion hath lay power to rest upon her,
Advancing virtue and suppressing vice.
For end, all good, all grace there freely grows,
Had people grace it gratefully to use.

But England does not use its grace gratefully. The poet steps carefully. Raleigh is complimented throughout, a token of Spenser's appreciation; the great ladies of the Court are lauded; English poets are praised; and of course, Elizabeth is exempted from any criticism:

And long while after I am dead and rotten:
Amongst the shepherds daughters dancing round,
My lays made of her shall not be forgotten.
But sung by them with flowery garlands crowned.
And ye, who so ye be, that shall survive:
When as ye hear her memory renewed,
Be witness of her bounty here alive,
Which she to Colin her poor shepherd showed.

Obeisance done, Colin tells why he will not live in England and why the life of a poor shepherd in Munster is to be preferred. It concerns a discovery made: the frightening emptiness of worldly success, the corrupting influence of power and wealth. Spenser had climbed far from humble birth; in *Colin Clouts* he drew the inevitable line, content with what he has and has achieved. The shepherds and shepherdesses of the pastoral ask him repeatedly why he returns an exile to Munster when England has opened its opportunities to him. By one example or another, he answers that the life of the Court is hollow, sterile, without passion. Fullness of life lies not in ease, but in a marrying of opposites, in a disorderly collision of vital forces, in eternal yearning and struggle. "Love" is his word for this creative process. In a word, the "love" of *Colin Clouts* is completeness, and Spenser found completeness in the precarious world of Kilcolman. He is asked whether or not they love at Court and replies: "For all the walls and windows there are writ / All full of love, and love, and love my dear, / And all their talk and study is of it." This is the love of fine clothes and titles, of power, and enticement. It is nothing to build a life on, Colin suggests. Elizabeth is Queen and surely a great Empress; England is sound and a nation of puissance and virtue, but Spenser recognizes the point of divergence between ambition and private fulfillment and declines the opportunity to climb farther. As Colin, the shepherd, he returns to Kilcolman and his humble condition, content to hold what his hands have made.

The brittleness of authority, when it pits itself against permanent forces, is illustrated in the poem by a curious parable drawn from the surroundings of Kilcolman and Gaelic nature myth. The song Colin sings for Raleigh is about the marriage of the rivers Mulla and Bregog, the Mulla being the Awbeg called after the ancient name for Buttevant—Kilnemullah—and the Bregog being a rock-strewn, sluggish stream in the fields by Kilcolman. According to local lore, the Mulla, daughter of Father Mole, or the Ballyhoura Hills, was given in marriage to the Allo, or Blackwater River. From the dawn of creation, however, she had been loved by the Bregog, whose name means "deceitful" in Irish, and the Bregog, twisting and turning across the landscape, hoped to flow into her. Father Mole, seeing his intention, sought to stop the Bregog, but the stream disappeared underground in the soft limestone and emerged once again beside the Mulla. Next, Mole flung stones from his crest into the Bregog, scattering the water into marshy pools, yet slowly and inexorably the Bregog continued in its course and, though broken into rivulets, finally found its way into the Mulla near Buttevant.

The Awbeg and Bregog still behave near Kilcolman as they did in Spenser's day, the Bregog vanishing abruptly into the roots of an ancient oak tree. And the meaning Spenser found in them 400 years ago is easy to see. The fable spoke directly to Raleigh in his relations with the Queen, but certainly the story also suggests the main theme of Spenser's poem: how passion in many guises eludes restraint and surfaces where least expected. Passion, not reason alone, rules, and the worthwhile life unites the two in a bond of common purpose.

Intentionally or not, Spenser's tale contained a meaning for the Irish nation. The Irish resistance, diverted and driven underground Bregog-like by the conquest of Munster, was also moving slowly and inexorably toward a sudden emergence. If any Irish lord ever deserved the epithet "deceitful," Hugh O'Neill was surely the one, and while Spenser, for instance, was establishing himself at Kilcolman, the Earl of Tyrone was rapidly expanding his power. By underground preparation and cautious planning
O'Neill was laying the basis for the greatest of the Irish rebellions. The most cunning and politic Irishman of the age, he was destined to defeat Elizabeth and sweep away the world of the Munster settlers.

By 1589 the Earl of Tyrone's frequent hunts were notorious throughout the land. Unlike Desmond, he achieved an astonishing rapport with his people and would not lead them to war unready. Archbishop Lombard tells how Hugh O'Neill hunted: "Whenever he used to go out hunting or fowling, or on some other exercise of business, he ever arranged that some guns should be carried by his company, and seized an opportunity of chatting familiarly with any of the people he met in the district, and used to ask them sundry questions as to their lives and habits . . . and when they replied that they knew nothing except spears, and bows, and arrows and other such primitive weapons of their fathers, he would produce a gun and having briefly explained its use bid them try if they could manage it. He would praise anyone handy and give him a piece of money and sometimes would bestow the weapon itself." Hugh O'Neill was never to be in the position of leading kern or gallowglass against trained infantry. He would come out of the North in his day with regiments of regular troops, led by seasoned officers, and he would wheel them through the South with a skill Grey might have envied. Wherever Irishmen had lost their lands, he would find ready allies, and long before the Munster settlers knew the full enormity of his preparations, their servants, the McSheehys, were hiding the ball and powder he bought for them in Spain.

Edmund Spenser had determined by 1589 to set his ambitions no higher than Ireland or the wealth his service to the state and the first three books of *The Faerie Queene* had earned him. He proposed to finish that master work on his estate at Kilcolman and to continue performing his duties as the Clerk of Munster. But whether he could hold what he had gained was a question. Raleigh knew better than Spenser that to seek success once is always to have to seek it. When the storm finally broke from the North, Raleigh was in London, preparing for his voyages to the New World, and the poet was at Kilcolman, defenseless.

DUNGANNON, 1594

Lord of the North

Nothing marked the passing of a generation of government in Ireland more than the departure of Sir John Perrot. He had come to Ireland in the early years of the Queen's reign, at the outset of the First Desmond War, and he had stayed to heal the wounds of the Second Desmond War. He did not succeed, and in 1588 he left the country for the last time. Perrot's contemporaries in Ireland, Sir Henry Sidney, Sir William Drury, Sir Nicholas Maltby, were dead; those who had sent them—Leicester, Walsingham, Cecil—were in their last years. Ireland now belonged to Loftus and Wallop, Bingham and Fitzwilliams, and they confronted the Irish with more militancy than understanding. Perrot could say of his generation that they had one accomplishment: the Spanish Armada had finally come, and Ireland, always the weak link in England's defense, had held. Cecil's misgivings of 1579 had come to pass; England had veered toward extreme nationalism and was at war with Spain and Catholic Ireland, while France stood neutral. But Desmond Ireland had fortunately expired before King Philip could mount his assault. This was the slender achievement of twenty years' fighting.

Perhaps Perrot realized that worse dangers lay ahead, that the great challenge would come from within Ireland, from the North, supplied with Spanish arms. If he did, he was too old and eccentric by 1589 to be taken seriously. Sir John Perrot did not leave Ireland for tranquil retirement. He was recalled, charged with treason, and tried at Westminster. Every indication is that he was driven out of office and ruined by his political adversaries, and the means employed were fraud and perjury. Perrot stood fast against attempts to strip loyal Irish of their property, but he thwarted his own efforts by arrogance and irascibleness.

By 1587 he was on bad terms with Bingham, Bagenal, Fitzwilliams, Loftus, and Wallop. In the Council Chamber at Dublin he struck Sir Nicholas Bagenal, Elizabeth's aged marshal, in the face and knocked him to the floor. The reasons for the row are obscure, but the charge was made in letters to Walsingham that Perrot was drunk and took offense at Bagenal's manner of address. Whatever the reason, the animus loosed in the Council Chamber persisted for months, disrupting government and frustrating all attempts at reconciliation. During the enmity Sir John Norris' neutrality was severely tried, and the incident partially accounts for his attempts to be recalled. Rumors of the feud between the Lord Deputy and his chief lieutenants spread quickly throughout the land, undermining confidence in the government.

In 1587 a German visitor to Dublin reported of Perrot: "He is among the most majestic and grave leaders I have ever met, portly and immense in height and breadth of shoulders." In old age Perrot resembled no one more than his reputed father, Henry VIII, and was in demeanor as regal and as overbearing. Remarkably, his policy toward the Church of England in Ireland suggested the Great Dissolution, and his imperious treatment of Archbishop Loftus was strikingly familiar. Perrot wished to use the revenues of St. Patrick's Cathedral for the founding of Trinity College; Loftus argued privileges and threatened a version of excommunication if he tried. The Lord Deputy deplored the corruption of the clergy in Ireland, their wealth and inability to minister to the Irish. If he seemed on better terms with the Church of Rome than was advisable, his disgust with Loftus was sufficient to account for his attitude. Even Perrot's most outrageous epithets tend to support Spenser's contention that the Church of England had failed completely in the countryside. But to attack the Church of England was also to attack its temporal head, Elizabeth herself, and Perrot did not hesitate to rail publicly at the Queen, calling her coarse names, and describing her sword of state as "paltry," a sexual innuendo intended. Sir John was foulmouthed, had always been, and enjoyed disparaging those he considered the Queen's foppish companions. In the presence of Wallop and Fitzwilliams he declared her letters "filthy hypocrisy," would hear nothing of her plans further to advance the Munster Plantation, and wherever possible judged in favor of the Irish. Where he declined favor was in the North, distrusting O'Neill and O'Donnell from the first. These chieftains, however, were the ones most favored by the Crown, Wallop, and the Dublin administration.

Perrot enjoyed violent demonstrations. He threatened to thrash Loftus with a cudgel if the Archbishop dared to cross his path and then had the audacity to reprimand Bingham for excessive use of force. Under Perrot, the Queen's government in Ireland probably experienced some loss of dignity, yet where the government lost, the Irish generally gained, and Wallop was particularly galled by the widespread popularity of the Lord Deputy. Perhaps inevitably plots were hatched to effect Perrot's removal. His petty tyrannies could be tolerated, but not his irrationality, and difficulty certainly attaches to understanding some of his actions. Perrot suffered extreme pain from kidney stones, a common Elizabethan affliction, and in all likelihood anesthetized himself with drink. The charges of drunkenness and unprovoked rage would thereby be explained. As for his unconscionable persecution of Wallop and Loftus, he simply despised their greed and ostentatiousness, their weakness and ineptitude.

Perrot could not last. His own abandon opened him to charges of treason. And when, in 1588, he requested his recall, Whitehall obliged without delay. In February of the Armada year he left Dublin, and Fitzwilliams was immediately appointed his successor. On the quays in the River Liffey thousands of poor Irish gathered to bid Perrot farewell. Along the streets to the river people lined the way to cheer him, and contemporary accounts reveal no greater show of enthusiasm for an English official than that accorded Sir John. In his day he had never hesitated to hunt the Irish down in their bogs, to hang hundreds, to burn their homes and confiscate their cattle. Such had been his war, brutally direct, but he was also remembered for having offered an end to the killing. In peace he had understood the dilemmas of the conquered and, with only a few lapses, had ruled them with rough justice and an almost fatherly forbearance. He never shrank from the facts of Irish life or, after an attempt to suppress their customs, begrudged them their ways. He grew in his office as no other Englishman had and in his last years became trapped between his own countrymen and the rising power of the Celtic North.

In 1590 Perrot was summoned from his estate in Wales to Westminster and there reprimanded by the Council for his indiscretions in Ireland. The proceedings constituted an inquiry preparatory to indictment. For in the records of Dublin Castle, Lord Deputy Fitzwilliams had uncovered a letter in Perrot's hand which purportedly offered to Philip of Spain the kingdoms of Ireland and England. Sir John's treasonous abuse of the Queen was recalled, and his obstruction of English designs in Ireland. Late in 1591 he was arraigned before the Queen's Justices at Westminster and formally charged with high treason. As he was being committed to the Tower, he is said to have raged, "God's death, will the Queen suffer her own brother to be offered up as a sacrifice to the envy of his frisking adversaries?" This statement is Perrot's only known reference to their possible common paternity.

Traitors were discovered everywhere during these years, some unquestionably real. Sir William Stanley, the same who participated in the battles of Monaster and Glenmalure, who had received Desmond's head from O'Moriarty at Tralee, surrendered the town of Deventer in the Netherlands and turned coat. He had long wrestled with his growing belief in the righteousness of Rome and, depressed by Elizabeth's neglect of her soldiers and misrule of Ireland, finally deserted his country for his faith. Stanley's act instantly compromised Leicester's expedition by calling into doubt the determination and loyalty of English troops. Apparently Perrot's behavior was interpreted to resemble Stanley's; the letter to Philip was expected to prove the case, and did. But the letter was a patent forgery, the work of Charles Trevor, one of many Elizabethan counterfeiters. Who paid Trevor to make the document is not known, although Loftus, Wallop, and perhaps Fitzwilliams are suspected. They were never blamed, however, for in a travesty of justice almost as glaring as that which befell Teig McGilpatrick and Connor MacCormac, Perrot was tried and found guilty. The letter, which would not have convinced a jury of country dolts, was accepted as prima facie evidence by the Queen's Bench, and Perrot was duly sentenced to the block. The true nature of the proceedings now became known. The Queen had humiliated her detractor and declared that she wished no more than his imprisonment. She refused to sign his death warrant and let it be heard that she declined to confiscate his property or prevent his heirs from inheriting. Perrot was consigned to the Tower for an indefinite term, and there in 1592, protesting his innocence, he succumbed to kidney infection, compounded by grief. His end hardly became a soldier of such long and valiant service, but Perrot had overstepped many times; he had subjected the government to ridicule and criticism, and in Dublin the news of his decease was met with relief.

Nothing accounts for the relentless hounding of the man more than his interference in matters of Irish land lease and taxation. Beneath the spectacular improprieties of Perrot's administration lay an earnest determination to tax Ireland equitably and to restrain the worst depredations of its lords and officials. The Lord Deputy viewed gravely the Crown's avowed responsibility to protect its common subjects from extortion by their overlords. Yet as Perrot responded to the pleas of the common people, he uncovered a network of influence peddling, land fraud, and abuse of authority which led to every corner of his government. That conspiracies to defraud followed quickly on the surveying of Desmond's land is unquestioned, for through petitions and humble complaints even the

Crown gradually became aware of vast and illegal confiscations. By a variety of nefarious agreements, tax policy was made to favor certain lords and undertakers; the burden of their cess, or taxes, being paid by the poorer landholders, who were often unable to meet the levy. In this manner, honest Irish farmers saw their holdings foreclosed and then by regrant and purchase transferred to the richer lords and settlers. Three years after the end of the Desmond War, the Queen's revenues remained depressed, almost 50 percent below expectation. The tax base was shrinking rather than growing, despite all of the Crown's measures to repopulate and resettle Munster. Concomitantly, the number of destitute and dispossessed Irish families had increased alarmingly. Even Camden, in his official history of Elizabeth's reign, could not ignore the evidence: "Those who were supposed to survey and seize only the rebels' lands began to turn the faithful and loyal subjects out of their possessions with violence, so that the Queen was moved to refrain them lest their greed should kindle a new fire of rebellion." Out of Kerry came a warning from Sir William Herbert, one of the most conscientious and diligent undertakers: "Our pretence in the enterprise of plantation was to establish in these parts piety, justice, inhabitation and civility, with comfort and good example to the parts adjacent. Our drift now is, being here possessed of land, to extort, make the state of things turbulent, and live by prey and pay. . . . The oppression of the Queen's subjects in Ireland will but turn them out enemies to the Crown, less the avarice so lately shown by the settlers in Munster be called back." Herbert received his reply from Sir Edward Denny, an influential landholder and a close associate of Sir John Norris. Denny reminded him of the late and bitter war and the inveterate viciousness of the Irish and charged him with being "soft" on rebels. Sir Edward enjoyed an estate of more than 6000 acres in Kerry, and by 1592 his original grant had increased almost twofold.

Though the situation in Munster was fraught with danger, Perrot could not trust his highest officials and, therefore, could not police the establishment of the plantations. He might rail at the government and on occasion judge in favor of the Irish, but he lacked the enforcing instrument of previous Lord Deputies—an effective army. When he realized that the Crown's policy had again changed direction, that scarce resources were being directed to the Netherlands, he wrote despondently to Walsingham, asserting that the Munster scheme was out of control and without application and expenditure beyond recovery. The Queen's Secretary acknowledged the justness of his complaint but warned him also to do as he was told: "You might have lived in better season under Henry VIII, when princes were resolute in honourable attempts; but our age is given to other manner of proceedings . . . conform . . . as other men do."

Perrot's answer was that sweeping and almost revolutionary reassessment of land and taxes known as the Composition of Connaught. His opponents argued that Perrot chose Connaught for reform because he disliked Sir Richard Bingham, but just as likely the Lord Deputy saw in the province a suitable testing ground for reorganization of land lease and government. There, in one year, the Queen's revenues had dropped below 1000 pounds. The poor tenants were on the verge of a wide-scale rising, and the more predatory lords were richer than ever. Not only was the Composition intended to reassess taxable land and fix the limits of land ownership, but it was meant to bring English and Irish magnates alike under direct control of the Crown. Naturally, the Composition was steadily opposed. Bingham disputed many of its details, and the Irish Parliament balked at each step, but the plan was nonetheless original and positive, and in a letter to Walsingham, Perrot explained his determination: "I entered into consideration how this confusion and great enormity, whereof the poorer sort bore the whole charge, and the greater men went free, might be reformed, as well there in that province as throughout the whole Realm. I passed indentures . . . between the lords and their tenants, for a certain rent to be had out of every quarter of land there, the said province also being thereby divided into nine seigniories or honors . . . whereby in short time her Highness will reap yearly by this composition four thousand pounds sterling. . . . There is besides that such a general knot of obedience tied to her Majesty and the State thereby, as her Highness shall stand assured of a round revenue; the lords have thereby agreed with their tenants for a certain rent; the tenants understand what they are to perform to her Majesty and their lords, every man knowing what is his, and depending now upon the law, and not upon one another."

Perrot's determination that the country be governed by law rather than influence befitted his dignity as Lord Deputy; every worthy governor of Ireland had expressed the selfsame aim. Perrot's hardship, however, was to be hindered in matters of justice as much by his own countrymen as the native chieftains. Both were to blame, the Irish lords and the Anglo-Irish settlers, and not unexpectedly the Lord Deputy's staunchest support came from the common people. For a time he might have believed that the authority vested in him was adequate to oppose all sides; the greater was his disappointment, then, to discover that Elizabeth never intended anything like genuine reform or reconstruction.

In the first years of the new decade some redress was offered the Queen's Irish subjects as a response to nagging complaints. Restitution was made in several cases; here and there an undertaker surrendered a few plowlands, but for the most part correction was postponed interminably by administrative malfeasance. The case of Maurice, Lord Roche, Viscount of Fermoy, is illustrative. In 1586 Roche found his seigniory in the Awbeg Valley hemmed in on all sides by new settlers. Range which had been in his family unchallenged for centuries was suddenly assigned to the Desmond inheritance and granted to strangers. Although the Fermoy Roches had not taken sides in the late war, Maurice had been young and impulsive; for several weeks he had ridden with John of Desmond, until his father and Lord Justice Pelham managed to restrain him. Now, as a result of this lark, his family was unable to move either officials in Dublin or the Earl of Ormond to support their suit against the settlers. Roche claimed that plowlands belonging to him as a loyal subject—that is, an unindicted subject—had passed illegally into the possession of Hugh Cuffe, Edmund Spenser, Roger Keate, and Arthur Hyde, all undertakers in the Awbeg and Blackwater valleys under the protection of Thomas Norris, Vice President of Munster. Roche had recourse to courts in Cork and Dublin but, far from receiving satisfaction, was lucky to escape the experience with his freedom. In 1587, during the Armada scare, Thomas Norris arrested Patrick Condon; John Fitzedmund Fitzgerald, the Seneschal of Imokilly; and several pardoned lieutenants of Gerald Fitzgerald on suspicion of disloyalty. Maurice was fortunate to miss arrest. The Seneschal of Imokilly legitimately held 36,000 acres of land in Munster. He had been one of the first of the great Munster lords to associate himself with James Fitzmaurice's rebellion, and his bravery and intelligence had made him eventually more feared than the Earl of Desmond himself. In 1587 he was in retirement, clearly innocent of any plots, but Norris took advantage of the emergency to send him to Dublin Castle, where he remained until his death two years later. Wisely Roche allowed the Armada crisis to pass without intensifying his efforts to win back his property. But in late 1588, disobeying an injunction against leaving the country, he journeyed to London to present his case to the Queen.

Elizabeth was by this time aware of the legal embarrassments surrounding resettlement of Munster and, in a mood of conciliation, granted Roche an audience, thereafter promising to look into his grievances. The outcome, in Roche's own words, was endless irresolution and bureaucratic red tape: "Those whom her Majesty by letters willed to be favored were not always granted justice, for was a suitor's cause never so just and lawful, his forwardness in service never so apparent, or his letters never so gracious and effectual, so that anyone might judge the success of his suit to be assured, yet any bill wanting a word, either of form or matter, was thereby abated and rejected. A new one had then to be made, and those that wanted for the new bill had no redress. Those who had no bill had no redress at all, whereby the poor people and subjects, by reason of that hard course taken by the Justices, when as they chiefly expected to be reformed according to her Majesty's undoubted pleasure, were very much discouraged, and in a manner fallen into despair, being not able for want of ability to have recourse unto her Highness." In essence, any bill favoring an Irish petition had to be perfect in form and wording or be rejected, even if the bill originated with the Queen. Elizabeth might judge fairly in Irish disputes, but the bureaucrats in Dublin Castle were not always responsive to her commands.

Maurice, however, was exceptionally stubborn and headstrong and as much given to physical intimidation as to litigation. In the years following his return to Ireland from the Court, he petitioned the Queen's Secretaries continually, while also conniving with his tenants to annoy and discourage the new settlers. His accusations ranged widely over the English establishment in Ireland, but one particularly formal complaint, addressed to Walsingham, cited Spenser as a principal: "One Edmund Spenser, clerk of the council of Munster, by color of his office, and by making of corrupt bargains with certain persons pretending falsely to parcel of Lord Roche's lands, dispossessed the said Lord Roche of certain castles and sixteen plowlands. Also the said Spenser, by threatening and menacing of the said Lord Roche's tenants, and by taking their cattle pasturing upon his lordship's own inheritance, and by refusing and beating of his lordship's servants and bailiffs, hath made waste of six other plowlands of his lordship's lawful inheritance to his no small undoing." Evidently, Roche laid claim to Kilcolman Castle, as well as the adjacent meadows, and his servants found on the property were beaten off as trespassers. Spenser was, according to contemporary descriptions, a small, slight man and hardly accustomed to exercise of arms. In all likelihood his servingmen and those of the surrounding landlords stood together against Roche and, meeting McSheehys and Shynans in the fields, drove them off whenever they could. Skirmishes were fought along the boundaries of the Kilcolman estate with clubs and fists, and if no fatalities are recorded at this stage, Spenser's frequent reference to "bordrags and alarms" is certainly not a literary affection. While *Colin Clouts* and *Epithalamion* were being written, the fields of Kilcolman were not safe. Abductions, thefts, and firings were daily occurrences. Today no one is competent to judge the varying merits of the dispute. Surely, Roche believed in his case, and his tenant, Nicholas Shynan, was awarded two of Spenser's plowlands in 1592. But Roche also laid claim to land which had definitely been in the possession of John of Desmond, and to this extent his case is flawed. Whatever the verdict, however, no one doubts that a deep and irreconcilable political conflict underlay the increasing violence. When Spenser and his fellow settlers lodged their charges against Roche, their references were political and their justification was purely national: "Lord Roche, in July, 1586, and at sundry times before and after, relieved and maintained one Keadagh O'Kelly, his foster brother, a proclaimed traitor. Secretly, upon the first report of the coming of the Spaniards, he caused powder and munition to be made in his house. He speaketh ill of the government and hath uttered words of contempt of her Majesty's laws, calling them unjust. He hath imprisoned in his house sundry persons, viz., a man of Mr. Verdon's, a man of Mr. Spenser's, and other of the freeholders of this country. He apprehended one Ullig O'Keif for stealing nine cows, and later freed him, so that said Ullig would make feoffment to him of his land. He made proclamation in his country that none of his people should have any trade or conference with Mr. Spenser or Mr. Piers or any of their tenants. He killed a fat beef of Teig O'Lyne's because Mr. Spenser lay in his house one night as he came from the sessions at Limerick. He killed a beef of his smith's for mending Mr. Piers's plough-iron. He hath concealed from her majesty the manor of Crogh, the freehold of one who was a rebel, and has lately entered into the said rebel's other land, which he gave him in recompense thereof, as he allegeth."

Roche was accused of consorting with rebels, behavior difficult to avoid in a neighborhood of rebels. He was blamed for ostracizing the settlers, a form of resistance perfected in nineteenth-century Ireland against Charles Boycott, an English landlord. And he was charged with concealing arms and abetting criminals. But Roche was to reply that his life was in danger. In the vicinity of his castle at Castletownroche, a crossbowman in the hire of Mr. Piers tried to shoot him. As the years passed, the Munster settlers perhaps did attempt to frighten or murder Roche, and he responded in kind. He sent North to Hugh O'Neill for powder and ball, south to Spain for firearms and steel, and by 1595 had fairly turned the Awbeg Valley into an armed camp.

The true beneficiary of the troubles in Munster was Hugh O'Neill, the O'Neill, Earl of Tyrone, and virtual Prince of Ulster. Though in 1590 O'Neill took no visible interest in the South, every imprisonment and every confiscation contributed to his power. The destruction of the Geraldine lords had left a vacuum among the Irish of the South, and O'Neill filled this void, first through emissaries like Lord Roche and Tirlogh Mac-Sheehy, and then as the supreme war leader of an Irish nation. By the time of the Second Munster Plantation O'Neill was not just the most powerful Gael in Ireland, but the only Gael in Ireland with power, and the English had no one to blame for his ascendancy but themselves.

From the dwindled barony of Dungannon, his by birth, O'Neill rose to the earldom of Tyrone in 1586 and, of commensurate importance, to the chieftaincy of the North. He contrived to succeed Turlough Luineach, to become the heir of his uncle and mortal enemy Shane O'Neill, and, meanwhile, to ignore the desperate pleas of the Desmond Irish. While James Fitzmaurice and Gerald Fitzgerald fought and died in the South, Hugh O'Neill remained a loyal and cooperative ally of the Crown, more embroiled in the dynastic contentions of the North than in the struggle for Munster. The years would teach him that to be a great Irish lord was by necessity to be a great Irish rebel, but by the time the lesson was learned the Desmonds had fallen. Hugh was not born as Gerald was to power and influence, only to the sordid violence and ignoble family feuds of the Ulster O'Neills, and by the time he was fourteen he had already strangled a cousin with his own hands. Far from suspecting him, the Crown preserved his life as a matter of policy, and Sir Henry Sidney virtually adopted him. More was the surprise, therefore, when Hugh O'Neill inherited Desmond's mantle and surpassed Desmond in every way. By Elizabeth's own admission, O'Neill was her most formidable adversary, and during the last decade of her reign she raged against him variably as "my Arch Traitor," "my Monster of the North," "my Running Beast." He was the brilliant campaigner who avenged Monaster, Carrigafoyle, and Smerwick. He was the adept politician who, knowing and fearing English might, turned Elizabeth's strength against her. And he was the nemesis of the Munster settlers and the outposts of Elizabethan culture. More has been written about O'Neill than any other Irishman of the age, for he was in a sense the father to Irish nationhood, the last defender of the Gael. He was as well, and perhaps inevitably, the last of the great Irish lords.

There would perhaps have been no Rebel O'Neill had Shane not killed Hugh's father and brother and narrowly failed to murder Hugh himself. This was the same Shane who visited Elizabeth's Court in tribal splendor in 1562; the same who was called the Grand Disturber and who kept the North in foment until the O'Donnells slipped into his tent one night and cut him to pieces with their swords. He was the son of Con Bacach O'Neill, who had been translated by Henry VIII from "the O'Neill" to the first Earl of Tir-Oen. In his youth Bacach had enjoyed the charms of the wild North, and Shane always resented his father's inability to say no to alleged paternity. For it happened that by the lovely daughter of a blacksmith, Alison Kelly, Bacach begot a son named Matthew. Matthew was to be the father of Brian and Hugh, both of whom Shane believed were Kellys by birth, blacksmiths by inheritance, and bastards to boot. But Bacach's dalliance with Alison was no casual bedding. She became the avowed passion of his life, and years later he permitted himself the indulgence of disowning his legitimate son, *Sean an Diomais*, Shane the Proud, in favor of Matthew. By this stroke, Alison's son was within reach of becoming the O'Neill, the second Earl of Tyrone, and Shane's overlord. Shane's answer to Bacach's romantic recollection was to lock him up for good and murder Matthew. In confused dealing, shot through with betrayal and treachery, Shane managed to catch his half brother and hang him. Months later he captured Brian, Matthew's eldest son, and ordered his throat cut, and he was searching the neighborhood of Dungannon for his nephew Hugh when the Crown stepped in to end the slaughter.

In 1559 Sir Henry Sidney was campaigning in Ulster for the first time. His aim was to bend Shane to the Crown's will by a demonstration of force, and while he had no instructions to overthrow the Grand Disturber, who was by far the strongest lord in the North, he discovered the young horseboy Hugh in the wilderness around Dungannon. Sidney recognized the value of his find. If the Crown could keep Hugh O'Neill alive, they would have the natural counterpoise to Shane or any other tanist elected to the O'Neill chiefdom. An opportunity to groom the next Earl of Tyrone, or in any event a useful pretender, was too good to let slip. The only safe place for Hugh was England, and Sidney returned with the boy to Kent, to Penshurst Castle, where during the next seven years he would grow up beside Sir Philip Sidney.

Elizabeth's England did not lack for magnificent country palaces or satellite courts, but of those in which Hugh might have found a place, Penshurst, "not built to envious show," epitomized all that was most decent in English county life. Sir Henry was a kind and understanding master, his household well governed and hospitable, and to his door came the great and near great of the age. By birth and marriage the Sidneys were connected to the finest families of the realm. Their house stood halfway between London and Calais, a frequent lodging of diplomats and couriers. But all qualities of men journeyed to Penshurst and were welcome—poets and voyagers; scholars and divines; the high and lowly of state—and in the simple hall they sat together at meals, a microcosm of English society. The Sidneys were devout Protestants with a pronounced puritan leaning, but they were also citizens of a new Rome, humanists alive to art and tradition. If Penshurst lacked for no civilized amenities, the house was also not sumptuous. Grace and learning, gravity and noblesse were the articles of Sir Henry's creed, and young Hugh was reared in his faith. As page to Mary Sidney, O'Neill was taught manners by the grandam of courtesy, the mother of Philip Sidney, the perfect knight; the mother of Mary, Countess of Pembroke, patroness of Donne and Jonson. Between the ages of nine and sixteen, when he was returned to Ulster, O'Neill could have observed the architects of Elizabeth's Ireland gathered in the armory at Penshurst: Leicester and Walsingham; Sir John Perrot and the Earl of Ormond.

Desmond was a captive in London during Hugh's last years in Kent, and plans had already begun for Carew's First Munster Plantation. In later years Hugh O'Neill would give out that he had not been unhappy at Penshurst, though homesick, and he would express his gratitude to the man who had rescued him from Shane and Dungannon. He had every reason to be grateful; he had studied his enemies-to-be and understood them. He had experienced the English world as no chieftain could, trained in its schools, reared in its values, and if he returned to the ways and religion of his own land, he remained throughout his life at home in both cultures.

After, on the shores of Lough Neagh, O'Neill's Court blended the exotic customs of Ireland with the refinement of Renaissance England. He could look up from his simple meal on the ground beneath the pines and quote verse to English visitors, then, turning aside, in Gaelic send his henchmen to murder a kern. Upon the death of Shane, Hugh returned home, but he returned to disappointment, for Turlough Luineach O'Neill had meanwhile demonstrated the necessary support to win the earldom, and once again Hugh was confined to the barony of Dungannon. Years of plotting and calculation lay ahead, while Baron Dungannon maneuvered against his kinsman Turlough, placated his English masters, and sought out the seed of Shane the Proud. It took time for Luineach to drink himself to death, and in the interim Hugh revenged the deaths of his father and brother on Shane's heirs. Apparently he never despised the English as he despised his dead uncle or exercised half the ruthlessness in driving back Elizabeth that he expended against his half cousins. While the Desmond Wars raged in the South, Shane's children were assassinated one by one. The feud outlasted the century, often as much in O'Neill's mind as his war with the English, and its obsessive nature is revealing. Shane was not despised and murdered symbolically again and again just for his brutality or because, like the Titan Saturn, he gobbled up his offspring. The practice of tanistry made such crimes common. Rather, O'Neill grew to see in Shane and his kind the primitive inadequacy of traditional Celtic life, the insularity and ignorance which crippled Irish resistance to the English. Shane's life had been a monument to self-indulgence. Insatiable, inexhaustible, he was a leader of immense physical energy. His weeklong bouts with *uisce beathadh* (whiskey) and the daughters of Armagh were legendary, and the tale survives of Shane buried to his neck in cool, moist sand, a fabled cure for hangover and sexual exhaustion. Of course, Shane could also fight and often did so quite effectively, but the discipline of the heroic age was not the discipline which would overcome English marshals and English pikemen. The cold eye of the strategist, the reasoning mind, these O'Neill admired and cultivated, and if in the process he became more the

Earl of Tyrone than the O'Neill, he succeeded where Shane could not. He valued the wild, hot-tempered strain in Ulster, found both courage and passion in the O'Donnells and made them his lifelong allies, but he shaped his policy to a knowledge of the outside world. No Irish renegade of the century knew as many eminent Englishmen as O'Neill; at times in his career he had more friends among the invaders than among his own, and he never failed to call in debts of friendship. He started with Sidney and Leicester, attached himself to the elder Essex, married his daughter Margaret to Viscount Mountgarret. He mentioned as friends of his Lord Chancellor Hatton, Sir Francis Walsingham, Sir Anthony St. Leger, and Sir Robert Gardner; he wrote as a confidant to Lord Chancellor Loftus; Sir Geoffrey Fenton was almost invariably on his side, and he thanked Burghley for "good turns received." From 1580 until 1585, while the Desmond War and its aftermath was occupying the attention of everyone else in Ireland, he had been busy making useful friends like these.

But O'Neill's crowning triumph in the game of diplomacy and deception came with his marriage to the sister of Sir Henry Bagenal, the English general he would rout and kill at the Battle of Yellow Ford. To suggest that Tyrone married Mabel Bagenal as a ploy is perhaps too hard on him; evidence to the contrary, he appears to have genuinely cared for her at first and to have exerted all his considerable charm in wooing her from her father's house. Her father was Sir Nicholas Bagenal, the same who fought with Perrot in the Council Chamber at Dublin, and although his daughter was apt and eligible, marriage to an Irish warlord was not exactly the match he desired. The problem for the Bagenals was that they could not stop the marriage. As representatives of the Crown, they were expected to treat Tyrone with dignity, to allow him entrance to their homes, to oversee his exercise of power. Outside the rituals of state, he was far their superior in rank, and the government was inclined to encourage intermarriage with English gentlewomen as a civilizing measure where convenient. The Bagenals could not hide behind the Queen when Hugh O'Neill came courting.

For his part, O'Neill thought Sir Nicholas and his son to be fools and, determined to win Mabel, set out to have her at any price. He had noticed her many times on his visits to the garrison town of Newry, watching her grow from a girl into a graceful young woman. And likely he had had his fill of harsh Ulster wives. He was forty-one, Mabel was twenty, his second wife had just died, and now, as the Earl of Tyrone, Hugh was perhaps of a mind to establish the graces of England on Lough Neagh. To have done so would have required an English wife, though as matters turned out, more an English amazon than a frail young maiden. Mabel was swept off her feet without a thought to the world she was accepting. O'Neill courted her in the full regalia of an Irish peer. When he put on his courtier's clothes, his crimson gold-studded jacket and his lined cloak, and rode into the dusty little garrison town escorted by a hundred retainers in glittering mail, Mabel Bagenal succumbed. Differences of age and culture could be forgotten for a title. Besides, O'Neill was still a fine figure; with flaming red hair, a red spade beard, and broad shoulders, a vision of lordliness.

From the moment he made his intentions clear, not all the officials in Ireland could have kept Mabel from him, even had they dared. Only the Crown had the authority to dictate to Tyrone, and since the marriage of a wellborn Englishwoman to a Gaelic lord raised delicate points of precedent and policy, the matter was referred to the Queen. Whitehall deliberated for weeks, weighing the implications of the match, questioning its effects on the balance of power in Ulster. Meanwhile, the Bagenals and their well-wishers urged the Queen to uphold the statute of exclusion and proscribe the marriage. Tyrone, however, had advocates, too. From Dublin, Geoffrey Fenton wrote that he sincerely believed the match to be desirable and conducive to English interests. Archbishop Loftus concurred with Fenton. And Sir Robert Gardner and Garrett Moore, Tyrone's particular friends, testified that the marriage would hasten Ulster's acceptance of English ways. Elizabeth had grave doubts; she probed O'Neill's intentions carefully, yet finally, even she could discover no harm in the marriage and, more mindful of politics than Mabel Bagenal's welfare, granted her approval. A refusal would have been tantamount to outright provocation, and the Queen had little need to provoke further enmity in the North. She had delayed as long as possible, withholding her answer to the last moment, and when her permission arrived, it came late. While she debated, O'Neill had seduced and abducted his lady, and as her courier arrived in Dublin, he was enjoying his wedding feast at Lough Neagh. Not for the last time Tyrone deferred to the Queen's pleasure, only to do what he pleased before she could answer.

The bird had flown, and no purpose was served by closing the cage. The government felt acute embarrassment, but the girl seemed light and hardly worth a breach of the peace. The Bagenals were inconsolable; everywhere in Ireland English fathers looked to their daughters, but Mabel's honor was lost, and she was abandoned to her choice. And if she was happy at first, it was because she had no idea what it meant to be a chieftain's wife. In the world of the North she was not "lady Mabel, Countess of Tyrone," but "that English woman, Bagenal's wench," and all of Hugh's tenderness and solicitude could not reconcile her to the harshness of Gaelic society. Eventually the couple fought terribly, she goaded by jealous concubines and the warrior wives of O'Donnells and Maguires, and he exasperated by her airs and expectations. It is easy to remark that

O'Neill should have guessed, should have known in his maturity the futility of transplanting Mabel. He loved her perhaps, yet he also loved what she represented, the grace and refinement she could bring to Dungannon. She was chosen to transform Matthew O'Neill's dank castle into an English gentleman's home, the seat of Tyrone into a civilized household. To this end Hugh begrudged nothing, showering gifts on her extravagantly and even suffering her abuses publicly. The North laughed at the dance his Englishwoman led him, but O'Neill, silent and inscrutable, tossed his friends out of Dungannon and kept his wife.

Shortly after their marriage Hugh appeared in London. Though his presence was offensive to Elizabeth, he was not there on matters of state. He had come to buy Arras tapestries, fine plate, Brussels lace, French furnishings, and Flemish paintings. His purchases filled the hold of a merchantman bound for Belfast Lough, and they were meant for Mabel and the "new" Dungannon. He hired English artisans to return home with him and paid them excessively for their journey. The public was astonished to learn that he was planning a fine country house on the site of Dungannon and that he had voyaged to England to find labor and materials. O'Neill consulted with the foremost patron of architects, the master builder of Theobalds and Burghley House—William Cecil—and the old man was delighted at Tyrone's sudden conversion to sensible values.

They were a strange match these two, Burghley in his dotage, O'Neill at the height of his powers, and they were drawn together by a common bond and enthusiasm. Hugh claimed that he lacked lead for properly roofing his new house, for most great houses were roofed in lead, and Cecil agreed to clear the import to Ireland of several tons. Lead was a scarce commodity there, never easy to slip past Her Majesty's customs and awkwardly heavy to sneak ashore in the bays and loughs of the North. Importation was strictly controlled, for obvious reasons, and Cecil might well have been the only man in England capable of circumventing the restrictions. In any event, Hugh got his lead, a whole shipful, and for the next two years, while he planned his mansion, the metal lay in a stand of pines near Dungannon. Precisely when his plan became fiction, if indeed it had ever been genuine, is not known. Tyrone was by then married to a fourth wife and on the brink of war with the Crown. Before the Battle of Yellow Ford, Burghley's lead was melted down and molded into shot and ball. And on that field, where Tyrone's muskets raked the troops of his former brother-in-law, Sir Henry Bagenal, the few survivors had reason to resent Cecil's magnanimity.

Whether O'Neill's marriage was ultimately just a convenience and whether he seriously planned to create a shireland of Tyrone are questions which have long been debated. To those English settlers who faced the fury of the North a few years later, Tyrone would always be the arch-Machiavellian, an oath breaker, a master of deception. But just as likely he never intended war with the Crown. No Irish leader of the sixteenth century was more acutely aware of English supremacy. Unlike the Earl of Desmond, O'Neill was less a feudal magnate than a Gaelic captain, and consequently, he did not labor under comparable delusions of pride and prerogative. If he professed a desire to civilize Ulster, he also carried out changes which were unmistakably modern in design. Tribal council was replaced with the machinery of a rudimentary administration. Tyrone subdued warring factions by suppressing the practice of coynage and opened the way into the North for the Queen's justice by subordinating the Brehons. Underlying his many disputes with Dublin was the surety, in English minds, that O'Neill meant change and reform and that, in the end, he was the man to tame the wild Scots and Irish. Unlike his uncle, Shane, he was a presentable leader and therefore, like Ormond, an indispensable ally. O'Neill's difficulty was less that he hated the English than that in his eagerness to emulate them, he could not forsake his Irishness. He married an Englishwoman, imported English servants and advisors, even employed a Cornish Jew named Salomon as secretary, and yet at the last moment, when decision was irrevocable, fell back on the ways of a Gaelic chieftain. His most loyal gestures had a habit of resulting in treason. He abolished coyne and livery but substituted a peasant army, obedient only to him and to a dream of Irish nationhood. He proscribed Brehon Law but in its place became the sole law of the North. And the very administration for which Dublin praised him tied the warrior Maguires and O'Donnells closer to him. Clearly Tyrone, like Desmond before him, submitted to intolerable pressures. The zigzag course he followed over the years was less a reflection of indecisiveness or subterfuge than of irreconcilable desires. He was always aware of the grave consequences of disloyalty to one side or the other, but he was never able to bridge for long the differences between his world and the world of Mabel Bagenal, Sir Henry Sidney, and Penshurst. Not unexpectedly, he grew weary of trimming and dodging and in that mood declared unequivocally for Ulster. The precise turning point is not easy to discern. He negotiated, surrounded by increasing suspicion, until events forced decision on him, just as Fitzmaurice's landing once forced decision on Gerald. But the fate of Mabel Bagenal was an indication of the way he would eventually go, and the last account of them together, offered by a servant, is revealing: "Then Phelim McTurlough O'Neill met with Tyrone and they parted in an unfriendly way—the Earl stepping into his cot beside Mabel, and Phelim saying piteously, 'Well, God be with you, My Lord,' and Tyrone turning his back on him and saying, ominously, 'May God be at defiance with you until night.' The

O'Hagans who had been watching this conference with an uneasiness now came about Phelim. They stood and watched the Earl and his wife being rowed into the lake, and they put their arms about Phelim, and soothered him, and took him away into their camp, where at the gate they fell upon him. One slashed off his arm. The others fell upon him. One of his men ran for the river but they drowned him in it. In the evening Hugh O'Gallagher brought evening food to the Earl and his wife. 'Why have you been so long?' asked Tyrone. 'I was seeing the doing of an ill deed,' said Gallagher. 'What is that?' 'The killing of Phelim McTurlough.' 'And is he killed?' 'Aye.' 'And is Donal Oge killed too?' 'Aye, both killed and drowned.' 'What became of my shot that went over the river, yesterday?' asked Tyrone, changing the subject. And that moment, Mabel broke into hysterical speech, weeping and clapping her hands. She spoke in high voice and in English, admonishing the Earl, so that her speech could not be understood, and he turning on her, silenced her with a few harsh words. Together they rowed away into the dusk after this killing of Phelim McTurlough."

Phelim was condemned to death before Mabel's eyes not because he had committed crime, but because he was Shane's cousin and had sought the Crown's protection. For Mabel, the romance had gone out of Irish life. She was beginning to see the ruthless enforcement, to read the signs and gestures which meant murder, and she could no longer reconcile her suspicions with the husband she thought she knew. Out of her own fear, she protested too loudly. And of course, her protests were useless. Following Phelim's assassination, she was never again allowed in public. For two years more she languished inside Dungannon, virtually a prisoner, surrounded by hostile servants, until in 1595 she died forsaken by everyone. Nor did Hugh wait long to marry a fourth time. His new wife, however, was an Ulster woman, and her household was swept clean of all traces of Mabel and her fine designs. In 1595 O'Neill was on the verge of war with England, and two factors in particular had banished his indecision: the encroachment of English settlers onto the lands of the O'Donnells and the Queen's incessant interference in the politics of Ulster.

Elizabeth's attempts to curb the bloody rivalries in Ulster met with no more success than Mabel's. She was bound to try, however, and her intervention was largely reflex, stemming from the same considerations which had prompted the Crown to keep young Hugh alive while Shane ruled. The government was well served by pretenders, claimants, and malcontents; and since the election of chieftains by tanistry regularly resulted in feuds, the Crown seldom lacked for informers and willing tools. Tyrone's aim was to liquidate such threats to his security before they developed. Phelim was just such a threat, so also were the children of Shane. In return for their information about O'Neill's activities, the government extended them protection. And violation of protection was the principal area of contention between the Queen and her Earl of Tyrone. Phelim's elimination caused no little stir in Dublin, but the government was never able to pin the charge directly on O'Neill. The case of Shane's son Hugh was clearer. Fettered Hugh, so named because his mother bore him while in prison, turned informer in 1591, reporting to the Crown that Tyrone was plotting with Spain. His testimony was made more prejudicial by a certain trull's corroboration—she had entertained Hugh's Spanish visitors—and Dublin was able to add to its growing file another bit of evidence pointing to Hugh's perfidy. In exchange for his testimony, Fettered Hugh, or Hugh Gaveloch as he was also called, was extended the Queen's protection, and since he was a bandit as well as an informer, the protection was welcome. But when the Crown moved to arraign Tyrone on charges of conspiring to treason, it discovered that its lady of the night had vanished, and that Fettered Hugh was hanging dead from a thorntree outside Dungannon. Reliable witnesses claimed that O'Neill had caught him in the nearby woods, had him bound in chains, and then hanged him from the thorntree with his own hands. The Queen was furious when the news reached her. Immediately investigations were opened into the substance of the charges and the reasons for the hanging. O'Neill replied under questioning from Dublin that he had done nothing but good, in the best interests of the Queen. He had had Hugh hanged by Melaghin McMurrehey because "he was the son of a traitor and himself a traitor; because he was a murderer and the son of a murderer, a spoiler, and a killer of women and infants; a man of whom he had complained more than once to the Deputy and to his honourable friend, Sir Thomas Cecil." To allay the Queen's rage, Tyrone now volunteered to visit London and explain his version of the affair.

Privately he lamented the government's continual meddling in his business, but publicly he was all reason and obedience. Tyrone counted on Sir Christopher Hatton's support at Court and the good wishes of many gentlemen, but Elizabeth, whose splendid instincts suggested danger in the man, refused to see O'Neill. Instead of composing her differences with him, she ordered him arrested and detained in Sir Henry Wallop's house —a reminder of Desmond's fate—and bade him report to the Privy Council. The Queen fashioned the noose and left O'Neill to tighten it himself as he testified before the Secretaries. But she never counted on his honeyed tongue or his capacity to adjust to the mood and viewpoint of his accusors.

Before the Council he argued: "I acknowledge that by my education among the English I am not altogether ignorant, but that in the strict course of Her Majesty's laws I might be reprehensible for this execution. Nevertheless I humbly desire that consideration may be had to the place where this fact was done and to the person—a notable murderer—and to the ancient form of government among us in Ulster, where there is neither magistrate, judge, sheriff, nor course of the laws of this realm; but certain customs by which both [Turlough] O'Neill and I and others of our sort do govern our followers; neither have we been at any time restrained from execution of evildoers, nor of such as be invaders of our country, or professed enemies to the same." He concluded his defense by begging for the swift establishment of English magistrates in the North and by asking Her Majesty's grace and favor, "which is my greatest comfort and the chief cause of my coming over."

In effect, O'Neill now spoke for the whole of the North. He argued that protection could not be extended to known criminals without subverting what slight legitimacy existed in Ireland. And he concluded appropriately by joining with the Council in wishing a quick resolution to all disturbances in the country. Here was the skill which led his contemporaries to talk of "his profound dissembling heart," "his high dissembling, subtle and profound wit," which was to say his remarkable gift for words. O'Neill escaped London with only a warning and an injunction to desist from levying black rents against his vassals. He was off cheaply and especially so since Fettered Hugh had been right: O'Neill had been treating with the Spaniards and would seek their aid and intervention more actively in the future.

Between 1590 and 1595 the government found numerous occasions for interrogating O'Neill, and he was summoned often to Dublin at the pleasure of Lord Deputy Fitzwilliams. As the decade wore on, his friends began to doubt his loyalty, but no one was able to bring charges to bear. Suddenly Fenton wrote that he doubted Tyrone's innocence but did not know where to look for proof; he concluded that "so long as the Earl of Tyrone stands aloof, as he does, he will be a sponge to suck unto him all doubtful parts." At the time of Fenton's writing Hugh stood between the Maguires and Sir Richard Bingham's Connaught settlers, ostensibly to prevent war. But everywhere it was believed that Tyrone was counseling the Maguires to refrain from attacking the settlers until the Queen's forces in Ireland had deteriorated further. Supporting this belief were rumors of an Irish army being raised in the North. One report credited Tyrone with a force of 700 horse and 3000 foot. Another reckoned his strength as closer to 1000 horse and 7000 foot. What made these estimates particularly ominous was that the Queen's militia was at a historic ebb. Even had his life depended on it, Fitzwilliams could not have mustered 1000 trained soldiers. O'Neill gave no signs of hostility, yet this in itself was unsettling. Everywhere along the northern borders, into Fermanagh and Monaghan, the counties of the Maguires and O'Donnells, settlers were expanding their holdings under the Crown's protection. The North was primed to explode, and Tyrone was the fuse; he could not stand by indefinitely while the hunger for land spilled out of Munster and Connaught and into Ulster. That he did not act precipitously was only an indication of his deep preparations. The old Irish hands sensed the impending danger and argued caution, but none could penetrate the secrecy surrounding O'Neill. The first indication of what lay ahead occurred in 1593; in the hard winter of that year, Red Hugh O'Donnell was sprung from Dublin Castle, and with the O'Donnells thereafter aligned with the O'Neills and Maguires, Ulster achieved a unity unknown since the days of the Red Branch Kings.

Tradition has long held that Tyrone managed Red Hugh's escape, but the success of the adventure probably depended far more on O'Donnell's enterprise and remarkable constitution than on O'Neill's arrangements. Red Hugh had been kidnapped in Lough Swilly three years before on Sir John Perrot's orders. He had been lured aboard a coastal vessel with two companions, plied with wine, bound and trussed, and transported directly to the castle's Bermingham Tower. The reason for Perrot's trickery was simple and unconscionable: Hugh's father hated the Crown, his mother outspokenly despised the English race, and together they were closely allied with the new Earl of Tyrone. Red Hugh was thrown into a dungeon at fifteen because Perrot needed a hostage against the O'Donnells, but an extra dividend was the lesson taught O'Neill. If the new Earl thought he could outface the Lord Deputy, Perrot meant to show him that Gaelic chieftains had no corner on ruthlessness. For the most part the lesson was heeded, but the price was a young boy, who for the next three years endured darkness and malnutrition in a stone cell. The details of Red Hugh's imprisonment are obscure, but for the rest of his long life he never forgave or forgot the humiliations his captors inflicted on him. He was eighteen when he finally escaped and old for his years. By the time he was twenty-three he had become the most formidable captain of gallowglass of his generation.

Tyrone liked the boy and needed him. His father, Black Hugh O'Donnell, was no longer a healthy man, and his son was destined to succeed him as chief of the O'Donnells. O'Neill planned, therefore, to have the privy holes left open on Bermingham Tower one night in January. The castle privies emptied into the moat by conduits venting through the walls, and by sliding down a conduit and dropping into the icy water below, Red Hugh and the two youngsters taken with him, Henry and Art O'Neill, escaped into the night. They had aid outside the castle; Tyrone had sent his foster brothers the O'Hagans to lead the prisoners out of Dublin, and in a blinding snow storm the O'Hagans directed them into the Wicklows, where Fiach MacHugh was waiting to help. In the dreadful blizzard, over trails which had exhausted Grey's troops in fine weather years before, the renegades made their way into Glenmalure. There Hugh and Art O'Neill collapsed from weakness and exposure, and by the time the O'Hagans had dragged them to the warmth of Fiach's camp, Art had frozen to death. Of the three men who escaped, only Hugh survived, and he was soon carried North to be hidden safely in the wild glens of Donegal.

Fitzwilliams could never prove that O'Neill had conspired in the freeing of O'Donnell. Rumors were everywhere, but evidence scarce. The escape was the most daring in memory; North and South it became the talk of English and Irish alike, and most believed that the break was proof of Tyrone's long reach—extending into the very heart of English power in Ireland, Dublin Castle itself. Among the O'Donnells the deliverance of Red Hugh was deemed to fulfill an ancient prophecy; their bards sang the vision of the family of Conall up and down the North: "When two Hughs, the Black and the Red, lawfully and lineally succeed each other as O'Don-nells, the last Hugh shall be monarch of Ireland and banish the foreign invader." The prison break was a resounding defeat for the government, and since it gave to the North a great natural hero, an instrument ready to Tyrone's will, the final cost was truly incalculable.

Red Hugh was home no more than a year before he assumed his father's chiefdom and the title Baron Tyrconnel. To pursue him further was impolitic, if not outright folly, and the Crown resolved instead to wean him from O'Neill's influence. This charade continued into 1594, only ending with the recognition that Tyrconnel was Tyrone's protégé, his loyal lieutenant and principal stalking-horse. Under O'Neill's tutelage, Red Hugh played the young rebel, while his mentor lingered neutrally in the background, counseling restraint to Queen and countrymen alike. While the Maguires fought Bingham's settlers on the lakeshores of Erne, and while O'Donnell slowly strangled the English outpost at Enniskillen, Tyrone decried their acts and, traveling to Dublin, tendered his services as an intermediary. If many there suspected his sincerity, none was audacious enough to call him out. The very thought of the O'Neills in arms with the O'Donnells and Maguires was sufficient to intimidate Elizabeth, to say nothing of Fitzwilliams. Incredible though it seems, the Lord Deputy's answer to O'Neill's veiled threat was to favor the Maguires against Bingham, the Lord Lieutenant of Connaught. The Crown had plotted to turn Tyrconnel against Tyrone; now Tyrone turned the Lord Deputy against his own man and, encouraging him to appease the Northern counties, paved his way to disgrace and recall. In the spring of 1594 the Maguires broke through the Gap of the Erne and, overrunning the plain of Roscommon, routed Bingham's forces. Sir William Russell replaced Fitzwilliams that August, and while he intended to act forcefully, he soon discovered that he had little wherewith to fight. A few months later Red Hugh attacked an English relief column bound for Enniskillen. In a running battle along the banks of the Blackwater River the O'Donnells routed the column and scattered their supplies into the river at a place since called the Ford of Biscuits. By early 1595 the Irish of O'Donnell and Maguire had broken through the English garrison line stretching from Newry in the East to lower Lough Erne in the West. Newry remained in English hands, but the center of the line, Fort Monaghan, was encircled and in danger of submitting. In February, Sir Henry Bagenal led a party of reinforcements toward Monaghan, and though they fought their way into the fort with essential supplies, they were ambushed on withdrawing and severely mauled. The Battle of Clontibret, as this ambush became known, saw the O'Neills in the field for the first time, and at their head the Earl of Tyrone.

Clontibret struck a stunning blow against the government. The better part of an English company perished in the battle, but more damaging than their loss was the loss in confidence which followed disclosure of O'Neill's strength. Sir John Norris, who was returned to Ireland at this time with a regiment of Flanders veterans, studied the battle closely and concluded that O'Neill outnumbered Bagenal at least three to one. He recognized the difficult terrain over which Bagenal would have to march in order to penetrate County Tyrone and, weighing the government's slender resources, advised Russell to negotiate a peace. Norris was weary and in poor health. Long campaigns had sapped his strength, and the spectacle of corruption and incompetence among the Queen's troops further dissuaded him from offering battle. Sir John believed that Tyrone was content to remain penned in the North, that he was not likely to molest the pale, the Midlands, or Connaught if left alone. William Russell disagreed; the Lord Deputy knew of O'Neill's negotiations with Spain and believed that Spanish troops would land once more in the South. Almost alone among the Crown's high officials, Russell was convinced that Ireland was on the brink of an enormous rebellion which could engulf the entire country. He argued bitterly with Norris, and in 1596 Norris retired to his estate at Mallow, pleading illness. But the campaigns which now followed only lowered English stock in Ireland further. Russell lost Fort Monaghan. Red Hugh's followers pressed into Connaught and the Lord Deputy was compelled to raze his own lands in order to drive the Irish out. And the negotiations of 1595–1596 were no more successful. Tyrone and O'Donnell demanded "freedom of conscience" for the North, an open return to the religion of Rome, and when Russell demurred, they virtually dictated the language of the new truce. The document which Russell signed at Dundalk used the words "war" and "peace" instead of "rebellion" and "pardon," and Elizabeth turned livid with rage when she learned the details. Once more the Queen spent no money to enforce her will in Ireland, yet she demanded that Tyrone and his kind be made to show respect. In April, 1597, a new Lord Deputy arrived in Dublin to take Russell's place.

Thomas, Lord Burgh was the last Lord Deputy to sit at Dublin Castle during the century. He was nominated by Cecil, confirmed by the Queen, and undoubtedly was an appropriate choice for the mission. The army he was intended to lead stood then at under 2000 enlistments; it was starved and naked, defeated and rebellious, and confronting it stood O'Neill's 10,000 Irish patriots in various states of training and preparation. Large stores of powder and arms had recently arrived in the North from Danzig; Spain was committed to supporting the Catholic legions in Ulster; and artillery, never plentiful among the Irish, was arriving in Donegal from Corunna. Burgh was, therefore, advised to hold the forts along the northern borders as long as he could, buying time for the Crown to strengthen its position. Instead, he resuscitated his army and attacked. During the summer of 1597 he drove Tyrconnel out of Connaught, flung O'Neill's clansmen back from the Blackwater River, and within a few weeks restored a semblance of stability to the situation. He was a brusk, laconic soldier, much underestimated by the clever O'Neill, and after several disastrous skirmishes, Tyrone resolved to step back from the brink of war. He temporized, now buying time for his side, and shamelessly asked the Crown's pardon for his misdeeds. But Burgh was not given to compromises or treaties. His headlong ferocity is clear in a letter to Cecil: "The traitor holds our idleness in contempt. . . . Therefore be her Majesty's ensigns advanced. Our hopes many. If he will fight we have the cause, and to that end be we paid to execute the due of our profession: if he fly, pursuit must needs bring him into disdain. . . . And the waverers in this intermission and suspense will now, when the ensigns be displayed, bethink them of a prince's strength. . . . I will, God willing, stick to him, and if need be lie on the ground and drink water ten weeks, unless sooner blessings fall upon my labors."

Burgh was evidently a leader of matchless spirit, a worthy opponent of O'Neill and Tyrconnel, but as he began to hammer them back into Ulster, he also threw the army and officialdom of Dublin into turmoil. He attacked the corrupt captains, the sale of arms to the rebels, the extortion and blackmail by which fortunes were made in Ireland. And in October, 1597, just as he had begun a thorough reform, he died. Tyrone surely had reason and means to dispatch him, but there are doubts that the deed was done by an Irishman. The suspicion has long survived that Burgh was poisoned by his own countrymen, who, disliking his interference in lucrative practices, might have seized the moment to murder him. In any event Burgh's reforms died with him, and the advances he had made against Tyrone were soon lost through bungling and malfeasance. The Crown was left no choice but to turn again to Thomas Butler, and in 1598 the Earl of Ormond was named Lord General, while Thomas Norris, resident in Munster, was made Lord Justice.

By 1598 the playacting was over; the sides were drawn in the North, and indeed across Ireland, and negotiations had broken down completely. Ormond was no longer a young man; he desperately wanted peace, but O'Neill's terms were inadmissible: the complete and total restitution of all lands confiscated by the English and their allies in Munster, Leinster, Connaught, and Ulster. Such terms were beyond Butler's power to discuss, and he chided his countrymen for interfering in the business of other provinces. Finally, in July, as both sides continued their raids across the border, Ormond met with Tyrone outside Dundalk in one last attempt to forestall war. The troops which accompanied Butler were so shamefully ragged and undisciplined that he hid them in the streets of the town and went forward alone to meet Tyrone across a brook. The hills around the spot were dotted with O'Neill's men, and Ormond, now partly deaf, listened to Hugh as best he could from the far bank. O'Neill promised peace —he was then awaiting word from Spain—and he urged Ormond to return to Kilkenny and cease meddling in the North. Butler asked for hostages, Tyrone's two sons, as security against a breach of peace, and O'Neill denied him. The speech was recorded by a scribe at Ormond's side, and it is the most impassioned outburst O'Neill ever allowed himself. After years of verbal fencing, he spoke his mind, and his charges were equivalent to a declaration of war: "You do not know the North as I know it," he told Butler. "If my sons were out of this country their people would despise them. And if they were not here in Ulster how would *you* treat them? They would be treated as I was treated by Sir Henry Sidney when my father died. The people made Turlough the O'Neill—my father's enemy. And Sir Henry Sidney supported him against me. And he was supported by every Deputy ever till the day he died. Her Majesty never gave me anything but what belonged to me. And as for what I have gotten I got it by my own scratching of the world and not from her goodness. Have I not spent my blood for her? Have I not kept quiet for thirty years? Bounden to serve? To offer her my sons? You shall get none of my sons, but my word and oath for keeping the peace. I am resolved never to deliver any of my sons. And do you think that I esteem my sons so much? Between me and God if they were both in your hands all this while I would have done just the same that I have done." The exchange was in Gaelic, as befitted the two most powerful Irish lords in Ireland, and O'Neill's assertions were beyond Butler's capacity to answer or contradict. Like Gerald Fitzgerald, those many years before, O'Neill had chosen his course; Butler understood, perhaps even felt for what Tyrone had swallowed, but he could do nothing else than ride back to Dundalk and prepare for war.

Between 1595 and 1598 the Earl of Tyrone surrendered, pleaded, or treated for consideration no less than seven times. After each submission he was permitted to return to Dungannon. The Crown recognized his intransigence, even attainted him for a period, but consistently refused to mount an attack against the North. There were confusing negotiations, obscure maneuvers, and inevitable contradictions. In all likelihood, O'Neill's ascendancy could not have been stopped with the resources available in Ireland. The storm would have to break before the English nation would commit men and arms to Ireland, and by then the line of forts and garrisons, sealing the North off from the rest of Ireland, had been overrun and O'Neill was thrusting his forces deep into Munster and the Geraldine South.

WHITEHALL, 1599
The Passing

O'Neill is like a frozen snake picked up by a farmer which, growing warm, hisses at his benefactor," so Tyrone seemed to Spenser in the spring of 1596, a serpent "raised out of the dust by the
Queen, yet encompassing the most serious of all perils to Elizabeth's rule in Ireland." As Spenser searched the scanty and contradictory
reports from the North for reassurances, Sir John Norris lay on his deathbed five miles away at Mallow, and Thomas Norris verged on becoming
the most important civil officer in Munster. The province was then quiet
and productive. The troubles in the North were talked about everywhere,
but Munster was unusually tranquil. Some of the more casual undertakers
had quit their estates, sensing in the stillness fallen over the South the
scope of the approaching danger, but the gentlemen settlers of the Awbeg
Valley were committed to staying. They argued over the merits of Sir
John's advice to Russell, most favoring Russell's militancy, and while in
1595 Spenser included a dedication to "valiant" John Norris in the second
installment of *The Faerie Queene*, he omitted Norris' name entirely from
A View of the Present State of Ireland. The villains of that treatise were the
peacemakers who coddled the Irish and shrank from confronting them.

Munster seemed worth a war. Ten years had passed since the Crown
began apportioning Desmond's wealth, and in that period the level of

exports and domestic agriculture had climbed steadily. The major towns enjoyed a growing trade. Conflicts and disorders remained, but the famine of Desmond's last years was gone, and the countryside once again could support life. To many of the older undertakers the horrors of the Desmond Wars had faded with time, and they could no longer accept appeasement. They believed that Ireland's greatest age lay ahead, if only the Crown would lock the gateways of the North, and they bitterly resented the timid settlers, the peacemakers, and trimmers who stood in awe of Tyrone.

Munster was still a rough country, but in 1595 it showed signs of attaining the settled life of an English shire. Sir Henry Sidney's ambition to see the rich earth of the South under plow and husbandry was as close to fulfillment as it would ever be in Elizabeth's reign. How much was at stake is known partially from the records and accounts of the Munster Plantation, partially from Spenser's poetry. The love poetry in particular suggests the reality of the land, celebrating love and marriage against a backdrop of Munster's hills and valleys and blending actual with imagined advantages. No love poetry of the period is comparable in its use of place and community. For example, the sonnet cycle *Amoretti* is noted less for high-flown ardor and rhetorical ingenuity than for its simple story of requited love in an Irish setting. The action of the sonnets takes place between Kilcolman and Youghal. The subject is a real woman, Elizabeth Boyle, and because the lovers stand at the edge of the European world, settlers in every sense, it is fitting that their love is more in the nature of an accomplishment than an experience. There is little of the posing, the extravagant emotion, of sophisticated, courtly lyrics. *Amoretti* compares the poet's passion to the wildness of the Irish landscape, his lady's beauty to the fruitful plains. And in this respect, *Amoretti* is only a preamble to the great marriage ode which crowns Spenser's occasional verse and is his second statement about life in Ireland.

Colin Clouts offered his resolve to remain in Ireland apart from the scramble for wealth and power at Court, content to fashion a life of simple rural pursuits. *Epithalamion* was an extension of this mood, a song made "in lieu of many ornaments" with which his bride, Elizabeth Boyle, should have been decked. Their wedding was likely a modest ceremony, and the poem makes good the deficiencies through its splendor and richness of meaning; it is a marriage song more befitting a prince than a farmer/official. The plain service at Christ Church, Cork, becomes a high mass; Munster is endowed for the occasion with civilized towns, thronging celebrants, merchants' daughters, and all the festivity of a Roman wedding. The ruined town of Buttevant comes back to life, the hills send in nymphs and shepherdesses, the rivers give up their fish, and the roads are strewn with wine and flowers. This is marriage in the tradition of Virgil and Catullus, made all the more poignant by recognition of the scarcely civilized state of Ireland. The poem's sensualness is meant to compensate for the roughness of life at Kilcolman, the land is depicted not as it is but as it might be, and sustaining his visionary hope is Spenser's faith in natural order. Marriage is the highest expression of nature's harmony. Therefore all the elements of the physical world conspire in the uniting of the two. The poem is made up of one stanza for each hour of the day, all in perfect proportion to day and night. The wedding takes place on Barnabas Eve, the summer solstice, the longest day of the year, and the astrology of the moment is complete and authentic. Spenser makes the union of man and woman an event of cosmic significance. Through marriage and progeny the barren soil of Munster is expected to bring forth in fullness of time a generation of just and civil men. This is the reason then that this metaphorical marriage takes place in daylight, before a multitude, sanctioned by the community and consecrated to the public good. The life at stake is not Spenser's or Elizabeth Boyle's, but posterity's, and in posterity lies the hope of human improvement. The stirrings of chanceries and courts, the clash of issues and causes, are like nothing before the powers of procreation, and the groom, looking out of his window to watch the moon rise on their marriage night, invokes the only certain comfort in the world: "O fairest goddess . . . the chaste womb inform with timely seed . . . That may our comfort breed."

Epithalamion is not without political meaning. By inference, love is likened to obedience and service; lust, to rebellion. The first is natural and godly; the second, unnatural and diabolical. Spenser's ambition was to see the children of his lawful love inherit his land and people it with his own kind. Forgotten was the bloodshed on which the Munster venture was founded and the dispossessed hiding in the hills. These found their champion in the Earl of Tyrone. While Spenser courted and married Elizabeth Boyle, Hugh seduced and abducted Mabel Bagenal. When Spenser was writing his marriage ode, Tyrone was drafting nine demands for the restitution of Irish rights. God and nature were invoked to justify both causes, but the irreducible element of the conflict was not political or religious; it was a matter of who held the land. In 1595 Tyrone had been content to ask for liberty of conscience, the removal of garrisons, and a form of county administration for the North. In 1596 he demanded in effect what later centuries called Home Rule. His terms were dictated by the need to win Spanish support, but they constitute for whatever reason a revolutionary declaration:

That the Catholic, Apostolic and Roman religion be openly preached and taught throughout Ireland by bishops, seminary priests, Jesuits, and all other religious men.

That all cathedrals and parish churches, abbeys, and other religious houses, with all tithes and church lands, now in the hands of the English, be presently restored to Catholic churchmen.

That there be erected a university upon the Crown rents of Ireland, wherein all sciences shall be taught according to the manner of the Catholic Roman Church.

That the Lord Chancellor, Lord Treasurer, Lord Admiral, the Council of State, the Justices of the Laws, and all other officers appertaining to the Council and Law of Ireland, be Irishmen.

That all statutes made against the preferment of Irishmen, as well in their own country as abroad, be presently recalled.

That the Queen nor her successors may in no sort press an Irishman to serve them against his will.

That O'Neill, O'Donnell, the Earl of Desmond, with all their partakers, may peaceably enjoy all lands and privileges that did appertain to their predecessors 200 years past.

That all Irishmen may freely travel and traffic all merchandises in England as Englishmen, paying the same rights and tributes as the English do.

That all Irishmen may freely build ships of what burden they will, furnishing the same with artillery and all munition at their pleasure. . . .

Confronted with these demands, Elizabeth was furious; she categorically declined to have terms read to her by "a base bush-kern" or to yield one prerogative. When Cecil saw the full list of Tyrone's demands, he scrawled across the page "Ewtopia" and commented that "the man means to be head and monarch of Ireland." Implicit in the reaction of the Crown was the belief that, more than reform the state of Ireland, O'Neill intended to supplant Elizabeth, that he was driven to rebellion by pride and ambition. No one could conceive of his sincerity or envision a radically different Ireland under Tyrone and the King of Spain. Even Philip II, duly apprised of O'Neill's articles, overlooked their implications and saw his victories as merely advancing the Counter-Reformation. "I have been informed you are defending the Catholic cause against the English," Philip wrote to him in 1596, "that this is acceptable to God is proved by the signal victories which you have gained. I hope you will continue to prosper; and you need not doubt but I will render you any assistance you may require. Give credence to Fussius, the bearer, and acquaint him with your affairs and your wishes." In 1596 Elizabeth decided to ignore Tyrone's demands, while the King of Spain resolved to support him. The issue would be settled now only by arms, and in this event Tyrone possessed an initial advantage. He would take hostage the South, where the Elizabethans had spent so much gold and effort, and they in their turn would exhaust themselves attempting to penetrate his country.

◆

Remarried and settled at Kilcolman, Spenser was acutely aware, as were the other Munster settlers, of a new Earl of Desmond. Tyrone's article, calling for the restoration of Desmond lands, was a direct recognition of the claims of James FitzThomas Fitzgerald. The title which had remained in abeyance after Gerald's death had passed to James at Tyrone's instigation, not the Crown's, and overnight the new Earl found himself the recipient of Geraldine loyalties. James was Gerald's nephew. He had remained loyal to the Crown during the Desmond Wars in hope of succeeding to the earldom, but after his uncle's death he was forgotten, and his claim disallowed. Tyrone raised James from abject poverty, a willing instrument, and though the people of Munster jokingly titled him the Hayrope Earl, or "straw-man," they followed him with the same devotion they had shown the legitimate Desmonds down through the years. The Hayrope Earl lay hidden in Munster after 1596. He offered a rallying point to the McSheehys and McSweenys who had served Gerald, and he passed from one loyal household to another during those months recruiting support, soliciting money and supplies for the new rebel stronghold in the Aherlow Valley. He was often accompanied by a Jesuit named Archer and by a Hagan or an O'Donnell from the North.

The Hayrope Earl inspired the McSheehys in particular, and while Spenser was in London between 1595 and 1596, Thomas Norris hanged ninety of that family for various offenses ranging from murder and theft to concealment of arms and unlawful assembly. Lord Roche, pleasantly cognizant of the growing danger, now pleaded loyalty to the Crown incessantly, but his son, David, rode with the McSheehys to secure his father's credit with Tyrone as well. The geographical center of the growing disturbance was as always the Aherlow; in 1597 Thomas Norris was determined to scour that valley in search of hidden arms, but in all Munster he could raise no more than 700 poorly armed militia, and the rebels outnumbered him many times over. When fighting finally broke out, the Hayrope Earl would lead more men to the battle than Gerald had ever commanded— 8000 foot and 1000 horse. Such was the extent of disaffection caused by the Munster planters.

Other signs of disloyalty manifested themselves in the year immediately preceding the Battle of Yellow Ford. Bishop Lyon of Limerick was shocked to discover "the style and title" of the Queen torn out of all grammars—seventy-four in number—in one school within the city of Limerick. The westward buttress of English rule in Munster was infiltrated by rebels and on the verge of open disloyalty. The castle within the city walls was deserted and in hopeless disrepair. Kilmallock and Castlemaine were hardly better, and at Carrigafoyle and Castle Glynn the Irish were raising fortifications secretly under James FitzThomas' direction. The merchants of Limerick, as well as of Cork and Youghal, were trading actively with Spain, and the powder and lead finding its way into the interior were often brought across the docks of those cities. Everywhere the English looked Munster was unsound and treacherous. Sir Henry Wallop put the matter to Robert Cecil in February, 1596: "The state of the realm was never so dangerous in the memory of man as it is at this present, in regard of the uniting of O'Donnell, and all the chieftains of Ulster and Connacht with Tyrone, and the great combination which they have drawn together, stretching itself unto all the parts of this Kingdom, and the strength of the traitors through Tyrone's wealth, who is well furnished with all the habiliments of war. . . . They have so trained their men, they seem to be other enemies, and not those that in times past, were wont never to attempt her Majesty's forces in the plain field." In other words, the Irish had discovered the virtues of firepower. Peasants and kern alike carried matchlocks, and in every field and along every road the English settlers were likely to be shot in the back.

There is no question that the settlers felt deserted and betrayed as 1597 passed into 1598 without reinforcements or new garrisons arriving. They were appalled as the sick and aged Bingham replaced Burgh and then expired in office. They were no happier when Ormond took Bingham's place and negotiated a temporary truce with O'Neill. By then it was common knowledge that Tyrone spared nothing to win wavering chieftains to his side. The O'Connors reported his assertion that within a month he would kindle such a fire in Munster that Ormond would have no leisure to trouble the Irish in Ulster and Leinster. English officials at Dublin were aware of the pressures Tyrone brought to bear on such loyal and unwavering lords as Barry and McCarthy Reagh, but they were unable to make an equal demonstration of strength to restore flagging confidence. Lord Barry, for instance, received the following letter from Tyrone: "Your impiety to God, cruelty to your soul and body, tyranny and ingratitude both to your followers and country, are inexcusable and intolerable. You separated yourself from the unity of Christ, his mystical body, the Catholic Church. You know the sword of extirpation hangeth over your head as well as ours, if things fall out otherwise than well. You are the cause why all the nobility of the south from the east part to the west are not linked together to shake off the cruel yoke of heresy and tyranny, with which our souls and bodies are oppressed. . . ." Since Tyrone's forces, without his Spanish reinforcements, outnumbered the English army in Ireland five to one, his letter to Barry was more in the nature of a command than a request. Barry, nevertheless, stood firm, yet he was one of only four lords Norris could count as loyal in all Munster, and between the four, they could contribute ten men. Their servants had deserted en masse to the Hayrope Earl.

On February 7, 1598, Spenser was granted permission to postpone until the beginning of the following Easter term arrearages of rent due on Buttevant Abbey, "for that at this present moment, by reason of trouble in the way, he durst not bring down any money to Cork." The roads of Munster, clear and filled only two years before, were now interdicted by rebels. It was worth a man's life to venture out of his house in broad daylight or to open his door at night. For those English who were still in the countryside, flight was already impractical. They risked as much on the roads to the ports as locked up in their fortified houses. Thomas Norris distributed arms and powder to the settlers in early summer, fearing that the same would end up in rebel hands, and the several hundred families in Munster now waited apprehensively for the storm to break.

Tyrone accommodated them in July by laying siege to the English fort on the Ulster Blackwater, a threat to the heart of County Tyrone. At first, little happened; O'Neill's soldiers made some headway, the English garrison sent to Armagh for relief, and both sides summoned their strength. At stake was the Pass of the North, as the gap between Upper Lake Erne and the Armagh highlands was called, and at the end of the long road from Newry through Armagh lay Dungannon and Tyrone. The country between Armagh and the Blackwater Fort was firm and flat; it favored a strong advance and the sort of warfare the English preferred. On either side of the road was room for regiments of pikemen to deploy, for cavalry to maneuver, for artillery to be brought to play. Ormond was convinced that he could break through O'Neill to relieve the fort and, having once done so, open the way for an invasion of County Tyrone. The puzzle then was that he did not lead the advance himself, but sent Henry Bagenal in his stead. Ormond, it has been observed, was always solicitous of his own good, and while Bagenal prepared to depart northward, Butler traveled South to quell disturbances around his home at Kilkenny. Ormond was unquestionably an able soldier, and in all probability Yellow Ford would not have befallen him. Before he left, he warned Sir Henry to close the distance between his regiments when marching against Tyrone, excellent advice as events soon proved. But Bagenal, Henry of the Battleaxes as his troops named him, was not attentive to drill or formation; he was a headlong fighter and a commander of supreme confidence. He took up his position too close to the van of battle and, eager to get at his despised brother-in-law, allowed his regiments to string out behind him all the way back to Armagh.

The English force was composed of 4000 foot and 300 horse, formed into six regiments and supplied with a section of four cannon. The lead regiment was commanded by Captain Percy, a veteran of Flanders, with picked English troops recently arrived. Sir Henry himself commanded the second regiment, his own; Henry Cosby, the third; Sir Thomas Wingfield, the fourth and fifth; and Captain Billings, the sixth. Normally these regiments would have advanced along a road at 120 yards from each other, but they left Armagh separated by only 100 on Ormond's recommendation— a precaution against flank attacks and encirclement. Pikemen were slow and unwieldy in battle, and success could depend on consolidating them quickly to ward off a threat. Fortunately for the English, the road from Armagh to the Blackwater was relatively free of woods, offering little cover for the Irish to mass behind. The road crossed a small stream called the Callan River at a ford known by the yellow color of its banks and ran straight onward to the fort. This was not terrain the Irish were expected to contest. They had avoided open country in earlier skirmishes, and Bagenal believed they would continue to do so. What he and his lieutenants overlooked was the revolution in Irish arms and tactics O'Neill had achieved.

Tyrone had every intention of stopping the Marshal dead on the Armagh Road. He knew Bagenal was coming and had prepared defenses. Beyond the Callan River grew a line of hedgerows, running for several hundred yards and terminating in a small bog on the advancing army's left flank. Behind the hedges O'Neill dug trenches to shelter musketeers, the dense growth shielding them as effectively as if it were barbed wire, and on the road he sank pitfalls to snag wagon wheels and break up the marching formations. On either side of the Callan, at some yards distance from the road, he placed more musketeers and a body of cavalry. These would be bypassed by the English column and were intended to attack the rearmost regiments. For the first time in Irish warfare, the clans would fight at a distance from the enemy, not rushing the pike squares until heavy musket fire had decimated them. Tyrone was a master of ambush, and he employed the same relay sniping often used in the South for lack of guns. But although his forces were short of powder, they had an ample supply of firearms. Most English lost on the field of Yellow Ford were felled by gunshot. Down the road, a quarter of a mile beyond the little river, Tyrone massed his own pikemen. These were fully trained and drilled levies, not the gallowglass of the Desmond Wars, and they would sweep up the road into Bagenal's broken regiments as soon as the musketry had achieved full effect. To the rear of the long column Red Hugh O'Donnell took up his position. His cavalry and the Scots gallowglass of the Maguires and Mac-Donalds were intended to block any retreat by the enemy and to dispatch the wounded left behind. Tyrone's infantry outnumbered Bagenal's; he enjoyed a two-to-one superiority in muskets, and while the English were encumbered by their wagon train of supplies for the beleaguered fort, the Irish were well placed and flexible. O'Neill's task was to hold his men in check until they could be committed effectively. To this end he took personal command of the army, and his generalship extended to the smallest details of preparation and movement.

Bagenal is condemned in hindsight for his carelessness and indifference to the fighting style of the Ulster Irish. But what was about to happen on the Armagh Road had never happened before in Ireland. Yellow Ford was not an ambush. It was not over in a furious rush of axmen or kern. The battle lasted an afternoon; it was a leisurely engagement, the English regiments advancing slowly into a funnel of intensifying fire, and it did not end until smoke and darkness blanketed the field. The nightmare quality of Yellow Ford, attested to by English survivors, stemmed from a gradual, dawning recognition of Irish supremacy and from the sudden collapse and panic which followed the discovery.

Late on the morning of August 14, while Percy's lead regiment was about half a mile from the Callan, the English force came under fire. The popping of musketry was heard the length of the column, and Bagenal immediately ordered his regiments to close distance. His order came too late. The formations had gradually stretched out to 200- or 300-yard intervals, and as they hurried to rejoin, hidden muskets dropped their horses and oxen. As draft animals died in their traces and wagons careened into pitfalls, the marching columns were caught in a snarl of wounded animals, frightened drovers, and disoriented pikemen. Bagenal's two sakers, his largest cannon, fell into holes, shattering their carriages, and while the gunners struggled to extricate them, Wingfield's main body stopped in its tracks. The two foremost regiments pressed on out of contact with the main body. Captain Cosby, with the third regiment, saw the danger and realized that the army was under attack its full length, but he was unable to reach Bagenal, and as the first two regiments plunged into the caldron along the Callan, his was drawn along in support. By one o'clock Irish skirmishers had filtered into the gaps between the regiments on the Armagh Road. Billings, in the rear, was pinned down by O'Donnell; Wingfield was stalled and suffering mounting casualties; and in the front of the column, Percy's regiment had already ceased to exist.

Captain Percy drove his troops through the musket fire straight at the river. He crossed the Callan with some casualties, re-formed, and attacked in good order toward the hedgerows and trench. On his left flank a saker was lost in the bog, and a pike company engaged with Tyrone's cavalry, but along the main line of advance Percy fared better. He crossed the trench with little difficulty, entered a small wood, and was within sight of the Blackwater Fort. The regiment's banners could be seen from the ramparts, and the besieged and hungry soldiers sent up a loud cheer as they saw their relief breaking through. The English advance, however, had now reached its maximum extent. Just as the lead company entered the woods, the Irish to the rear in the trench and hedges emerged and opened fire. Tyrone seized the opportunity to unleash his own pikemen, and these, crashing through Percy's weary ranks, flung the first regiment back all along the road. The English were driven back into the hedges, where the Irish musketeers shot them down in droves. Percy was killed on the road by a fusillade, and a few moments later a tremendous explosion was heard as a keg of gunpowder exploded beside a wrecked supply wagon. Back with the main body, Wingfield saw the white pall rising high over the battle and sent forward to Cosby to learn what was happening. He received no answer and a half hour later assumed full command of the army.

Henry Bagenal crossed the Callan just as Percy advanced into the small woods. Like the lead regiment, his was suffering continual losses from sniping and flank attacks. He pressed on toward the hedgerows and had almost reached them when he saw terrified English troops breaking through the growth and pouring out onto the road in flight. At that moment he too heard and saw the explosion and realized that Percy's regiment had been destroyed. His only chance was to get back across the Callan as quickly as possible, and as he ordered the retreat, dispatching his aide the length of the column, a musketball struck him in the forehead. His men did not succeed in carrying his body out of the action, for Tyrone's infantry were already through the hedges and overwhelming the second regiment. The fighting was confused and terrifying. A fog of burned powder lay close to the ground, and men lost touch with their companies. Irish enlisted men in Bagenal's regiment took their chance to desert and join O'Neill's troops. The English companies lost their banners and direction, and many pikemen wandered into the bog, where they were shot or captured. Probably the only English officer who knew what was happening was Henry Cosby; he had reached the Callan and saw the remnants of the first two regiments thrashing through the bloody water to reach safety. Cosby had received Bagenal's order to retreat, but he hoped to catch up the shattered survivors of the first two regiments in his own and continued to advance. The third regiment crossed the Callan, losing contact with Wingfield and the main body, and disappeared into the haze. It was never seen again. Cosby was taken prisoner and spared only for the ransom he brought; almost all his men perished with Bagenal's and Percy's.

Sir Thomas Wingfield found himself alone and surrounded by midafternoon. If he attempted to advance and save the small pockets of English troops still fighting ahead of him, he would have been destroyed like Cosby. If he stayed where he was, he would have been slowly annihilated by long-range musketry and the occasional attacks of O'Neill's pikemen. Wingfield tried to bring his remaining cannon to bear, but as quickly as his gunners manned the piece, they were shot down. Then, as the fourth and fifth regiments began their slow retreat, another powder keg exploded in their midst, flinging soldiers off the road and burning many. O'Neill threw his remaining reserves at the retreating enemy, hoping to turn their withdrawal into a rout, but Wingfield held his companies together and, abandoning his wounded and equipment, fell back onto Billings. Firsthand accounts of the battle praise Captain Montague and the English cavalry for screening Wingfield's retreat, and in all likelihood the entire army would have been destroyed except for the courage and determination of the cavalry. O'Neill's horse outnumbered Montague's, but the Irish persisted in riding without stirrups and thereby lost leverage with lance and sword. Montague broke the Irish cavalry and opened a way out of the trap for Wingfield and Billings.

In the rear of the column Billings had withstood O'Donnell's gallow-glass. He drew his men and wagons into a circle and fought through the afternoon at even losses with the enemy. Now, as Wingfield joined him, they abandoned the wagons and began a retreat back toward Armagh. In the three surviving regiments few musketeers were left alive, and the Irish took this opportunity to close in and rake the enemy at will. At several points Wingfield and Billings almost lost control of their men. The rear regiments were composed of recruits and recent arrivals. They were green and frightened. The Irish appeared on the hillocks along the road, waving captured banners and jeering, and back where the fighting had been fiercest, kern had begun to decapitate the dead and wounded. Though a majority of the last three regiments were to reach safety, they were so shaken by their experience that few would ever fight again.

Wingfield led his men into Armagh ahead of the Irish; they labored up a hill in the center of the town, staining the roadway with the blood of their wounds, and barricaded themselves inside St. Patrick's Cathedral. This stone church was among the oldest in Ireland. Its hilltop site had been presented to Patrick by the Irish Queen Macha, and the crypt below was the resting place of King Brian Boru, buried there after his great victory over the Viking invaders at Clontarf. Now Wingfield turned the church into his fortress and hospital, and the Irish, who took the town below, refrained from attacking him there. O'Neill would gain concessions by negotiating their release. That Wingfield ever reached Armagh is a feat attributed to his excellent generalship and Montague's courage. But the

Irish had also run out of powder along the road, and since they took Armagh behind the English and had Wingfield trapped, they have always claimed destruction of the entire army. The dispute is not important; the Battle of Yellow Ford resulted in just under 2000 English battlefield deaths, perhaps the loss of another 1000 through wounds and desertion, and the total surrender of all cannon, arms, and supplies.

Yellow Ford was not just a victory; it was a national triumph. The defeat of Bagenal precipitated the surrender of the Blackwater Fort and Armagh; it destroyed the Queen's Irish army; it opened all Ireland to Tyrone's war of liberation. For the first time an Irish force had met the English on their own terms and crushed them. Bagenal had been out-gunned, outmaneuvered, and destroyed piecemeal on a fine bright day in open terrain. Tyrone had proved to all Europe that Irishmen could be trained and disciplined into an effective conventional army. And Europe, when it learned of Yellow Ford, celebrated O'Neill's genius. In a congratulatory letter, Philip of Spain hailed Tyrone as "the Prince of Ireland," and the Pontiff wrote that he had commissioned a gold crown to be fashioned in expectation of O'Neill's coronation as "King of the Irish." As much as the battle buoyed the Irish, it depressed the English, and when Montague finally broke out of Armagh on August 17 to tell Dublin the fate of its army, the city went wild, and the price of passage to England shot up tenfold.

Yellow Ford was the worst defeat English arms ever sustained in Ireland. The defeat was the greatest military disaster of Elizabeth's reign and provoked a crisis second in magnitude only to the Armada scare. Elizabeth was not on the brink of losing Ireland after Yellow Ford; she had already lost it and now would spend a princely fortune trying to regain it.

One man was spared the shame and anxiety of the aftermath. William Cecil, Lord Burghley, died August 4. He was seventy-nine and racked by infirmities. At the end he did not fear the grave; he was worn out by cares and long service and complained to his chaplain, "Oh what a heart have I that will not die." The Queen came to his bedside to feed and console him. He offered to resign his offices; she refused to accept them. When news of Ireland finally reached her, she had not yet accepted the loss of her old friend and counselor. On the first day of his funeral, as 500 notables of the realm marched behind his hearse through the streets of London to Westminster Abbey, the first complete report of the battle near Armagh arrived at Whitehall. The tidings, though expected, were worse than anticipated and tended to confirm Cecil's lifelong distrust of military solutions. The god of war was fickle and the issues too important to be left to soldiers like Bagenal. The Irish situation plunged the Court into gloom. Rumors of Spanish attacks and plots against the Queen's life sprang up immediately, and with Cecil gone, no one remained to restrain the hotheads or encourage Elizabeth's native caution. She was surrounded by young men who doubted her competence and resolution. She had outlived her age, and time showed in her face. The French diplomat De Maisse, present during the crisis at Whitehall, remembered how her features were white and drawn, her teeth yellow with many missing, and he wondered how she talked as well as she did. As in the beginning, in the days of Leicester and Alençon, love intruded, compounding her difficulties. That August Elizabeth was at odds with her favorite, Robert Devereux, the Earl of Essex, and their quarrel had come to overshadow the Irish question. A few weeks before Yellow Ford they had argued over a Lord Deputy for Ireland. Essex turned his back on her in anger, she struck him, he reached for his sword, and only the intervention of the Lord Admiral forestalled an irreparable mistake. Now, while the Crown wrestled with the Irish dilemma, the politics of love and favor impeded a decision.

Essex was always forward in war, counseling a strong force in Ireland and maritime attacks on Spain. He had inherited Leicester's mantle and had distinguished himself on a raid to Cádiz. His principal opponents were the two Cecils, Burghley and his son Robert, for if Burghley could accept Devereux's dalliance with the aging Queen, he could not accept his adventurous policies. While Burghley lived, England prosecuted the Spanish War with restraint and economy. The distrust of daring and gallantry was still there. In the face of Tyrone's provocations Cecil held to his conviction that Ireland could not be subdued at a cost acceptable to the Crown. At most, the Spanish might be kept out. But Cecil was ill and crotchety, he came to Court infrequently, and his attention was known to wander. It grew easy to discount his advice. He had lived through Carew and Perrot, Grey and Bingham, and to his mind Ormond was adequate to secure Ireland. The Spanish war was already expensive enough. Philip, too, was old and ailing, and his son and heir was not the fanatical soldier of Christ his father had been. Cecil counted on time and the cumulative effects of a measured resistance. He had never been proud or arrogant, and in his last months he seldom appeared in public without his prayerbook. In April he confronted Essex for the last time. The place was the Council Chamber at Whitehall. As Essex denounced peace with Spain as fraudulent and dishonorable, Burghley interrupted him, saying that "he breathed forth nothing but war, slaughter, and blood"; then, taking out his prayerbook, he opened it and pointed silently to the twenty-third verse of Psalm 55: "Bloodthirsty and deceitful men shall not live out half their days." Cecil's last rejoinder was prophetic.

These were the sides that Elizabeth had once again to reconcile. Cecil was gone and Essex estranged from her, but their arguments stood and attracted alternating sides of her nature. She had tested the ground between the two positions, and her compromises had given her Yellow Ford. Now her course was decided by one consideration—Tyrone—injured pride driving her. The issue was plain; she would gladly have given O'Neill all Ireland, to have and rule, so long as he was ruled in the end by her. She had no feelings for that country; it could not interest or sway her. But O'Neill's rebellion was mortifying, as he knew well, and she prepared to hunt him down at any cost to her treasury. Where before Yellow Ford she might have stooped to any expedient to be rid of her Irish problems, she now determined to raise the largest expeditionary force of her reign, and over the next three years to send more than 25,000 English troops into the country if necessary to pursue Tyrone. At the start they would be commanded by the ardent Essex. He had wanted war, and he was to have it; Ireland would test his loyalty and subordination.

While the new army was being raised, Elizabeth turned with ferocity on survivors of her Irish government. Cousin Ormond was sunk in defeatism, and the Queen rebuked him for his negligence in the field and for the endemic corruption which was as much her doing as his. "It was strange to us," she wrote, "that when almost the whole forces of our kingdom were drawn to a head, and a main blow like to be struck for our honor against the capital rebel, that you, whose person would have better daunted the traitors, and would have carried with it another manner of reputation, and strength of the nobility of the kingdom, should employ yourself in action of less importance and leave that to a mean conduct." Besides wanting to know where Ormond was during the Battle of Yellow Ford, Elizabeth asked where were the many regiments she was feeding and arming. She also wanted to know why, when her pay ships were delayed by contrary winds, the English captains paid themselves out of their troops' food allocations. Her questions were long overdue, but easily answered. There were more Irish regiments on paper than in existence. Allotments for food and arms were excessive because many men on the company musters were dead, discharged, deserted, or had never existed. As for Ormond's whereabouts, he had turned southward to shield Leinster and Munster and probably for this reason was still alive. The Queen tended vastly to overestimate her forces in Ireland and the "strength of the nobility." Although Ormond argued his situation, Elizabeth commanded that he make his army ready for battle and, "in the meanwhile, follow the wars of Leinster which is in the heart of our Kingdom, this winter, to the end that those inward provinces of the Realm may be freed." The Queen had studied the map of Ireland, but she refused to see the extent of the crisis. In a helpful vein she advised Ormond that if his English soldiers attempted to flee the enemy and desert for home, remember "all must return by sea, which is not easy, if such good orders were taken as should be, that no soldier were suffered to embark in any our port towns, without good warrant for their passage." By the time Elizabeth thought of closing the ports those of her troops who had escaped Yellow Ford and a dozen minor ambushes were already embarked for Wales, France, and even Flanders.

Ormond not only was penned in Kilkenny, fighting for survival, but had lost contact with Norris in Munster and Clifford Conyers in Connaught. By September Norris had been persuaded to send what few men were available for the defense of Munster to Conyers in the West. With Thomas' brother, Henry, Conyers proposed to strike at O'Donnell through County Sligo, halting Red Hugh's advance to the south and drawing O'Neill away from vulnerable Dublin. The expedition delayed for months, and when Conyers finally launched his attack, the results were more disastrous than Yellow Ford. Henry Norris and Conyers died with their men in a mountain defile, set upon by O'Donnell's gallowglass and kern. Ormond ventured out of Kilkenny several times during the autumn of 1598; each time he was beaten and driven back onto his defenses. In the great, general rebellion which now gripped the South, Butler was helpless and isolated. He watched the Munster colony, the labor of two decades, swept away, and was powerless to intervene.

Unavoidably at first, and then by intention, Munster was sacrificed to buy time for the government. The settlers were on their own; they could fight for their homes or fight to reach the safety of the coastal cities, but no army would come for months and little encouragement. As the Munster Plantation collapsed in a storm of fire and looting, Whitehall fixed the blame for the catastrophe on the settlers themselves. The official view was stated by Fynes Moryson, after he journeyed through the ashes in 1601: "To speak the truth, the Munster undertakers were in great part cause of their own fatal miseries. For whereas they should have built castles and brought over colonies of English, and have admitted no Irish tenants, but only English, these and like covenants were in no part performed by them. If the covenants had been kept by them, they of themselves might have made 2000 able men, whereas the Lord President could not find above 200 of English birth among them, when the rebels first entered the Province. Neither did these gentle undertakers make any resistance to the rebels, but left their dwellings and fled to walled towns; yea, when there was such danger in flight, as greater could not have been in defending their own, whereof many of them had woeful experience being surprised with their wives and children in flight." Elizabeth always contended that if her orders to exclude the Irish race from Munster had been followed, the destruction of the plantation would not have occurred. But had her orders been carried out, there would have been no plantation. She, not the settlers, failed to encourage development of her Irish domain. In retrospect, Moryson was insensitive to the suffering and loss of his countrymen. He failed to grasp the extent of the confusion, the rumors and final fright, which drove the settlers like a herd toward Cork. And he was not present to see the wagons burning along the roads, the dazed women wandering over the fields naked and in shock, the mutilated bodies filling the ditches. On most points, his account conflicted with eyewitness reports, but it is an example of the callousness with which the Crown accepted the loss of its Munster colony.

What really happened in the South that autumn is evident from the disposition of O'Neill's forces. Immediately following Yellow Ford, he sent 2000 insurgents across Leinster into Munster. This force, mounted and well armed, was commanded by Captain Richard Tyrrell, "of English race but a bold and unnatural enemy to his country and people." Tyrrell caught Ormond napping outside Kilkenny and battered him badly. He then swept South to establish a base of operations in the Aherlow Valley, from which he stripped the surrounding countryside bare, laying siege to castles, driving in cattle, and seizing the harvest for transport to the North. O'Neill counted on Tyrrell's select force to secure the supplies he would need in the winter campaign; these men were not renegades, but seasoned cavalry, more than able to brush aside any resistance. They lent backbone to the irregular levies of Geraldines commanded by the Hayrope Earl. Tyrrell's companies overran Counties Cork and Limerick, but they were not the main participants in the massacre of the settlers. O'Neill directed his best soldiers to envelop the major towns—Kilmallock, Limerick, Cork, and Waterford—and left the destruction of the English enclaves to the local Irish.

As soon as Tyrrell was arrived in the Aherlow, the Geraldines rose across the South. In Kerry they joined Owen O'More in capturing Tralee, Castlemaine, and Killarney. In County Cork they pillaged the Awbeg Valley, the Blackwater Valley, and most of the coastline between Cork and Youghal. Conservative estimates place the size of the Hayrope Earl's following at 6000, but more remarkable than the size of the rebellion was the speed with which it rose. Most of the English settlements were taken by surprise. Irish servants opened gates to their countrymen in the dead of night. Tenants burned their cottages and drove off their masters' livestock. Simple churls took arms against their bailiffs. The resentment of decades poured out against the women, children, and possessions of the English overlords, and in their fury the country people, Geraldines or not, destroyed everything in their path. The rebellion broke out before noon on October 6, and how it appeared to a Munster undertaker is found in a letter from Hugh Cuffe. Cuffe was Spenser's neighbor five miles to the north. "After the Ulster rebels had entered the Province, . . . the rebels of Munster, all the Province through, rose instantly before noon, and made spoil and prey, with fire and sword, upon all English subjects. At which time my wife, for safety of her life, with her children fled to Cork, most dangerously escaping their hands, being assisted with the help of the Lord Barry; in which morning the rebels took all such cattle, which were upon my lands, of mine and my English tenants. But my wife having left a ward in my castle for the defense of the same with all my goods therein, my goods were all preserved till the 19th of this month . . . On which day, in the morning, the new proclaimed Earl of Desmond; Derby McOwen, son-in-law to the Lord Roche; Donogh McCormac, son-in-law to the White Knight, and Piers Lacy, new made Seneschal of Imokilly, which are the chief of Munster rebels, together with Owen O'More, chief leaders and Captains of Ulster rebels, being in all of Munster and Ulster four thousand, came to the castle and assaulted it, and played against it with their shot, till the 22nd following; and, having burnt the town by it, with the houses and corn about it, and also burnt down the top of the castle, and also breached the wall through, the warders, divers of them wounded, and all wearied out with watching and fighting, and having no possible means to be assisted by any of Her Majesty's forces, and the Lord General then being passed from them out of the Province, were compelled to yield the castle, upon Desmond's promise that they should depart with their lives, and the carrying away of their own wearing apparel; who, being passed but a mile from the castle toward Cork, were robbed, and stripped to their naked bodies, by the Lord Roche's tenants, but were not slain, as at their first taking it was bruited. The warders were eighteen."

Cuffe saw the hand of Lord Roche in all that happened to him. Indeed, the hour was Roche's, yet not surprisingly, Maurice did not join or lead the rebels in person; he cautiously preserved the appearance of neutrality, while his son, David, and his tenants and servants carried out his bidding. Elizabeth had boasted to Ormond that her nobility was strongest and most numerous in Ireland and should be employed against O'Neill. With the sole exception of Lord Barry, her nobles were actually employed in stripping her colonists of their livestock and possessions. The day had come for the lords to be revenged on upstarts, and loyal to O'Neill or not, they abetted the common Irish in their fury. They locked up their castles and villages against the fleeing settlers and countenanced the worst atrocities. William Saxey, Chief Justice of Munster, wrote of the misery and suffering: "About the 5th of October, some 3000 rebels came into the country of Limerick, sent from the archtraitor Tyrone, under the leading of John FitzThomas . . . son of the elder brother to the last attainted Earl of

Desmond . . . and burnt and spoiled most of the towns and villages there.
. . . These combinations and revolts have effected many execrable murders
and cruelties upon the English, as well in the county of Limerick, as in the
counties of Cork and Kerry and elsewhere; infants taken from their nurses'
breasts, and their brains dashed against the walls; the heart plucked out of
the body of the husband in the view of the wife, who was forced to yield
the use of her apron to wipe off the blood from the murderer's fingers; an
English gentleman at midday in a town cruelly murdered, and his head
cleft in diverse pieces; divers sent into Youghal amongst the English, some
with their throats cut, but not killed, some with their tongues cut out of
their heads, others with their noses off; by view whereof the English might
the more bitterly lament the misery of their countrymen, and fear the like
to befall themselves." During the weeks following October 6 the rebels
took to inflicting the maximum indignity on their helpless victims. Murder
lost its efficacy, and captives were sent toward Cork mutilated and
stripped, their nudeness a mark of shame and warning in the eyes of the
country people. The savagery of the land, so long subdued, broke out
everywhere. Gentlewomen, raped and naked, their nostrils slit, were
jeered and whipped along the roads by gangs of country louts. Children
played at bowling with the heads of murdered settlers. Any act that could
diminish or humiliate the colonists was done in those weeks, until an
absolute terror gripped the survivors and none dared to venture beyond
the walls of the coastal towns.

English Munster died overnight. Clerics were invariably put to the
sword, their schools and churches burned. The castles of officials were
frequently demolished stone by stone, and even the improvements of the
land, hedgerows and orchards, uprooted and leveled. Here and there a
stronghold held out, like Mallow Castle, but towns surrounding the castles
were usually destroyed. The Munster uprising pitted the countryside,
predominantly Irish, against the villages, predominantly English, and by
the end of the year the great Kilmore wilderness, the Ballyhoura Hills and
the Aherlow Woods, overflowed with household goods and luxuries. Askeaton was founded again, by the rebels, and the Hayrope Earl made his
residence there or at Castlemaine. Meanwhile, the province was ruled
from the Aherlow, where Tyrrell established his headquarters, and
through the Aherlow, from Dungannon. Munster had been overrun before, once by Fitzmaurice and once by Gerald, but never had it been
administered by a rebel with such total effectiveness. The hard core of
Ulstermen in the South bridled the independent lords and quashed petty
rivalries.

The awesome devastation of the English colony surpassed official
belief. At Whitehall the reports of refugees were dismissed as exaggera-

tions; the waste they described did not seem believable in so short a time. But the list of wealthy castles and dwelling houses abandoned that autumn, with all furniture and stock, would soon arrive and convince skeptics. Sir Henry Ughtred abandoned his Kerry estates, Maine and Pallas, and fled to Limerick with his wife; Edward Fitton, the county Sheriff, fled to England; Sir George Bourchier lost his estates in Limerick through treachery; Sir William Courtney abandoned Newcastle; Justice Goold left Foynes, Shanid, and Tarbert; Aylmer fled from Kilfinnane; Thornton from Adare and Bruff. "Generally, all the English in Kerry ran away," a government report states, "and in Cork, the President Norris ran away first from Mallow and discouraged all the Englishry about him." This slander was undeserved; Norris held out in Mallow Castle throughout the autumn, leaving it only to convoy settlers from Mallow to Cork. Still, the destruction in his neighborhood was alarming. Tracton, Castlemahon, Mallow, and all the English villages of the seigniory of Sir Walter Raleigh and Sir Warham St. Leger were razed. Mogeely and Rosscarbery were laid waste. The Bishop of Cork narrowly escaped into the city, his estates burning behind him, and Chief Justice Saxey did not stop running until he reached London in mid-November. Stovel lost Carrigrohane in the shadow of Cork's walls, proving that the rebels controlled every yard of ground right up to the city gates. These were only a few of the more notable casualties in Counties Cork and Limerick, hardly a complete catalogue. In Counties Waterford and Tipperary the losses were repeated, and throughout Offaly and Kildare, wherever the Butlers held power. At Enniscorthy the Irish put to the sword more than 100 household retainers of Sir Henry Wallop. The onetime Lord Justice was fortunate to escape to Waterford with his family and a few possessions. With him fled Lodowick Bryskett. Early the next year Bryskett was in London, exhausted and ailing, sick at heart for his lost friends in Ireland. Warham St. Leger, despite his age, succeeded in reaching safety, but his lands too were ruined, and he would not live long enough to see them restored to his family. Thus, out of the number of friends to whom Bryskett played host at his cottage near Dublin, the only two not definitely known to have suffered at the hands of Tyrone allies were Master Smith, the apothecary, and the Archbishop of Armagh. The rest of Grey's protégés lost their lands, their livelihoods, or their lives in the final upheaval.

On October 16 the McSheehys made an end to Kilcolman Castle. They slipped out of the woods on the northern edge of Spenser's pasture and probably attacked just before dawn. If the family had any warning, it was short and came from the lower Blackwater, where Hugh Cuffe's place was already under siege. Not much is known about the last hours of Kilcolman. That there was some resistance is evident from an anonymous account in the government records "that Edmund McSheehy was killed by an Englishman at the spoil of Kilcolman." The castle was certainly burned, and the stone house beside it, but how Spenser and his wife escaped and reached Mallow is not clear. Even today the road between Kilcolman and Mallow is desolate, and then it ran through the ruined town of Buttevant, past deserted Ballybeg Abbey, and down into wooded defiles. If Spenser fled his estate in this direction, he likely did so in darkness and on horseback. He was lodged at Mallow until the third week in October and finally convoyed with his wife to Cork, penniless and with only the clothes on his back. The last he would ever see of his home and the world of Munster was flame and smoke. An old grudge was being settled. John of Desmond's lands had returned to the McSheehys, and south and west of Kilcolman the Hyde, Piers, Keate, and Vernon families were driven from their estates. Very few of them ever reached the safety of Mallow or Lord Barry's stronghold at Liscarroll. The poet's dream of a golden age in Munster, of a new Britain rising out of the fields of ancient Ireland, had ended. He was fifty-one, had lost every possession and, more essentially, a purpose to life. He may also have lost the culminating achievement of his epithalamion. Many years after, Ben Jonson remarked to William Drummond "that the Irish having robbed Spenser's goods and burnt his house and a little child new born, he and his wife escaped." Whether in fact a child died in the sack of Kilcolman, and whether indeed that child was Elizabeth Boyle's, has never been substantiated. The catastrophe which overtook the Munster Plantation was so sudden, the losses so complete, that the private tragedies of the settlers will never be known.

The city of Cork had not grown appreciably since the time of the Desmond Wars, and the refugees flocking into the city were many times more numerous in 1598 than they had been in 1569 or 1579. Consequently, the living conditions in the city were more miserable than ever. A new fort was rising to the southwest of the walls, but it was not complete, and the workmen had fled. In November 1000 troops arrived in the city to reinforce the province, and they were quartered on the townsfolk while the refugees crowded the back alleys, muddy byways, and church porches. The rains fell incessantly throughout November, and the weather was cold. Exhausted survivors, many of them injured, lay in the open, cold, hungry, and untended. Criers passed among them, searching for relatives and kinsfolk. By the burial pits in Christ churchyard settlers studied the faces of the dead for family members lost or separated during the flight. Apparently little sympathy was shown the survivors. Soldiers pouring in from English ports made no attempt to distinguish them from the Irish, and the townspeople spurned them as a cause of danger to the city. Ormond visited Cork in November and decried the cowardice and negligence of the undertakers; for time being, they, not Tyrone, were made the cause of the English defeat.

Spenser and his wife probably fared better than many settlers inside Cork. Elizabeth's uncle, Richard Boyle, the future Great Earl of Cork, was in the city and already well provided. He would not have allowed his niece to be turned out into the streets. Spenser, in his own right, was still Clerk of the Munster Council, and although that body was now effectively defunct, he also learned on arrival that he had been preferred to the office of Sheriff of Munster. This reward for his services came late. The previous Sheriff had fled to England several weeks before, lucky to escape the rebels with his life. After the sack of Kilcolman the appointment must have seemed an especially bitter jest; the notice read that he was "a man endowed with good knowledge in learning, and not without experience in the service of the wars." He was England's foremost poet, and experience in the wars had ruined him. The appointment had been issued before the destruction of the Munster Plantation and now entitled the holder only to a warm shelter in the city. On every side the Crown was in retreat; aid was months away, and the Queen in her anger had turned on her own people in Ireland. From the misery and degradation of Cork, Spenser wrote to Her Majesty: "Out of the ashes of desolation and wasteness of this your wretched realm of Ireland . . . receive the voices of a few most unhappy ghosts . . . who lie buried in oblivion. . . . Surely should any stranger hear that the English nation, so mighty and puissant, so far abroad in a country of your own dominion, lying hard under the lap of England, should by so base and barbarous a people as the Irish, so untrained in wars, so inexperienced of all government and good policies, be so suddenly trodden down and blown away with a blast, they would forever condemn us, not knowing the means how the same is come to pass." Spenser explained to Elizabeth the faults of her policy: "The deviser of the settlement of Munster perhaps thought that the civil example of the English being set before the Irish, and their daily conversing with them, would have brought them by dislike of their own savage life to the liking and embracing of better civility. But it is far otherwise, for instead of following them, they fly the English, and most hatefully shun them, for two causes: first, because they have ever been brought up licentiously and to live as each one listeth; secondly, because they naturally hate the English, so that their fashions they also hate." This was the admittance of a disappointed pedagogue; the barbarians were unteachable, Ireland was lost, and now only the Queen could intervene to save her missionaries: "In the mean season, we poor wretches, who now bear the burden of all oversights, pour out our most humble and piteous plaint to your most excellent Majesty, that it may please you to cast your gracious mind unto the regard of our miseries

. . . we have spent all the small portion of our abilities in building and erecting, and now have nothing left but to cry unto you for timely aid." The despair of the letter, called a *Brief Note of Ireland,* was not characteristic of Spenser; it is testimony to his frame of mind and the condition of the settlers. Unfortunately, it came to the attention of a preoccupied Queen. Elizabeth was mindful of the need to destroy Tyrone, but her preparations were only half done, and the cause of the Munster undertakers would have to wait.

The poet could not have spent more than a few weeks at rest in Cork. Norris was fighting every day to keep open the road to Mallow, and beyond to Liscarroll and Kilmallock. By October 23 Kilmallock had been under siege for three weeks, and every available reinforcement was rushed westward into the sprawling battle. The 1000 troops who arrived from the Low Countries in November were soon used up in countless skirmishes with Tyrrell, and couriers traveled back and forth to Westminster, begging support and delivering urgent dispatches. Spenser became a courier. He hated sea passages and the long ride from the West ports to London, but Norris trusted him to carry confidential reports and deliver them to the proper persons. He may have made the trip in November or early December, and his last journey brought him to Court at Westminster at Christmastide. The letters he carried were uncompromising appraisals. The last ones, delivered to Sir Robert Cecil at Whitehall on Sunday, December 24, told that the rebellion in Munster had gained such headway, and been so strengthened by the daily efforts of Roman priests, that Norris believed extreme measures would be necessary to bring the people back to loyalty. A return to loyalty would, of course, never occur, and Norris' request took its place beside Sidney's request of 1569, Maltby's of 1579, Grey's of 1583.

Spenser presented the letters and was paid eight pounds for bringing them over. He needed the money. The testimony is overwhelming that he arrived in England a poor man, poor at least in available funds. He was not destitute, as has sometimes been argued, but hard pressed to afford lodgings in the crowded city. He had not been in London for two years, and time had worked great changes in his circle of friends. Patrons were gone, lost in Ireland or spent with the years, and in the commotion raised by the new war, he and other refugees were shunted aside. They were the losers; a new generation had arrived to try its hand in Ireland. Under the circumstances it was probably difficult to be heard, even to find access to Court officials. Cecil, the opponent of twenty years before, was gone, and the friends Leicester, Walsingham, the Sidneys. Raleigh was deep in the intrigues of the succession, and Essex lived, as Grey had once, surrounded by knights and courtiers eager to distinguish themselves in the wars. On

January 4 Essex wrote to Lord Willoughby: "Now for myself. Into Ireland I go. The Queen hath irrevocably decreed it; the Council do passionately urge it; and I am tied in mine own reputation to use no tergiversation." Like Grey, Essex was not keen for Ireland; he had been advanced as his country's hope and dared not refuse. If possible, the war fervor of 1599 outdid that of 1579. Churchyard, among the longest-lived English poets, wrote commendatory verses for the occasion; this was his third Irish war, and he recalled sending Essex's father off to the first one. The news of the year was predominantly about defeats and victories in Ireland, matters of recruitment and desertion, victualing and transport. A great army was mustering in the West, and the logistical heart of the effort was Whitehall. The Queen was in residence at the palace throughout the New Year and met daily with her Council. Just beyond the palace gates, the inns and hostels of King Street, Westminster, were packed with couriers, consulars, and soldiers, and Spenser found a room at an inn a few yards beyond King's Gate.

Here, during the first week in January, he fell into a fever, his illness aggravated by exhaustion and the shocks of the last few months. Death was a common occurrence in the crowded inns, and Spenser was probably neglected since his wife was in Cork and he had no relatives then living in London. He was bedridden for ten days before any high officials heard or took note of his condition. Unseasonably frigid temperatures hastened his decline, for the weather was cold that December and January, the Thames iced over from bank to bank for the first time in thirty years. Those who might have come to the inn out of deference or respect stayed home, and on the morning of January 16, attended by a landlady and a messenger, the poet died. His Irish sojourn ended a short stroll from the lodging house where it began in 1579.

Whether Spenser succumbed to pneumonia or some other malady is not known and was not important. His contemporaries agreed that he died of a broken heart. The first mention of his death appeared four days later in a letter: "Spenser, our principal poet, coming lately out of Ireland, died at Westminster on Saturday last." Nothing more was said, yet the news spread quickly through literary circles, and in early February a funeral notice appeared: "Master Edmund Spenser is dead at Westminster on the 16th of this month and is interred in the Collegiate Church near to Chaucer at the charge of the Earl of Essex, his hearse being attended by poets, and mournful elegies and poems with the pens that wrote them thrown into his tomb. . . . He surpassed all the English poets of former times, not excepting Chaucer himself; but by a fate which still followeth poets, he wrestled always with poverty. . . . For scarce had he settled in Ireland in a retired privacy and got leisure to write, when he is by the rebels thrown out of his dwelling, plundered of his goods, and returned into England a poor man, less than a month since." At Essex's expense, the poet was buried in Westminster Abbey, and following the practice of the times, the literary world turned out to throw their scribblings into his grave. Dying, he was forgotten to the last moment; dead, he was the prince of poets, the father of English poesy.

In the years following, the rumor spread that he had been offered help on his deathbed by the Earl of Essex. "He died for lack of bread in King Street," Jonson told Drummond, "and refused twenty pieces sent to him by my Lord of Essex, and said that he was sorry he had no time to spend them." As a poet usually poor, and seldom above self-pity, Jonson had a vested interest in stretching the truth. But the irony of Spenser's death scene appealed widely and was repeated over the subsequent years. King Street was then the wealthiest thoroughfare in the realm, Essex the richest lord, and England's foremost poet died of need in their shadow.

Spenser, however, was not killed by poverty so much as by Ireland and, more specifically, by the McSheehys. He was a casualty of the Irish wars as certainly as young Cheke had been at Smerwick, Bagenal had been at Yellow Ford, or Drury, Perrot, and Grey in their sicknesses and ruined reputations. His generation had borne the cost of the wars against Spain and Catholic Europe and had suffered most miserably in Ireland. In the spring of 1599 Hugh O'Neill ruled more of that island than Elizabeth; he would hold it virtually entire until 1601, and thereafter, in retreat until the end of the reign. In the summer following Spenser's death, near Kilmallock, still the killing ground of Irish wars, a Desmond gallowglass broke through Thomas Norris' breastplate with his spear, and several weeks later the President of Munster died of gangrene at Mallow. He was the fourth of six brothers to die in Ireland. One had been killed in action in Brittany, and the last was brought home from Munster at the Queen's command to console his parents in their bereavement and old age. This was the way of the Irish wars, devouring the strength of the realm slowly, sapping its energy and idealism. Four more years of killing would pass before Ireland would again sink into an exhausted passivity, and by then Elizabeth would be gone. That she knew in the last years of her life the bitterness of conquering her own domains is proved by her unceasing grief for Burghley. "He was our great pilot on whom all cast their eyes and sought their safety," she said on one occasion. Witnesses describe how she "did often speak of him in tears and turn aside when he was discoursed of; nay, even forbidding any mention to be made of his name in the Council." Cecil had advised against the Irish adventure in 1569 and the Irish war in 1579.

Spenser's death coincided with the end of an age, a time of great hopes and lofty ambitions. He was a man of the High Renaissance, imbued with an ardor for order and national achievement. Not incidentally, he was also part of one of the most energetic governments in English history. In London new poets were emerging, and these, Shakespeare, Jonson, Donne, would speak more dramatically to the concerns of modern men. They would never be truly public poets, though, in the sense that Spenser had been, defining the ideals and guiding principles of their age.

The meaning of the great effort made in Ireland after 1579 was never lost on him. And the summary of his experience was committed to paper sometime before his death. In 1606 his printer published the fragmentary beginning of a new book to *The Faerie Queene*, ever since called "The Mutability Cantos," and these interpret the decline and fall of Munster. They are about change, not orderly change, but what Elizabethans feared most, random happening, and they describe the susceptibility of all things to time and decay. The cantos are set in Ireland and conclude with a heavenly inquisition held high above the ruined Aherlow Valley, where the gods and Dame Nature are called to explain why nothing that is good lasts. The gods do not know, but Nature does, and she explains that while everything changes, nothing changes. The things of the world "by their change their being do dilate, / And turning to themselves at length again, / Do work their own perfection so by fate." Human experience is repetitive and indestructible. The Aherlow would in time flower and be fruitful again, only to fade once more. England would never be finished with Ireland, or Ireland with England, until the great God Himself called a halt to time. The only rest in the process of life is death, and prophetically the fragment ends with the poet's readiness: "All that moveth doth in change delight; / But thenceforth all shall rest eternally / With him that is the God of Sabbath hight. / O that great Sabbath God, grant me that Sabbath's sight." Spenser was dead seven years when his third statement about Ireland appeared, and the truth of his prediction was by then apparent.

But in 1600 the Irish had won Ireland back. O'Neill held all but the principal coastal cities and the pale, and as Spanish troops came ashore, he was prepared to negotiate for these. The only obstacle between him and the kingship of Ireland was an old, frail woman, Elizabeth, who would not give up. She bent her every thought and action to trapping Tyrone and destroying him, and in her proclamation of 1599 she declared the total war she had always before declined in Ireland: "Although our actions and carriage in the whole course of our government, ever since it pleased God to call us to the succession of this crown, doth clearly witness how earnestly we have affected the peace and tranquillity of the people of our dominions, and how much we have preferred clemency. . . . Notwithstanding it hath fallen out to our great discontent that this our gracious intention hath not wrought in all men's minds a like effect, nor brought forth everywhere that fruit of obedience which we expected, and namely in our kingdom and people of Ireland. . . . This is therefore the cause that after so long patience we have been compelled to take resolution to reduce that kingdom to obedience by using an extraordinary power and force against them. . . . We do profess hereby to the world, that we are so far from purposing conquest, or an utter extirpation and rooting out of that nation, as is the opinion put into them by the heads of this rebellion. . . ." The Queen could not admit freely that her own domains had been so misruled as to stand in need of reconquest, but in March, 1599, Essex finally sailed for Ireland with 16,000 troops under instructions to destroy the rebels at any cost. As the many accounts of Elizabeth and Essex make clear, her hopes were in vain; she had selected a man of unbounded ambition, and in her doting, she only encouraged his presumptuousness.

Essex was ordered to go North against O'Neill; instead, he swung South in a foolish effort to succor Ormond in Munster. The damage was already done in the South, the settlers overwhelmed, and Essex's slight victory over Tyrrell's horse in the Pass of the Plumes was small compensation for a stinging defeat experienced by his infantry in the Wicklow Mountains. While he frittered away his opportunity to attack Tyrone directly, his army began the process of evaporation so common in Ireland. By summer he mustered only half the troops he had brought with him, and by then he no longer had the superiority to strike at Ulster. Essex deplored the damp Irish weather, the uncivilized nature of campaigning in that country, and, to amuse himself in camp, advanced his young lieutenants to knighthoods at a whim. In her letters the Queen railed at him for debasing the nobility and for delaying a decisive action. She was appalled at his inaction, at the shrinkage of his force, and, in July, commanded him to attack northward without delay or excuse. Essex, in reply, summoned the commanders of his army, and after deliberations, they certified in the Earl's defense that the army was not fit to attack the rebels. The minutes of this council were signed by a formidable list of English aristocrats: the Earls of Southampton and Kildare, Henry Docwra, Thomas Jermyn, Henry Danvers, Francis Darcy, Arthur Champernowne, Robert Drury, Richard Wilmot, and Edward Herbert. On the strength of their advice Essex sat comfortably in Dublin and left the countryside to the Irish. He was not in the style of old campaigners, a Maltby or a Perrot, who would march the bogs to flush an enemy; he was the spoiled child of a better era, and when he finally did act in September, he idled northward without purpose.

Tyrone had not been similarly inactive. He held the upper hand but also knew that time was against him. Philip II had died, as Cecil predicted, soon after Yellow Ford; Spanish troops were on the high seas bound for Ireland, but if Tyrone did not secure the island quickly, Spanish resolve might falter. As Essex moved North, O'Neill had the force to meet him, but he had also taken the measure of the Earl and knew well how to avert a decisive engagement. He determined to negotiate, to delay, until Spanish forces were ashore in strength at Tralee. Then, as the English wheeled southward to fend off an attack on Cork, he was positioned to attack their rear and the city of Dublin. Tactical dangers such as these did not occur to Essex. Neither he nor his key officers had conducted a sustained campaign before; they were trained by the raids on Cádiz and in the isolated and glorious actions of the Flanders army. The Earl proposed to act boldly when the time came, but in the meanwhile, he complained about the miseries of Ireland, the Queen's harshness to him, the insults he suffered at the hands of her counselors. All this Tyrone knew or sensed, and as the English regiments marched North, he shadowed them with his superior force, often encamping across rivers from them or on adjacent hills and always ready to brush aside an attack and retreat again.

Early in September a clash became inevitable, and in the vicinity of Louth, a few miles south of Dundalk, the two armies came to rest facing each other. Inconsequential skirmishing followed, but no clear action. The English force was outnumbered two to one, but Tyrone refrained from throwing his main body at them. Finally, on September 5, O'Neill called for a parley, and against all instructions from Elizabeth, Essex consented to meet Tyrone at the ford of Bellaclynthe. The famous meeting took place on the following morning, the Earl in the middle of the stream, his horse lapped in water to his belly, and O'Neill across from him on the bank. Each man was escorted by six retainers, and after salutations Tyrone rode forward into the stream to speak privately with his enemy. What was discussed and decided at Bellaclynthe will never be known. The parley lasted for several minutes, and when it was over, Essex returned to the English camp and commanded his regiments to break bivouac and turn southward. In defiance of the Queen and her Council, Essex granted Tyrone a truce.

The reasons for the truce have never been convincing. Essex argued that his army needed reinforcements, that the winter was coming, that he did not dare leave Dublin open to attack. He granted Tyrone until the following May, and in that time reinforcements would arrive—Spanish soldiers—intended for the Irish army. The Queen would not learn for several weeks what had passed at Bellaclynthe, but curiously, she had anticipated something of the kind. Waiting in Dublin was a letter for Essex which undercut every one of his alibis: "If sickness of the army be the reason why action is not undertaken, why was there not action when the army was in better state? If winter's approach, why were the summer months of July and August lost? If the spring were too soon, and the summer that followed otherwise spent, if the harvest time that succeeded were so neglected as nothing hath been done, then surely we must conclude that none of the four quarters of the year will be in season for you and your council to agree on Tyrone's persecution, for which all our charge is intended." Elizabeth was not to be hoodwinked; in effect, she accused her commander of being either a coward or a fool. She wanted battle and would not hear otherwise. The letter proved too much for Essex. On September 24 he caused a commission to be drawn up constituting Chancellor Loftus and Sir George Carew, Lord Justices, of Ireland and, with a party of his closest followers, embarked secretly for England. He thereby deserted his army without orders and returned home to plot against the Queen. Events were in motion which led to his rebellion months later and which ended finally on a cold February morning at the Tower, where a clumsy headsman needed six blows to sever Essex's head from his body.

The fall of the great Earl of Essex began in Ireland, his proud nature frustrated by that country, and Tyrone could claim a decisive, if bloodless, victory over him. O'Neill was likely a fox too wily for unseasoned soldiers, yet the suspicion remains that he and Essex discussed more than a truce in their meeting at Bellaclynthe. In the closing months of the century one issue above all dominated war and policy—the succession. Elizabeth was an old woman; she could not last much longer. And on this chance O'Neill founded all his hopes. Tenuous evidence links him to James Stuart, James VI of Scotland, and the possibility cannot be discounted that he was in negotiation with the Queen's heir. If indeed, he may have been in a position to bargain with Essex, the favors of a new reign against a few months' truce in a hopeless war. In the aftermath of Bellaclynthe several rebel chiefs proclaimed Essex an ally, and rebels across Ireland took heart in believing that the Queen's commander had come over to them. Whether their hopes were ill conceived, a misinterpretation of the Earl's actions, or a product of Tyrone's instigation is not known. All that is certain is that O'Neill had set his course to outlast the Queen, and therefore, it is probable that he did not ignore her designated successor.

While Elizabeth dealt with her rebellious favorite and his highborn followers, her Lord Justices, Loftus and Carew, blundered ahead. Fighting was continual and costly; the war deteriorated into a dozen inconclusive skirmishes across the provinces, and little glory was won by either side. Ormond was captured in Kerry. Tyrrell took Kilmallock, or appeared to, and lost it again. And early in 1600 Sir George Carew broached his plan for overturning the Hayrope Earl in Munster. The scheme promised to erode support for James FitzThomas by reinstating the legitimate descendant of the Desmonds, Gerald's son. The boy whom Justice Drury had fetched to Dublin Castle was a grown man now, still a prisoner in London. Eleanor, the Countess of Desmond, had been granted a small pension by the Queen, and if she was poor and ragged, she and her five other children were still alive and serviceable as a ready-made noble family. All that remained was to bring the young Earl over and encourage the Geraldines to flock to his banner. Under the circumstances Elizabeth must have been ready to grasp at straws, and she approved the venture. "The Queen's Earl of Desmond," as Gerald's son was known, arrived in Youghal in the summer of 1600, under the guidance and direction of Captain Simon Price. He was received by the Munster folk with enthusiasm, the Mayor of Cork expressed grave doubts on meeting him, but at Kilmallock the men, women, and children upset each other in the streets to see the restored exile. A guard of soldiers lined the way, but the crowds broke the line, showering down salt and wheat on him as he passed. The next day was Sunday. Ostentatiously Price led the Protestant Earl to the Protestant church, and as they entered, the cheers outside turned to jeers. When he came out after services, he was cursed and spat at. The fiction had evaporated. The Earl of Desmond had not returned to lead his people; only a pretender, a wooden image, had come back to them. The English were disappointed with their Earl. Not only was he too frail and bookish after long confinement to grasp the opportunities around him, but woman-starved, he seized the moment to fall in love with a handsome widow, whom Carew had no intention of allowing him to marry. Early in 1601 he was returned to England—penniless, despised. He died nine months later, the last legitimate Desmond of Munster.

Far from discrediting the Hayrope Earl, Carew's crude ruse added more adherents to the rebel cause. Two years were to pass before James FitzThomas fell into English hands and was confined for life to the Tower. In the meanwhile, the war dragged on in Counties Cork and Limerick. Kerry was virtually abandoned, and much of Connaught. Signs had begun to appear of famine and plague. Tyrone continued to pray for Elizabeth's timely decease, but she did not weaken or relent in her determination to break him. The Queen poured thousands of reinforcements into Cork and Dublin, and as before, the maladministration of her army drove them to wholesale desertion. O'Neill received arms and men from Spain; he fought with the blessings of Catholic Europe; he had achieved a truly international importance, the first Irishman of his age to do so. But he could not take the English cities. Outnumbering the English, he still had neither the weight of number nor an effective navy to capture Cork, Limerick, or Dublin. And by late 1600 Elizabeth had finally found the commander she was seeking. Charles Blount, Lord Mountjoy, was described by his friends as a quiet, diffident, even foppish courtier, but in the field he proved a model of efficiency. During the first months of 1601 he brought new discipline and vigor to the army, and by the fall of that year the army needed the new skills he had taught it.

The crisis of the third Irish war came in September at Kinsale, just south of Cork. Don Juan del Aguila landed below the city with a Spanish force 4000 strong. Tyrone raced southward to join him, as Mountjoy bottled up the Spanish on the promontory at Kinsale, a spot reminiscent of Smerwick. In the dash South O'Neill defeated every attempt to block him, but in attacking the English siege lines, he was defeated. Del Aguila surrendered in December. The three-month battle was over; it had become the slugging match Tyrone could ill afford, a contest of trenches in which his troops lost their principal advantages—mobility and surprise. In the wake of the battle the English counted 1200 Irish dead; many more had been killed or wounded, and of the nearly 900 Irish prisoners taken, all but a few of highest rank were hanged. The Spanish survivors were generally spared.

Kinsale is seen as the decisive battle of the Irish wars. A long, complicated engagement, it was in effect an Irish Hastings, a battle which lost a nation. The new Irish state was dead in its infancy. Henceforth Tyrone fought only for terms, for self-preservation, waiting for Elizabeth to die or to grow weary of the expense of chasing him. Still formidable, he withdrew into the fastnesses of Ulster, abandoning the provinces to local rebels, and he sent Red Hugh O'Donnell into Spain to beg a new army from his allies. At Madrid, in 1602, O'Donnell was poisoned, presumably murdered by an English agent, and Tyrone, like Desmond before him, would wait in vain for a Spanish salvation.

Though the war was lost, the fighting did not end. In the year following Kinsale, Ireland sank into a state of darkness and ruin exceeding the worst conditions of the Desmond Wars. Then famine had been restricted largely to Munster; now hunger spread across Ireland, and with it plague, lawlessness, and chaos. The English blamed Tyrone, Tyrone the English, but both sides were powerless to save the population. Once more war had exhausted the country's slender reserves of grain and cattle. In the frightfulness of the time men believed they saw a Day of Judgment come, an end of time and human nature, for the sights in the countryside were beyond description or imagining. Fynes Moryson was a witness, and his account only suggests the horror: "No doubt the famine was great because the rebel soldiers took all the common people had to feed on . . . the common sort of the rebels were driven to unspeakable extremities (beyond the record of most histories that ever I did read in that kind). . . . Captain Trevor and many honest gentlemen living in Newry can witness, that some old women of those parts, used to make a fire in the fields, and divers little children driving out the cattle in the cold mornings, and coming thither to warm them, were by them surprised, killed and eaten, which at last was discovered by a great girl breaking from them . . . and Captain Trevor sending out soldiers to know the truth, they found children's skulls and bones, and apprehended the old women, who were executed for the fact. The captains of Carrickfergus, and the adjacent garrisons of the northern parts can witness, that upon the making of peace, and receiving the rebels to mercy, it was a common practice among the common sort of them . . . to thrust long needles into the horses of our English troops, and they dying thereupon, to be ready to tear out one another's throat for a share of them. And no spectacle was more frequent in the ditches of towns, and especially in wasted countries, than to see multitudes of these poor people dead with their mouths all colored green by eating nettles, docks, and all things they could rend up above ground. These and very many like lamentable effects followed their rebellion, and no doubt the rebels had been utterly destroyed by famine, had not a general peace shortly followed Tyrone's submission . . . by which the rebels had liberty to seek relief among the subjects of Ireland, and to be transported into England and France, where great multitudes of them lived for some years after the peace made."

No Irish lord ever lost a rebellion without his countrymen's paying a dreadful price for the failure. O'Neill stood the results as long as he could. He had numerous close escapes in the neighborhood of Lough Neagh; he struck back where he could, but his force was diminishing quickly, and the Queen's soldiers were scouring the hills and woods of the North for him. By 1603 the war was over elsewhere in Ireland.

Three months into the new year Tyrone was persuaded to surrender. He had promises of terms, and he came to Blount at Mellifont Abbey on March 30, disarmed and submissive, his commanding features lined with wrinkles, his beard grizzled. The moment of his surrender was recorded by several observers, and all corroborate the account by Thomas Gainsford: "At the first entrance into the room, even at the threshold of the door, he prostrated himself grovelling to the earth, with such a dejected countenance, that the standers-by were amazed and my Lord Mountjoy had much ado to remember the work in hand . . . it was one of the deplorablest sights that ever I saw: and to look upon such a person, the author of so much trouble, and so formerly glorious, so dejected, would have wrought many changes in the stoutest heart, and did, no doubt, at this instant raise a certain commiseration in his greatest adversary. . . . Thus was Tyrone made the tennis-ball of fortune, and abandoned by Spain's over-prized greatness." According to Moryson, who was also present, O'Neill was kept kneeling before Blount for one hour. At the end of the audience he was dismissed and not brought in again until the following day. On April 1 he was made to submit to the lords of the Irish Council, and on April 3 to representatives of the Irish Parliament in Dublin. Then after the ceremony at Dublin Castle, he was finally told: the Queen had died on March 24; James of Scotland was monarch of England. Moryson describes the immediate effect on O'Neill: "The Earl of Tyrone upon first hearing the Lord Deputy's relation of the Queen's death, could not contain himself from shedding tears, in such quantity as it could not well be concealed, especially in him, upon whose face all men's eyes were cast. . . . There needed no Oedipus to find out the true cause of his tears, for no doubt, the most humble submission he made to the Queen he had so highly and proudly offended, meant nothing, if he had held out till her death."

Mountjoy tricked Tyrone as Tyrone had often tricked Lord Deputies. The Archrebel and his nation had outlasted their wrathful Queen and never knew until too late. In the years to follow, Ireland's rebel lords abandoned their lands for the Continent, and King James permitted them to go. The Irish annalists are eloquent in their catalogue of those who chose to go and not look back: "Maguire and Donough, the son of Mahon, son of the Bishop O'Brien, brought a ship with them to Ireland, and put in at the harbor of Swilly. They took with them from Ireland the Earl O'Neill, and the Earl O'Donnell, Rory, the son of Hugh, son of Manus, with a great number of the chieftains of the province of Ulster. These were they who went with O'Neill, namely, the Countess Catherina, the daughter of Magennis, Hugh the Baron, John, and Brian; Art Oge, the son of Cormac, son of the Baron; Fedorcha, son of Con, son of O'Neill; Hugh Oge, the son of Brian, son of Art O'Neill. And these were they who went with the Earl O'Donnell: Caffar; Nuala; Rose, the daughter of O'Doherty. . . . They entered the ship on the festival of the Holy Cross, in autumn." The list continues for pages, a litany for Gaelic Ireland, and it is proof that an age had passed in the history of the Irish. O'Neill died in Rome thirteen years later. Most of the exiles never returned. But change, as Spenser knew, is like the wind on the sea; water moves but never alters. In 1642 Owen O'Neill, nephew of Hugh, returned home to lead his countrymen against the Puritan Parliament.

GENEALOGIES

SELECT CHAPTER BIBLIOGRAPHIES

INDEX

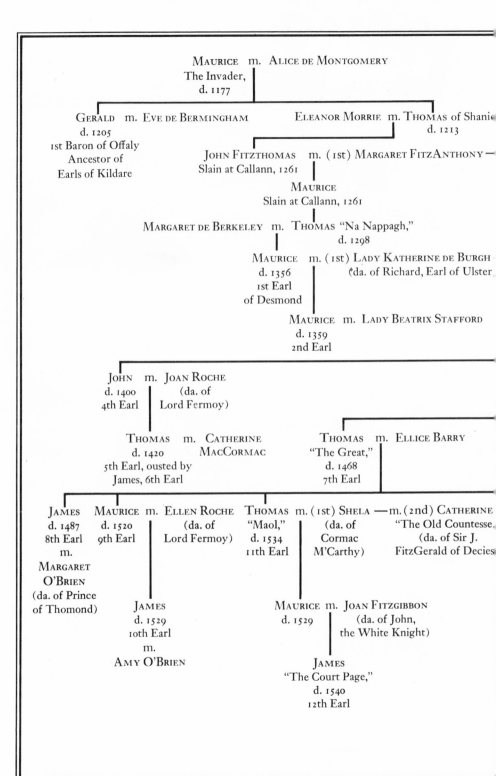

MAURICE   m.   ALICE DE MONTGOMERY
The Invader,
d. 1177

GERALD   m.   EVE DE BERMINGHAM
d. 1205
1st Baron of Offaly
Ancestor of
Earls of Kildare

ELEANOR MORRIE   m.   THOMAS of Shani‹
d. 1213

JOHN FITZTHOMAS   m. (1st) MARGARET FITZANTHONY —
Slain at Callann, 1261

MAURICE
Slain at Callann, 1261

MARGARET DE BERKELEY   m.   THOMAS "Na Nappagh,"
d. 1298

MAURICE   m. (1st) LADY KATHERINE DE BURGH
d. 1356   (da. of Richard, Earl of Ulster
1st Earl
of Desmond

MAURICE   m.   LADY BEATRIX STAFFORD
d. 1359
2nd Earl

JOHN   m.   JOAN ROCHE
d. 1400   (da. of
4th Earl   Lord Fermoy)

THOMAS   m.   CATHERINE
d. 1420   MACCORMAC
5th Earl, ousted by
James, 6th Earl

THOMAS   m.   ELLICE BARRY
"The Great,"
d. 1468
7th Earl

JAMES   MAURICE   m.   ELLEN ROCHE
d. 1487   d. 1520   (da. of
8th Earl   9th Earl   Lord Fermoy)
m.
MARGARET
O'BRIEN
(da. of Prince
of Thomond)

THOMAS   m. (1st) SHELA —m. (2nd) CATHERINE
"Maol,"   (da. of   "The Old Countesse.
d. 1534   Cormac   (da. of Sir J.
11th Earl   M'Carthy)   FitzGerald of Decies

JAMES
d. 1529
10th Earl
m.
AMY O'BRIEN

MAURICE   m.   JOAN FITZGIBBON
d. 1529   (da. of John,
the White Knight)

JAMES
"The Court Page,"
d. 1540
12th Earl

The Earls of Desmond

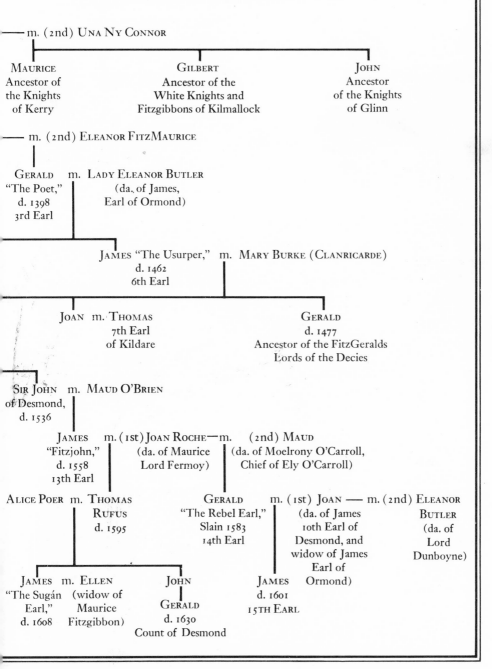

———— m. (2nd) UNA NY CONNOR

MAURICE Ancestor of the Knights of Kerry	**GILBERT** Ancestor of the White Knights and Fitzgibbons of Kilmallock	**JOHN** Ancestor of the Knights of Glinn

———— m. (2nd) ELEANOR FITZMAURICE

GERALD "The Poet," d. 1398 3rd Earl   m. LADY ELEANOR BUTLER (da. of James, Earl of Ormond)

JAMES "The Usurper," d. 1462 6th Earl   m. MARY BURKE (CLANRICARDE)

JOAN m. THOMAS 7th Earl of Kildare

GERALD d. 1477 Ancestor of the FitzGeralds Lords of the Decies

SIR JOHN of Desmond, d. 1536   m. MAUD O'BRIEN

JAMES "Fitzjohn," d. 1558 13th Earl   m. (1st) JOAN ROCHE (da. of Maurice Lord Fermoy)   m. (2nd) MAUD (da. of Moelrony O'Carroll, Chief of Ely O'Carroll)

ALICE POER m. THOMAS RUFUS d. 1595

GERALD "The Rebel Earl," Slain 1583 14th Earl   m. (1st) JOAN (da. of James 10th Earl of Desmond, and widow of James Earl of Ormond)   m. (2nd) ELEANOR BUTLER (da. of Lord Dunboyne)

JAMES m. ELLEN "The Sugán (widow of Earl," Maurice d. 1608 Fitzgibbon)

JOHN
GERALD d. 1630 Count of Desmond

JAMES d. 1601 15TH EARL

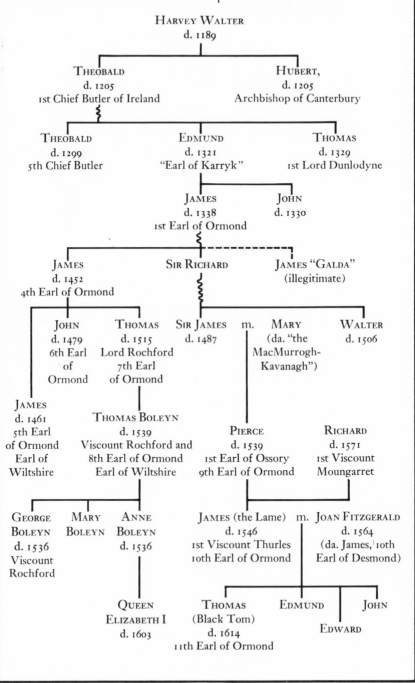

The Earls of Ormond

HARVEY WALTER
d. 1189

THEOBALD
d. 1205
1st Chief Butler of Ireland

HUBERT,
d. 1205
Archbishop of Canterbury

THEOBALD
d. 1299
5th Chief Butler

EDMUND
d. 1321
"Earl of Karryk"

THOMAS
d. 1329
1st Lord Dunlodyne

JAMES
d. 1338
1st Earl of Ormond

JOHN
d. 1330

JAMES
d. 1452
4th Earl of Ormond

SIR RICHARD

JAMES "GALDA"
(illegitimate)

JOHN
d. 1479
6th Earl
of
Ormond

THOMAS
d. 1515
Lord Rochford
7th Earl
of Ormond

SIR JAMES
d. 1487

m.

MARY
(da. "the
MacMurrogh-
Kavanagh")

WALTER
d. 1506

JAMES
d. 1461
5th Earl
of Ormond
Earl of
Wiltshire

THOMAS BOLEYN
d. 1539
Viscount Rochford and
8th Earl of Ormond
Earl of Wiltshire

PIERCE
d. 1539
1st Earl of Ossory
9th Earl of Ormond

RICHARD
d. 1571
1st Viscount
Moungarret

GEORGE
BOLEYN
d. 1536
Viscount
Rochford

MARY
BOLEYN

ANNE
BOLEYN
d. 1536

JAMES (the Lame)
d. 1546
1st Viscount Thurles
10th Earl of Ormond

m.

JOAN FITZGERALD
d. 1564
(da. James, 10th
Earl of Desmond)

QUEEN
ELIZABETH I
d. 1603

THOMAS
(Black Tom)
d. 1614
11th Earl of Ormond

EDMUND

EDWARD

JOHN

The Earls of Tyrone

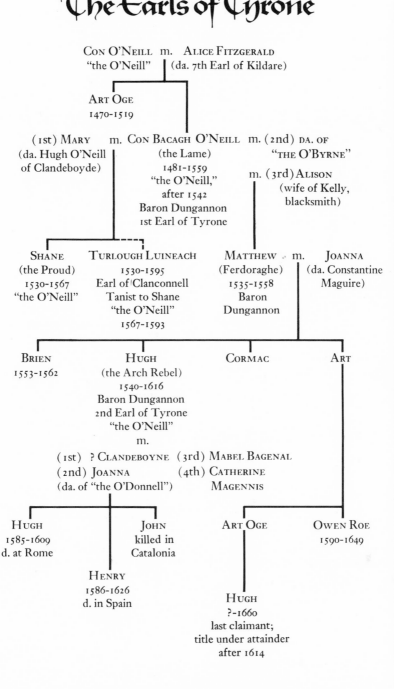

CON O'NEILL   m.   ALICE FITZGERALD
"the O'Neill"   (da. 7th Earl of Kildare)

ART OGE
1470-1519

(1st) MARY   m. CON BACAGH O'NEILL   m. (2nd) DA. OF
(da. Hugh O'Neill   (the Lame)   "THE O'BYRNE"
of Clandeboyde)   1481-1559
         "the O'Neill,"   m. (3rd) ALISON
         after 1542   (wife of Kelly,
         Baron Dungannon   blacksmith)
         1st Earl of Tyrone

SHANE   TURLOUGH LUINEACH   MATTHEW   m.   JOANNA
(the Proud)   1530-1595   (Ferdoraghe)   (da. Constantine
1530-1567   Earl of Clanconnell   1535-1558   Maguire)
"the O'Neill"   Tanist to Shane   Baron
         "the O'Neill"   Dungannon
         1567-1593

BRIEN   HUGH   CORMAC   ART
1553-1562   (the Arch Rebel)
         1540-1616
         Baron Dungannon
         2nd Earl of Tyrone
         "the O'Neill"
         m.

(1st) ? CLANDEBOYNE   (3rd) MABEL BAGENAL
(2nd) JOANNA   (4th) CATHERINE
(da. of "the O'Donnell")   MAGENNIS

HUGH   JOHN   ART OGE   OWEN ROE
1585-1609   killed in   1590-1649
d. at Rome   Catalonia

        HENRY
        1586-1626
        d. in Spain   HUGH
                       ?-1660
                    last claimant;
              title under attainder
                 after 1614

III

The Sidneys

SIR WILLIAM SIDNEY m. ANNE PAGENHAM
1482-1554

LADY MARY DUDLEY m. SIR HENRY
(da. of John Dudley,   SIDNEY, K.G.
Duke of Northumberland)   1529-1586

├ MARY m.
│   SIR WILLIAM DORMER
├ LUCY m.
│   SIR JAMES HARRINGTON
├ ANNE m.
│   SIR WILLIAM FITZWILLIAM
└ FRANCES m.
     3RD EARL OF SUSSEX

(1st) SIR m. FRANCES WALSINGHAM
PHILIP   (da. of Sir Francis
SIDNEY   Walsingham)
1554-1586   m. (2nd)
             ROBERT DEVEREAUX
             2nd Earl of Essex
             m. (3rd)
             RICHARD DE BORGH
             Earl of Clanricarde

THOMAS   MARY
             m.
         2ND EARL OF PEMBROKE

FRANCES   SIR ROBERT SIDNEY, K.G. m. BARBARA
b. 1584   1563-1626   (da. of
m.   cr. Baron Sidney 1603   John Gamage
5TH EARL OF RUTLAND Viscount Lisle 1605   of Coity,
                   Earl of Leicester 1618   Glamorgan)
SIR WILLIAM SIDNEY
d. 1613

LADY DOROTHY PERCY m. ROBERT
(da. of 9th Earl   1595-1677
of Northumberland)   2nd Earl of
                         Leicester,
                         K.B.

├ MARY m.
│   SIR ROBERT WROTH
├ CATHERINE m.
│   SIR LEWIS MANSEL, BT.
├ PHILIPPA m.
│   SIR JOHN HOBART, BT.
└ BARBARA m.
     1ST VISCOUNT STRANGFORD

PHILIP   ALGERNON   HENRY
1619-1698   1622-1683   1641-1704
3rd Earl of   cr. Earl
Leicester   of Romney
m.   ROBERT
LADY CATHERINE   1626-1668
CECIL
(da. of 2nd Earl
of Salisbury)

├ DOROTHY m.
│   1ST EARL OF SUNDERLAND
├ LUCY m.
│   SIR JOHN PELHAM, BT.
├ ANNE m.
│   REV. J. CART
├ ISABELLA m.
│   2ND VISCOUNT STRANGFORD
└ ELIZABETH

IV

Select Chapter Bibliographies

WHITEHALL, 1579 *The English*

Biographies of Elizabeth and histories of her reign are, of course, legion. For the years at issue here the reader might consult J. E. Neale's authoritative *Queen Elizabeth I* (London, 1934); B. W. Beckingsale's *Elizabeth I* (London, 1963); Neville Williams' *Elizabeth, Queen of England* (London, 1967); or Paul Johnson's recent *Elizabeth I* (London, 1974). My authority for the Queen's infatuation during 1579 derives principally from Neale.

The political history of the period is dealt with in J. E. Neale's *Elizabeth I and Her Parliaments, 1559–1581* (New York, 1958). Outstanding among general histories are S. T. Bindoff's *Tudor England* (Baltimore, 1967) and G. R. Elton's *England under the Tudors* (Cambridge, 1969). Accounts of Elizabethan society are numerous, but A. L. Rowse's *The England of Elizabeth* (New York, 1968) has the merit of being both complete and readable.

The attitudes of Leicester's circle, and of the Sidneys, are well documented in James M. Osborn's *Young Philip Sidney* (New Haven, 1972), while discussions of the puritan influence on certain Elizabethan writers and university men can be found in the following: A. C. Judson, *Life of Edmund Spenser* (Baltimore, 1966); Ralph M. Sargent, *The Life and Lyrics of Sir Edward Dyer* (Oxford, 1935); Joan Rees, *Fulke Greville, Lord Brooke, 1554–1628* (Berkeley, Calif., 1971); John Bakeless, *Christopher Marlowe: The Man in His Time* (New York, 1937); Henry Plomer and Tom Peete Cross, *The Life and Correspondence of Lodowick Bryskett* (Chicago, 1934).

The diplomatic crises of the late seventies and early eighties are covered exhaustively in Conyers Read's *Mr. Secretary Walsingham and the Policy of Queen Elizabeth*, 3 vols. (Oxford, 1925) and in *Lord Burghley and Queen Elizabeth* (London, 1960). B. W. Beckingsale's *Burghley: Tudor Statesman* (London, 1967) is a concise and useful biography.

The account of John Stubbs's involvement in the marriage crisis, the London setting of his actions, and their results are laid out in Lloyd E. Barry's *John Stubbs's Gaping Gulf with Letters and Other Relevant Documents*, The Folger Shakespeare Library (Charlottesville, Va., 1968).

Finally, Arthur F. Kinney's comprehensive *Titled Elizabethans: A Directory of Elizabethan State and Church Officers and Knights with Peers of England, Scotland, and Ireland* (Hamden, Conn., 1973) is an invaluable guide to the officialdom of the period.

MUNSTER, 1565 *The Irish*

For a modern outline, with analysis, of events leading to Desmond's attainder and the First Desmond War, consult the ponderous *A New History of Ireland*, edited by T. W. Moody, F. X. Martin, and F. J. Byrne (Oxford, 1976). For a broadly historical and anecdotal account of Gerald and his imprisonment, Brian Fitz-Gerald's *Geraldines* (New York, 1952) is a colorful and dramatic source. The bare bones of Gerald's career up to and following his imprisonment are found in the *Calendar of State Papers, Ireland*, edited by H. C. Hamilton and R. P. Mahaffy, 11 vols. (London, 1860–1912). This source should be supplemented by articles and monographs of the Royal Society of Antiquaries, Dublin, and by articles relating to the Desmonds found in the issues of the *Kilkenny Archaeological Journal*.

The Irish source most closely equivalent to the English *Calendar of State Papers, Ireland*, is *Annals of the Kingdom of Ireland by the Four Masters . . .* , translated and edited by John O'Donovan, 5 vols. (Dublin, 1854), which is throughout this book for convenience referred to as the Irish Chronicle. Notes to the Donovan edition provide voluminous detail on the affairs of the Geraldines.

The activities of Sir Peter Carew, James Fitzmaurice, and the conduct of the First Desmond War are presented in their full detail in Richard Bagwell's *Ireland under the Tudors* (London, 1885–1890, reprint 1963). Bagwell remains the cardinal historian of this period in Irish history, and any work surveying the Elizabethan conquest must be indebted to him. The pattern of confiscation during this period is also treated in F. R. M. Hitchcock's sketchy *The Midland Septs and the Pale* (Dublin, 1908) and in William F. T. Butler's *Confiscation in Irish History* (London, 1917).

A general introduction to the legal, political, and social institutions of Gaelic Ireland is provided by James Lydon's *Ireland in the Later Middle Ages* (Dublin, 1973), wherein the intact structures of the society are presented with a minimum of scholarly obfuscation. For an account of these structures in decay, a century later, the pertinent chapters of A. L. Rowse's *The Expansion of Elizabethan England* (London, 1955) are important. Indeed, how far into decline Irish society had fallen is bitterly disputed. I tend to credit Elizabethan descriptions of but to disagree with Elizabethan reasons for the decline.

ASKEATON, 1573 *Lord of the South*

In addition to Bagwell, FitzGerald, the *Calendar of State Papers*, and the Irish Chronicle, this chapter draws on Kathleen Hughes's *Early Christian Ireland* (Ithaca, N.Y., 1972) for Irish background. Constantia Maxwell's *Irish History from Contempo-*

rary Sources (London, 1923) has been useful for contemporary opinion, and *The Fugger News-Letters,* edited by Victor von Klarwell (New York, 1925), for international opinion.

An amusing, if biased, account of Stukeley is found in a contemporary pamphlet, *The Famous History and Life of Captain Thomas Stukeley* (London, 1603).

YOUGHAL, 1579 *Resolution*

Military appreciations are owed to G. A. Hayes-McCoy's *The Irish at War* (Cork, 1964); Cyril Falls's invaluable *Elizabeth's Irish Wars* (London, 1950), on which I have especially relied, and C. G. Cruikshank's *Elizabeth's Army* (Oxford, 1966). That Elizabeth's parsimony crippled the effectiveness of her army is challenged by Lindsay Boynton's *The Elizabethan Militia, 1558–1638* (Newton Abbot, Eng., 1971), but I have not found his arguments applicable to the Irish situation. Finally, contemporary woodcuts of the Irish in action are to be found in John Derricke's *The Image of Ireland* (London, 1581), and in the edition edited by J. Small (London, 1883).

The Geraldine story was recorded from the Irish point of view a generation later in Philip O'Sullivan Beare's *Historiae catholicae Ibernia compendium* (Lisbon, 1621) and in the edition edited by Matthew Kelly (Dublin, 1850), and in Dominicus De Rosario O'Daly's *Initium, incrementa et exitus familiae Geraldinorum* . . . (Lisbon, 1655). These sources are highly inaccurate but, between them, they communicate the passion of the Geraldines.

A useful compendium of English experiences is found in Edward M. Hinton's *Ireland Through Tudor Eyes* (Philadelphia, 1935).

KILMORE, 1580 *Pursuit*

The ravaging of Munster is widely attested to in contemporary accounts. Bagwell is the best guide to the month by month campaign, and Maxwell, Hinton, Rowse, and the Irish Chronicle offer ample corroboration of the tragedy.

SMERWICK, 1580 *Siege*

Grey's arrival in Dublin and the conditions of his army are presented in A. C. Judson's *The Life of Edmund Spenser.* The life of a typical infantry captain, then in Ireland, is offered in Rachel Lloyd's sentimental *Elizabethan Adventurer: A Life of Captain Christopher Carleill* (London, 1974).

Cyril Falls provides much of the background for the Battle of Glenmalure.

Treatment of the siege of Smerwick is *de rigueur* in "lives" of Sir Walter Raleigh. Raleigh's career in Ireland is as fascinating as it is embarrassing to his admirers and the following provide the full gamut of explanation: Willard M. Wallace, *Sir Walter Raleigh* (Princeton, 1959); Norman Lloyd Williams, *Sir Walter Raleigh* (London, 1962); J. H. Adamson and H. F. Folland, *The Shepherd of the Ocean* (Boston, 1969); Robert Lacey, *Sir Walter Ralegh* (New York, 1974). Adamson and

Folland have the temerity to treat the episode of Del Oro at length, Lacey likewise declines to shun it, and their accounts are all generally valuable. Insightful remarks on Raleigh are offered by C. A. Patrides in his edition of Raleigh's *The History of the World* (Philadelphia, 1971).

Additional information on Grey and Spenser, the conduct of the siege, and subsequent controversy can be found in learned articles by Raymond Jenkins, Rudolf Gottfried, and Alfred O'Rahilly.

SLIEVE MISH, 1583 *Ruin*

The passing of Gerald Fitzgerald is dramatically summarized in Brian Fitz-Gerald's *Geraldines* and in Bagwell's definitive account of the last years of the Desmond War. Embellishments are found in O'Daly and O'Sullivan Beare and in contemporary Elizabethan reports.

Curious and out of the way facts and notions are provided in St. John D. Seymour's *Irish Witchcraft and Demonology* (New York, 1973 reprint), which concludes confidently that the real devil in Ireland was the English tyrant.

KILCOLMAN, 1588 *The Broken Land*

Besides Judson's *Life of Edmund Spenser*, Pauline Henley's *Spenser in Ireland* (Dublin and Cork, 1928) is a valuable source of information on Kilcolman and the surrounding Munster settlements.

The story of John Norris is illuminated by Rowse, whose *Expansion of Elizabethan England* provides the background of the Dutch wars and the struggle for Ireland.

Perrot's illegitimate son, James (1571–1637), wrote *The Chronicle of Ireland, 1584–1608*, edited by Herbert Wood (Dublin, 1933), which helps to illuminate some of his father's actions. A manuscript life of Sir John Perrot, dating from the close of Elizabeth's reign and commonly attributed to Rawlinson, was published in Dublin in 1728. I have only seen fragments of this last. Perrot was nothing during his lifetime if not controversial, and great difficulty attaches to interpreting the stories about him and the views attributed to him.

For Hugh O'Neill's activities parallel to the Second Munster Plantation, Sean O'Faolain's *The Great O'Neill* (London, 1942) is the most stirring and intimate account. *The Great O'Neill* encapsulates much of the Southern troubles, from Peter Carew through Gerald Fitzgerald.

DUNGANNON, 1594 *Lord of the North*

The conflict between Perrot and his associates is documented in Bagwell's *Ireland under the Tudors*, while the neighborly disputes in the vicinity of Kilcolman have been researched by Robert Dunlop and Raymond Heffner, their findings summarized in Judson's *Life of Edmund Spenser*.

Select Chapter Bibliographies

O'Neill's early career is touched on in all the general histories, but O'Faolain's biography remains the most complete source and I have relied heavily on him for the years before the outbreak of war.

WHITEHALL, 1599 *The Passing*

For month by month developments after January, 1591, the three volumes of G. B. Harrison's *An Elizabethan Journal, 1591–1603* (London, 1974) are a fascinating guide, presenting news of the Irish crisis in the context of London, the Court, and general foreign and domestic affairs. Elizabeth's Proclamation of 1599, "On sending over the Army into Ireland," is presented in its context in Arthur F. Kinney's *Elizabethan Backgrounds: Historical Documents of the Age of Elizabeth I* (Hamden, Conn., 1975), while O'Neill's demands can be found in Maxwell's *Irish History from Contemporary Sources.*

Numerous books are available on the Earl of Essex and Elizabeth, but I have turned most often to an old one for accounts of Cecil's relations with Essex, Essex in Ireland, and Essex and O'Neill: G. B. Harrison's *Robert Devereux, Earl of Essex* (New York, 1937).

Index

Index

Butler, Thomas, Earl of Ormond (Black Tom), 25, 44, 54, 63, 80, 81, 104, 119, 125, 144, 184; at Affane, 35–6, 38; captured, 289; criticism of, 178, 179–80, 182; discharged, 177, 182–3; and Eustace, 145, 146, 157; and Gerald Fitzgerald, 81, 82, 108, 115–16, 121, 124, 129, 130, 133, 138, 140, 149, 200; meeting of Hugh O'Neill and, 260–1; named Lord General, 260; pardons given by, 201; and Peter Carew, 48, 49, 50, 52; property owned by, 219; and Raleigh, 181–2; and Smerwick, 162, 164, 165; surrender of Countess of Desmond to, 202; and Ulster rebellion, 267, 268, 275–6, 277, 281

Calendar of State Papers, 54, 117, 119, 188, 200
Camden, William, 132, 228; on Butler, 54; on Carew, 52; on Grey, 171; on Hugh O'Neill, 24, 25; on mutilation of Stubbs, 30; on Sanders, 92; on siege of Del Oro, 176; on tax policy, 241; verses to Elizabeth, 216
Campion, Edmund, 19–20, 71
Carew, George, 147, 158, 159, 289
Carew, Peter, xiv, 25, 41, 42–3, 44, 45–52, 78, 159, 160–1, 180
Carew, Peter, the younger, 47, 147
Carleill, Christopher, 156, 198
Carrigafoyle Castle, siege of, 136–9, 267
Carter, Arthur, 88, 90, 91, 92, 93
Cartwright, Thomas, 11, 28
Casimir, Count, 8
Castleisland, 139; sack of, 140
Castlemaine, 67, 69, 90, 128, 266–7, 279; fall of, 73, 140, 277
Castlemartyr, 67, 69, 73
Catherine de Medici, 6
Cecil, Robert, 274
Cecil, William, Lord Burghley, 15, 16–18, 20, 22, 118, 176, 233, 237; belief of, in legal reform, 71, 154; and Butler, 182, 201; contempt of, for Irish law, 77;

and Cheke's death, 168; death of, 273; and Drury, 99; and Essex, 274; faith of, in diplomacy, 94; and Gerald Fitzgerald, 66, 69, 70, 108, 112, 115; and Grey, 153; and Hugh O'Neill, 249, 251, 265; and the Irish crisis, 19, 44, 72, 121, 125, 217; and the marriage crisis, 6, 7, 30, 31; and *Mother Hubberds Tale,* 33, 151; slander of, 32, 33; and Stubbs, 27
Cheke, John, 167–8
chieftaincies, 23, 37, 45, 46, 47, 72
Churchyard, Thomas, 152, 284
Chylde, Machabyas, 230
Clancar, Earl of, *see* More, MacCarthy
Clanricarde, Earl of, 38, 53, 59, 183
clan system, *see* Irish political organization
Clontibret, Battle of, 258
Coke, Edward, 28
Colclough, Anthony, 185
Coleman, Richard, 99
Colin Clouts Come Home Again (Spenser), 232, 233–5, 263
colonization, xiv, 16, 25, 41, 43, 52, 208, 217–18, 242–4
Commentary of the Services . . . of William, Lord Grey de Wilton (Grey), 153
Common Law, 38, 46, 71–2
Composition of Connaught, 242
Condon, Patrick, 202, 208, 243
Connaught: Composition of, 242; massacre in, 209–10
conscription, 55
conscience: freedom of, 258–9; Irish, 197
Conyers, Clifford, 276
Cork (city), 55–6, 191, 281
Cosby, Francis, 158–9, 161
Cosby, Henry, 269, 270, 271
Counter-Reformation, 89, 112, 170, 265
Courtenay, Thomas, 90–1, 119
Courtney, William, 219, 280
coyne and livery, 69, 209, 210, 252
Cuellar, Francisco, 136
Cuffe, Hugh, 219, 230, 243, 278
Cullen, Castle, 69–70, 88

Index

Fenton, James, 188

Fermoy, Viscount of, see Roche, Maurice, Lord

feudalism, 23, 46, 76; see also Irish political organization

firepower, 267, 268

Fitton, Edward, 104, 280

FitzEdmond, Eustace, 180, 181

Fitzgerald, Eleanor, Countess of Desmond, 38, 40, 66, 73–4, 82, 140, 141, 148, 190; and Butler, 202; and Drury, 103–4, 192; plea of, before Pelham, 142; resettled, 208, 290; sent back to Gerald, 195–6; surrender of, to Grey, 192–4

Fitzgerald, Gerald, Earl of Desmond, xiii, 15, 78–9, 89, 93, 150, 192; at Affane, 35–6; at Askeaton, 75, 76, 77, 82–3, 114; and Carrigafoyle, 137, 138, 139; death of, 204; and Drury, 99–100; and Elizabeth, 67, 68–9, 71, 72–3, 108; England's case against, 109–12; and Fitzmaurice, 25, 73, 74, 83, 87–8, 91; flight and pursuit of, 140–3, 148–9, 190, 193, 194–6, 201, 202–3; foreign aid to, 73, 117; imprisoned in London, 36–41, 82; legends attached to, 143, 149, 205–6; and Maltby, 113–14, 115; marriages of, 80–1, 82; proclaimed a traitor, 73, 122; rebellion led by, 26, 77, 81, 96, 116–17, 118, 121, 126–7, 128, 129, 184; renewal of fight by, 177–8, 185–6; return of, to Ireland, 66–7; and Smerwick, 90, 91, 101, 103, 164, 168–9; at Youghal, 121–4; youth of, 79–80

Fitzgerald, James (brother of Gerald), 38, 69, 92, 93, 108, 147–8

Fitzgerald, James (father of Gerald), 79

Fitzgerald, James (son of Gerald), 40, 73, 100, 103, 194, 290

Fitzgerald, James FitzThomas, (new) Earl of Desmond (Hayrope Earl), 266, 277, 278, 279, 290

Fitzgerald, Joan Butler, 80–1, 82

Fitzgerald, John (brother of Gerald), 69, 96, 99, 100, 101, 107, 108, 117, 141, 161, 162, 169; arrest of, 38; and Davells, 90, 92; death of, 188–90; and Fitzmaurice, 93, 94–5

Fitzgerald, John Fitzedmund, Seneschal of Imokilly, 69, 189, 202, 208, 243

Fitzgerald, Thomas (of Desmond), 178, 202

Fitzjohn, James, 184, 189, 190

Fitzmaurice, Gerald, 157

Fitzmaurice, James, Captain of Desmond, xiii, 12, 25–6, 162, 163; army of, 56–8; death of, 26, 95–6, 203; and Eleanor Fitzgerald, 74; escape of, to France, 65; in First Desmond War, 14, 51, 52–3, 128; foreign encouragement for, 53, 83, 84, 85, 86; Kilmallock taken by, 58–60; meeting of Burke and, 95–6; and Perrot, 63–5; return of, to Ireland, 13, 15–16, 86–7, 88

Fitzmaurice, James, of Decies, 140, 169

Fitzwilliams, Lord Deputy, 72, 237, 239, 256, 257

France: encouragement of rebels by, 84; English hostility to, 7, 27–8; lost to England, 216; and Mary Stuart, 18, 44; neutrality of, 237; as refuge for rebels, 178

Francis of Valois, Duke of Alençon, 5, 6, 12, 18, 27–8, 29, 31

"freedom of conscience": demanded for the North by Tyrone and O'Donnell, 258–9

Frobisher, Martin, 40, 163

Gaelic society: customs of, 20, 135, 136; decay of clan system, 23, 38; political organization and legal system of, 23–4, 45, 46–7, 71–2, 77, 205; racial bias toward, 22, 38; as tribal culture, 19, 23; see also Ireland; Irish customs; etc.

Gainsford, Thomas, 292

gallowglass, 57, 91, 93, 101, 102, 106, 107, 148, 193, 223; annihilation of, 208–10

Gaping Gulf (The Discovery of a Gaping Gulf . . .) (Stubbs), 26–7, 28, 29

A Note About the Author

Richard Berleth has traveled widely in Ireland and England. He holds a Ph.D. in Renaissance Literature and is presently a publishing executive in New York City, where he lives with his wife, Emily, and daughter, Kate.

―――――――――◆―――――――――

A Note on the Type

This book was set via computer-driven cathode ray tube in Video Janson, a design made from type cast from matrices long thought to have been made by the Dutchman Anton Janson, who was a practicing type founder in Leipzig during the years 1668–87. However, it has been conclusively demonstrated that these types are actually the work of Nicholas Kis (1650–1702), a Hungarian, who most probably learned his trade from the master Dutch type founder Dirk Voskens. The type is an excellent example of the influential and sturdy Dutch types that prevailed in England up to the time William Caslon developed his own incomparable designs from them.

Composed by The Haddon Craftsmen Inc., ComCom Division, Allentown, Pennsylvania.

Printed and bound by American Book–Stratford Press, Saddle Brook, New Jersey.

Designed by Gwen Townsend

089861